Abel Hovelacque, Augustus Henry Keane

The Science of Language

Linguistics, Philology, Etymology

Abel Hovelacque, Augustus Henry Keane

The Science of Language
Linguistics, Philology, Etymology

ISBN/EAN: 9783743394728

Manufactured in Europe, USA, Canada, Australia, Japa

Cover: Foto ©Thomas Meinert / pixelio.de

Manufactured and distributed by brebook publishing software (www.brebook.com)

Abel Hovelacque, Augustus Henry Keane

The Science of Language

THE AUTHOR'S PREFACE.

To the last years of the eighteenth century was reserved the privilege of giving birth to the true methods of scientific research. The undertaking was immense; but the men by whom it was attempted were fully equal to the task. The Encyclopedists led the way in the new era by introducing the modern system of experimental science.

The methodic spirit recast the processes of research and of instruction hitherto pursued, while mathematics, chemistry, the physical sciences, broke at last, once for all, with metaphysics.

The Science of Language, to which this volume is devoted, is neither the least important nor the least interesting of contemporary sciences. Our purpose is to show its real place in the natural history of man. And at the very outset we shall have to define its scope and nature. The most delicate questions of this science are daily discussed and solved by persons ignorant alike of its object and of its method. This, however, is but the general fate of all the natural sciences. The lack of deep study, based on experience, is supplied by assertions of a purely sentimental character. It is thus that we constantly hear people boldly proclaiming themselves polygenists or monogenists, friends or foes of the doctrine of evolution, without having ever set foot in an anthropological museum.

We shall not seek to shirk the question of the origin of speech, which is in itself a purely anthropological one. Without troubling ourselves with the fancies it has given rise to, we shall treat it solely on the standpoint of natural history—that is to say, of anatomy and physiology. Articulate speech is a natural fact, subject, like all others, to free and unprejudiced inquiry; hence there is nothing rash in attempting to broach the question of its origin. To put it aside under the pretext that all inquiry into "first origins" must be proscribed, is of itself an admission of the possibility of these first causes, which mathematics and chemistry themselves have amply vindicated.

By the side of questions purely philological, we have here and there, though sparingly, introduced certain linguistic matters directly connected with them. We have more readily discussed some points of linguistic ethnography, though in a very incomplete manner, with the intention of returning to the subject. Even the strictly philological questions themselves, the nature and aim of this series has compelled us to treat in a very cursory way, and it is to be hoped that the reader will make allowance for this difficulty.

In conclusion, we may be permitted to express our thanks to MM. Picot and Vinson for their co-operation in the work. To them we are much indebted for notes, information, and, above all, for their safe and methodical suggestions.

TRANSLATOR'S PREFACE.

CASTING about for a suitable title to his "Introduction à l'Étude de la Science du Langage," Domenico Pozzi asks almost in despair: "How, then, shall we name it? Linguistics with many French writers, or Glottics and Glottology with some Germans?" And after, on various grounds, rejecting these and other still more incongruous terms, he ends by adopting the expression, "Science of Language." Yet it is obvious that, after all, this is rather an explanation of a title than a title in the strict sense that botany or zoology are titles. It tells us in so many words what this particular branch of knowledge is, describing it as a science, dealing with language as its subject matter. Still the expression has been sanctioned by the authority of some great names, and is, on the whole, the best that has been yet suggested. In the absence of any better equivalent for the German term "Sprachwissenschaft," it will probably continue to hold its ground, and has been accordingly adopted as the title of this English edition of M. Hovelacque's work. It has the great advantage of being sufficiently general without being vague, and of being perfectly intelligible without committing us to any special theories—no slight consideration in the present state of the science.

TRANSLATOR'S PREFACE.

The distinguished Author belongs to the advanced school of anthropologists, and as such, of course, treats language as strictly and exclusively a physical science. Many of his views will, doubtless, fail to meet with universal acceptance, while it must be confessed that some of his conclusions are utterly unwarranted, at least in the present state of our knowledge. This is particularly true of his argument for the original plurality of the human race, based upon the assumed original plurality of human speech. (Ch. vi. § 2, pp. 304–7.) In the actual state of the science, philology can no more prove the primeval diversity than it can the primeval unity of articulate speech itself; and until this point is settled, it can tell us absolutely nothing about the original unity or plurality of mankind.

But, although this and one or two collateral questions are really foreign to the subject, the Translator did not on that account consider himself justified in tampering with the text. The preferable course in all such cases seemed to be to let the Author set forth his own views in his own way, and then, where desirable, point out their fallacies, and warn the reader against their illogical nature. All such comments, as well as all other supplementary matter, for which the Translator alone is responsible, will be found either in special notes or interspersed, in square and round brackets, throughout the work.

With the view of rendering it, as far as possible, a complete handbook of the subject, he has also supplied an Appendix, illustrated by a philological map, presenting, so to say, a birdseye view of all known languages, living and dead, and thus forming a clearly tabulated summary of its varied contents.

Some thought has also been given to the important matter of the spelling of foreign names. It would, of course, be hopeless to look for uniformity amidst the chaos at present prevailing amongst English writers. But we may still aim at least at consistency, and avoid the absurdities of those who at one moment somewhat ostentatiously write Kimon for Cimon, and the very next give us Thucydides for Thukydides. Besides this modest virtue of consistency, the Translator has further endeavoured to be *correct*, in all cases giving preference to what he considered the better forms, where two or more were in current use. Thus it is that he writes *Kafir*, not *Kaffir*, the *f* not being doubled in the Arabic كافر = *Kāfir* = infidel. So also *u* long everywhere supersedes the clumsy *oo* and the French *ou*, whence *Rumanian*, *Beluch*, *Bantu*, &c., and not *Roumanian*, *Belooch*, *Bantoo*, &c. Diacritical marks, however, have been very sparingly used, being always cumbersome and mostly needless. Thus there is no danger that anyone will give the same sound to the first syllable of *Rumanian* that he does to the English word *rum*, although the *u* does not bear the usual mark of the long vowel sound. On the other hand, eccentricities are avoided, such eccentricities, for instance, as would lead us to write the strictly correct *khalīfah* and *kārāwan-sarāe* for our old friends *calif* and *caravansaries*.

It remains to be mentioned that, though based on the first edition of the original, this translation has been carefully compared with the proofs of the second now being issued. All improvements and important additions have been embodied in the text, which it is hoped will thus be found to present a faithful picture of the present state of philological studies.

A. H. K.

11, AINGER TERRACE, N.W.,
January 3rd, 1877.

CONTENTS.

	PAGE
THE AUTHOR'S PREFACE	v
TRANSLATOR'S PREFACE	vii

CHAPTER I.—Linguistics—Philology—Etymology 1
    § 1. Difference between Linguistics and Philology ... 1
    § 2. The Life of Languages 8
    § 3. Linguistics and Philology mutually useful to each other 10
    § 4. The Polyglot 11
    § 5. The Dangers of Etymology ... 13

CHAPTER II.—The Faculty of Articulate Speech—Its Locality and importance in Natural History ... 17

CHAPTER III.—First Form of Speech—Monosyllabic or Isolating Languages 31
    § 1. Chinese ... 34
    § 2. Annamese ... 41
    § 3. Siamese or Thai 42
    § 4. Burman ... 42
    § 5. Tibetan ... 43

CONTENTS.

	PAGE
CHAPTER IV.—Second Form of Speech—Agglutination—The Agglutinating Languages	44
§1. What is Agglutination?	45
§2. South African Languages	47
(1) Hottentot	47
(2) Bushman Dialects	51
§3. Languages of the African Negroes	51
(1) Wolof	52
(2) Mande group	56
(3) Felup group ...	56
(4) Sonraï	56
(5) Hausa, or Hawsa	56
(6) Bornu group	58
(7) Kruh group	58
(8) Ewe, or Ifc group ...	58
§4. Bantu, or Kafir Family ...	59
§5. The Fulu group	64
§6. The Nubian Languages ...	66
§7. Languages of the Negritos ...	66
§8. Languages of the Papuas ...	66
§9. Australian Languages ...	67
§10. The Malayo-Polynesian Idioms	68
§11. Japanese ...	72
§12. Corean	76
§13. The Dravidian Tongues	77
§14. The Finno-Tataric, or Uralo-Altaïc Languages ...	88
§15. Basque	109
§16. The American Languages ...	123
§17. The Sub-Arctic Languages	135
§18. Languages of the Caucasus	136

Chapter IV. (continued).

	PAGE
§ 19. On some little known idioms classified with the Agglutinating Languages ...	137
(1) Sinhalese, or Elu	137
(2) Munda ...	138
(3) Brahui ...	138
(4) The Pretended Scythian Language ...	138
(5) The Language of the Second Column of the Cuneiform Inscriptions ...	139
(6) The so-called Sumerian or Accadian Language ...	141
§ 20. The Theory of the Turanian Languages ...	144

Chapter V.—Third Form of Speech—Inflection ... 146

§ 1. What is Inflection? ...	147
§ 2. Aryan and Semitic Inflection ...	148
A. The Semitic Languages ...	151
§ 3. The Semite and the Semitic Languages collectively	151
§ 4. The Aramæo-Assyrian group ...	155
(1) Chaldee and Syriac ...	155
(2) Assyrian ...	157
§ 5. The Canaanitic group ...	160
(1) Hebrew	160
(2) Phœnician	164
§ 6. The Arabic group ...	166
(1) Arabic ...	167
(2) Languages of South Arabia and Abyssinia ...	170
§ 7. Individuality of the Semitic idioms—Their Primeval home ...	172

Chapter V. (continued).

B. The Hamitic Languages	174
§1. The Egyptian group	175
§2. The Libyan group	179
§3. The Ethiopian group	180
C. The Aryan Languages	181
§1. The Common Aryan mother-tongue	182
§2. The Indic branch	189
(1) The Ancient Hindu Languages	190
(2) Modern Indian Languages	193
(3) Gipsy Dialects	195
§3. The Iranic branch	196
(1) Zend	197
(2) Old Persian	200
(3) Armenian	202
(4) Huzvâresh	203
(5) Parsi	205
(6) Persian	206
(7) Ossetian, Kurdic, Belúchi, Afghan, &c.	207
§4. The Hellenic branch	208
§5. The Italic branch	217
(1) Primitive Italic Languages	218
(2) The Neo-Latin Languages	227
(α) French	233
(β) Provençal	236
(γ) Italian	237
(δ) Ladin	238
(ε) Spanish	239
(ζ) Portuguese	240
(η) Rumanian	240

CONTENTS.

CHAPTER V. (*continued*).

	PAGE
§ 6. The Keltic Languages...	242
§ 7. The Teutonic Tongues	252
(1) Gothic	254
(2) The Norse Tongues	255
(3) The Low German group	257
(4) The High German group	264
§ 8. The Slavonic Languages	268
§ 9. The Lettic group	285
(1) Lithuanian	285
(2) Lettish	288
(3) Old Prussian	288
§ 10. Unclassified Aryan Tongues...	289
(1) Etruscan...	290
(2) Dacian	291
(3) The Aryan Languages of Asia Minor...	292
(4) The so-called "Scythic" Aryan Tongues	293
(5) Albanian...	293
§ 11. On the ramification of the Common Aryan Speech, and on its primitive home...	294

CHAPTER VI.—Original Plurality of Speech, and Transmutation of Linguistic Systems ... 302

§ 1. How to recognise Linguistic Affinities	302
§ 2. Original plurality of Linguistic groups and consequences thereof	304
§ 3. In their historic life Language and Race may cease to be convertible terms	307
§ 4. The Permutation of Species in Philology	308

THE SCIENCE OF LANGUAGE.

CHAPTER I.

LINGUISTICS—PHILOLOGY—ETYMOLOGY.

§ 1.—*Difference between Linguistics and Philology.**

It is seldom that in ordinary language, or even in scientific works, any distinction is observed between the two terms *linguistics* and *philology*. They are usually employed one for the other, almost at haphazard, and according to the more or less urgent euphonic requirements of a phrase or a sentence. The best writers, and even scientific men themselves, constantly confuse them; too often treating philology and linguistics as nothing more than the study of etymologies, and describing those engaged in such pursuits as *philologists* or *linguists* indifferently. The inquiry into the pos-

---

* In what follows, the terms *linguistics* and *philology*, owing to the different usage of the two languages, have necessarily changed sides. Philology and comparative philology, according to the English practice, now mean what is more comprehensively understood by the Science of Language, linguistics being more usually restricted to the critical study of a given language. But the more correct French writers use *la philologie* in this sense of linguistics, and *la linguistique* in the sense of the Science of Language; these two terms thus forming respectively the French and the English titles of the present work. It may be added that in this translation the terms Science of Language, Philology, and Comparative Philology, are used as practically synonymous. In the words of Schleicher, quoted further on, "philology is nothing unless comparative."—*Note by Translator.*

sible relationship of two Australian idioms, or the revision of a text of Plautus, would be spoken of by them either as a linguistic or philological work indistinctly.

But this is very far from being the case, and we must at the outset endeavour to combat such a serious error.

Philology is a natural, linguistics an historical science.

In his dictionary of the French language, M. Littré, using the term *linguistique* in the sense now usually given by English writers to the word *philology*, describes it as "the study of languages, considered in their principles, their relations, and as an involuntary product of the mind of man." In spite of all its vagueness, this definition possesses the great merit of not being quite so easily applicable to the word *linguistics* (in the English sense). On the other hand, to the term *philology*—by it partly understanding *linguistics*—he assigns three different meanings: 1st, A kind of general learning, respecting belles-lettres, languages, criticism, &c.; 2nd, More definitely, the study and knowledge of a language in so far as it is the instrument or medium of literature; 3rd, Comparative philology, a study applied to several languages, which are explained by being mutually compared with each other.

Of these three definitions the first two are correct, but the third can scarcely be accepted, according to the present use of the term by French writers. The author justly distinguishes between philology, properly so-called, and linguistics; but, without sufficient reason, sanctions the unjustifiable practice which confuses the science of comparative philology with mere linguistics.

It is difficult to understand how, by becoming comparative, the one could be changed to the other. Comparative physiology embracing, for instance, the relations of the animal and vegetable kingdoms, does not surely cease to be physiology. And so with the comparative anatomy of the various races of mankind, or even of man and the other *primates*, which still claims the title of anatomy. It is clearly the same with philology, which by becoming comparative cannot by any means thereby forfeit its true and proper designation.

Rollin defined linguists as "those who have studied the old

writers for the purpose of examining, correcting, explaining, and expounding them," and this definition is still largely applicable. It corresponds, as we have seen, to M. Littré's two first meanings of philology; and in truth, the province of the linguist is the critical study of literature from the standpoint of archæology, art, and mythology; the inquiry into the history of languages, and incidentally into their geographical extension; the discovery of the elements they have mutually borrowed from each other during the course of ages; the restoration and the correction of texts.

This is on the face of it an historical science, and an important branch of learning. Before the modern development of the natural sciences, languages could be regarded only from this historical point —that is to say, linguistics necessarily long preceded philolophy.

Strictly speaking, linguistics are concerned with one language only. This it criticises, interprets its records, improves extant texts, according to the data and materials furnished by this one language itself. When this study becomes extended to two different languages, or to several branches of the same language, it becomes so far comparative. Thus what we understand by *classical* linguistics are most commonly comparative studies, because occupied with both Greek and Latin texts. In the same way, Romance, Teutonic, and Slavonic linguistics are all comparative. They will treat, for instance, of the influence exercised by the Euphuists of the sixteenth century on the current speech of succeeding generations; of the part played by Luther's version of the Bible in the formation of New High German; of the westward spread of the Slavonic tongues during the Middle Ages, and of their subsequent retirement towards the East.

Equally comparative are "oriental linguistics," as they are called, and which embrace three languages scientifically distinct—Persian, Arabic, and Turkish. Lastly, Buddhism in India and the extreme East has given birth to yet another branch of comparative linguistics.

We are indebted more particularly to Schleicher,* Curtius,†

---

* "Die deutsche Sprache," Introduction, chap. vi.
† "Philologie und Sprachwissenschaft."

Kuhn, Chavée,* and Spiegel,† for this important distinction between the two sciences of linguistics and philology. All these writers agree on the cardinal point—that the one belongs to the province of historic knowledge, and the other to that of the natural sciences.

The Science of Language, or Philology, may be defined: The study of the constituent elements of articulate speech, and of the various forms by which these elements are or may be affected. In other words, philology is the two-fold study of the phonetics and of the structure of languages.

It is easy to see how philology trenches on physiology by the study of the phonetic material of languages—that is, of their sounds. The first care of the philologist is to arrange the vowels and the consonants of the languages he is studying, and to establish the laws of their changes or modifications, and the discovery of these laws will be all the more easy for him according to his acquaintance with the action of the vocal organs.

Vowels and consonants make up the fundamental elements of language. There are others growing out of these, which are at times, strictly speaking, described as *simple elements*, although often in fact already compound; these are the monosyllables usually called *roots*.

Inquiry will show us that these monosyllables lie at the bottom of all philological systems. Sometimes they are formed by one pure element, that is by a single vowel: *i = to go* in the Aryan languages. Sometimes they are formed by the union of several fundamental elements: *ta* corresponding in Chinese to the various conceptions of *greatness*. But their meaning must always be very general, never being limited by any consideration of gender, case, number, person, time, or mood.

The study of these elements forms, as stated, one of the first cares of the philologist. To this study succeeds the examination of the forms by which such elements are or may be affected. This

---

* "Bulletins de la Société d'Anthropologie de Paris," 1862, p. 198.
† "Die traditionelle Literatur der Parsen," p. 48.

new study receives the name of *morphology*. We shall treat farther on of the several morphological varieties in language, that is of the different kinds of structure that languages may present. It will then be seen that idioms classified in this relation in one and the same group, as for instance the *agglutinating* languages, may possibly be otherwise, and, in respect of their constituent elements, entirely strangers to each other. Thus the Aryan and the Semitic languages, whose roots are totally different and incapable of being identified, are both found in the same morphological division; so also with Turkish, Basque, Japanese, and Tamil, which present the same general structure, but the roots of which are so essentially different that it becomes impossible to reduce them to one common stock or origin.

This subject will claim all due attention in its proper place. Meanwhile our object is thoroughly to establish the cardinal fact that philology belongs to the group of natural sciences, and that to classify it with the historical sciences we must ignore at once its aim and its method.

It is to Augustus Schleicher (*ob.* 1868, at Jena, where he taught) that we are indebted for the clearest and most conclusive writings on this important subject. Schleicher was especially distinguished amongst his fellow-countrymen for a turn of mind altogether free from metaphysical reveries. Like so many others, he had waded through the schools of the transcendentalists, and followed the expounders of hyperphysicism and "theourgies," but their subtleties had failed to allure his positive intellect, which could ill rest satisfied with dogmatic and empty assertions. His was essentially an experimental and methodic mind. He was confessedly the first to draw up the general scheme of the phonetics and structure of the Aryan languages, whose relationship had been definitely proclaimed by Sir W. Jones at the end of the last, and scientifically demonstrated by Bopp at the beginning of the present century. As Schleicher was himself wont to remark, his extensive botanical information was of the greatest service to him in his researches into the morphology of languages, so entirely identical are the processes of analysis and comparison in the study of all the natural sciences.

Here the ingenious analogy deserves to be quoted, which, in order to render clear the difference between the science of language and linguistics, he was fond of establishing between the philologist and the botanist on the one hand, and the linguist and horticulturist on the other.*

"Linguistics," he writes, "are a historical science, a science which has no place except where we are in possession of a literature and a history. In the absence of monuments or of a literary culture, there is no room for the linguist. In a word, linguistics are applicable to historic documents alone. It is very different with philology, whose sole object is language itself, whose sole study is the examination of language in itself and for itself. The historical changes of languages, the more or less accidental development of the vocabulary, often even their syntactical processes, are all but of secondary importance for the philologist. He devotes his whole attention to the study of the phenomenon itself of articulate speech; a natural function, inevitable and determined, from which there is no escape, and which, like all other functions, is of inexorable necessity. It little matters to the philologist that a language may have prevailed for centuries over vast empires; that it may have produced the most glorious literary monuments; that it may have yielded to the requirements of the most delicate and refined intellectual culture. He little cares, on the other hand, that an obscure idiom may have perished without fruits or issue, stifled by other tongues and ignored utterly by the mere linguist. Literature is unquestionably a powerful aid, thanks to which it becomes easy to grasp the language itself, to recognise the succession of its forms, the phases of its development, a valuable, but by no means an indispensable ally. Moreover, the knowledge of a single language is insufficient for the philologist, and herein he is again distinguished from the linguist. There exists a Latin linguistic science, for instance, totally independent of the Greek; a Hebrew equally independent of the Arabic or Assyrian. But we cannot speak of a purely Latin

---

* "Die deutsche Sprache," Introduction.

or a purely Hebrew philology. Philology, as above stated, is nothing unless comparative. In fact, we cannot explain one form without comparing it with others. Hence linguistics may be special, and restricted to one language. But when there is question of the constituent elements, and of the structure of a language, we must be previously familiar with the phonetics, and the structure of a certain number of other tongues. Let us repeat it once more: the researches of the philologist are consequently always and essentially comparative, whereas those of the linguist may be quite special."

It is here that Schleicher introduces his ingenious and reasonable comparison. "The philologist," he remarks, "is a naturalist. He studies languages as the botanist studies plants. The botanist must embrace at a glance the totality of vegetable organisms. He inquires into the laws of their structure and of their development; but he is in no way concerned with their greater or less intrinsic worth, with their more or less valuable uses, the more or less acknowledged pleasure afforded by them. In his eyes, the first wild flower to hand may have a far higher value than the loveliest rose, or the choicest lily. The province of the linguist is far different. It is not with the botanist, but with the horticulturist that he must be compared. The latter devotes his attention only to such or such species that may be the object of special attraction; what he seeks is beauty of form, colour, and perfume. A useless plant has no value in his eyes; he has nothing to do with the laws of structure or development, and a vegetable that in this respect may possess the greatest value, may possibly be for him nothing but a common weed."

The comparison is correct, and, better than any more or less lucid explanation, points out clearly enough that the philologist studies in man the phenomenon of articulate speech and its results, just as all physiologists study such other functions as locomotion, smell, sight, digestion, or circulation of the blood. And not only does he inquire into and determine the normal laws peculiar to this phenomenon, but he also discovers and describes the changes, really pathological in their nature, which are frequently presented during the course of the life of languages.

§ 2.—*The Life of Languages.*

For in point of fact languages are born, grow, decay, and perish, like all other living things. They pass first through an embryonic period, then reach their highest development, and lastly enter on a stage of retrogressive disintegration. It is precisely this conception of the *life* of language that, as already remarked, distinguishes the modern science of language from the unmethodical speculations of the past.

In another chapter we shall speak of the birth of languages, and of the origin of the faculty of articulate speech. We shall also see, farther on, how the most intricate philological systems grow out of rudimentary systems; how, in a word, the highest morphological stratifications ever rest upon others of a lower order.

Languages once born, cannot be said to enter at once on their historic career, if by this we are to understand that their development becomes henceforth subject to the whims and caprice of fashion. To suppose so would be a serious error, for their development is determined beforehand, and the course of their life can by no conceivable departure from the natural laws escape from the necessities common to all living things. Under the influence of favourable or adverse circumstances, they may undergo more or less serious modifications, they may advance more or less precipitately to decrepitude and extinction, but nothing can ever bend or change their organic tendencies. They are, in a word, what their nature compels them to be.

There are, for instance, no such things as mixed languages, nor is it possible to conceive, say, an Aryan tongue, whose grammar is partly Slavonic, partly Latin. English again, into which have been introduced so many foreign and especially French (and Latin) elements, remains none the less as it will remain to the last, a true Teutonic tongue. Basque is similarly circumstanced, its constant borrowings from two Romance tongues never having been able to affect its inner structure. In the same way the Husváresh, or Pahlavi, remained throughout medieval times an Aryan language, notwithstanding the large amount of Semitic elements which found their way into it.

But it cannot be doubted that such intellectual commerce, and that such borrowings, the inevitable results of civilisation, in a marked manner hasten on or promote the life of languages. To this truth the most evident and tangible facts bear witness. Thus amongst the Teutonic tongues English has run a singularly rapid course, whilst Icelandic has often preserved some very primitive forms with striking fidelity. The obscure Lithuanian may be looked upon as the best preserved of all Aryan languages in Europe, and in all probability would still for a long time to come challenge our admiration of its ancient and precious forms, did not the rough competition of German threaten it with approaching extinction. It is thus that such unequal but inevitable struggles daily cause the destruction of beings full of life and health, and which under less disastrous conditions would have enjoyed a long term of existence, instead of perishing miserably and without issue.

It is difficult to believe that a philological system, once it has attained its most flourishing state and its highest development, does not forthwith enter on its downward course, and it is equally hard to suppose that this period is not itself characterised in a special manner by an ever-increasing tendency towards independence on the part of the various idioms of such a system. We know, for instance, that the Indo-European or Aryan tongues—Indic, Iranic, Hellenic, Italic, Keltic, Teutonic, Slavonic, Lettic—spring from a common mother, whose phonetic elements it has been possible to determine, and whose morphology and structure have been recovered, at least in all their essential features. Now, it may be assumed that the period of formation, to which must in all likelihood be assigned a very protracted duration, was brought to a close as soon as dialectic divergencies began to make their appearance, and that no sensible interval elapsed between the first stage and the period of retrogressive change. One of the most important duties of philology is precisely to determine, or rather to restore, the forms of mother-tongues possessing no written monuments, at the time when they were breaking up into dialectic subdivisions. The task as stated, has been all but accomplished for the Aryan system; but it has scarcely yet been roughly sketched for the Semitic family—Chaldee, Syriac, Hebrew, Phœnician, Arabic, &c.—while all has yet to be done for the other systems; as, for instance, the so-called Hamitic (ancient Egyptian, Coptic, Ta-Masheq, Galla, &c.), and that of the Dravidian tongues, such as Tamil, Telugu, &c.

However, the life of languages is not a matter to be disposed of in a few pages. To do it justice would require a whole volume, and a long series of examples drawn from the various families of languages respectively. The matter cannot be here further dwelt upon; and we must rest satisfied with having pointed out the general and persistent fact of this life, of this material energy, under one of its most curious and instructive aspects.

§ 3.—*Linguistics and Philology mutually useful to each other.*

It cannot be denied that philology finds at times a powerful ally in the employment of the historic method. This latter is in fact indispensable when we come to enter upon the still almost virgin soil of syntax, where a more or less sensible individual influence may make itself felt. Let us, however, repeat that the natural science of philology and the historical science of linguistics are not rivals, and that there is nothing to justify the assumption that they are two hostile sciences. In truth, two branches of knowledge, however different in their nature, cannot lead to contradictory results, nor can two true sciences, really worthy of the name, be in any sense enemies of each other. The various sciences are on the contrary the complements one of the other, each being at once both debtor and creditor of all the rest.

Such is especially the case both with philology and linguistics. The latter must, at least in a general way, recognise the results obtained by the former. If it knows nothing of speech itself, which is such a powerful aid to progress, if it ignores its structure and constituent elements, it can never form an adequate judgment on the acquisitions of this agent. As well say that an ethnographist might derive profit from a collection of elementary data respecting the anatomy of races, without taking them even into calculation. This is almost a truism, and yet there are many linguists whom it has so far failed to convince. Hence those interminable and abstract discussions, without object, without sound knowledge, and mostly pedantic, that medley of idle hairsplitting, in which declamation competes with shallowness and inanity.

On the other hand, the linguist himself collects valuable materials for the philologist. He facilitates a knowledge of the historic forms of languages, and reveals all that he has been able to discover respecting their chronology and succession. Lastly, he discloses all the dialectical divergencies which are so pregnant with valuable instruction.

Hence, if it is necessary carefully to distinguish these two sciences in their aim and their method, it is no less important to acknowledge that they are both of them destined to render each other mutual, and possibly very considerable assistance. Thus it is that history has frequently furnished useful materials for the study of the races of mankind, and that anthropology has, in its turn, thrown light upon many historic events.

§ 4.—*The Polyglot.*

The practical knowledge of languages, or, to speak more exactly, the art of speaking them fluently and correctly, depends mainly on natural capacity, which is itself developed by a more or less protracted exercise. But it would be a mistake ever to regard it as a science. One is often surprised to meet with an author of numerous and sound philological works, who is incapable of conversing in three or four different languages, and we are still more astonished to find that he is perhaps unable to make use of any language except his own with ease and fluency. But this arises from a misunderstanding. The philologist is not a polyglot, or at least he need not be one. The polyglot, again, has no claim based on his art to the title of philologist; yet we constantly hear this name given to persons who, thanks to some exceptional circumstances, and especially to the individual aptitude above mentioned, discourse with more or less ease in ten or twelve languages, occasionally even in a still greater number, without at the same time possessing the least notion of their inner structure.

What has been above stated concerning the nature of philology and of philological studies obviates the necessity of dwelling further on this common confusion of ideas. At the same time, however, we are of opinion that the results of philology may to a certain point facilitate the study of the art here in question. Let us take, for instance, the Romance tongues, which flow directly from vulgar Latin. It cannot be denied that we may pass from one to another of these idioms, according to tolerably fixed rules, in all that more especially concerns their phonetics and the interchange of consonants. A very small number of general principles gives the key to the more usual equivalents, showing that the resemblance of French, Italian, and Spanish words is not accidental. By this treatment it becomes logical and rational, rendering the study of the languages themselves all the more rapid the less it is given up to mere chance and routine.

In the same way the Teutonic idioms possess laws in common which are generally definite. For instance, to such or such German consonants correspond such or such English, Dutch, or Swedish letters uniformly. And so with the Slavonic group, where Bohemian, Russian, Croatian have a perfectly settled phonology, permitting us to pass without much trouble from the forms of any one of these languages to those of the kindred tongues. Nor are any great mental efforts needed in order to reach these results, nothing more being required than a knowledge of a few elementary principles. Unfortunately there are still wanting practical manuals free from all scientific parade, and planned in such a way as to clearly, and, if needs be, somewhat empirically summarise these few and extremely simple laws. Such little works would be of inestimable aid to the complicate and obsolete systems still in use.*

§ 5.—*The Dangers of Etymology.*

If a special capacity for the practical acquisition of languages is not a science, etymology, on the other hand, can be looked upon neither as a science nor an art. In itself it is nothing but a sort of trick or sleight-of-hand, the greatest and most relentless foe to which is the genuine philologist. In a word, etymology, in itself and for itself, is mere guess-work, ignoring all experience, over-riding all objections, and resting satisfied with specious show, and with results which are scarcely probable, or even at all possible. At first sight the German words, *haben*, to have; *bereit*, ready; *ähnlich*, like; *abenteuer*, adventure, seem to answer, letter for letter, with the Latin *habere*, *paratus*, the Greek ἀνάλογος, and the French *aventure*, as the English *to call* does to the Greek καλεῖν. And yet appearances are here deceptive, philological analysis showing the futility of such comparisons as these, which in fact cannot for a moment stand the test of sound criticism.

---

* This passage is suppressed in the second edition, and the following substituted: "Let us not be too sanguine as to the amount of success likely to be attendant on the introduction of a few elementary notions of comparative Grammar into the lower classes. A lad of ten, twelve, or fifteen years can scarcely show any sustained interest in the laws regulating the interchange of letters in the languages he is studying. He tries to learn Greek and Latin as he has learned his mother-tongue, that is by dint of sheer practice, without paying any heed to rules more or less crudely framed. But would it not be very useful, for those at least who are engaged in teaching, to be acquainted with the existence of these laws, and to have some knowledge of the principal and most elementary of them? In our opinion it would not be going too far to insist upon so much." But the original passage is here retained in the text, because it points, however timidly, at a great principle, which is gradually, but surely, making its way. The translator has himself devoted many years to the solution of the problem, how best to utilise the conclusions of comparative philology in facilitating the acquirement of languages. In spite of much opposition, and much ignorant contempt, he has at least succeeded in convincing some few intelligent teachers that the problem admits of solution, and that the day is perhaps not distant when science will be happily and advantageously combined with routine in the teaching of languages.—*Note by Translator.*

It is by means of such-like fantastic methods that attempts have been made to compare languages absolutely unconnected with each other—the Semitic with the Aryan tongues, Irish with Basque. The most distinguished Semites, who have rendered the greatest services to the philology of the Syro-Arabic languages, have frequently allowed themselves to fall into this trap, and a large number of their works swarm with uncritical comparisons with Aryan roots and words. The celebrated Gesenius himself has not escaped from the misapprehension, so that it is not perhaps surprising that, following in his steps, orthodox interpreters have yielded to it with a keen relish. There is nothing more risky than to get hold of two ready-made words and compare them together. What at first sight seems to establish the most convincing relationship is often the most deceptive.

On the other hand, forms that we should never dream of comparing together are often found to be most intimately related with each other. Since their primitive connection and identity in one and the same form, each of them has been subjected to different modifying laws. But these laws are now discovered, and the absolute unity of the forms themselves placed beyond doubt. Thus, for instance, we reduce to one and the same primitive form the Greek ἡδύς and the Latin *suavis*; the Latin *solus*, and the old Persian *harura*, all; the old Irish *il* and the Sanskrit *purus*, numerous; the Greek ἰός, poison, and the Latin *virus*; the English *fire* and the Croatian *pet*; the Dutch *rader* and the Armenian *hayr*; the Armenian *sé*, I, and the Croatian *ja*. It is thus, also, that words belonging to one and the same language, and which at the first blush seem to be in no way connected, belong in reality to one and the same root. For instance, in French, *solide*, *soldier*, *soldat*, *seul*, *serf*; *jeu*, *bon*, *jour*, *divin*; *auspice*, *sceptique*, *évêque*, *épice*, *répit*; *assister*, *coûter*, *étable*, *obstacle*. We should be exceeding the limits assigned to this treatise were we to set forth in detail the principles that connect all these forms together, and which mere guess-work would, doubtless, never suspect of being so related.

What then is etymology?—or, rather, what ought it to be, to deserve consideration and lay claim to any scientific value?

It is simply a result—a result both of philology and of linguistics.

In the first case it is deductive; in the second, historical.

The history of the French language teaches us for example that *dinde*, turkey, is a contraction of *poule d'Inde*; that *hussard* comes indirectly from the Hungarian *húsz*, meaning *twenty*; that the English *jockey* represents the Old French *jaquet*. These are all so many examples of linguistic, or, if you will, of historic etymologies. In this department, in fact, it is historical criticism alone that can decide on the reasonableness or likelihood of suppositions, on their improbability or incorrectness. It is historical criticism that deals with the multitude of etymologies relying on so many whys and wherefores, amongst which there are many which, however obvious at the first glance, must nevertheless be looked upon as absolutely arbitrary. Thus, according to the Latin jurists, the slave, *servus*, was so called because through the clemency of the victor he had been saved, *preserved*, from the death-blow. But the fact is, the primitive meaning of the word is that of *protector* or *guardian*, in its nominative singular form corresponding closely to the Zend *haurvô*, keeper, *paçus-haurvô*, guard or keeper of cattle in the Avesta. It is by means of the why-and-wherefore argument that *fut*, defunct, is derived from *fuit*, he was. One step more and *cadaver* will come from *ca* [ro] *da* [ta] *ver* [mibus] = *caro data vermibus*; *nobilis* from *non vilis*; and *dignus* from *di-genus* = a kind of God.

Philological is quite as dangerous—perhaps even more dangerous than linguistic etymology. "Do you know," asks the learned doctor, "whence comes the expression *galant homme?*"—Le Barbouillé: "Whether it came from Villejuif or d'Aubervilliers, I care little." The Doctor: "Know that the expression *galant homme* comes from *élégant*; taking the *g* and the *a* from the last syllable, we get *ga*; and then taking the *l*, adding an *a* and the two last letters, that makes *galant*; and then adding *homme*, that makes *galant homme*."

The least indifferent of such etymologies, if all are not alike worthless, may be said without exaggeration to be but little superior to this. Thus, it is not more reasonable to compare the Greek μορφή, form, figure, appearance, with the Latin *forma*, by assuming that the consonants *m* and *f* have simply changed place, than it is to derive *galant homme* from *élégant*. The Latin consonant *f* initial, as will be seen farther on, answers to an aspirated explosive (*bh*, *dh*, or *gh*) of the primitive Aryan form, here to *dh*, which gives us the Sanskrit *dharma*, meaning *jus*, *justitia*, and which explains the force of the Latin diminutive *formula* = form, rule, precept, whereas μορφή is akin to μάρπτω = I seize, a totally different root. Yet how many take as perfectly natural this pretended and fallacious resemblance of μορφή to *forma*, who are the first to laugh at Ménage for deriving *rat* from the Latin *mus* by means of the assumed intermediate form *muratus*, whence *ratus*.

The idea of looking on the philologist as a mere manufacturer of etymologies is far too common, though it can be entertained by those alone who have no notion either of the scope or the method of philology. In truth, the scientific linguist looks on the more or less striking resemblances that give rise to the so-called elegant etymological explanations as the very opposite of conclusive. Experience has shown him how far they may be deceptive; but before and above all it has taught him that languages are not the result of mere chance, but, like all other functions, correspond to an organic necessity; that the laws regulating them reveal a precision all the more striking in proportion as they are the more methodically studied; that these laws, in a word, in many cases discover and explain the direct or indirect relationship of words; but that the inquiry into such relationship is but an accessory, an accidental fact, void of all scientific interest.

The etymologist, it has been said, makes little account of the consonants, and neglects the vowels altogether. But this is not all. Hopelessly to shut the eyes to the true nature of linguistics, and, if possible, to be still more blind to the nature of philology—such is the basis, such the *raison d'être* of the pretended science of etymology. It is by means of such etymological processes that Basque has been brought into relationship with Irish, that French and Provençal have been converted into Keltic dialects, that Latin has been derived from Greek, that Phœnician has been transformed into anything or everything. It is by means of etymology that even now attempts are made to characterise the language of the ancient Iberians with the help of a few geographical terms taken at random; it is by the same medium that the Etruscan inscriptions have been recently read off fluently in two or three different languages.

It cannot be too often insisted upon that philology has nothing in common with these mental gymnastics. The very first shoal that it guards its followers against, is the temptation to deal with words ready made. The etymologist is fain to yield to this temptation, precisely because it forms the basis of his operations; and the philologist himself must doubtless at times rest satisfied with mere assumptions. But these will have no weight either on his conclusions or his method of research. What he aims at discovering and studying are the simple elements of speech and their manner of coalescing together, the functions of organic forms, the laws that regulate the development and subsequent modifications of these forms.

Philology is therefore nothing but a natural science, a truth which will be further confirmed by the consideration of a fresh subject connected with it.

CHAPTER II

THE FACULTY OF ARTICULATE SPEECH—ITS LOCALITY AND IMPORTANCE IN NATURAL HISTORY.

Man is man in virtue of the faculty of articulate speech. This proposition, at one time received with suspicion, has now become a truism, at least for those who believe that metaphysics have run their course. Though it may not be a very convincing argument to appeal even to the best known authorities, we may still be permitted to quote, in connection with this subject, the opinion of some authors, of whom science is justly proud. Such, for instance, is that of M. Charles Martins: "Articulate language is the distinctive character of man."* That of Ch. Darwin: "Articulate speech is peculiar to man, although, like other animals, he may be able to express his intentions by inarticulate cries, by gestures, and by the muscular movements of his features."† That of M. Hunfaly: "The origin of man ought to be considered coincident with that of speech."‡ That of M. Haeckel: "Nothing can have transformed and ennobled the faculties and the brain of man so much as the acquisition of language. The most complete differentiation of the brain, its perfection and that of its noblest functions, that is to say, of the intellectual faculties, while reciprocally influencing each other, still kept pace with their manifestation in speech. It is therefore with good reason that the most distinguished cultivators of comparative philology look upon human speech as the most decisive step man has taken to separate himself from his animal ancestors. This is a point that Schleicher has ably handled in his work on the importance of language in the natural history of man. There is seen the connecting link between zoology and comparative philology, the doctrine of evolution, enabling each of these sciences to follow step by step the origin of language." And farther on, "This man-ape did not yet possess true speech, that is articulate language expressing ideas."§

We shall return at the proper time to the question of the coincidence of the birth of man with that of the faculty of articulate speech. For the present, let us be satisfied with insisting on the capital point, that the faculty in question constitutes the one absolute characteristic of humanity.

. In studying the comparative anatomy of man and other inferior animals, all attempts have failed to discover any difference

---

* "La Création du Monde Organisé," in the "Revue des Deux Mondes," December 15th, 1871, p. 778.
† "The Descent of Man and Sexual Selection," vol. i. p. 58.
‡ "International Congress of Prehistoric Anthropology and Archæology, Fifth Session," vol. i. p. 58.
§ "History of the Creation of Organised Beings, according to Natural Laws." French translation, by Ch. Letourneau, pp. 592 and 614.

beyond one of degree between the two. And even this divergence has been greatly diminished in the eyes of all unprejudiced observers, since the discovery of the African anthropoids. The sentimental theory of the supremacy of man may be said to be at an end, and to have at last fallen into utter discredit. Man is no longer distinguished from the anthropoids, either by the structure of the teeth, the character of the intermaxillary bone, the formation of the hands and feet, the constitution and functions of the vertebral column, the structure of pelvis and sternum, the muscular system, the facts connected with the external sensorial apparatus, the digestive organs, or the anatomical and morphological characters of the brain.*

Nay more, there exists in this respect a far more serious gap between the inferior apes and the anthropoids, than between these latter and man.† Reliance was accordingly then placed on the so-called non-physical characters. But the inferior animals also were found to possess foresight, memory, imagination, the reasoning faculty, the amount of will compatible with their organic systems, giving the most unequivocal proofs of feelings of pity, wonder, ambition, affection, love of rule, and method in their work.

At last recourse was finally had to the two arguments hitherto held in reserve—that is, to those based on *religion* and *morality*, though with but indifferent success. And in truth it is easy to subject the religious sentiment to the same critique that takes cognisance of all other mental phases, and to show that it has its origin in fear, the dread of the unknown: *primus in orbe deos*

---

* Broca, " Discours sur l'Homme et les Animaux," in the " Bulletins of the Paris Anthropological Society," 1866, p. 53 ; " L'Ordre des Primates," *ib.* 1869, p. 228 ; " Études sur la Constitution des Vertèbres caudales chez les Primates sans Queue," in the " Revue d'Anthropologie," ii. 577. See also Vogt, " Leçons sur l'Homme," eighth lesson ; Schaffhausen, " Les Questions Anthropologiques de notre Temps," " Revue Scientifique," 1868, p. 769 ; Paul Bert, " Bulletins de la Société d'Anthropologie de Paris," 1862, p. 473 ; Bertillon, *ib.* 1865, p. 605 ; Magitot, *ib.* 1869, p. 113.

† Broca, " L'Ordre des Primates, &c.," *op. cit. passim* ; Dally, " L'Ordre des Primates et le Transformisme," in the " Bulletins de la Société d'Anthropologie," 1868, p. 673.

fecit timor. The child is not born into the world endowed with the religious faculty: "On this point he knows what he is taught, but he guesses nothing; he has no intuitive perception."* All this has been excellently set forth by M. Broca: "The author of a religious conception brings into play certain active faculties, amongst which the imagination often occupies the chief place. Here we have a first species of religiosity which I will call the active religious sentiment. But this manifests itself in a very limited number of individuals only. The greater part, the vast majority of men, have nothing beyond a passive religion, which consists merely in believing what they are told to believe, without being required to understand it; and this feeling itself is for the most part nothing but the result of education. From his earliest infancy the child is reared in the midst of certain beliefs, to which his mind is moulded without his being in a position to argue or to reason on the matter. No intellect can escape from the action of such systematic instruction, planned and perfected during the course of ages. The child submits in all cases, and frequently once for all. He believes without inquiry, because still incapable of examining for himself, and because in all matters, whether religious or not, he refers blindly to the authority of his instructors.

In all this there is nothing to reveal the existence of a faculty, of a capacity, or of any special promptings of the mind. But with years, experience, and especially study, this passive state always gives place to a certain degree of scepticism. We begin to lose confidence to a greater or less extent in the statements of others; it is no longer enough merely to hear a thing asserted in order to accept it; we ask for proofs, and when any one takes for granted everything that he is told, we say of him that he is credulous as a child.

* Letourneau, "De la Religiosité et des Religions au point de Vue anthropologique," in the "Bulletins de la Société d'Anthropologie," 1865, p. 581; "Sur la Méthode qui a conduit à établir un Règne Humain," *ib.* 1866, p. 269; Lagneau, *ib.* 1865, p. 648; Condereau, *ib.* 1866, p. 329; Broca, "Discours," &c., *ib.* 1866, pp. 59 and 74; Dally, "Du Règne Humain et de la Religiosité," *ib.*, 1866, p. 121.

The spirit of criticism, which grows with the growth of the intellect itself, is at first concerned with material actions, the events of everyday life, in many cases never getting beyond this order of phenomena. But in many others, without at all changing its character, it widens its circle so as to embrace metaphysical and religious thought. Hence in every country, and especially in those where the mind of man is cultivated, we meet with a great number of individuals who little by little give up a part or even the whole of their religious views. Has then this human sentiment, which you call religiosity, been effaced from their minds? Would you place on a level with brute creation those men, who are often distinguished by the extent of their learning and the vigour of their mental powers?

Thus, from whatever point of view we consider this religious element, it becomes impossible to look upon it as a universal fact, inseparable from the nature of man. The active sentiment, which gives birth to religious conceptions, exists in a few individuals only. The passive sentiment, which is but a form of obedience to authority, or of the adaptation of the mind to its surroundings, though indefinitely more diffused, is still very far from being universal. Were it otherwise, the zealots of the various forms of religion would not keep thundering as they do against unbelief.

It should be carefully borne in mind that this pretended sentiment is not only not shared in by a great many men of science, but is further absolutely non-existent amongst a good many reputed savage peoples. It is needless here to reproduce the emphatic statements of a crowd of unprejudiced observers—statements which have been vainly called in question. Tribes living without definite faiths or forms of worship have been supposed to believe at least in supernatural forces and manifestations. But it is certain—in fact, self-evident—that the very inferiority of these races renders them incapable of at all distinguishing between the natural and the so-called supernatural. Hence the necessity of in all cases again ultimately falling back on that fear, in itself easily enough accounted for, which has been above spoken of—the fear of an unknown, or rather of the unknown. But if in this we are to recognise a religion, then there is no animal, however low, to whom the religious sentiment can be denied.

It is needless to dwell upon the last objection—the assumed sentiment of *morality*. It is an ascertained fact that it does not exist amongst a multitude of savage tribes, as the records of ethnology clearly prove; while on the other hand, it is unmistakably to be detected in the acts of a large number of animals, at least of the social order.

Thus it is the faculty of articulate speech that ultimately and conclusively distinguishes man from the inferior creation, where no trace of this faculty has ever been detected. No argument can of course be based on the power of parrots to repeat words—words which are no doubt articulate, but the utterance of which is totally disconnected with any corresponding mental conception. This very correspondence and intimate association between the word and the thought precisely constitutes the true character of articulate human speech, which the parrot does but unconsciously echo.

This characteristic, again, is common to all the races of mankind, which is in itself conclusive. However rude the idioms of the lowest types may appear, they have none the less a full claim to the title of true speech; and the greater or less degree of harmony and grace possessed by them in no way affects their true nature. Besides, it should be observed that it is only the utterance and sounds of their languages that may seem strange, their structure being often far from rudimentary.

But it is objected that individuals not possessing this pretended distinctive human character, the deaf and dumb, for instance, from their birth, or persons stricken with speechlessness in consequence of some injury to the brain, could not in this case be considered as human beings, though on the other hand their claim to the title cannot be gainsaid.

This two-fold objection, though scarcely possessing the force of a specious argument, may still be worth refuting.

What the mute lacks at birth is by no means the faculty here in question, but the power of exercising it. He is dumb only because he is deaf, his deafness alone preventing him from making use of the faculty of speech. Besides, careful instruction may remove this obstacle, and in point of fact those born deaf and dumb do learn to speak and make use of the inherent gift of articulate speech. "The mute, properly so-called, is no more affected in the cerebral or vocal organs of speech than is a person whose legs are tied in the organs of locomotion. Neither the one nor the other lacks the native faculty. They lack nothing but the liberty of exercising it, and this itself is due to a circumstance foreign to the faculty itself."*

We shall consider more fully the case of a cerebral lesion resulting in the loss of speech. Assuredly there can be no doubt that persons so affected retain their right to be considered as human beings, even when speechlessness is complete. But the results of the important studies made in France on this subject do not yet seem to be sufficiently known; hence it is well, and even necessary, here to proclaim them. It may at the same time help to throw further light on the true nature of philological research.

The attempts made during the last century to localise the cerebral faculties were based on a sound principle, but they were necessarily rendered unsuccessful through the want of experimental processes. At the present day the question has been resumed by pathological anatomy, and it is difficult to overlook the great importance of the results arrived at by M. Broca in this domain.† We shall here pass them rapidly in review. ‡

---

* Vaïsse, "Bulletins de la Société d'Anthropologie de Paris," 1866, p. 146.

† "Bulletins de la Société Anatomique," 1861, 1863; "Bulletins de la Société de Chirurgie," 1864; "Bulletins de la Société d'Anthropologie de Paris," 1861, 1863, 1865, 1866; "Exposé des Titres et Travaux Scientifiques," 1868.

‡ What follows may be rendered more intelligible to the unscientific reader by a brief account of the parts of the encephalon alluded to. The cerebrum, or brain proper, as distinguished from the cerebellum, on which it partly rests, is divided by the great longitudinal fissure into two lateral halves, known respectively as the *right* and *left hemispheres*. The under surface of each hemisphere is marked off into three parts or *lobes*—anterior, middle, and posterior, according to their position; the posterior being that part overlapping the cerebellum, while the anterior and middle are clearly

The exercise of the faculty of articulate speech would seem to be dependent " on the integrity of a very circumscribed portion of the cerebral hemispheres, and more especially of the left. This portion is situated on the upper border of the Sylvian fissure, opposite the Island of Reil, occupying the posterior half, or probably not more than the third part of the third frontal convolution." It was the autopsy of those subject to aphasia, that is, of those the muscles of whose articulation are not in the least paralysed, that has demonstrated this localisation. In truth, this autopsy almost constantly reveals "a very decided lesion of the posterior half of the right or left third frontal convolution," nearly always, or about nineteen in twenty times on the left side. A serious lesion of the right has in many cases not affected the power of speech; but "this faculty has never been known to survive in the case of those whose autopsy has disclosed a deep lesion of the two convolutions in question."

We need not here mention the series of operations bearing on this point, which, in our opinion, are entirely conclusive, and which have been placed on record by a number of anatomists. Those who are curious in the matter, will find them in the works quoted in the last note. The interesting question, however, presents itself, why the exercise of the faculty of articulate speech should depend so much more particularly on a convolution of the left cerebral hemisphere, than on the corresponding one on the right, although the functions of both hemispheres do not seem to be radically different. This curious phenomenon is due to the fact, that the convolutions of the left hemisphere have in general a much more rapid development

divided by a deep cleft known as the *Fissure of Sylvius*, or *Sylvian fissure*. On opening this fissure there is exposed to view a triangular prominent portion of the cerebral mass, called the *Island of Reil*, marked by small and short convolutions, or *gyri operti*. These convolutions, concealed in the Sylvian fissure, are amongst the earliest to be developed, and are themselves surrounded by a very large convolution forming the lips of the Sylvian fissure, and known as the *Convolution of the Sylvian fissure*. Lastly, both hemispheres are moulded into numerous smooth and tortuous eminences, also called convolutions or gyri, and marked off from each other by deep furrows, sulci, or anfractuosities.—*Note by Translator.*

than those of the right.* "The first are already clearly planned," remarks M. Broca,† "at a time when the others are not yet perceptible." The left hemisphere, on which depend the movements of the right members of the body, is therefore more precociously developed than the opposite one. Thus we see why the child, from the first moments of existence, more readily makes use of those members, whose nervous system is then more perfect; why, in other words, he becomes right-handed. The upper right member, being from the first stronger and more apt than the left, is on that very account brought more frequently into play, thus acquiring at the outset greater strength and skill, which of course goes on increasing with years. Hitherto I have called those *right-handed*, who more readily make use of the right, and *left-handed*, those who more readily make use of the left hand. But these expressions are drawn from the outward manifestation of the phenomenon, which, when considered in relation to the brain, rather than to its mechanical agents, teaches us that the greater part of mankind are naturally left-handed, so far as the brain itself is concerned, and that some few, those known as left-handed, are, on the contrary, exceptionally right-handed in the same sense. . . .

"The fundamental phenomenon of articulate speech lies neither in the muscles, nor in the motor nerves, nor in the motor organs of the brain, such as the optical layers or the striate bodies. Were there nothing beyond these organs, speech would be impossible; for they exist at times in a perfectly healthy and normal state in individuals that have become totally speechless, or in idiots who have never been able either to learn or understand a language. Articulate speech therefore depends on the portion of the brain connected with intellectual phenomena, of which the motor organs of the brain are in a way nothing but the agents. Now this function of the intellectual order, governing the dynamic no less than the mechanical part of articulation, seems to be the almost invariable concomitant of the convolutions of the left hemisphere, since the

* Gratiolet, MM. Bertillon, Baillarger.
† "On the Seat of the Faculty of Articulate Speech," in the "Bulletins de la Société d'Anthropologie de Paris," 1865, p. 383.

lesions productive of speechlessness are nearly always found to exist in this hemisphere. This is as much as to say that, so far as speech is concerned, we are left-handed (if such a term can be applied to the brain); we speak, so to say, with the left hemisphere. It is a habit we acquire from our earliest infancy. Of all the things we have to learn, articulate speech is perhaps the most difficult. Our other faculties exist, at least, in a rudimentary state, amongst other animals. But although they undoubtedly possess thoughts, and although they are able to communicate them by the medium of a veritable language, articulate speech is itself altogether beyond them. It is this intricate and difficult task that the child has to grapple with from his most tender years, and he succeeds in mastering it by dint of much groping, and by brain work of the most complicate order. Now, this very task is imposed on him at a period almost coincident with those embryonic stages in which the left hemisphere is in a more advanced state of development than the right. Hence there is nothing inconsistent in admitting that the most developed and most precocious cerebral hemisphere is in a better position than the other to guide the execution and co-ordination of the acts, at once intellectual and muscular, that constitute articulate speech. Thus arises the habit of speaking with the left hemisphere, a habit which at last becomes so much a part of our nature, that, once deprived of the functions of this hemisphere, we lose the power of making ourselves understood by speech. But from this it does not follow that the left hemisphere is the exclusive seat of the abstract faculty of speech, which consists in establishing a fixed relation between an idea and a sign, nor even of the special faculty of articulate speech, which consists in establishing a definite relation between an idea and an articulate word. The right hemisphere is no more alien to this special faculty than the left, and the proof is that the individual rendered speechless by a serious lesion of the left hemisphere is, generally speaking, deprived only of the power of himself reproducing the articulate sounds of language. He continues to understand what is addressed to him, consequently he perfectly grasps the relations between the idea and the word. In other words, the faculty of perceiving these relations belongs at once to both hemispheres, which in case of disease may reciprocally supplement each other; but the faculty of expressing these relations by co-ordinate movements—a habit to be acquired only after long practice—seems to belong to one hemisphere only, which is nearly always the left.

"Now, as there are left-handed people, with whom the innate pre-eminence of the motor forces of the right hemisphere imparts a natural and ineradicable pre-eminence to the functions of the left hand, in the same way we see how there may be a certain number of persons with whom the natural pre-eminence of the convolutions of the right hemisphere will reverse the order of phenomena here indicated. In their case the faculty of co-ordinating the movements of articulate speech will, in consequence of a habit contracted in infancy, devolve definitely on the right hemisphere. These exceptional beings in respect of language may be compared to those who are left-handed in respect of the functions of the hand. Both alike are right-handed in respect of the brain. . . . . The existence of a few individuals exceptionally speaking with the right hemisphere would very well explain the exceptional cases in which speechlessness is the result of a lesion of this hemisphere. It follows from the foregoing statement that a subject, whose third left frontal convolution (the ordinary seat of articulate speech) happened to be in a state of atrophy from birth, would learn to speak, and would speak, with the third right frontal convolution, just as a child born without the right hand becomes as skilful with the left hand as others usually are with the right."*

To this quotation, which sums up the state of the question, we have but one remark to add. It is, that the observations hitherto recorded, which are very numerous, all go to confirm the doctrine of the locality of speech. This main point is more conclusive than all the rest, when the question is to show that the study of arti-

---

* See also Adr. Proust, "Altérations de la Parole," in the "Bulletins de la Société d'Anthropologie de Paris," 1873, p. 786; and by the same author, "De l'Aphasie," in the "Archives Générales de Médecine," Paris, 1872.

culate speech is really a branch of natural history, as we have endeavoured to make clear in the preceding chapter.

At the same time the possession of the mere faculty itself can tell us nothing as to how it will be applied by the individual endowed with it. This application is, in fact, an art, and a very difficult one. The child stammers and stutters for a long time, until, thanks to a certain intellectual development, and to the habit thus acquired, he succeeds at last in using his native faculty like those around him. In other words, the faculty is natural, but its exercise is an art; the former being well expressed by the Greek term ἐνέργεια, as the latter is by ἔργον. Hence those purely automatic acts so constantly exhibited in the exercise of the function in question, no less in its normal manifestations than in its pathologic state.*

This distinction is important, and by overlooking it we would run the risk of forming the most extravagant and unscientific notions on the origin of speech.

In the second book of his history, Herodotus relates that Psammeticus, king of Egypt, wishing to find out who were the oldest inhabitants of the earth, entrusted two new-born infants to the keeping of a shepherd, with injunctions to bring them up in seclusion, and never allow them to hear a human voice. Goats supplied them with nourishment, and after a lapse of two years the shepherd was hailed by them with the repeated cry of βέκος. Psammeticus, on inquiry, ascertained that this was a Phrygian word, meaning *bread*; whereupon the Egyptians acknowledged the right of the Phrygians to be considered the most ancient people.

This absurd story, which represents two children, ignorant of every other word, inventing and seemingly declining an undoubtedly derivative noun, gives us a tolerably fair estimate of the philological criticism of the ancients. The experience of Psammeticus implies a total ignorance of the essential and indisputable fact, that the exercise of the lingual faculty is a difficult

---

* Onimus, "Du Langage," in the "Bulletins de la Société d'Anthropologie de Paris," 1873, p. 759, and following.

art—one that is acquired and handed down from generation to generation. To separate from his like a new-born and of course utterly inexperienced infant, and expect him to hammer out a glottic system of his own, betrays a state of mind absolutely devoid of methodic principles. A language, that has already passed through several phases of its existence, cannot be invented; for here, as in all things else, the present is the result of the past. How could an isolated individual of himself possibly again build up that long series of different stages that all languages have undergone? A linguistic system is not a thing that can be manufactured; it is formed and developed of itself step by step; but it is formed when man is born—not the individual man, but man taken in the aggregate, the human race, if you will. As above stated, the appearance of the faculty of articulate speech determines the point of evolution when one of the primates becomes entitled to the name of man.

Schleicher, in his cursive though solid essay on the importance of language for the natural history of man, and in his no less remarkable treatise on the Darwinian theory and the science of language, has discussed this coincidence of the birth of man with the dawn of articulate speech. " If," he says, " it is language that constitutes man, then our first progenitors were not real human beings, and did not become such till language was formed in virtue of the development of the brain and of the organs of speech." Philology, like all the other natural sciences, compels us to admit that man takes his origin in the evolution of inferior forms. We have ourselves alluded to this subject in connection with the excellent communication on "The Precursor of Man," made by M. de Mortillet to the French Association for the Advancement of the Sciences,* on the occasion of the finding of the chipped flints in the marl deposits of the limestone period at Beauce. According to the laws of paleontology, actual man could not have existed at that epoch. The succession of the fauna in the various geological eras is, in fact, now well established. From age to age animals

---

* Second Session, held at Lyons in August, 1873.

become modified, and their varieties fall off all the more rapidly in proportion to the greater intricacy of their organisation. Three times at least the fauna have been renewed since the formation of the above-mentioned limestone deposit at Beauce, and the mammalians contemporary with the flints in question belong to extinct genera, the precursors of, but distinct from, those now living. It is not reasonable to suppose that man alone has escaped from these modifications—man, above all, whose organisation is precisely of all others the most complicate. Hence the chipped flints of the middle tertiary epoch would belong to a genus the forerunner of present man. This opinion is in our eyes extremely probable, and corresponds in every respect with the doctrine set forth by Schleicher in the above-mentioned treatise.

If it cannot be admitted, without falling into metaphysical and childish conceptions, that the lingual faculty was acquired all of a sudden, without cause, without origin—in fact, *ex nihilo*—it must be allowed to be the result of a progressive development of the organs of speech. This assumes before man—that is, before the being distinguished by the faculty of articulate language—another being on the way towards its acquisition; that is to say, on the way towards becoming man. As Schleicher teaches, we must admit that a certain number only of such beings succeeded in acquiring the faculty under the influence of favourable circumstances, from which time they also acquired the right to the title of men; while others again, less favoured by circumstances, broke down in their onward progress, and fell back into a retrograde metamorphosis. Their representatives we may possibly have to recognise in the anthropomorphic creatures, the gorilla, the chimpanzee, the ourang-outang, the gibbon, and the like. We shall see farther on, when passing in review the various phases of languages, that these different stages bear witness, in the most unmistakable manner, to constant progress, to natural development, and regular tendency towards perfection.

Thus, then, in the presence of this perpetual spectacle of evolution unfolding itself before our eyes everywhere throughout nature, we cannot but acknowledge that the faculty of articulate speech has been acquired little by little, in virtue of a progressive development of the organs of speech. It matters little whether this development be due to the various kinds of selection, natural or sexual, or proceed from other hitherto unascertained causes. This, however, is a matter on which we cannot now dwell. It belongs rather to the general study of the variations and permutation of species, which we can do no more than allude to. Here, doubtless, as in everything else, the function has had much to do with the progress of the organ itself; but here also, as elsewhere, the organ, such as it is—that is, the organ in its actual form—must have necessarily proceeded from some lower organism.

It must be therefore definitely admitted that this distinctive property of man is purely relative. We detect its origin and its rudimentary state;* we see that our progenitors acquired it only by degrees, in the struggle for excellence, in which they were destined to prove victorious.

But, though relative only, this faculty is not the less special and peculiar to man, and it is in virtue of it alone that the first of the primates is entitled to this name, which he has earned by incessant struggles, fought out during the course of ages.

CHAPTER III.

FIRST FORM OF SPEECH—MONOSYLLABIC—THE ISOLATING LANGUAGES.

Of all the various forms that languages or groups of languages may present, the monosyllabic is the simplest. In this elementary state all the terms are mere root-words, or word-roots, corresponding in their essence with general conceptions, and unrestricted by any ideas of person, gender, number; of time or mood; of relationship,

---

* Lamarck, "Philosophie Zoologique," éd. Ch. Martins, i. 316, Paris, 1873; Darwin, "Descent of Man," i. p. 59; Hæckel, "Histoire de la Création des Êtres organisés," trad. fr., p. 591.

prepositions, or conjunctions. In this first stage the language is made up of elements only, the sense of which is essentially general, without suffixes, prefixes, or any modification whatsoever, by which any kind of relation might be implied. Hence, in this first state, the simplest of all others, the sentence is made up of the formula: root + root + root, &c. &c., and it is particularly to be noted that these successive roots are always unchangeable.

From this brief statement it becomes clear why the languages of this class have received the name of *monosyllabic* or *isolating*, their words being in fact composed of simple monosyllabic roots, isolated, and, as a rule, independent of each other.

It may be well to state at once that all linguistic systems have passed through this monosyllabic period. The languages whose forms are the most complicate, that is those liable to inflection—as, for instance, the Aryan family—when subjected to scientific analysis betray unmistakable traces of a monosyllabic origin, remote and indirect it may be, but which cannot for a moment be gainsaid, as will be shown in its proper place. We shall also see that the intermediate stage, the period of agglutination—that for instance of Basque, Japanese, and the Dravidian group—has given rise to the inflectional system, whilst itself deriving from the lower stage, that is the monosyllabic—with which we are now occupied.

Not that it can be asserted that all agglutinating idioms must some day become inflectional, or that all the isolating and monosyllabic ones must pass into the agglutinative state. Many tongues belonging to the two lower orders have perished, and it is certain that amongst those now living, whether monosyllabic or agglutinative, the greater number are definitely fixed in those states. Thus, it may be unhesitatingly asserted that Basque and the idioms of North America will perish in their present form.

Besides, it is not without determining causes that such and such languages have definitely assumed their actual forms, whether monosyllabic or agglutinative, while showing but very feeble and rare tendencies to work into the higher stage. These causes may possibly have been multiplied, and may be of very different kinds, the discovery of which is an arduous task, not yet even attempted.

Yet it must in the end prove successful, for the simple reason that there is a cause for everything, and we are making daily advances from the known to the unknown.

Doubtless the most powerful cause of the effect here spoken of is the fact that these languages have entered on their historic life, and have become the instruments of literature. This fact of itself alone proves that the language, such as it was, felt itself equal to the requirements of a developed nationality. In this sense it is not incorrect to say that, at his first step into historic life, man reaches the period which in natural history is called the period of retrogressive metamorphosis. This, however, may or may not be confirmed by the future; nor is it possible, in the present state of scientific knowledge, to indulge in much more than purely conjectural assertions on the point.

It is easy to understand that a system of successive roots, all implying the most general ideas, could offer but a very limited resource to language. On the other hand, the imperious necessity of expressing the various relations of ideas must have made itself felt at a very early stage. But we have seen that the essence of the root-words was the negation and even exclusion of the relational elements, such as active and passive, unity and plurality, past, present, and future. Yet such a period must have necessarily existed. It must, doubtless, be removed back to extremely remote prehistoric ages, and in all probability, it succeeded itself to a still more primitive period, during which the roots were formed by the cohesion of the simple phonetic elements.

In course of time an ingenious expedient was devised as a remedy for the intolerable defect of precision. This consisted in rigorously fixing the position of the roots, that is of the words, in the sentence. Thus syntax was born before accidence or grammar, properly so-called. As we shall have to show farther on, this expedient of rigidly fixing the position of the words in the sentence ultimately gave rise to the second, or agglutinative stage. By passing in rapid review the various monosyllabic languages, we shall see how this important result was turned to account, as well as how its origin may have gradually become obscured.

However this be, we already see that the grammar of all monosyllabic or isolating idioms is necessarily and entirely a question of syntax. In fact, the word in these tongues is inflexible; in spite of all changes of position in the sentence, it remains invariable and always the same, position alone determining its value or force, as subject or predicate, noun or adnoun, substantive or verb, and so on.

It should also be noted, in a general way, that intonation is an important element in monosyllabic languages, a point which does not seem to have received sufficient attention in the various works on this class of idioms. Not the least important function of tone is the differentiation according to circumstances of a large number of homophones, that is of words identical in form, but different in their respective applications, a point we shall presently have to enter into somewhat more fully.

The principal monosyllabic languages—that is, those that constitute or represent an independent glottic system—are five in number: *Chinese, Annamese, Siamese, Burman,* and *Tibetan.* To these, however, must be added a considerable number of isolated idioms in Transgangetic or Further India, such as the *Pegu* in British Burma, and the *Kassia,* confined to a small district in the south of Assam, on the left bank of the Brahmaputra, and about two hundred miles from the head of the Bay of Bengal. These, however, are not of sufficient importance to claim further notice here.

It is not our intention, nor would it here be possible, to treat in minute detail all these different languages. It will be enough to give some general information respecting each of them, while dwelling more particularly on Chinese, the most characteristic of all the languages of this class.

§ 1.—*Chinese.*

Its three great divisions are: the Mandarine, vernacular in the central provinces, and employed as a cultivated language throughout the empire; the dialect of Canton; and that of Fo-Kien. All three, while belonging to the same language, are vastly different, so that the natives of the northern and southern provinces have the greatest difficulty in understanding each other.

The study of Chinese is composed of two clearly-defined branches—the writing system, and the language itself. Let us first speak of the latter.

As already stated, it is purely and simply syntactic. The first rock it had to avoid, in common with all the isolating tongues, was the constant uncertainty of meaning, arising from the multiplicity of senses which one and the same form is susceptible of. Thus the form *tao* means indifferently: *to reach, to ravish, to cover, banner, corn. to lead, way*, without reckoning two or three other senses in which it may be taken. The syllable *lu* stands for: *to turn aside, vehicle, precious stone, dew, to forge, way*, besides three or four others.

It was a somewhat artless, yet very exact expedient, to place side by side two terms capable of being synonymous in some one of their meanings, as for instance *tao* and *lu*, both answering to the idea of *way*. Thus, while *tao* by itself might leave us to choose between nine or ten senses, *tao lu* can mean nothing but *way* or *road*. Is this, as has been assumed, a case of real composition? By no means, for a compound term always implies relationship, while we have here nothing but a heaping-up of homonyms. Not even the juxtaposition of two such words as *fu*, father, and *mu*, mother = parents, can be looked on as forming a true compound, though at the first glance it may seem to be one; and so with *yuan*, distant, and *kin*, near = distance. In point of fact, in this sort of coupling of words together, the first no more depends on the second than the second does on the first.

It may well be supposed that gender also can be determined only by means of a second term. Recourse, for instance, is had to *nan*, male, masculine; *niu*, female, feminine—whence *nan tse* = son; *niu tse* = daughter; *niu jin* = woman. In the case of animals, the distinguishing terms are different, but the process is the same. Nothing can be simpler than this expedient, which we shall again meet with in the agglutinating languages, such as Wolof, Japanese, &c., and even in the most highly-developed forms of speech. In Latin, for instance, there occur the forms *mas canis, femina canis, femina porcus, anguis femina*, and many analogous expressions. Thus it is that many phenomena peculiar to the first phase of speech have struggled on through the course of ages into the last and highest stage of all.

Number is expressed, in principle, by the general context only. Still, at times use is made of some word expressive of *multitude*, *totality*: *to jin* = a crowd of people, many persons, people.

The subject is at once denoted by the fact that it is always the first word in the proposition. The direct object also, in simple sentences, is indicated by its always following the word expressing the action, much as we should say, "James strikes John," and "John strikes James." But in other circumstances the direct object is determined by the employment of certain accessory words; which help-words, however, can in no case be looked on as true prepositions. They are always pure root-words, the only kind of words known* in Chinese, as already remarked; but that they always and constantly retain their proper and independent value in the mind of those who employ them can scarcely be admitted. This value becomes gradually weakened and ever more subordinate; and it is this very subordination that in time converts isolating into agglutinating languages.

The ideas of locality, of dativity, instrumentality, privation, and the like, are also conveyed either by the aid of certain words, or by position in the sentence. It will, doubtless, be enough to indicate this general fact, without entering into the analysis of a series of examples, which may be found in special works on the subject. The genitive is clearly expressed by placing the leading term after the relative, as in *tien tsє*, heaven son = son of heaven; or in the Mandarine language, by introducing the syllable *ti* between the two words placed in the same order as before.

The conceptions of quality and comparison are expressed in perfectly analogous ways. Lastly, that of action, on which the whole proposition turns, is also denoted by a purely syntactical process, or else will have to be deduced from the general sense of the context. Thus, there is nothing in Chinese answering to our imperfect forms, and the future also must at times be evolved out of the context. As to the moods, the Romance conditional is recognised by its syntactical position, while the subjunctive and the optative are eked out by auxiliaries.

In Chinese there is no more room for a verb than for a noun, and it cannot be too often repeated, that syntax alone defines the sense. Out of its place in the sentence the word is nothing but a root taken in the vaguest possible way. In position alone, it awakens precise ideas of individuality, of quality, relation, action. Thus, for instance, the single syllable *ngan* means *to obtain rest, to enjoy rest, in the manner stated, repose*. So with *ta = great, greatly, greatness, to make great*; another = *round, a ball, to round off, in a circle*; another = *to be, truly, he, the letter, thus*.

As above stated, and as we shall have again to repeat, the use of accessory words, in order to impart the required precision to the principal terms, is the path that leads from the monosyllabic to the agglutinative state. The meaning of these auxiliaries becomes gradually obscured, until the time comes when they acquire a value partly arbitrary. But there was a period, the golden age, so to say, of the monosyllabic system, when their true sense, their full and independent signification, suggested itself at once to the mind. This is a fact that the Chinese themselves have observed with astonishing shrewdness, when they divided the roots into two distinct classes—the *full* and the *empty* words (*chi-tsen* and *lin-tsen*). By the first, they understood those roots that retained their full and independent meaning; the roots that reappear in a translation as nouns and verbs. They called *empty* words those roots whose proper value was becoming gradually obscured, and which, little by little, acquired the function of fixing precisely the extremely vague idea of the full words, whose primitive sense was still fully preserved. In this they showed a remarkable power of discernment, which, better than many other discoveries, gave proof of a rare degree of perspicacity. "What is grammar?" the Chinese teacher asks his pupil. "It is a very useful art," replies the pupil; "an art that teaches us to distinguish between the full and empty words."

The different *tones* occurring not very frequently in Chinese, form so many methods of accentuation, extremely useful where it becomes necessary to distinguish the meanings, at times very different, of syllables made up of the same phonetic elements. The Chinese vocabulary, of almost Academic authority, gives 42,000 different ideographic symbols, each of which has its pronunciation sharply determined. But as the spoken language possesses only about 1,200 consonances, " it follows that the same utterance must be given on an average to thirty characters" —(d'Hervey Saint-Denys). From this we see that if intonation has not been able to meet every difficulty, it was, at all events, of great service. This circumstance, as stated, is common to all the monosyllabic tongues. Special works quote a number of examples which need not here be repeated, and without entering into further details, it will perhaps suffice to describe this ingenious and very practical process.

The Chinese phonetic system is not very intricate, without, however, ranking with the most simple. Amongst the consonants *g*, *d*, and *b* are missing in the Mandarine dialect, but *d* only in that of Fo-Kien; but in the latter the sibilants are less varied than in the former. The absence of *r* is a well-known fact. The vowels call for no special remark: they are often met with in the form of diphthongs, and frequently also nasalised.

It is a characteristic fact that the monosyllables begin with a consonant and close with a vowel, the signs *n* or *ng*, met with at the end of Chinese words transcribed in Roman letters, merely indicating the nasalisation of the preceding vowels. There is but one solitary word that has escaped from this strict rule of an initial consonant and final vowel—*eul* = *two* and *ear*.

Purely graphic questions do not come within the province of philology. They form a special study, doubtless very interesting, but quite distinct and independent. It may still be useful to say a few words on the Chinese graphic system, and to show with what skill this people have contrived to adapt to their singular speech a collection of characters seemingly but little suited for the service required of them.

Considering the great number of homophones in a monosyllabic language, that is, of syllables formed of the same phonetic elements, but answering to totally different ideas, it became a serious difficulty how to determine the various meanings of such monads, in a written system. The Chinese solved the puzzle by employing two sorts of signs.

The first is composed of nothing but images, or true designs—the picture of a tree, a mountain, or a dog—at times employed independently, at others, coupled together to reproduce a more or less complex idea. Thus, the image of water and that of the eye placed in juxtaposition convey the idea of *tears*. A door and an ear give the notion of *listening* or *hearing*; while the sun and the moon stand for *brightness*.

Amongst the true designs must also be included the grouping together of lines or points, expressing either number—one, two, three—or superiority, inferiority, inclination to one side or another, and so on. There was a time when these ideographs, thanks to the correctness of their drawing, directly awakened the conception they were intended to represent. But these simple and truthful symbols gradually lost their original outlines, and in the signs now standing for the notions of dog, sun, moon, mountain, we can no longer, at the first glance, detect the primitive images that directly awakened these different ideas. The characters of this first category have been calculated at least at about 200.[*]

The second class is more intricate, involving two elements, a phonetic and an ideographic. From all that has been said, it will be readily understood that the object of the latter is to determine the, at times, very diverse value of the phonetic element. This last, if left standing alone, might leave the reader's mind wavering between a multiplicity of homophones. The ideographic element puts an end to this uncertainty, by suggesting a definite conception, or at least a category of ideas. Thus, the character taken in its totality denotes both the pronunciation and the meaning, each part being complementary to the other. One of them, however, is looked on as of no account as far as its phonetic value is concerned, the utterance

---

[*] Abel Rémusat, "Recherches sur l'Origine et la Formation de la Langue Chinoise," in "Mémoires de l'Acad. des Inscriptions et Belles-lettres," 1820.

being determined by the other alone. If, for instance, the sign *chen*, vessel, is placed before those representing *huo*, fire, and *ma*, horse, these last two will lose their phonetic value, and the whole will be read off as *chen*, but this *chen* will no longer mean *vessel*. In consequence of the character following it, its meaning will be either the flickering of a flame or a particular kind of horse.*

The Chinese have limited to 214 the number of signs which they call "tribunals," and to which European grammarians have given the name of "keys" or "radicals." Besides the 169 ideographs, whose object in association with a non-phonetic element has been explained above, these 214 keys comprise a small number of signs that are purely graphic, or simple pictures. They contain the elements of all the Chinese characters, of which there are about 50,000 (43,496 according to a calculation based on the Imperial Chinese Dictionary), and to the keys all the rest must, therefore, be subordinate. This is what the Chinese have done in their lexical classification, taking care to arrange the keys in consecutive order, according as they are composed of one, two, three, or more strokes, the last of all (*jah*, a musical instrument) being made up of seventeen such strokes. This arbitrary classification, it is evident, has nothing to do with the language itself. In fact, as above stated, the study of Chinese embraces two distinct parts—that of the language, and the written system. Hence the serious difficulties met with by those beginning to study Chinese.

Let us add that all the signs may on certain occasions be employed as purely phonetic symbols. It is in this way that the Chinese are able to write foreign words or names, such as *'Ia si 'ia*, Asia; *'In ki li*, English; *Wi ki to lia*, Victoria. We also know that it was from the Chinese characters, treated as phonetic signs, that was derived the Japanese system of writing, while the Japanese language is so totally different from the Chinese.

* Stephan Endlicher's Chinese Grammar is the simplest we are acquainted with, though too often displaying a lack of criticism.—"Anfangsgründe der Chinesischen Grammatik," Vienna, 1815. The rules for the position of the words in the sentence may be profitably studied in the "Syntax nouvelle de la Langue Chinoise," by Stanislas Julien. Paris, 1869.

As to the Chinese signs themselves, we have already seen that they arose out of a genuine pictorial system. They are still met in this primitive form on some old monuments, so that it becomes possible step by step to follow the gradual changes they have undergone during the course of ages. Several graphic systems have been very clearly determined and employed during periods of many centuries, owing their more or less serious subsequent modifications entirely to accidental circumstances. There, moreover, exist among the Chinese several other kinds of writing, amongst which is a very rapid cursive hand in common use.

But we cannot enter further into the question of the Chinese characters, which is merely incidental to the subject, as we are not concerned with graphic systems, but with the structure and phonetic elements of speech.

§ 2.—*Annamese.*

This is the language of the extreme eastern portion of Further India, that is, of Cochin-China on the south and of Tonkin on the north. It is separated, at least towards the south-west, from the Siamese by the Cambodian, on the nature of which it is still very difficult to form an opinion. A very interesting ethnographic chart of the south-eastern portion of this peninsula has been drawn up by Francis Garnier.*

The Annamese language is absolutely independent of Chinese, both in its phonetic system and its roots, that is to say, its words, since the root constitutes the word itself in all monosyllabic tongues. Gender and number are expressed, as in Chinese, by adding to the principal syllable others with the meaning of *male, female, all, many,* and the like. The adjective is recognised by its position after the noun it qualifies. Lastly, in the verb, tense and mood are denoted by the simultaneous employment of the root on which the sentence turns, and of others, the general meaning of which is that of past, future, and so on.

What has been said of the structure of Chinese is, therefore,

* " Journal Asiatique," Août-Septembre, 1872.

applicable in all its details to Annamese. Here, also, the tonic system plays a chief part, as in Chinese, distinguishing words, the utterance of which would be exactly alike, although their sense may be quite different. There are in Annamese six tones—the *acute*, very hard to describe; the *interrogative*; the *pitched* or *rising*, not very different from the interrogative; the *subdued* or *lowering*; the *grave*; and the *equal* or *uniform*.

The Annamite writing system is figurative, that is, ideographic, and was at a remote period borrowed from the Chinese, but has undergone serious modifications and numerous additions.

The language itself has also borrowed largely from Chinese, especially from the southern dialect. This fact has deceived some writers, who have endeavoured to compare the two languages, and derive them from one common source. But however great be the number of such borrowed words, they have nothing to do with the essence of the language, or with its proper roots. These, even were they much less numerous than they are, would still suffice to establish the undoubted originality and independence of Annamese.

§ 3.—*Siamese or Thai.*

Siamese occupies the region to the north of the Gulf of Siam, extending to some distance into the interior, and also along the western shore of the gulf. Towards the east, it comes in contact with the still but little-known language of Cambodia; and towards the west, with the Burmese, also a monosyllabic language. The name *Thai*, or Siamese, is peculiar to a certain people, but has been extended to the neighbouring and kindred races, as, for instance, to those of Laos to the north.

The Siamese phonetic system is one of the richest, especially in aspirates and sibilants. Its grammar, like the Chinese and Annamese, is purely monosyllabic, and it has four different intonations, serving to distinguish words of like form but different meaning.

§ 4.—*Burman.*

Spoken in the north-west of the peninsula, between Siamese and the Aryan languages of India. Its phonetic elements are not so numerous as the Siamese, and it reckons but one sibilant. Its intonations also are less numerous than the Chinese and Annamese, whilst its grammatical expedients and processes are absolutely the same.

§ 5.—*Tibetan.*

Tibet is indebted to the Buddhism of India for most of its intellectual culture, including its alphabet and its not inconsiderable literature. It is difficult to say what Tibetan literature may have been before the great religious movement entirely revolutionised it. There are no documents dating from that period, and the Buddhist missionaries' first care was to translate into Tibetan the religious works composed in Sanskrit (or Pali). The alphabet employed by them, and which is still in use, was (a modification of the Devanāgari) current in Northern India. Its origin is perfectly clear; and anyone who can read Devanāgari may in a few hours learn Tibetan, which derives directly from it.

The different authors that have written on Tibetan have not made its monosyllabic character sufficiently clear. The processes employed by it are analogous to those made use of in Chinese, Annamese, and the other isolating languages. Thus it possesses neither number nor gender, expressing the latter by the addition of another word meaning male or female: *ra pho*, he-goat; *ra ma*, she-goat. And so with number, denoted by the help of some second term, generally implying the idea of *all* or *multitude*. The pretended Tibetan cases are no more cases than are those that have been attributed to Chinese and Annamese. Here also the *full* root is determined by words which become *empty*, that is, which lose a part of their primary sense, and serve as adjuncts to the principal word.

In itself the term is no more a simple noun (or adjective) than it is a verb, its nature being in each case determined either by its position in the sentence or by the addition of some *empty* root.

After what has been said of the monosyllabic tongues in general, and of Chinese in particular, it seems needless to go more minutely into the structure of Tibetan. It does not differ from that of the other isolating tongues, and we must not be led astray by what grammarians without judgment tell us of its pretended gender, number, cases, persons, moods, and tenses. These are merely so many ways of speaking, which should not be taken literally; and all traces of which will disappear in the comparative syntax of the various monosyllabic languages, which will doubtless soon be composed. Anyone undertaking this task, without attempting to reduce to a common form the essentially different roots of these idioms, would supply one of the first *desiderata* of philology. It would above all be necessary that the idea be thoroughly disseminated that, in order to study any monosyllabic language whatsoever, we forget for a moment all that we know concerning the structure and processes of our flexional forms of speech. Unfortunately, this would seem to be no slight difficulty.

CHAPTER IV.

SECOND FORM OF SPEECH—AGGLUTINATION.

The Agglutinating Languages.

OF all known languages, those that by their form belong to this second class are by far the most numerous. Beyond all manner of doubt they belong to a great many stocks, very distinct, independent, and incapable of being reduced to a common source. Professed etymologists may have attempted to bring them back to one origin, herein more or less wittingly ministering to the tendency of theological systems; but their efforts have been crowned with no better success than they deserved. Doubtless, all etymologists will lend themselves to a comparison of Magyar and Basque, of Tamil and Algonquin, of Japanese and the Australian dialects. But what is etymology? We have already explained that it is a mass of fictions and delusions, an intellectual trifling, a constant defiance of the most rudimentary principles of method, and most frequently of the first elements of common sense.

§ 1.—*What is Agglutination.*

While in the idioms of the first form, Chinese, Siamese, &c., the words are invariably monosyllabic forms, following each other without the least fusion or connection, and each retaining its proper force; in those of the second category many elements are placed in close association, in a way agglutinating, or agglomerating together, whence the name of *agglutinating*, or *agglomerating* languages. Of these diverse elements, one alone contains the leading idea, the main thought or conception, the others losing their independent value altogether. They certainly still retain a personal or individual sense, but this is now entirely relative. The element preserving its primitive force, *strike*, *take*, *keep*, becomes surrounded by others determining its manner of being or manner of action, while these other elements themselves, thus tacked on to the primary one, play the exclusive part of so determining its manner of being or action.

Making R, the initial of the word "root," stand for the essential element of the word, and r r r, for those that have sunk to the condition of mere elements of relationship, we may assume in an agglutinating language the following formulæ: r R, where the primary root is preceded by a prefix of relationship; R r where it is followed by a suffix; r R r, where it stands between two relational terms; r R r r, and so on.

Two or three examples from the Magyar language will make this explanation clear. In the indicative present *kértek*, you pray, *kér* is the root, that is the element whose meaning remains unclouded, while *tek* is the relational element, denoting person. Hence the formula here is R r. In the present optative *kérnétek*, may you pray, where the *né* is also a relational sign, showing that the general and prevailing idea of *kér* is taken in an optative sense, the formula will be R r r.

Now let us take the root *zár*, to shut, and let us consider some of its so-called derivatives, which, in fact, are nothing but cases of agglutination or juxtaposition. They put in the clearest light the real nature of this process. Here are a few of its forms in the third person singular, where the element implying *he* or *she* is understood: *zárhat*, he can shut, formula R R ; *zároyat*, he often shuts, same formula ; *zárogathat*, he can often shut, formula R R R ; *zárat*, he causes to shut, formula R R ; *záratgat*, he causes often to shut, formula R R R ; *záratgathat*, he can often cause to shut, formula R R R R.

Thus we see that two characteristic facts distinguish the agglutinating from the isolating class. In the former the word is no longer composed of the root alone, but is formed by the union of several roots. In the second place, one only of these roots thus agglomerated retains its real value, in the others the individual meaning becoming obscured and passing into the second rank. They serve now only to fix precisely the manner of being or of action of the leading root, whose primitive meaning remains unaffected.

The primary root being thus retained in its primitive form, the others lose their independence, and fall into their place side by side of each other; and this is precisely what constitutes agglutination. Here the word is formed by the union of several different elements or roots, and thus becomes complex. It is this that distinguishes it from the word as conceived in the isolating languages, where it is composed of the root itself and of that alone.

In any case, let us state at once that in the agglutinating tongues there is no true declension or conjugation. The use of these terms, as well as of the corresponding words *case*, *nominative*, *accusative*, *genitive*, and so on, when speaking of Japanese, Basque, Wolof, &c., is merely a conventional way of expressing oneself, not, perhaps, to be absolutely condemned, but yet to be taken with great reserve.

We have stated that the agglutinating idioms are very numerous, in fact embracing the great majority of known languages. We shall now proceed to notice at least such of them as seem best to illustrate the principal agglutinating systems. Some we shall have to treat very summarily, such as the Corean and those of the African negroes. But we shall have to enter more fully into the details of some others, such as the different languages of the Uralo-Altaïc group, the Basque and the American languages. The relatively greater importance of the latter will probably be a sufficient justification of the greater attention they must command at our hands.

After mentioning the principal agglutinating systems, we shall have a word to say on the "Turanian" theory, on the pretended "Turanian languages," and on the principal speculations that this theory has given rise to.

We shall begin with the agglomerating languages of Africa — those of the Hottentots, the Bushmen, the true Negroes, the Katirs, the Fula tribes, and the Nubians. Proceeding eastwards, we shall then treat of the Negritos, the Papuas, and the Australians. Returning northwards, we shall meet the Malayo-Polynesian system; and still farther north, the Japanese and Corean, on the extreme east of the Asiatic continent. Retracing our steps westwards, we shall take the Dravidian group in the south of India; the Uralo-Altaïc family in Asia and Europe; the Basque at the foot of the Western Pyrenees; and, crossing the Atlantic, the languages of the New World. We shall conclude with the idioms of the Caucasus, and certain other tongues either little known or not yet classified.

The first part of this category is purely geographical, but we have had certain grammatical reasons for arranging consecutively the Dravidian, the Uralo-Altaïc, Basque, and American systems. It would be, perhaps, difficult here to explain these reasons, but they will become apparent later on, and more particularly when we come to treat of the American languages.

§ 2.—*South African Languages.*

Under this heading we do not include the idioms of the "Bantu" system, which will be treated of farther on, under the name of "Kafir languages." By South African, as here used, we understand the languages of the Hottentots and of the Bushmen only.

(1) *Hottentot.*

The origin of this race is involved in great obscurity, nor is that of their language at all better known. Attempts have unsuccessfully been made to group it with the Hametic system, Old Egyptian, Coptic, &c.; but, as it stands, it seems to be isolated and independent of all other tongues. It is, however, clearly agglutinating.

Of the Hottentot there are three dialects: *Nama* or *Namaqua*, *Khora*, and *Cape Hottentot*.

Of these, the first, spoken by some twenty thousand persons, is the most important. Converging northwards on the Herero (a Bantu idiom, of which presently), and limited on the south by the Orange River, Namaqua Land is bounded westwards by the Atlantic, and eastwards by the Kalahari desert.*

Khora, or *Khorana*, is spoken much farther to the east, in the district watered by the Vaal, Modder, and Caledon, about the 29° south latitude. It bears a certain affinity to the Namaqua tongue, but is rapidly dying out.

Cape Hottentot is well-nigh extinct. It was formerly diffused throughout the colony, bordering north-eastwards on the idioms of the Kafir system, northwards on the Khora, and on the northwest on the Namaqua. At present there remain but a small number of Griquas, who still speak Hottentot amongst themselves, Dutch, English, and Kafir having elsewhere almost entirely extinguished it.

However, all these dialects differ but little from each other, so that the Griquas have no great difficulty in understanding the Namaqua of the Atlantic seaboard.

The Hottentot in his own language calls himself *Khoïkhoïb*, in the plural *Khoïkhoïn*, a word which means "man of men," or "friend of friends."—(Hahn, *op. cit.*, p. 8).

The Namaqua phonetics are very varied, possessing a very delicately graduated series of vowels, all of which are capable of being nasalised. There are also a considerable number of diphthongs— about twelve altogether.

It is no less rich in consonants, besides the ordinary explosives

---

* Th. Hahn, "Die Sprache der Nama," Leipzig, 1870; Tyndall, "A Grammar and Vocabulary of the Namaqua-Hottentot Language;" Bleek, "A Comparative Grammar of the South African Languages," London, 1869.

(*p, t, k,* and *b, d, g*), including *k, h,* and several other gutturals; the sibilants *s* and *z* (as in *sister, zeal*); a peculiar nasal, somewhat resembling the nasal sound heard in the German word *enge*; *v, r, h,* and a palatal, which, however, does not occur in the Namaqua dialect.

To these various consonants must be added four others of a special order—the so-called *clicks*. The *dental* click, denoted by a vertical stroke |, or, according to some writers, by the letter *c*; the *palatal*, marked by two horizontal bars crossing a vertical one, ⧧, or by the letter *v*; the *cerebral*, represented by a sign of exclamation, !, or by the letter *q*; the *lateral*, expressed by two vertical bars, ‖, or by the letter *x*. These click-letters, though sounding strange to an European ear, are yet capable of being imitated. They will be found fully described in special grammars, all, at least, except the fourth, which is very peculiar, and is so called because the side teeth play an important part in its utterance.

The click-letters may precede the gutturals *n, h,* and all the vowels, and they occur moreover every moment—in fact, almost in every word.

Word-formation is extremely simple: root followed by a suffix —that is, by some derivative element.

Let us observe at once that these derivative elements have each a three-fold form: one for the word when subject; another for the word when object, whether direct or indirect—the first receiving the name of *subjective*, the second that of *objective*; the third form is the *vocative* or *interjective*.

Again, these suffixes have a singular, a dual, and a plural form, making for one and the same element altogether nine forms; as there may be a subjective singular, an objective dual, an interjective plural, and so on.

We find ourselves on the other hand confronted by a triple supposition: The derivative element of the root may be an element of the first person (*I, we two, we*), or of the second (*thou, ye two, ye*), or else a common or third personal element; and on this depends the nature of the suffix itself.

In the first two cases, words are formed with the sense, for instance, of " I king, I who am king," "thou who art queen," and so on. In a word, the element, as already stated, changes nine times for one and the same word, according as the form is subjective, objective, interjective, singular, dual, or plural.

Let us add that the suffix varies according as the individual is masculine, feminine, or neuter.

Passing from words derived by an element of the first or second person to those formed by a common or impersonal suffix, we find the subjoined endings in the Namaqua dialect, to which these remarks are restricted :

		Mas.	Fem.	Neut.
Singular	Subjective	b	s	i
	Objective	ba	sa	ô
Dual	Subjective	kha	ra	kha or va.
	Objective	khâ	ra	,, ,,
Plural	Subjective	gu	ti	n
	Objective	gà	te	na

Glancing at this scheme, we at once see that the word *taras*, woman, is subjective, singular feminine. In the expression " I see the woman," it will become *tarasa*; in "the two women say," it will be *tarara*; and so on. The form *khoib*, man, will be used in the sentences, "the man says," "the man strikes ;" in "the men say," "the men strike," it will be *khoigu*, and in "they strike the men," *khoigà*. All this, doubtless, requires a little attention and practice, but is otherwise easy enough.

Secondary derivation is effected by adding fresh suffixes to those already attached to the root ; and it is also by means of fresh elements thus added to the end of the word that are expressed the relations of locative, ablative, instrument, and the like. Adjectives also are derived from substantives by the same process.

Causatives, diminutives, intensitives, desideratives, are all formed by adding secondary or derivative elements to the principal root. As to the pretended verbal forms, they simply consist in the agglomeration of elements, one expressing person, another the principal root, a third, time—present, past, or future.

Lastly, Hottentot, like the monosyllabic tongues, distinguishes its homophones by uttering them in various tones. Of these tones there are three, as in the word *ikaib*, meaning either *darkness*, *place*, or *linen*, according to its intonation. Such homophones, however, are not very numerous.

On the other hand, the true accent falls invariably on the radical syllable, that is, on the first, the Hottentot formula always being: root + suffix, or root + suffixes. In the case of compound words, the accent falls on the principal component.

(2) *Bushman Dialects*.

The Bushmen, who are scattered in a great number of small tribes over the country, have no generic name for their race. The Hottentots call them *Sán*, that is, aboriginal or indigenous; and the designation of Bushmen was first given them by the Dutch.

But little is known of the various idioms spoken by the Bushmen. If there is any common affinity between them, great differences at least prevail amongst some of their tribes, while the attempt to connect them with the Hottentots has been unsuccessful. As far as we know them, the Bushmen dialects are, in fact, quite independent of those of the Hottentots. In any case, they belong to the agglutinating order of languages, and are said to possess six or seven click-letters.

It is not easy to fix their geographical limits. They are met with on the east of the Herero district, north-east of Namaqualand, and north of the Kalahari desert; while some tribes are found south of this desert and of the Orange River, in the north-west of Cape Colony. In fact, according to Fritsch, they must have at one time spread over the whole of South Africa, from the Cape to the Zambesi, and even beyond that river,* whence they seem to have been gradually driven by the pressure of more powerful races.

§ 3.—*Languages of the African Negroes*.

The north of Africa is occupied partly by Arabic, which belongs to the Semitic, and partly by Berber, which belongs to the Hamitic

---

* "Die Eingeborenen Süd-Afrika's." Breslau, 1872.

family. On the east coast there are also Semitic tongues, more especially related to the Arabic branch; and farther south, that is, immediately north of the equator, some Hamitic idioms, grouped under the general designation of Ethiopian languages. The whole of the south-east, and a large portion of the south-west coast, are occupied by the Kafir tongues, forming a distinct family in themselves; while the Bushman and Hottentot dialects stretch thence southwards to the Cape. In the centre of the continent, going from the south of Upper Egypt westwards, we meet with the Nubian and Fula groups, neither of which have anything in common with the others here mentioned.

The rest of Africa, that is, the middle of the west coast, and a great portion of the centre, is in possession of idioms spoken by the negroes proper, who are anthropologically to be distinguished from the Kafir race.

The number of these negro dialects is considerable. Some of them are closely enough related to constitute together certain well-defined groups, though the common origin of these various groups cannot yet be scientifically proved. They all, doubtless, belong to the agglutinating order, but this in no way implies a common source. Notwithstanding numerous reciprocal borrowings, both their vocabularies, and especially their grammars, differ greatly. In the actual state of our information, we may say that there are a certain number of negro languages, or groups of languages, entirely distinct and independent of each other.

Fr. Müller reckons twenty-one of such groups, but whether this number will be increased or diminished by further research, it is impossible to say. For the present it will be enough to point out that the expression "Languages of the African Negroes," forming the title of this paragraph, is purely geographical, involving no necessary affinity between these languages themselves. We shall take them as nearly as possible in their geographical order, proceeding from the north southwards, and from the west eastwards.

(1) *Wolof.*

There are a number of grammatical treatises on this language, whose accidence and vocabulary are tolerably well known. Still all these works are deficient in method and critical acumen. They supply us with the materials for a scientific Wolof grammar; but such a work has yet to be written, nor can it be looked for from the missionaries labouring in this field. Their numerous publications betray the most complete ignorance of the principles of the modern science of language, and they seem to be wholly unconscious of the true nature of an agglutinating tongue.

The phonetics of the Wolof are tolerably rich, possessing, besides the short vowels *a, e* (sharp), *i, o, u,* the long sounds *â, î, ô, û, ê* and a sharp *e,* also long, besides another *e,* seemingly answering to the *e* of the French *je, te, le,* and a short *a,* which seems intermediate between the French *a* and *e.* In a few words there occurs a nasal *a,* answering to *an* in the French *grand;* but, as a rule, the vowel preceding *n* is not nasal. Wolof also possesses the French *u* as in *tu, lu,* but only in words borrowed from that language.

The consonantal system is equally rich, possessing, besides the three pairs of simple explosives (*k g; t d; p b*), a *t* and a *d* liquid, transcribed by *t' d';* the nasals *m n n'* (*gn* French) and a nasal described as guttural, which is both initial, medial, and final; further, a very soft *h* and a guttural *h',* answering to the German *ch* in *nach* : *y, r, l,* the hard fricative *s* and a *z,* for words taken from the French ; lastly, the fricative *f* and a *w,* very difficult to be grasped by European ears. The groups *mp, mb, nt, nd, ng* are very frequent, but they are mere combinations, not distinct sounds.

Nouns and adjectives are undeclinable, as in all agglutinating tongues, the case endings of inflexional languages being expressed by particles or prepositions. When, however, the direct and indirect object come together, as in "Give a book to John," the particle *to* is not expressed at all, recourse being then had to a purely syntactical process, as in the isolating idioms. In fact, the sense is deduced from the position of the word in the sentence, the indirect always preceding the direct object. Nouns dependent on other nouns, as in "the king's son," are placed after them, the conjunction *u* intervening, though this particle is sometimes understood.

Gender is expressed by the addition of some other term meaning *male* or *female*, connected with the qualified word by means of a relational particle. The form of the word is otherwise invariable, even for number, the plural also being denoted by the particle *i*, which, in the case of a noun with a complement is inserted between the two words, thus replacing the above-mentioned particle *u*, this latter being restricted to the singular.

The noun is often accompanied by a determinating suffixed particle, composed of a consonant and a vowel. The consonant varies according to a euphonic law, regulated by the nature of the initial letter of the word so determined, as thus : *báy-ba* = father-the, *fás-vă* = horse-the, *kăr-gă* = house-the. The vowel also varies according as the determined object is present (*i*), near, but not present (*u*), at a distance (*ă*), at a great distance (*ă*). Thus, *kăr-gă*, as above, implies that the house spoken of is at a distance; whereas it would become *kăr-gi* were the house close by, and so on. In the plural, again, the suffixed particle is also modified according to the four cases of greater or less distance; thus becoming *yi, yă, yu*, &c., and in certain cases, *n'i n'u* (*n* liquid): *kăr-yi* = the houses close at hand, &c. This determinating plural particle *yi, yă, yu*, obviously contains the above-mentioned plural sign *i*, whence we may conclude that in the singular particles *gi, bă, ku*, &c., the real determinating element is the vowel, though the part played by the initial consonant *g, b, k*, &c., has not yet been clearly ascertained.

By means of these hints the learner begins to understand such elementary expressions as : *fás u băr* = horse-of-king ; *fás u băr-ba* = the horse-of-the king ; *fás u băr-yă* = the horse-of-the kings ; *fás i băr* = horses-of-king ; *fás i băr-ba* = the horses-of-the king ; *fás i băr-yă* = the horses-of-the kings. Apart from the determinating element of this suffixed particle, the process is very elementary and easily grasped. From these examples it appears that the first noun does not take the determinating sign, so that if the second is undetermined neither of them take it : *fás u băr*; *dăh' u muy* = butter-of-cow.

Another means of still more closely determining the word, is by transposing the determinating particle : *bi-báy, bă-báy, bu-báy* =

this father; or by suffixing the particle *lé* to the word already determined by the usual process: *báy-bi-lé, báy-bu-le*, &c., and even *bi-lé-báy, bu-lé-báy*, and so on; these forms of course becoming in the plural *yi-báy, báy-yi-lé* = these fathers.

It need scarcely be said that the Wolof verb is no more capable of being conjugated, than is the noun of being declined. The so-called verbal forms occurring in the endless schemes of Wolof grammars, drawn up on Greek and Latin models, are nothing but an accumulation of independent words placed side by side, as in all other agglutinating tongues. The root always retains its general or abstract force, and to it are tacked on, either as prefixes or suffixes, certain particles expressing the various relational ideas of past, future, conditional, subjunctive, &c. In all this there is no real change, the words so placed in juxtaposition never varying in form. Hence, in this so-called conjugation we have merely to supply the required pronouns, *I, thou, he*, &c.; which, however, are placed, according to circumstances, in various positions in this agglomeration of words.

The number of such combinations is considerable, two-thirds of all Wolof grammars being usually devoted to this pretended conjugation. Yet all that is needed, is a knowledge of a certain number of accessory words or particles, and of the place they occupy in the general scheme. Thus, the particle *on*, answering to the imperfect tense, is placed after the principal word and before the personal pronoun: *más-ná* = have-I; *más-on-ná* = having-was-I. The forms, however, are usually much more complicated than this, at first sight appearing very intricate, and often involving six, seven, eight, or even more accessory elements. Thus *más-águ-nu-won-sopá-sopá-la* = we have not yet made a show of loving, is but one compound term, made up of sundry agglutinated particles, all fused together, but each playing a fixed part, and occupying a settled place in the agglomeration. The last three elements mean "not to make a show of loving;" the first (*más*) expresses the action itself; *agu* implies that the action has not yet begun; *nu* is the personal element, and *won* the sign of the imperfect. We may add that this is by no means an exceptional case, and many other far more intricate examples might be quoted, but the formative process is always the same.

Of all the pure Negro tongues, Wolof is one of the most important, so far as concerns the interests of European civilisation. The French Senegal settlements are in daily contact with the Wolofs, who have borrowed a number of words from the French language. All along the river Senegal, Wolof borders on the Arabic spoken on its right bank, and stretches southwards over a large portion of Senegambia. It is the current speech of Jolof, Kayor, Walo, Dakar, and is also spoken in Baol, Sine, and Gambia.

(2) *Mande Group*.

Mandingan occupies the southern portion of Senegambia, and the region of Upper Guinea. *Bambara* is spoken a little more to the north, and east of central Senegambia. To the same family belong the *Susu*, *Vei*, *Tene*, *Gbandi*, *Landoro*, *Mende*, *Gbese*, *Toma*, and *Mano*.

(3) *Felup Group*

Also occupies the southern parts of Senegambia and the districts a little farther south. It touches at various points on the Mandingan, and comprises a number of dialects, such as *Felup*, on the Gambia; *Filham*, on the Casamanze; *Bola*, *Serere*, *Pepel*, in the *Bissagos* islands; Biafada, on the river Geba; *Pajade*, *Baga*, *Kallum*, *Timne*, *Bullom*, *Sherbro*, *Kissi*.

(4) *Sonrai*

Occupies an isolated position on the Niger, south-east of Timbuctu, about the 15° north latitude. It is therefore spoken in a portion of South Sahara, its domain confining on that of the Tuaric, which stretches more northwards. Speaking generally, it may be said to be spoken in the district lying between Timbuctu and Agades.

(5) *Hausa, or Haussa,*

Which is split up into a considerable number of dialects, may be described as the proper language of Soudan (or, more correctly, of the region lying between the Niger on the west and Lake Chad on the east). No other idiom of Central Africa is so diffused as the Hausa, which is the commercial speech of this part of the continent. It is now tolerably well known, thanks especially to the writings of the English missionary, the Rev. James F. Schön.

Its vowel system is rich; besides *a, i, u*, long and short, possessing *o, e*, an *e* and an *i* very short, not easily distinguished from each other, a labial intermediate between *u* and *o*, which may be lengthened, lastly *a* and *e* obscure and guttural. The consonantal system is less complicated, consisting of *p, t, k; b, d, g, m, n; r, l; f, s, z, s' (sh); j* French; *ch, j, w*, and a nasal analogous to the English *ng* in *king*.

Gender is distinguished not only by some secondary term meaning *male* or *female*, but also by the ending *ia* or *nia*, the force of which has not yet been quite cleared up: *sa* = bull; *sania* = cow. Its origin, however, is doubtless the same as that of the other process. Number also is denoted either by a particle, of which there are several varieties, or by doubling the last syllable of the word. In practice this process presents certain difficulties, but is in itself simple and intelligible enough.

There is no true declension in Hausa any more than in any other agglutinating tongues. The various relations of the Greek and Latin cases are expressed either by the position of the word in the sentence, or by the help of particles joined to the noun: *ma-sa* = to him; *ma-ta* = her; *gare-sa* = of or from him. The subject and the object are also denoted by their position, the latter naturally following the former. Lastly, the idea of possession is expressed by placing the principal word immediately before the other, or else by connecting the two with the particle *na* or *n* masculine, *ta* feminine.

As in other agglutinating idioms, the pretended moods and tenses of the Hausa verb are formed by means of distinct words that have reached the stage of particles. The system seems at first somewhat complex, but it presents no difficulties that cannot be overcome by means of a little scientific analysis.

(6) *Bornu Group*

Is situated in the neighbourhood of Lake Chad, to the east of the Hausa, and comprises some half-dozen dialects, amongst which *Kanem*, *Teda* (or *Tebu*), both spoken by Tebu tribes, north and north-east of the lake, *Kanuri*, *Murio*, and *Nguru*.

(7) *Kruh Group*,

Including *Grebo* (Basa, &c.), brings us to the Windward and Grain Coast, near the river St. Paul (in Liberia).

(8) *Ewe or Ife Group*

Occupies the western portion of the Gulf of Guinea, about the 7° north latitude, and somewhat farther north. It embraces four idioms, all akin to each other—*Ewe*, *Yoruba*, *Oji* (or *O-tyi*), and *Gã* or *Akra*.

Besides these groups there remain to be mentioned the *Ibo* and *Nupe* spoken, the first in the north, the second in the south of the Niger Delta.

Michi, an isolated idiom, a little to the east of the foregoing, about the 7° north latitude.

Mosgu, *Batta*, and *Logone*, still farther east, south of the *Bornu* group and of Lake Chad, and forming a group of themselves.

Baghirmi, to the east of the preceding, in the very heart of Africa, and stretching south-east from Lake Chad (in the direction of Darfur).

Maba, in the same direction, and unconnected with the surrounding dialects.

Lastly, eastwards of Central Africa, south of Nubia, and west of Abyssinia, another negro group, known as that of the *Upper Nile*, and comprising the *Shiluk*, on the west bank of the Bahr-el-Abiad; *Dinka*, on the right bank of the same river; *Nuer*, immediately below *Shiluk* and *Bari*, about the 5° north latitude (or between Gondokoro and the great equatorial lake system).

In conclusion, let us repeat that the various groups of languages, spoken by the negroes of Senegambia, Soudan, and Upper Guinea, are all independent of each other. We have here mentioned the majority of the one-and-twenty groups hitherto recognised; but these groups do not constitute so many branches or ramifications of some one linguistic family. They are no doubt all agglutinating, but, as already stated, this analogy establishes no sort of affinity between languages so constituted. In a word, *Wolof, Hausa, Sonraï*, and *Bari* are no more cognate tongues than are Basque and Japanese, or Magyar and Tamil.

§ 4.—*Bantu or Kafir Family.*

Occupies a wide domain, roughly comprising the whole of the south-east of the continent, reaching southwards to the neighbourhood of the Cape, and northwards a little beyond the equator, where it meets the Ethiopian group of the Hamitic family, and the dialects of the negroes of Guinea, thus spreading north and south over about one-half of the whole continent.

About one-fourth of the natives of Africa speak the various dialects of this family. These are very numerous, and are derived all from one common source, which, as we have seen, is far from being the case with the languages spoken by the negro tribes in the centre and west of the continent. The mother-tongue of this great family is utterly unknown, but it may possibly yet be restored in all its essential grammatical and lexical features.

The general name of Kafir, often given to the Bantu family, is purely conventional. The word, which is Arabic, and means *infidel*, was at first applied to all the tribes of south-east Africa, but was gradually limited, until it has now come to be restricted to those stretching from the north-east of Cape Colony to Delagoa Bay. Hence it cannot with propriety be any longer applied to such languages as the Kisuaheli, spoken in Zanzibar, or to the Fernandian, in the Gulf of Guinea.

The term *Bantu* is in every way preferable. It is the plural of the word meaning *man*, has the sense of *men, population, people*, and may readily be extended to the language itself.

The phonetic system of the whole family is one of the richest, nor is it lacking in harmony. As a rule words are modified not by suffixing, but by prefixing the various elements of relationship.

It is divided into three great branches—a western, a central, and an eastern, each of which is again subdivided into a number of minor groups. They are thus classified by Fr. Müller and Hahn*:

Eastern Branch.—Languages of the Zanzibar district; languages of the Zambesi; Zulu-Kafir group.

Central Branch.—Sechuana and Tegeza.

Western Branch.—Kongo; Herero, &c.

The principal dialects of the north-eastern or Zanzibar district are the *Ki-Pokomo*, a little to the south of the equator; *Ki-Suaheli*, about the 5° south latitude; *Ki-Nika*, *Ki-Kamba*, *Ki-Hiau*, about the 13° south latitude. Of the tribes speaking these idioms, the Suaheli is the best known.

Somewhat farther south are the Zambesi languages, *Tette*, *Sena*, and others. *Makua*, a little more to the north-east, is spoken in the Mozambique country.

Still farther south are the *Kafir* proper and the *Zulu*, closely related to each other, and tolerably well known through the writings of the English missionaries.† Zulu is spoken by the Amazulus, in Zulu-land and Natal; Kafir, by the Amakhosas or Kafirs proper, south of Natal. To these is related the *Fingu*, spoken by the Amafingus, the Amasuazis, and some other obscure tribes. Thus this Kafir group reaches from Cape Colony to Delagoa Bay.

Of the two languages of the central group, *Tegeza* is the least known.

Sechuana, with which we are much better acquainted, is the language of the Bechuanas, north of the 20° and south of the 25° latitude. It includes eastwards the *Sesuto*, spoken by the Basutos; westwards, the *Serolong* and *Sehlapi*, spoken by the Barolongs and the Bahlapis.

Coming to the west or Atlantic coast, we find the Bantu system less prevalent here than on the east coast.

Northwards it stretches four or five degrees beyond the equator, thus bordering on the languages of the Negroes proper.

The northern division of this western branch comprises the

* " Grundzüge einer Grammatik des Herero," p. 5. Berlin, 1857.
† Appleyard, " The Kafir Language." London, 1850.

dialects of *Fernando Po*, *Mpongwe*, *Di-Kele*, *Isubu*, *Dualla*, and *Kongo*, which last is the most important of the group.

More to the south are the *Bunda* (in Angola), *Benguela*, *Londa*, and *Herero*, about the 19° south latitude, and reaching southwards as far as the Hottentot Namaqua dialect.

Bleek classifies all these languages somewhat differently, dividing them into three distinct branches.*

The first comprises *Kafir*, *Zulu*, *Schlapi*, *Sesuto*, and *Tegeza*.

The second embraces five subdivisions: 1, *Tette*, *Sena*, *Makua*, *Ki-Hiau*; 2, *Ki-Kamba*, *Ki-Nika*, *Ki-Suaheli*, *Ki-Sambala*; 3, *Bayeiye* (in the interior); 4, *Herero*, *Sindonga* (spoken by the Ovambo), *Nano* (in Benguela), *Angola*; 5, *Kongo*, *Mpongwe*.

The third division includes the *Di-Kele*, *Benga* (in the islands of Corisco Bay), *Dualla*, *Isubu*, *Fernandian*.

It is difficult to venture an opinion on this arrangement, many languages in the interior of South Africa being unknown. But fresh discoveries and researches will doubtless enable us to classify more exactly the idioms already known.

The phonetics of the Bantu family call for no particular remark, except that the vowels are liable to contraction, to euphonic suppressions, and to rather numerous variations, but always in accordance with well-determined principles. In this respect the Kafir idioms are more refined than many other agglutinating tongues; instances occurring in them of true vowel harmony, that is of the vowel of one syllable assimilating to that of another in the same word.

The consonantal system seems somewhat complex, owing especially to the great number of double consonants, whose first element is a nasal: *nt*, *nd*, *mp*, &c. &c.

On the other hand we again meet here with some of the click-letters described when treating of the Hottentot phonetics. The Kafirs seem to have borrowed them from their Hottentot neighbours, as they occur in those Kafir dialects only that border on the Hottentot domain, as, for instance, in those of the Zulu branch.

* Bleek, "A Comparative Grammar of South African Languages," p. 5. London, 1869.

The farther we proceed from this neighbourhood, the less frequent these letters become; hence they do not occur at all in Mpongwe. Nor can the clicks precede other consonants in Kafir as they can in Hottentot; and of the four Hottentot clicks, two only (especially the dental) are of frequent occurrence. Of the other two, one is very rare and the other altogether unknown.

The number of other consonants is very considerable. They are subject to fixed euphonic laws, and interchange regularly between the various members of the Bantu family, a great many of such concordances being already well known and determined.* Kafir seems the most highly developed of the cognate tongues in its euphonic system.

All these languages have this in common: that the word is built up by elements not suffixed, but prefixed to the principal root. Thus the agglutinating formula in Kafir, Tegeza, Herero, &c., is R R (see p. 45).

Of these prefixes, some denote the singular, others the plural. Thus, in Kafir, the singular prefixes are: *ili, izi, u, ulu, um*; those of the plural: *aba, ama, imi, izi, izim, izin, o*. Thus *umuntu* = man, *abantu* = men; *ulude* = sister, *odude* = sisters.

These various formative prefixes of course differ in the various idioms of the Bantu family, but they all, nevertheless, derive from older common forms. At some unknown period there existed a common Bantu tongue, which subsequently broke up into different dialects, all characterised by special euphonic laws. Hence the various prefixes of this primitive speech were naturally modified in the various idioms derived from it.

A comparison with the other members of the family shows that the initial vowel of the Kafir prefixes *um aba*, above referred to, really constitutes another prefix. The words *umuntu, abantu* would thus be decomposed into *u-m-ntu, a-ba-ntu*; the elements *m, ba*, being, in this instance, the true derivative elements of the word. In Sesuto (a Sechuana dialect) the singular, *motu*, becomes plural, *batu*; in Sena, *munto* and *ranttu*; in Ki-Hian (the Zanzibar dialect) *mundu* and *vandu* respectively. But in Herero, as in Kafir, we

* Bleek, *op. cit.*, p. 81.

CHAP. IV.] SECOND FORM OF SPEECH—AGGLUTINATION. 63

meet with another element prefixed : *omuntu, ovandu* ; so also in Kongo: *omuntu, oantu*. Hence, those writers that employ the word *Abantu* as the general designation of the whole family, would do better to use the form *Bantu* for this purpose, this being the first or most direct derivative of the term.

Subjoined is a table of the singular and plural forms of this word in some of the languages in question :

	Sing.	Pl.
Ki-Suaheli	mtu	watu.
Ki-Nika	mutu	atu.
Ki-Kamba	mundu	andu.
Ki-Sambala	muntu	wantu.
Ki-Hiau	mundu	vandu.
Sena	muntto	vanttu.
Makua	mûttu	attu.
Kafir	umntu	abantu.
Zulu	umuntu	abantu.
Sehlapi	mothu	bathu.
Sesuto	motu	batu.
Tegeza	amuno	vano.
Herero	omuudu	ovandu.
Sindonga	umtu	oantu.
Nano	omuno	omano.
Angola	omutu	oatu.
Congo	omuntu	oantu.
Benga	moto	bato.
Duabla	motu	batu.
Isubu	motu	batu.

The case elements are also prefixed. Thus in Herero, the instrumental sign being *na*, we get *nomuudu* or *namundu* = with or by the man. Here a euphonic law comes into play, the first form being *nomuudu* for *na + omuudu*. So in Kafir, *umntu* = man, and *abantu* = men, become *ngomuntu* = with the man, *ngabantu* = with the men. Here the instrumental sign is *nga*, answering to the Herero *na*, and we see how it is prefixed to the word formed by a primary derivative element singular and plural.

The adjective is formed with the same derivative element as the noun it qualifies, or if there be a difference it is at least very slight. In Kafir, *kulu* being *great*, *umntu omkulu* will be *great man* ;

abantu abakulu, great men. The word *into* = thing, being *izinto* in the plural, *into enkulu* = great thing; *izinto ezinkulu* = great things. In a word, the adjective necessarily agrees, even in its formation with its noun.

Thus the word *kulu* = great, may, in a sentence, have four or five different prefixes, if it happen to be repeated so many times as qualifying so many words also formed by means of these prefixes. This process is common to all the members of the Bantu family, whence the title of alliteral languages, which has been given them.

The method of expressing the relations of mood and tense seems, at first sight, somewhat intricate, but is really quite simple, consisting, as is usual in agglutinating tongues, in tacking independent particles on to the principal root. But, as already stated, the special feature of the Bantu family is the formation of words by means of prefixes, hence the secondary elements are here placed, not after, but before the chief radical.

§ 5.—*The Fula Group.*

The Fulas (also Pul or Peul) occupy the centre of Africa, between the tenth and twentieth degrees of north latitude; on the west, approaching the coast of Senegal, and stretching eastwards towards Lake Chad. It is a vast region, about 750 leagues in length, and divided into two nearly equal parts by the Niger. Its mean breadth is about 125 leagues, between the tenth and fifteenth degrees of north latitude. The principal Fula dialects are the *Futatoro*, the *Futajallo*, the *Bondu*, and the *Sokoto*.

The phonetic system of this group is not very complex, possessing neither *sh*, the French *j*, nor the Semitic gutturals.

Fula knows no distinction between the masculine and feminine genders, but still divides beings into two classes. It distinguishes, on the one hand, everything belonging to humanity, and on the other, everything else—the brute creation and inanimate objects.

M. Faidherbe calls these two classes the *human* and the *brute genders*.[*] This distinction is essential for the Fula grammar.

[*] "Genre hominin et Genre brute," in his "Essai sur la Langue Poule." Paris, 1875.

Words referring to human beings, whether nouns, adjectives, or participles, all end in the singular, in *o*, which is nothing but a pronominal root agglutinated: *gorko* = *man*. This class ends in the plural, in *bé*, which again is the pronoun *they* (masculine and feminine). In the brute gender, the singular ends either with a vowel, an *l*, or *am*, *o* being very rare. The plural seems more complex, and certain euphonic laws seem to play a great part in agglutinating endings to the root. The initial consonants of words in the singular are liable to interchange with others in the plural. The verb, however, is much simpler, its different tenses, as in all agglutinating idioms, being formed by the agglomeration of sundry elements, whose analysis remains always perfectly clear.

The Fula syntax is not very intricate, the order of the succession of ideas determining, in principle, the order of the words in the sentence. Thus, the name of the possessor is preceded by that of the thing possessed, and the object, whether direct or indirect, follows the verb (in the active voice). In fact, the whole difficulty of Fula consists in the great variety of its euphonic laws, but this is no slight difficulty.

With the adoption of Mohammedanism, the Fulas took over a certain number of Arabic words, religious, legal, and such like. But setting this element aside, it remained to be seen whether there were any, and if so, what kind of relationship between certain Senegal idioms, such as the Wolof and the Serer, and the Fula. No one, of course, pretends to deny that they have all a certain number of words in common. But in the actual state of our knowledge it would be at least rash to base an assumed, and, in itself, a very problematical affinity on a rather weak lexical agreement. M. Faidherbe is, with good reason, very reserved on this pretended connection of the Fula with the Wolof and Serer. Theoretically it is the very reverse of probable; practically, it remains still to be proved. We know that the Fulas reached Senegal only after having crossed Central Africa, and, in all likelihood, their primitive stock is to be looked for in Eastern Africa, where there may be found idioms related to theirs, if any still survive.

§ 6.—*The Nubian Languages.*

Ethnologists treat the Nubians and the Fulas as one race, of which the first forms an eastern, the second a western division. But however this be, the languages spoken by them seem to be different.

Nubian proper, that is, the speech of the Barabras, is spoken in the Nile Valley, between the twenty-first and twenty-fourth degrees north latitude, by about 40,000 people.

Dongola, spoken somewhat farther south, differs but little from it.

Tumal is spoken in the south of Kordofan, north of Shiluk, and is a negro dialect.

Konjari, also spoken in parts of Dar Fur and Kordofan, has been included in this group, but the point is not yet quite settled. There may be also other idioms related to it, but in the absence of complete information, it is impossible to speak very positively on the subject.

§ 7.—*Languages of the Negritos.*

But little is known concerning the dialects spoken by the various Negrito tribes, so that for the present we can do no more than mention them.

The Negritos—by some writers connected with the Papuas, but by others, seemingly with more reason, distinguished from them—are met with in the Peninsula of Malacca, in the Andaman and Nicobar Islands, and in certain districts of the Sundas and the Philippines. They have been traced farther northwards towards Japan, and are even supposed to exist in Central India. The geographical area occupied by the Negritos has been discussed by MM. de Quatrefages and Hamy, in their "Crania Ethnica," and in the first numbers of the "Revue d'Anthropologie."

§ 8.—*Languages of the Papuas.*

These, also, are but indifferently known. Spoken to the east of the Malay, north of the Australian idioms, in New Guinea, and in a number of the adjacent islands, they form several dialects more or less differing from each other.

But sufficient is known to pronounce them decidedly agglutinative. Thus, in one of their dialects, the plural element being *si*, the words *snûn* = man, *bien* = woman, become, in the plural, *snûnsi*, *biensi*. The particles answering to the case-endings of inflectional tongues are here prefixed to the word: *rosnûn* = of the man; *besnûn* = to the man; *rosnûnsi* = of the men; *besnûnsi* = to the men.

The languages of the Papuas have been treated by Mayer in the 67th vol. of the "Journal of the Vienna Academy."

§ 9.—*Australian Languages.*

The numerous Australian idioms seem all related to each other, but have no affinity with any other linguistic family.

Their phonetics are extremely simple, possessing neither sibilants nor aspirates. In nearly all of these idioms the idea of number is but little developed, and that of gender not at all. On the other hand, there is a certain wealth of suffixes expressive of nominal relations, constituting what are improperly called cases in the agglutinating tongues.

The Australian idioms are divided into three groups. The eastern branch, on the Pacific seaboard, is spoken in parts of Queensland and of New South Wales, and includes the *Kamiloroi* or *Kamilroi*, near the river Barwan; the *Koinberri*, the *Wiraturoi*, the *Wailwun*, in the region of the Barwan, towards Fort Bourke; the *Kokai*, farther north, on the rivers Maranoa and Kogun; the *Wolaroi*; the *Pikumbul*; the *Paiamba*; the *Kinki*; the *Dippil*, north of Moreton Bay; the *Turrubul*, near the river Brisbane.

The central group comprises the idioms spoken north of Adelaide, in South Australia.

The western group includes the dialects spoken in the south of Western Australia, to the east and south of Perth.

Thus all these languages belong to the southern portion of the Australian continent. Those of the centre and north may be said to be as yet utterly unknown.

The phonetics of the Australian tongues are very simple, including but a small number of vowels and consonants. They seem to possess the soft explosives only (*b, d, g*). Words are formed by means of suffixes alone, the formative element being placed always at the end of the word, as in Aryan, and never at the beginning, as in the Bantu system: *tippin* = bird; *tippinko* = to the bird; *punnul* = sun; *punnulko* = to the sun.

The numeral system is one of the most limited. They reckon up to four inclusive, but after that they use some general term expressive of multitude, or a great quantity.

The language of the Tasmanians seems to have been related to those of the mainland; but our information regarding it is very incomplete, and, as is well known, the Tasmanians are now extinct, Truganina, the last of the race, having died in 1876.

§ 10.—*The Malayo-Polynesian Idioms.*

These are sometimes called *Oceanic*, although including some spoken in Africa (or its islands), such as the Malagasse, and others in Asia, such as the Formosan.

They are thus classified by Frederic Müller, in his account of the cruise of the "Novara" round the globe,* and in his "Allgemeine Ethnographie":

Melanesian Group.—Figi, Annatom, Erromango, Tana, Mallikolo, Lifoo, Baladea, Bauro, Guadalkanar.

Polynesian Group.—Samoa, Tonga, Maori, Tahiti, Rarotonga, Marquesas dialects, Hawaii or Sandwich.

Malay Group.—Tagala branch: Language of the Philippines (Tagala, Bisaya, Pampanga, Bicol, &c.); Ladrone or Marianne dialects; Malagasse of Madagascar; Formosan. Malayo-Javanese branch: Malay, Javanese, language of the Sunda Islands, Madura, Mankasar, Alfooroo, Battak, Dayak.

Two facts seem now firmly established: (1) That the Malayo-Polynesian idioms have all a common origin; (2) That they are independent of all other linguistic systems. Bopp made an ill-

---

* "Reise der österreichischen Fregatte."

starred attempt to connect them with the Aryan family; while others have fancied that they belong to a pretended Turanian group, of which we shall have something to say in § 19 of the present chapter. But all this was labour lost. Their phonetic system is quite distinct from that of all others; their roots are thoroughly original, and afford no elements of comparison with those of the Aryan, Uralo-Altaïc, or any other system whatsoever.

According to Frederic Müller, the primitive Malayo-Polynesian phonetic system was composed of three explosives, k, t, p; three corresponding nasals; h, r; the fricatives s, f, v; and the vowels a, i, u ($=$ oo), e, o. It was not till a later period that the other sounds appeared—for instance, g, d, b, ch, j, y, l, &c.

The elements attached to the root to form words are sometimes prefixed, and sometimes suffixed, while in certain dialects they are intercalated, that is, incorporated in the body of the word.

Of the three Malayo-Polynesian groups, the Malayan seems to present the fullest and most highly-developed forms, the Tagala branch being especially distinguished in this respect. Next comes the Melanesian; and last of all, the Polynesian, which shows great poverty when compared with the Tagala, Formosan, and Malagasse. But this would not justify the statement that the Malay group more faithfully represents the common forms that have given birth to the Tagala and the Javanese, as well as to the Tahitian and the Marquesas dialect. The view to take of the matter is that the Polynesian group was detached from the parent stock at a period when the language was not yet very developed, and that the state of its civilisation did not permit of its further development. "Whilst the inflectional languages," says Frederic Müller, "broke up into separate divisions at an epoch when their structure was already perfect, whilst their history henceforth reveals nothing but a continuous modification of their forms, the uninflectional idioms seem, on the contrary, to have split up at a time when their structure was still in an unfinished state. Thus each of them, after having become detached from its congeners, was obliged to make provision out of its own resources for the completion of its inner structure. Hence the identity of roots and of their formative elements; but hence also the rare coincidence of the ready-made words."*

The grammar of the Malayo-Polynesian idioms is like that of all other agglutinating tongues. There is no true declension, particles performing the functions of the Latin and Greek case-endings, and of our prepositions. Thus, in New Caledonian,† belonging to the Melanesian group, *vangaevu* = lord, the lord; *o vangaevu* = of the lord; *vangaevu oi* = the lords; *o vangaevu oi* = of the lords. In Maori (Polynesian group), *te tanata* = the man; *a te tanata* = of the man; *ki te tanata* = to the man.

No special element is agglutinated to the noun in order to denote number. In Fiji, for instance, *a tamata* means both *man* and *men*; in Erromango, *niteni* = son and *sons*. Hence plurality is expressed by certain artificial processes, as in the Melanesian dialect of *Mare*, where the word *nodei* = crowd, is placed before the noun to make it plural: *nyome* = a man; *nodei gnome* = men. In New Caledonian the noun is either preceded by the collective *va*, or followed by *oi*; *vangaevu* = the lord; *vangaevu oi* = the lords. In the Malay group the noun is either doubled or else accompanied by some collective term. The repetition of the word is regulated by special laws, as in Formosan, which doubles the first syllable: *sjien* = the tooth; *sisjien* = the teeth; while in Javanese the whole word may be doubled: *ratu* = the prince; *raturatu* = the princes.

Gender also is denoted not by agglutination but by some secondary word, as in Fiji, *tagane* = male; *aleva* = female; *a gone tagane* = boy; *a gone aleva* = girl. In Tahiti *metua* means *parent*, of either sex, *father* and *mother* being distinguished by the accompanying words *tane* and *vahine* respectively. In the case of animals two other terms are used, such as *oni* and *ufa*. Thus: *moa oni* = cock; *moa ufa* = hen.‡ Neither is there any true

* "Allgemeine Ethnographie," p. 285.
† H. V. D. Gabelentz, "Die Melanesischen Sprachen," "Memoirs of the Saxony Academy," Philosophy and History sections, vol. iii. Leipzig, 1861.
‡ Gaussin, "Du Dialecte de Tahiti, de celui des îles Marquises, et, en général, de la Langue Polynésienne." Paris, 1853.

conjugation, the notions of tense and mood being expressed by means of affixes, or words no longer possessing anything more than a subordinate sense. As a rule, the verb itself comes last, as in the Melanesian dialect of Anatom:

> Ek asaig = I say.
> Ek mun asaig = I have said.
> Ekis asaig = I was saying.
> Ekis mun asaig = I had said.
> Ekpu asaig = I shall say.
> Eku vit asaig = If I say, &c. &c.

Still this is by no means an invariable rule.

It has just been said that the secondary or relational elements may be placed either before the principal word, as in the Bantu family, or after it, as in the Aryan tongues, or, lastly, embodied in the word itself.

Thus in Mare (Melanesian group) from *rose* = to tie, and *menenge* = to dwell, are formed *namenenge* = a dwelling; *narose* = a place, where the derivation is effected by means of prefixes; so also in the New Caledonian: *nguvie* = warrior; *nguveka* = giver—from *vie* = to fight, *veka* = to give; and in the Malay: *herpákei* = dressed; *berbini* = married—from *pákei* = clothes, *bini* = woman.

In Tagala, on the contrary, derivation is effected by means of suffixes, as in *putian* = whiteness—from *puti* = white; *bigayan* = gift —from *bigay* = giver.

Lastly, in the Malay group the derivative element is sometimes incorporated in the radical itself; but this incorporating process will be more fully discussed in the chapter devoted to the American languages.

The Malayo-Polynesian tongues have all of them a more or less developed literature. The natives of Polynesia possess a great number of stories, tales, and traditional songs.* Malay literature

---

* A most valuable contribution to the study of Polynesian oral literature has just been made by the Rev. William Wyatt Gill, by his "Myths and Songs from the South Pacific," London, 1876. The interest and importance of this work are not a little enhanced by the admirable preface, from the pen of Professor Max Müller.—*Note by Translator.*

itself is tolerably rich,* owing partly to its extensive borrowings. Its philosophic writings have been inspired by those of the Hindus or the Mussulmans. But its tales and romances are often indigenous, and its poetry is nearly altogether original. It embraces not only fugitive pieces, dialogues, proverbs, and fables, but genuine epic and dramatic poems.

Javanese possesses a literature which is largely indebted to Sanskrit, not only for its general tone and spirit, but also for its vocabulary. It has also its original poems, songs, fables, and legends.

Malay is written with the Arabic characters, introduced with the Mohammedan religion, and the nature of its original writing system is now unknown. The other idioms of the Malay group, Tagala, Javanese, Mankasar, &c., have borrowed their different systems from an ancient Indian alphabet, as has been shown by Frederic Müller.†

§ 11.—*Japanese.*

The attempt has been too frequently made to compare Japanese with the Uralo-Altaïc group—Mongolian, Turkish, Magyar, Suomi, and the cognate tongues. No doubt the Japanese race must have originally passed over from the Asiatic continent to the islands now occupied by them. But does it follow from this, that their language must have a common origin with those of the mainland, even situated nearest to them? By no means, nor is a mere assertion enough to establish such a conclusion. Hitherto, apart from some fruitless and unmethodical attempts, little heed has been paid to any sound arguments that might otherwise demonstrate this pretended relationship. In vain lists have been complacently drawn up of fifty, a hundred, or a hundred and fifty words, which seem to offer more or less analogy with each other. This is nothing but etymology, not philology. We could freely give up the five hundred Mongolo-Japanese quasi-homonyms, without reckoning the five hundred or a

---

* L. de Backer, " L'Archipel Indien. Origines, langues, littératures, &c." Paris, 1874.

† " Ueber den Ursprung der Schrift der Malayschen Völker," in the " Bulletins of the Vienna Academy," 1865.

thousand others that might be discovered in two hours of wasted time, for the startling coincidence of the Portuguese definite article with the Magyar article *a* and the Basque article *a*. This is doubtless quite as little to the purpose, but appearances are here at least far better respected. And if we argue on the large number of assumed agreements between Japanese and Mongolian or Magyar words, the case will be made only the more hopeless; the more such whims are indulged in, the less excusable we become. In vain also that such and such syntactical analogies are appealed to. Would the Bulgarian, which places after the noun the article it has developed within itself, be on that account related to the Moldo-Wallachian, which also postpones the article to the noun? To expect syntax, whose laws are quite secondary, to throw any light on the affinities of languages, is but again to show the greatest ignorance of the true scientific method. Where the roots are not common, there is positively nothing from which we can hope for any serious proof of the common origin of two or more languages. Assumed syntactical resemblances are of no greater value than the comparison of a multitude of words already fully developed. The more we heap them up, the more we give proof of scientific inconsistency.

Until there is scientific proof of the contrary, we shall therefore continue to look upon the Japanese as an isolated language, independent of all other linguistic systems, so far, of course, as the individuality and irreductibility of its roots are concerned.

Japanese occupies the southern and central portions of the archipelago lying between the Sea of Japan and the Pacific. It comprises a number of dialects, which, however, do not seem materially to differ from each other.

The present writing system, which is not free from certain difficulties for those commencing the study of Japanese, is derived from the Chinese characters, and is referred to about the third century of the Christian era. Strange to say, this ideographic writing seems to have been substituted in the place of an alphabetic system adopted from the Coreans at a still earlier epoch. A fresh and very desirable change, that is the adoption of the Roman letters, seems likely to take place at any day.

At the first assembly of the Congress of Orientalists, this point was discussed, and the general impression seemed to be that this great undertaking had some hope of success.* At the same time, however, the urgent necessity was once more made evident of introducing some new and simple founts into our typographic establishments, for the purpose of avoiding dangerous misunderstandings in transcribing languages that do not make use of the Roman characters.† For instance, *sh*, which is the French *ch*, the German *sch*, the Polish *sz*, and the Hungarian *s*, would require to be represented by a single type, in the transcription of a text written in foreign characters. This might very well be the sign employed by the Croatians and the Bohemians. But without pretending to arrive at absolute simplicity, some practical system might perhaps be devised, to which Japanese (and other Oriental tongues) would adapt themselves without much difficulty.‡

Japanese phonetics are simple enough, and the formation of the words enables us clearly to show what an agglutinating language really is. The cases are very distinctly expressed by adding to the primary root certain secondary ones, that have lost their independence, and now serve to denote relational ideas only. In transcribing Japanese texts, some writers would be inclined to separate by a hyphen the stem from these relational elements:

* Oriental Congress, Paris, 1873.

† E. Picot, "Tableau Phonétique des principales Langues usuelles," in the "Revue de Linguistique," vi. p. 362.

‡ A good foundation of such a system is offered by the little known but really admirable scheme of Colonel Henry Clinton, as explained and illustrated by him in his "International Pronunciation Table, proposed as a basis for the establishment of a uniform method of denoting and describing the pronunciation of many of the sounds, separate and combined, used in human speech," London, 1870. This scheme is so simple, and yet so elastic, that, as the ingenious author justly remarks, "it might be translated into any language in which instruction in pronunciation is to be given; when, *mutatis mutandis*, it might serve to aid in establishing, for popular use, a general system of denoting the pronunciation of all the most usual sounds of many languages." Its object is, of course, different from the more elaborate and better known, though, for international purposes, not quite so serviceable, scheme of Mr. A. J. Ellis.—*Note by Translator*.

hito-no, of the man; *hito-de*, with the man; but this plan can no more be justified than could that of separating, for instance, our plural sign *s*, and writing *book-s*, *wall-s*, *stone-s*. The closest juxtaposition is the proper feature of agglutinating languages, nor can they be represented in writing, otherwise than they exist in speech, without effacing the strikingly characteristic manner in which words are formed in these idioms. At the most, the prefixes *o*, *me*, denoting gender, might be so separated: *neko*, cat; *o-neko*, tom-cat; *me-neko*, she-cat. The particles of number, such as *tatsi*, ought to be attached, like those of case, immediately to the stem: *hitotatsino*, of the men; *hitotatside*, with the men; as in the singular: *hitono*, *hitode*.

Like all agglutinating verbs, the Japanese verb admits of those series of elements placed in juxtaposition, which have already been spoken of, and which more or less precisely determine the sense of the primary root—negative, causative, optative elements, and the like. It seems needless to give a list of examples, which would be absolutely analogous to those already quoted, or to others we shall have to introduce, when speaking more in detail of the Uralo-Altaïc group.

Japanese literature, though evidently interesting, has not yet found a historian. It is largely occupied with history, historical novels, stories, and romance in general. There are also a great number of works on religious philosophy and poetry, and amongst the sciences, linguistics and botany have been cultivated. It will, doubtless, be no easy matter in these compositions to separate the purely national element from what is due to Chinese influence, which made itself felt more particularly about the third century of our era. Still, we may hope that this undertaking may be accomplished at no very remote period.

All the Chinese words introduced through this literary predominance have been subjected to the principle of juxtaposition, just as the Romance and Latin words have conformed to the exigencies of Low German accidence in English: *conform-ed*, *conform-ing*, *rapid-ly*, and so on.

We have stated that the present alphabet is derived from the

Chinese ideographic system; and, like it, the characters are written in parallel columns from right to left. Besides this cursive writing, which is called *hirakana*, and is everywhere current, there is another, the *katakana*, vastly more simple, but employed mainly by foreigners little acquainted with the other system.

[This *katakana* system—the *i-ro-fa*, as it is called, from the names of the first three signs—is strictly *syllabic*, consisting of forty-seven characters, each representing *a full syllable*: *ri*, *ru*; *wo*, *wa*, &c. Of these, five are purely vowel sounds: *i*, *u*, *o*, *a*, *e*; the rest combinations in which the consonant in all cases precedes the vowel: *ro*, *fu*, *ni*, and so on. By the addition of the soft accent, *nigori*, consisting of two minute strokes to the right, of the hard accent, *maru*—a little dot or circle also to the right—and of a sign for the solitary *true* consonant *n*, the original forty-seven characters are raised to seventy-three, and are then differently arranged. There are a few other orthographic signs, such as *koto*, *tama*, *site*, &c., but the whole system is so simple and ingenious that the wonder is it has not long ago superseded the cumbrous, half-ideographic, half-phonetic systems, that still prevail everywhere throughout the country.]

§ 12.—*Corean.*

This language has been grouped with various agglutinating idioms, more particularly with the Japanese. Without absolutely denying the possibility of such a connection, before admitting it we must wait till it is supported by some methodic arguments, which have so far not been forthcoming.

Of all the languages of the extreme east, Corean is the least known and the least studied. It possesses a true alphabet, composed of detached vowels and consonants, which is simple enough, and dates probably from the fourth century of our era. But in spite of all the hypotheses propounded on the subject, its origin is still clouded in mystery.

In Corean, as in other agglutinating idioms, suffixes are used to express the various relational ideas denoted by case-endings in the inflectional languages. Number is denoted either by repeating the word, or by the addition of some secondary term meaning *all* or *many*.

In the Corean vocabulary there are a great number of Chinese words, which, however, are easily recognised, though their pronunciation is by no means uniform.

§ 13.—*The Dravidian Tongues.*

This group, which is also spoken of as the Tamulu, the Tamil, and the Malabaric family, derives its name from a Sanskrit word, originally denoting those Hindus who had settled in that part of India known afterwards as the Deccan. In course of time the word was applied to the country itself, and more particularly to that part of it where Tamil was spoken, which is the most important member of the group.

These languages occupy the whole southern portion of India proper, from the Vindhay mountains and the river Nerbudda to Cape Comorin. In this vast region, containing a population of about 50,000,000 inhabitants, there are a few European and Mussulman settlements; but the number of those speaking the Dravidian idioms exclusively may be estimated at upwards of 45,000,000.

In his important work on the Dravidian tongues, Caldwell divides them into two groups, according as they are cultivated or not. The first consists of six languages: *Tamil*, *Malayālam*, *Telugu*, *Kanarese*, *Tulu*, and *Kudagu*. The second also comprises six dialects, which will be presently mentioned.

The *Tamil*, also (but improperly) *Tamul* (the second vowel in the native spelling being distinctly a short *i*, not a *u*), occupies in many respects the same position in the Dravidian group that Sanskrit does in the Aryan, surpassing, as it does, all the others in the richness of its vocabulary, the purity and antiquity of its forms, and in its higher literary cultivation. It is the ordinary speech of 14,500,000 people, occupying the whole plain to the east of the Western Ghats, from Pulicat to Cape Comorin, and the west coast as far as Trivandram. There are also numerous Tamil communities in the north-west of Ceylon, and in the Nizam's Dominions.

The long strip stretching along the coast between the Ghats and the Arabian Sea, from Trivandram to Mangalore, is the home of the *Malayālam*, or *Malayajma*, spoken by about 3,000,000 of natives. It is looked on as an older dialect of the Tamil, into which a large number of Sanskrit words have found their way.

The *Tulu*, formerly spreading north of the Malayālam, is now confined to the neighbourhood of Mangalore, on the coast east of the Ghats, and is spoken by probably not more than 300,000. Though sometimes considered as a dialect of the Malayālam, it differs very decidedly from that language; and, in fact, constitutes a real branch of the Dravidian family.

The *Kanarese*, or *Kannada*, occupies the north Dravidian district, extending over the plateau of Mysore and the western portion of the Nizam's Dominions. The number of those by whom it is spoken is now estimated at about 9,000,000. This language is extremely interesting, as it often retains forms more antique and purer even than those of the Tamil.

The *Telugu*, also *Telinga*, is the *Andhra* of Sanskrit writers. It limits the Dravidian group on the east and the north, and is spoken by 15,500,000 natives. Its forms have been less faithfully preserved than those of its congeners, and its phonetic system has also been greatly changed, under the influence of harmonic laws, that have earned for it the name of the Italian of the Deccan.

Of all the cultivated Dravidian tongues, *Kudagu* is the least important, being spoken by not more than 150,000 natives, west of Mysore. Caldwell, who had formerly looked on it as a dialect of the Kanarese, gives it an independent position in the second edition (1875) of his "Dravidian Grammar."

Amongst the secondary dialects may be mentioned the *Kota*, the *Tuda*, the *Gond*, the *Ku* or *Khond*, and perhaps the *Rājmahal*, and the *Urāon*.

The *Kota* is spoken by a half-savage tribe, reckoned at about 1,100, in the gorges of the Neilgherries. The *Tuda* is the dialect of another Neilgherry tribe, consisting of not more than 750. The

SECOND FORM OF SPEECH—AGGLUTINATION.

Gond is the language of 1,600,000 in the hilly districts in the territories of Gondvāna, Nagpore, Sangor, and the Nerbudda. The *Ku*, or *Khond*, is spoken at Goomsur, on the hills of Orissa, and in the eastern parts of Gondvāna, by about 270,000. The *Rājmahal*, or *Māler*, and *Urāon*, are spoken in Central India—the first by 40,000, the second by upwards of 260,000—and both of these dialects are somewhat closely related to each other. Some writers add to this list the *Badaga*, current in a corner of the Neilgherries; but Caldwell treats it merely as an old dialect of the Kanarese, without any claim to be separately classified.

The territories still owned by France in these vast regions, which once rang with the names of a Dupleix, a Bussy, and a Lally-Tollendal, are so disposed that four of them are comprised within the Dravidian province. The two most important, *Pondicherry* and *Karikal*, are in Tamil land; *Mahé* is on the Malayālam coast, and *Yanoan* in the Telugu country.

In this rapid sketch of the limits still occupied by the Dravidian tongues, the question arises, Were they always so circumscribed? And are we to assume that they have been driven into their present domain by the first Aryan immigrations? This, though likely enough in itself, has so far not been clearly proved. It has been merely conjectured that the non-Aryan elements of the idioms spoken in Northern India may have a Dravidian origin. But, apart from the fact that they are very few and of but little importance, it is very difficult not only to analyse, but even to determine them. In the Dravidian family itself, a great deal of the vocabulary of certain rude varieties is of unknown origin. We should, therefore, accept with considerable reserve all statements made regarding a possible former expansion of the Dravidian languages. Farther on we shall have to speak of the language of Ceylon, whither Tamil has been extended, in comparatively recent times, possibly about the epoch of the great Buddhist emigration.

The Dravidian tongues may safely be regarded as an independent group, related to no other linguistic family. They have doubtless been connected, at one time, with the mythical Scythian languages; at another with the Uralo-Altaïc group, and again with the Aryan, the Semitic, and many others. But all such comparisons were absolutely void of scientific method. A number of Tamil or Telugu words were compared with certain Sanskrit or Hebrew words, or with others taken from any other quarter whatever—this being the usual method of those who confound fanciful etymological resemblances with true philological affinity. It is not Tamil or Telugu that we have to compare with Sanskrit or Hebrew. The first thing to be done is to restore the primitive Dravidian type, by the comparison alone of which with other families can any satisfactory conclusions be arrived at. We repeat, however, that the deductions already firmly established, seem more than sufficient to show the absolute independence of the Dravidian family from any other.

Attention has long been directed to the Dravidian tongues, which were discovered some time before the Sanskrit, by the Dutch, Danish, French, and English adventurers. They were acquired by Europeans, at first, for trading purposes, and afterwards as a means of spreading Christianity among the natives. The Protestant missionaries were the first to compose grammars and dictionaries, most of which never have been published. The first Tamil grammar* is that of the Danish missionary Ziegenbald, written in Latin, and printed in 1716; but the first Malayâlam grammar had already appeared in India in the year 1780. W. Carey did not publish his Telugu and Kanarese grammars till 1814 and 1817, at Serampore. Tulu has had to wait till 1872, when it was taken in hand by M. Brigel, of the Basel missions, whose printing establishment at Mangalore issues a number of sound works on the study of the Dravidian tongues.

* That is, the first composed in an European tongue. The first in Tamil, known as the Tolkâpyam, dates from about the eighth century of our era, and is, perhaps, the very oldest Tamil work extant. It was written by Trinadhûmagnî, one of the followers of Agastya, who is popularly supposed to have invented the Tamil language, in opposition to the Sanskrit of the north. The Tolkâpyam, itself, however, is rather a treatise on grammar, composed in Tamil, than a Tamil grammar in the strict sense; and though not written in Sanskrit must still be considered as an Aindra work, that is the work of a disciple of the Aindra school of Sanskrit grammarians.—*Note by Translator.*

They are also now cultivated in Europe by a certain number of linguists, and in France, especially by M. J. Vinson, to whom we are indebted for some valuable details on this subject. Dravidian scholars are by no means rare in England, and we may refer, before all others, to Caldwell, whose excellent treatise, although encumbered with too many metaphysical theories on the so-called Turanian theory, and on the assumed probability of a common origin for all languages, has justly become a standard work on the Dravidian group of languages.*

Dravidian grammar may be said to be remarkably simple, its phonetic system presenting no serious difficulties, and being composed of not over-numerous elements. In the whole group of the five literary languages, there exist only the five vowels *a, e, i, o, u*, long and short, which seem primitive, besides the two diphthongs *ai* and *au*, of which the latter at least does not belong to the common Dravidian stock. In the course of time these vowels became weak and attenuated in their utterance, whence arose a certain number of intermediate sounds, unrepresented in their written systems. Thus it happens that the spoken Tamil differs very sensibly from the literary language.

The consonants also are limited in number. They include five groups of strong and weak explosives—guttural, palatal, lingual, dental, and labial—with their corresponding nasals; *y, r, l, v, r strong*; two cerebrals; and one sibilant, *s*. There may be added a new class of explosives peculiar to Tamil and Telugu, transcribed by Caldwell as *tr, dr*, but which M. Vinson looks on as dentals preceded by a "*mouillement*." The aspirates are unknown in these idioms, whose primitive consonantal system seems to have been even still more simple than at present. Thus, M. Vinson thinks that the palatals—*ch, j*—are comparatively recent. However, these consonants, like the vowels, have been modified in the spoken language. Thus, both in Tamil and Malayālam, the dentals are now showing a decided tendency towards the English *th*

* "Comparative Grammar of the Dravidian Languages." London, 1858-76.

G

soft,* while in Telugu the *ch* and the *j* become at times *ts* and *dz*.

The utterance of these different sounds presents no very great difficulty, those linguals alone, perhaps, excepted which are generally but wrongly described as cerebrals. The final *l* in the English syllable *ble* gives an approximate idea of these lingual consonants, of which there are five altogether: *t*, *d*, *n*, *j*, and *r*, transcribed in Roman letters with a dot below. Sanskrit also possesses lingual consonants, but not organic, so that these letters would seem to form a distinctive feature of the Dravidian group.

Of the phonetic laws resulting from a comparison of these various idioms and their dialects, we shall mention but one, which is common also to the Aryan family. The Kanarese *k* often answers to the Telugu *ch* and to a Tamil *c* or *s*. Thus the word *ear*, which is *sèvi* in Tamil and *chevi* in Telugu, becomes *kevi* in Kanarese, and this last must have been the primitive form. [Compare the Latin, Italian, and French *cœlum*, *cielo*, *ciel*, where the initial, *as pronounced*, would be represented by the English letters *k*, *ch*, and *s* respectively.]

There are two other interesting facts peculiar to the Dravidian group. The letter *r* does not occur as an initial, hence, foreign words beginning with this letter must be preceded by a vowel. Thus the Sanskrit word *râjâ* appears in Tamil, as *irâyan* or *irâsan*. Again, no word can begin with a soft explosive, *b*, *d*, &c., while no hard explosive can occur alone, or isolated, in the body of the word. Hence Tamil, in borrowing the Sanskrit word *guti*, renders it by *kudi*, in accordance with this double rule.

But the phonetic laws of these important idioms have not been yet sufficiently studied to enable us definitely to fix the laws that have been brought into play in the formation of words. Enough, however, is known to allow of our classifying the Tamil, Telugu,

---

* The Dravidian cerebral *r* also has been identified by Mr. F. T. Ellworthy with the south-western or west Somersetshire *r*; he further shows how completely it differs from the trilled *r* of the north, from the French *r grasseyé*, and the Danish uvular *r*. See his "Dialect of West Somersetshire." Publications of the English Dialect Society, Series D.—*Note by Translator.*

and their congeners, and ascertaining their relative ages. Dravidian words seem ultimately reducible to roots, or better, to dissyllabic roots, nominal and verbal. By a further comparison of these roots with each other, we see that they, in their turn, can be reduced to still more elementary groups, each comprising several of the radicals in question. This study has so far been little more than just entered on; but it may be said to have already rendered highly probable the theory of the primitive monosyllabic nature of the Dravidian roots.

Derivatives are formed by the strictly agglutinating process, in which the fresh elements are always suffixed.* Thus, to a verbal root will be added a syllable denoting present time, then another implying negation, then the sign of personality, this agglomeration resulting in a word meaning, for instance, *thou dost not see*, but which should be thus transcribed: *to see + now + not + thou*. The sense of each of these elements is always present to the mind of the Dravidian, who treats them just as we do our pronouns, articles, and prepositions. Doubtless a large number of these derivatives have become so disguised that their primitive form can no longer be recognised. But many others, especially those intended to be placed last, and most of those serving to distinguish the so-called *cases*, are still independent words, retaining their natural sense of rest, contact, vicinity, consequence, &c. &c. Many of these derivative elements pass from one allied language to another, which sufficiently establishes the original independence of their suffixes.†

If it is easy to perceive the great advantage languages of this class have over the purely monosyllabic ones, where the roots are not thus subordinate to each other, it is, on the other hand, equally

---

* Not always suffixed, the vowels *a*, *e*, *i* (which are the initials of *avan* that one; *ivan* = this one; and *evan* = which one?) being prefixed, as in the Tamil: *atu* = that thing; *ithu* = this thing; *ethu* = which thing?—*Note by Translator*.

† No doubt these suffixes were originally independent words, as were the corresponding Semitic and Aryan case-endings. But in the present state of the Tamil language, a native has no more sense of the primitive and

evident how surpassed they must be by inflectional tongues, in all that pertains to clearness and precision of expression. A certain vagueness is the logical consequence of the multiplicity of forms in certain agglutinating idioms. Hence, also, certain combinations peculiar to them, which seem very strange to us, accustomed as we are to the comparative simplicity of the Indo-European languages. In these last, the elements of personal relationship—*amat*, he loves; *amamus*, we love—are confined to verbal inflection or conjugation. In the same way the elements intended to denote subject, object, position in space, are restricted to nominal inflection, or declension: *filius*, son (subject); *filium* (direct object). But the agglutinative system allows of mixed processes. Thus we find in a great number of agglutinating tongues nouns combined with personal suffixes; these are true possessive substantives. In Magyar, for example, the noun *haz*, house, and the personal suffix *am*, in the verb denoting the first person, produce the noun *hazam*, my house.

We meet with the same thing in the Dravidian group; but here, in words of this sort, the personal element imparts, so to say, an attributive sense, an assertion of existence. Thus, in Tamil, *tevarīr* (from *tevar*, God, honorific plural; and *ir*, second personal ending in the verb) means, *you are God*; and, in fact, may be declined in the sense of *you who are God*. Here is another significant and curious fact, though now occurring only in the older texts, especially in ancient Tamil poetry, where we meet with forms such as *sārndāyhku, to thee that hast approached*—which must be thus analysed: *sār*, to reach, approach, arrive; *n*, euphonic; *d*, sign of

independent meaning of the accusative *ei*, the dative *ku*, or the genitive *in*, than a Roman had of the corresponding *em*, *i*, and *is*, as in—

    Tamil. Latin.
  Acc. Kallai = lapidem = a stone (object).
  Dat. Kallukku = lapidi = to a stone.
  Gen. Kallin = lapidis = of a stone.
  Nom. Kal = lapis = a stone (agent).

Nor is the essential difference between agglutination and true inflection at all so clear in such cases as is generally assumed. But the subject is too extensive and too technical to be here discussed.—*Note by Translator*.

the past; *āy*, thee, thou, verbal second personal suffix; *k*, euphonic; and *ku*, to, nominal dative suffix.

Tulu, one of the least important of the Dravidian group, offers a peculiarity which cannot be overlooked. In Tamil, Telugu, Kanarese, and Malayālam, every verb gives rise to a causative, by the insertion of a certain syllable between the radical and the element of tense. Thus, in Tamil, from *seyven* = I will do, we get *seyvippen* = I will cause to do. But in Tulu the number of such secondary forms is far more considerable. Thus, *mālpuvé* = I do, gives *mālpévé* = I usually do (frequentative); *mālpāvé* = I cause to do (causative); *māltruvé* = I do do (intensive). By the insertion of a fresh element, each of these derivatives may become negative: *mālpāvuji* = I do not cause to do, and so on. This phenomenon is again met with in Turkish, where the verbs teem with examples of this process, and where one single word expresses, I cause to love, I can love, I love myself, they love one another; and so on.

The Dravidian group has no article, although in old documents instances occasionally occur of the demonstrative pronoun being employed in a determinative sense. The adjective, always unchangeable (as in English), is generally a mere noun of quality, invariably preceding the noun it qualifies. Distinction of gender must have originally been unknown, and even now it is applied only to human beings that have arrived at the years of discretion. The nouns referring to children are neuter in all the group, as are also the names of women in the singular in most of them. The verb has three tenses only—present, past, and indefinite future—and one mood, the indicative. Grammarians speak of two voices, a positive and a negative; but this last is easily reduced to its primitive form, being made up merely of a negative particle, personal suffixes, and the simple radical verb.

The Dravidian vocabulary implies rather a low order of civilisation. Notwithstanding the pretended consensus of all mankind, before the arrival of the Aryan race the Dravidians possessed neither "God," nor "soul;" neither "temple," nor "priest." It is, on the other hand, true that they lacked words for "book," "writing," "grammar," and "will." They could not count as far as 1,000; and Telugu, the only Dravidian tongue possessing a special word for this number, has derived it from *ve* = ardour, multiplication. None of them can render the abstract sense of the verbs *to be, to have*.

After this sketch the reader, we may hope, will be able to form some idea of the nature of the Dravidian tongues. They are agglutinating idioms arrested in the development of their forms at a, so to say, premature period, and this check was, in all probability, due to the Aryan invasion. But however that be, it is easy to assign to the Dravidian system its natural place in the scale of the agglutinating idioms. They must be comprised among the first in the ascending order, that is among those immediately following the isolating system, and anterior to Turkish, Magyar, Basque, and the American languages. They show no trace of inflection, and the vocal modifications that they allow of are purely phonetic. These modifications in no way answer to any corresponding change of sense in the word so modified.

We have said that contact with the Aryans was the probable cause of the Dravidians entering on their historic life. In fact everything points to the Aryans as at once the conquerors of the plains and forests of the Deccan, and the civilisers of their savage occupants. A few wandering and wretched tribes, rude and difficult of access, still inhabit some scarcely yet fully explored districts of this fertile region. If we can but conjecture that the Dravidians were civilised by the Aryan invasion, it is at least certain that they owe to it their writing system. Their five literary languages are usually transcribed by means of three different alphabets. Tulu employs the same characters as the Kanarese—Kanarese itself and Telugu being written in two varieties of the same alphabet, the forms of their letters presenting very little difference. This alphabet is characterised by the general round form of its signs. Tamil, on the contrary, possesses a special alphabet in which the square form prevails. It has, moreover, twenty-eight letters only, while the others faithfully reproduce the order and full number of the Sanskrit system. Hence, in writing Sanskrit, the Tamil Brahmans make use of a special alphabet called *Grantham*, derived from the *Devanāgari*, and from which the ordinary Tamil alphabet is itself derived. Intermediate between the Tamil and Kanaro-Telugu comes the Malayālam, also derived directly from the Grantham. The old Dravidian inscriptions are written in two different characters, one peculiar to Tamil, the other used in writing Sanskrit and the indigenous tongues, and closely resembling the old Devanāgari forms. The latter would seem to be the prototype of all the alphabets of the Deccan, while the former, according to Burnell, was borrowed directly from the Semitic.

It may be asked whether races without a writing system can be said to possess a literature properly so called. Many instances occur of utterly illiterate peoples, amongst whom long compositions, always in poetry, have been orally handed down through successive generations, and there are everywhere to be found popular songs and legends that have never been committed to writing. Though it cannot be positively asserted that this was the case amongst the ancient Dravidians, still their literature is very rich. At the same time all the works of which it is composed, down to the smallest fragment, are long posterior to their first contact with the Aryans. So far as number and worth are concerned, the Tamil and Telugu compositions far surpass the others; though Kanarese still offers a curious and not yet explored mine of wealth to the researches of the learned.

But in any case the Tamil literature remains the most copious, the most fruitful, the most interesting, and, at the same time, the most ancient. Nor is it merely a simple reflex of the Sanskrit, without any originality of its own. It has had the good fortune to have been for a long time the language of the Shiva sectaries, as well as of the Jaina and Buddhist heretics, who wrote much, and whose works are the masterpieces of ancient Tamil poetry. It should be added that all the old Dravidian monuments, or at least those possessing any intrinsic worth, are always written in verse. Tamil poetry is purer in point of style and more correct than the prose, and much more rigorously excludes foreign words. The opposite is the case in Telugu, Kanarese, and Malayālam poetry, in which Aryan words abound. The Tamil vocabulary is, moreover, very rich, and possesses a large number of synonyms.

Dravidian literature is particularly rich in moral poems, and in collections of wise saws and aphorisms, which constitute the most ancient monuments of Tamil poetry. It has also produced long epic poems, remarkable for the exaggeration and minuteness of their details, and otherwise not very attractive to Europeans. To a more recent period must be referred a number of lyric songs, full of energy, some monotonous religious hymns, and erotic tales of a very licentious character. Still more recently were composed some scientific works, almost exclusively medical. At the present day the Dravidians can do no more than hash up their venerable poetry, faithful to the conservative instinct which Caldwell justly condemns, and which one of their most celebrated grammarians has thus formulated: "Propriety of composition consists in writing on the same subjects, with the same expressions, and in accordance with the same plan, as the classic writers."

§ 14.—*The Finno-Tataric or Uralo-Altaïc Languages.*

Let us state at once that these are divided into five groups: *Samoyedic, Finnic, Turkic or Tataric, Mongolian, Tungusian.*

They are entitled to special attention in this work, not only on account of the historical importance of some amongst them, but also because of their structure itself, which is so frequently and so justly appealed to in illustration of the agglutinating stage generally of articulate speech. The simplest plan will be to pass first in review the five groups and the languages comprised in them, and then proceed to discuss the questions of their affinity, of the best name by which to embrace them all, and lastly, of the extravagant "Turanian" theory, which it is to be hoped there will soon be no longer any necessity even of refuting.

The various idioms composing the five groups present great differences, as well in their structure as in their vocabulary. Still, whatever opinion we may form of the actual degree of their affinity to each other, it is easy to see that they have certain morphological features in common, sufficiently marked to allow of their being comprised in a general notice of this sort. Thus they all in some way or other suffix the possessive pronoun to the noun, and divide the conjugation into definite and indefinite, the first being marked by the union of the direct pronominal object to the verb. They are alike also in the main features of their syntax, in their method of determining the noun, lastly, and above all, in their vocalic harmony, a most important fact, which will challenge special notice in its proper place.

(1) *The Samoyedic Group*

Stretches from the White Sea eastwards along the shores of the Arctic Ocean in Europe, and the western portion of the coast of Siberia in Asia. About 20,000 people speak Samoyede, of which there are five principal dialects, nearly all of which are again split up into a number of sub-dialects.

Yurak is spoken in European Russia and in the north-west of Siberia as far as the river Yenisei.

Yenisei Samoyede occupies the region watered by the Lower Yenisei.

Tagwi is spoken more to the east, as far as the mouth of the Khatanga.

Ostyak Samoyede lies more to the south-west, about the Middle Obi, and in the direction of the Tom and Chulim.

Kamassic is spoken by a small tribe in South Siberia.

The Finn Castrén, one of the founders of Uralo-Altaïc philology, has published a comprehensive and scientific treatise on the Samoyede dialects, in which he carefully compares them together.* In his opinion Samoyede is more closely related to Finnish than to any other Uralo-Altaïc group, both in its structure and component elements.

The vowel system is simple enough, whereas that of the consonants is highly developed. Of these there are more than thirty, amongst them the liquids *t, d, l, s,* and *z*.

We shall speak farther on of progressive vowel harmony, a feature of the Uralo-Altaïc system, which is far from being uniformly

* "Grammatik der Samojedischen Sprachen." St. Petersburg, 1854.

carried out in the Samoyede group, being in fact fairly developed in the Kamassic dialect alone. Here the strong vowels (*a*, *u*, *o*) cannot occur together with the weak (*ä*, *ü*, *ö*), while the neutrals (*i*, *e*) may readily occur in connection with either the strong or the weak.

As in the other Uralo-Altaïc tongues, declension is effected in Samoyede by agglutinating secondary or relational particles to the principal root. Thus, in Ostyak Samoyede the suffix *n* expressing possession, *loga*, fox, and *kule*, raven, make *logan*, of the fox, *kulen*, of the raven. If to these themes be added the plural element, *la*, we get *logala*, the foxes, *logalan*, of the foxes; *kulela*, the ravens, *kulelan*, of the ravens; than which process nothing can be simpler.

(2) *The Finnic Group*

Is of far greater interest than the preceding, occupying a more prominent position than any other of the whole family. It has been called *Ugrian*, or *Finno-Ugric*, or *Ugro-Finnic*, but the languages composing it have not yet been definitely distinguished from each other. Still, most writers recognise five sub-groups, thus classified by Donner:

West Finnic: Suomi, Karelian, Wepsic, Livonian, Krewinian, Esthonian, Wotic.

Lapponic.

Finno-Permian: Siryenian, Permian, Wotyak.

Volga-Finnic: Mordvinian, Cheremissian.

Ugric: Magyaric, Wogulic, Ostyak.

Some writers reduce these five groups to four, by including Lapponic with the West Finnic.

Suomi occupies the greater part of Finland, but does not stretch along the whole coast of the Gulf of Bothnia, where Swedish is spoken at some points, as about Vasa. On the south it touches only a few unimportant points of the Gulf of Finland, the northern shores of which, as about Helsingfors, are also Swedish. There are, moreover, some Finns in the neighbourhood of St. Petersburg, but altogether they cannot number 2,000,000.

With the Suomi are grouped the *Karelian*, reaching northwards to Lapland, southwards to the Gulf of Finland and Lake Ladoga, and east to the White Sea and Lake Onega; the *Chudic*, situated in a very scattered district south of Lake Onega; the *Wepsic*, which is northern Chudic; and *Wotic*, which is southern Chudic; lastly, *Krewinian*, spoken in Courland.

Esthonian, or rather *Ehste* or *Este*, is much less widely diffused than Suomi, being restricted to the greater part of the south coast of the Gulf of Finland and the northern half of Livonia (Dorpat). Its literature also is much inferior to the Suomi. There are two principal dialects, those of Revel and Dorpat, which are again divided into several sub-dialects, but have never succeeded in producing a common literary standard, notwithstanding the attempt made to develop such a standard towards the close of the seventeenth century.* Hence Esthonian literature is far inferior to that of the Suomi.

Livonian is now almost confined to the north-west corner of Courland, a tract some few leagues in extent. Landwards it is continually encroached upon by Lettic, an Aryan tongue allied to Lithuanian.

Let us here say a few words on the grammar, first of the Suomi,† and then of the Esthonian.

The Suomi consonantal system is very simple. Besides the explosives k, t, p, it possesses r, l, m, n; another nasal like that of the German *lang*; s, h, v, y (written j); but it rejects both the aspirated explosives and f. The weak explosives, g, d, b, occur, but rather as foreign elements, or replacing the older letters k, t, p.

Suomi is fond of the hiatus, and any vowel may, as a rule, close the word, except e; but this is not true of the consonants, n being most frequently met with at the end of words.

Nowhere else is the principle of vowel harmony more developed than in Suomi. If the vowel of the root be strong, those of the

---

* Wiedemann, "Grammatik der Eshtnischen Sprache." St. Petersburg, 1875.

† Kellgren, "Die Grundzüge der Finnischen Sprache mit Rücksicht auf den Ural-Altaischen Sprachstamme." Berlin, 1847.

suffixes must also be strong; if weak, the suffixes must similarly be weak; and if neutral, the suffixes must still be weak.

Words are never formed of prefixes, so that the principal root always stands first; and it is on this syllable also, as in Magyar, that the leading accent falls. Altogether, Suomi is an extremely harmonious language, readily assimilating consonants, especially those that end the root, with the initials of the formative elements. No doubt this assimilation is not constant, but when it does not take place another process is adopted, to avoid the clash of two consonants of different orders. This consists in introducing (at least in speaking, if not in writing) a very short vowel between such letters. Thus *pitkä* is pronounced *pitikä*.

The case-endings of inflectional languages are expressed, as in other agglutinating tongues, by means of suffixes attached to the radical. Thus *n* denotes the genitive, as in *karhu* = the bear; *karhun* = of the bear. The plural sign is *t* for the subject, but otherwise *i*, inserted between the root and the relational suffix. Thus the theme *lapse* = child, gives *lapsen* = of the child; *lapset* = the children; *lapsein* = of the children.

. The personal pronouns are added to the noun in order to express the person to which it refers. The first person so affixed is *ni*, singular; *mme*, plural; second, *si* and *nne*; the third, *nsa* (or *nsä*, according to the exigencies of vowel harmony), for both numbers. Thus *tapa* = custom, gives *tapani* = my custom; *tapamme* = our customs; *tapansa* = his custom, or their customs.

Verbal modifications are also effected by suffixes, the root always coming first, after which the causative, diminutive, or frequentative elements; then the modal; the personal; and lastly, the subject of the action.

The Esthonian consonantal system presents nothing very unusual, except that *t, d, n, r, l, s, z,* become liquid under certain conditions, in which case they take a small stroke to the right *d', n',* &c. The Dorpat dialect utters *g, d,* and *b,* more forcibly than the others, occasionally changing them to the corresponding *k, t, p.* Amongst the nine vowels is the French *u,* written *ü,* besides a special sound between *ö* and *e*. These vowels are both long and short, and sometimes form diphthongs.

Vowel harmony is far from being uniformly developed in Esthonian, in fact, occurring only in the eastern Dorpat dialect, though traces of it are evident in the western, as well as to the west and south of the Revel dialect.

The principal accent falls on the first syllable, this, as in Suomi, being the radical.

The so-called cases are formed in the same way as in other agglutinating tongues, their number being limited only by the number of post-positions that may be attached to the noun. Hence they are fixed by one writer at twelve, by another at twenty, this very uncertainty being of itself sufficient to show how essentially such pretended cases differ from the true cases of the Aryan system.

Conjugation also is entirely analogous to that of the Suomi.

Lapponic occupies the extreme north-west of Russia, to the north of Karelian, and some regions in the north of Sweden and Norway. It presents four dialectic varieties, and its grammar closely resembles that of the cognate tongues, Suomi and Esthonian.

The *Volga-Finnic* idioms are divided into two branches: *Cheremissian* and *Mordvinian*. The first is spoken by some 200,000 persons, on the left bank of the Volga, a little to the west of Kasan and east of Nijni Novgorod, without, however, reaching very closely to the environs of either city. There is a highland and lowland variety. Mordvinian is spoken by nearly 700,000 people, on either side of the Volga, about Simborsk, Samara, Stavropol, and some points still farther south. It is divided into two dialects, the *Erze* and *Moksha*. Between the Mordvinian and the Cheremissian is the Chuvak, belonging not to the Finnic, but to the Turkic group.

Farther north are the *Permian*, spoken by about 60,000; the *Siryenian*, by 80,000; and the *Wotyak*, by upwards of 200,000 people. Wotyak occupies a relatively compact district to the north-east of the Cheremissian, and south of Glatzov. *Permian* stretches to the north of the Wotyak, west of the river Kama, as far north as Solikansk. *Siryenian*, still farther north of its congeners, occupies a much more extended territory, reaching northwards to the Samoyede zone, and, touching on the *Wogulic*, which, with *Magyaric* and *Ostyak*, forms the *Ugric* group. Wogul is spoken by about 7,000, and Ostyak by some 20,000 persons; the first lying east of Siryenian, the second still farther east, along a considerable stretch of the river Obi, as far north as the Samoyede. Wogul comprises at least two dialects, while there are varieties of the Ostyak at Irkutsk, Surgut, and Obdorsk.

Magyaric must occupy us more at length. Its geographical position, the political relations of the five millions speaking it, and its somewhat interesting literature, entitle it to a special place in the Finnic group.

Magyar, or Hungarian, occupies two regions of unequal extent, and separated from each other by a tract some forty-five or fifty leagues wide. The principal or western division forms an irregular pentagon, at whose angles are the towns of Presburg (in Magyar, Porsony), Unghvar (which is Slovak), Nagi Banya (Magyar), Novi Sad (in German, Neusatz, where Syrmian Serbo joins it), and Limbach, a little to the north of Warasdin in Croatia. Thus the extreme length of this pentagon is a hundred and odd leagues by some eighty in breadth. It does not, however, form a compact territory, being encroached upon on the north by the Slovak, by Servian on the south, and German on the west and south. The eastern division is more homogeneous, though only about a sixth in extent of the western. It is situated in the very heart of the Rumanian region, with two German tracts on its western frontier (Mediasch and Kronstadt). It forms the extreme south-east portion of the kingdom of Hungary, including no places of any particular note (Maros, Vasarhely, Udvarhely, &c.).

Many unsuccessful attempts have been made to explain the word *Magyar*. *Hungarian* would seem to mean *Hun-ugrian*, which agrees well enough with their origin, and with what we know of their arrival in Central Europe in the ninth century.* The inva-

---

* Sayous, "Les Origines et l'Époque Païenne de l'Histoire des Hongrois," Paris, 1874; Riedl, "Magyarische Grammatik," Vienna, 1858, Introduction; Castrén, "Über die Ursitze des Finnischen Volkes," Helsingfors, 1849.

sion of Attila is with much probability supposed to have been but a first incursion of races closely allied to the present Magyars.

But in any case, these are now totally isolated from the other Finnic peoples, and are hemmed in on all sides by the German, Rumanian, and various Slavonic tongues, and there can be little doubt that their language must ultimately die out, notwithstanding the great advantages secured to it by political circumstances. But it will not disappear without having left a worthy history behind it. Its most ancient record dates from the end of the twelfth century, since when it has been regularly traced, though its productions have mostly remained sealed books for the generality of the foreign men of letters.

There are a good many Magyar dialects, some spoken in Lower, others in Upper Hungary. However, they differ but slightly from each other, and it may even be said that the language has not undergone any considerable change from the date of its oldest historic monuments, though a large amount of foreign elements has been absorbed, chiefly from Slavonic, and a few from German.

All the languages here briefly touched upon are undoubtedly related and derived from some common source. The true comparative method has so far been but partially applied to them, the labour of doing so being all the more delicate, inasmuch as idioms are here dealt with that have been separated from each other for many centuries, and have been subjected to the almost continual influence of the Aryan tongues, whose inner structure is superior to their own.

A comparison of the various Finnic idioms reveals some singular phonetic variations, though presenting, on the whole, nothing very novel. Here are some cases in point: The *hand* in Suomi is *käte*, in Wepsic *käzi*, in Wotic *tchäsi*, in Esthonian *käsi*, in Livonian *käiz*, in Lapp *giet* and *küt*, in Siryenian, Permian, and Wotyak *ki*, in Mordvinian *ked*, in Cheremissian *ket*, in Ostyak *ket* or *köt*, in Wogul *kat*, and in Magyar *kéz*. *Fish* is *kala* in Suomi, *guolle* in Lapp, *kal* in Mordvinian, *kul* in Wogul, *hal* in Magyar.

In general, Magyar seems to have reduced or shortened the primitive words, whilst Suomi shows a very decided tendency to multiply the vowels. A comparison of old with modern Magyar shows analogous facts, proving that it has within itself undergone changes that now normally take place between it and its congeners.

Amongst these idioms, the best studied are the Suomi, Magyar, and Esthonian, very little having so far been done for the others.

Magyar literature is rich, its most interesting and original works being in poetry. Since the kingdom of Hungary has acquired fresh importance at the expense of the adjoining Servian and Rumanian provinces, its language also has at least in this respect grown into greater consideration. But its works have been too frequently thought out in German, strongly reflecting the foreign education of the writers. Besides the Magyar, Suomi literature is almost the only other that offers any interest. Its principal monument is the great mythological epic of the "Kalévala."

It is impossible here to attempt anything like a complete summary of the grammatical structure of these languages, but we may briefly describe their more general features. Beginning with some details of the Magyar phonetic system, we shall then devote a few words to the particular sounds of the other members of the group, concluding with a glance at their formative processes.

Magyar phonetics are not very complex. Seven short vowels, a, e (more or less open), i, o, u, $ö$ = French eu, $ü$ = French u, with their seven corresponding long vowels, these last being distinguished in writing by a stroke to the right: a', e', o', u'. The consonants are not very numerous, but some, such as ty, gy, are peculiar. It might, perhaps, be better to use one sign for their notation, which is otherwise detestable, as, for instance, in its use of sz, zs, and s. Sz is our ordinary s, zs is the Croatian and Bohemian z, that is the French j, and s is the English sh. Unfortunately it would be now useless to attempt a reform of this vicious system. The Slavs have long been alive to the importance of some change for the better, and have to a great extent realised it; but national prejudice still stands in the way of any reform in Magyar orthography. Émile Picot has drawn up a synoptical table of the correspondence of written symbols for a number of the more important languages, which may be consulted with advantage, especially in connection with geographical names.

In it the Uralo-Altaïc family is represented by Magyar and Turkish.*

As in Suomi, the root in Magyar comes first, and is rarely preceded by a prefix, such cases being probably due to Aryan influence. At least the history of the language shows that they are recent. As in Suomi also, the accent falls on the radical, or rather always on the first syllable of the word, even when that syllable happens to be a prefix.

Magyar derivation is extremely simple. The plural is denoted by an agglutinated element: *ház-ak* = the houses; *atyá-k* = the fathers; and the case elements are placed after this plural particle: *atya* = *pater*; *atyat* = *patrem*; *atyák* = *patres* (nom.); *atyákat* = *patres* (acc.).

Magyar has developed an article—*a* before consonants, *az* before vowels: *az ember* = the man.

It is rich in verbal elements, incorporating the third person, when it is the direct object, as is the case with all other members of the Finnish group. Thus:

    Vár = he awaits;
    Várja = he awaits him;
    Várjuk = they await him;

where *ja* denotes the direct pronominal object, and *k* the plural.

But Magyar is capable even of incorporating the second pronominal object, though only when the subject is the first person singular: *várok* = I await; *várlak* = I await thee. This is a point to be carefully noted, and we shall see farther on that Basque goes even farther, incorporating both the direct and the indirect personal objects, so as to express in one word not only "I give it," but "I give it to thee."

M. Budenz reckons in the Ugrian group collectively nine vowels and thirty-three consonants, amongst which the French *j*, the twofold German *ch*, the semi-linguals of the Ostyak, the weak and sibilant Lapp *d*, and the liquid consonants. None of these idioms has a really indigenous graphic system.

* Picot, "Tableau Phonétique des Principales Langues usuelles," in "Revue de Linguistique et de Philologie Comparée," vi. p. 363. Paris, 1874.

The Finnic tongues ignore gender, but possess the three numbers, dual and plural being expressed by different suffixes. The article is used in accordance with our practice in Magyar alone, where it is *az* before vowels, and *a* before consonants. Mordvinian, however, is able to determine the nouns, as in Basque, by suffixing to them the demonstrative pronoun *sä* or *se* of the third person. Siryenian and Wotyak have something analogous to this, and Budenz finds traces of it in other members also of the same family. Thus in Magyar the affix of the third person *a* or *é* = his, her, is a derivative element common enough, as in *Pest varosa* = the city of Pest, literally, Pest its city.

As in all other true agglutinating tongues, here also real declension is wanting. Post-positions and particles are used, answering in sense to our prepositions, but tacked on at the end of the word, without any separating mark in writing. In the same way are formed the augmentatives, diminutives, and superlatives, but the suffixes answering to the Aryan case-endings always come last, for the simple reason that they do not affect the inner sense of the root, merely indicating its manner of being (to, at, in, with, of, &c.) in relation to the other terms of the proposition. The number of these particles being considerable, writers who have conceived the eccentric idea of composing grammars of the agglutinating tongues on the classic model, have given them a number of pretended cases, for which they have invented the most fantastic names in *ive*, utterly ignoring the nature of speech in general, and of the agglutinating type of language in particular.

In this last the verb presents itself with an endless suite of forms, whose derivation, however, offers no difficulty. In the first place the root, expressing the idea of action in a general way, may receive successive additions, showing that the action is done or suffered, possible, compulsory, or voluntary, and so on. Thus arise secondary radicals, that is so many derived forms. Add to this the incorporation of the third personal pronoun when it is direct object —*I see him*, for instance, thus becoming one word. All the Finnic idioms make use of this incorporation, while Magyar further incorporates the second person objective, when the first person is subject. Wogul does the same whatever be the subject, and, lastly, Mordvinian is able so to express even the first person objective. We shall have, for example, in the Moksha dialect, *palasa*, I embrace him; *af palatansa*, he does not embrace thee; *palamait*, thou didst embrace me. Forms, however, exist in which the object is not so incorporated, nor can any of them incorporate the indirect object, as does the Basque, when it throws into one word the phrase, *I give it to thee*.

These few remarks, notwithstanding their brevity, will, we trust, suffice to render clear the mechanism of these interesting members of the Finnic group.

(3) *The Turkic Group*,

Known also by the name of *Tatar*, by a sorry play of words (or misconception) changed to *Tartar*. The tribes speaking its numerous dialects now stretch from the shores of the Mediterranean to the banks of the Lena in Eastern Siberia. Their original point of departure is generally said to be Turkestan, whence within the historic period countless daring hordes have gone forth, overrunning vast regions in Asia, and penetrating westwards through Europe as far as French territory.*

Philologically considered, the Turks, in the widest sense of the word, are divided into five families, each speaking a distinct language, which in its turn is itself split up into a greater or less number of dialectic varieties. Coming westwards and southwards, these five branches are: The *Yakutic*, *Kirghiz*, *Uiguric*, *Nogairic*, and *Turkish*.

Yakutic is spoken by about 200,000 people in the midst of Tungusian tribes in the north-east of Siberia.

The *Black Kirghiz*, or *Burut*, occupy that part of Turkestan attached to the Chinese empire. The *Kazak Kirghiz* extend more westwards, as far as the Aral Sea and to the north of the Caspian.

Of the *Uiguric* there are three varieties: The *Uigur* proper,

---

* Abel Rémusat, "Recherches sur les Langues Tatares," p. 328. Paris, 1820.

the *Jagataic*, and the *Turkoman* (or Turkmenian). Of all its congeners Uïguric has attained the highest degree of literary culture. It was reduced to writing so early as the fifth century, as evidenced by Chinese authors, employing an original alphabet, since lost, and replaced under the influence of the Nestorian missionaries by a system based on the Syriac alphabet, as is also that of the Mandchus, the Kalmuks, and the Mongolians.

Nogairic is spoken by about 50,000 persons toward the north of the Volga, at Astrakhan, in some districts between the Black Sea and the Caspian, in a small tract north of the Sea of Azov, and throughout the Crimea. It is the language of the Russian Tatars, properly so called. The *Kumuk* variety is spoken on the north-east of the Caucasus.

The fifth family is that of the Turkish dialects proper, with which is included the *Chuvak*, spoken, as above stated, between the two Finnic idioms, Mordvinian and Cheremissian. It occupies a somewhat compact territory to the south-west of Kazan, and a great number of detached points in the neighbourhood of Simbirsk. Chuvak presents some remarkable features, though it cannot be looked on with some writers as a mixture of Turkish and Finnic. M. Schott has clearly shown that it belongs to the Turkish group, some connecting it rather with Nogairic than with Turkish proper.

Turkish, which for most Europeans is the most interesting member of this fifth group, is not, however, to be considered as the purest and most correct. It varies very strikingly in the different localities where it is spoken, the form current in Constantinople, for instance, being much freer from Arabic elements than the official and learned *Osmanli*. Of this we shall give a rapid sketch. Such is the clearness and precision of its structure that it may be regarded as the most striking type of an agglutinating language. There is no lack of Turkish grammars, mostly, however, wanting in critical discernment. In our remarks we shall avail ourselves mainly of that of Redhouse.*

Turkish is written with the Arabic alphabet, though this is but

* " Grammaire Raisonnée de la Langue Ottomane." Paris, 1846.

little suited to the purpose. It has already been stated, and will be again presently repeated, that in the Uralo-Altaïc group the vowels play a chief part, whereas the Arabic graphic system lends itself very indifferently to vowel notation. The Turkish alphabet consists of thirty-one characters, each susceptible of twelve modifying marks, some representing the several vowels, others doubling the consonant or suppressing it altogether. But apart from this, the phonetic elements proper consist of seven simple vowels : *a, e, ó, u, eu, u* French, short and long; the French nasal *in* of *maintien*; the semi-vowel *y*; and twenty-two consonants, including some gutturals, fricatives, and a few sibilants. Redhouse treats the vowel system somewhat differently from this, and Picot's tables, quoted above, may be advantageously consulted on the point.

The Turkish language is entirely subject to an imperious law of vowel harmony, which will again engage our attention farther on, and which is here extended even to the words borrowed from Arabic and Persian. In virtue of this law the infinitive ending is *maq* if the accented vowel of the root is *hard*, but *meq* if *soft*. Thus, *to love* is *sevmeq*, but *to write* = *yazmaq*.

The distinction of gender observed in Turkish for Persian or Arabic words is otherwise entirely foreign to the Tatar languages. There are but two numbers, the singular and plural, but Arabic words retain their dual form. Like all the Uralo-Altaïc idioms, Turkish expresses the Aryan case-endings by means of post-positions or independent syllables at the end of the word, and joined to it in writing. The plural sign, *lar* or *ler*, according to the prevailing vowel of the radical, is intercalated between the noun and the post-positions, thus : *dil*, tongue ; *dile*, to the tongue ; *dillere*, to the tongues. These terminal suffixes answer so completely to our prepositions that one of them suffices for a series of subordinate words, as, for instance, a noun coupled with a number of adjectives. Besides, some of them are independent words still used as common nouns in the ordinary language.

The adjective, which is a mere qualifying noun, comes always before the word it qualifies, and the degrees of comparison are expressed by words meaning *more, further, less*, &c.

The pronouns are both isolated and attached, the latter coming naturally after the plural sign: *boghaz-c*, his throat; *taraq-lar-e*, their combs.

The Turkish verb is often quoted for the richness and variety of its forms, in which the agglutinating system, so to say, runs riot. Yet, notwithstanding the vast framework of tenses, moods, and derivative voices piled up by the grammarians, the Finnic tongues must be allowed herein to surpass even the Turkish. Magyar, by incorporating the direct object, says in a single word *I see him*, which Turkish cannot compass. Its marked speciality consists in the play of the so-called derived voices, that is, of forms expressing various shades of the manner of being of the same action. These secondary forms are obtained by adding to the simple root a number of suffixes, whose vowels are of course modified according to the laws of progressive harmony. Thus *ma*, *me*, being the negative particle, the infinitive *sevmek*, to love, will yield *sevmemek*, not to love; *dir* denotes causality, *il* the passive, and *in* the reflex idea; hence *sevdirmek* = to cause to love; *sevilmek* = to be loved, and *sevinmek* = to love oneself. But these and other such suffixes may be combined together, resulting in such forms as, *sevinmemek* = not to love oneself. In this way every root might furnish some fifty derived forms.

What are called the tenses and moods are similarly formed by the insertion of certain elements between the root and the personal ending. But besides this natural conjugation, there is another that may be called the indirect, or periphrastic—that is, in which the simple forms are replaced by circumlocutions. It is based on the union of the various participles with the auxiliary *to be*, and by means of it may be expressed a multiplicity of exceedingly minute shades of meaning.

The limits of this work prevent us from casting even a glance at Turkish syntax. We can merely observe that it is all the more complex in consequence of the great change effected in the language by the intrusion of foreign words. Hence the grammars are full of rules, some restricted to Persian, others to Arabic words, and some again common to both, while still inapplicable to the native element. The vocabulary is deeply affected by Semitic and Aryan words, introduced successively by the Persians and the Arabs.

In Asia, Turkish is spoken in the interior of Asia Minor; the north and south coasts, as well as that of the Sea of Marmora, being Greek. In Europe it occupies but a small portion of the Ottoman empire; its more important points being situated on the south and east, at Larissa in Thessaly, here and there in Thrace, and in some tracts scattered up and down Bulgaria, such as the neighbourhood of Philippopoli, and especially the north-east of the Balkan peninsula, below Silistria. In Candia it still possesses a somewhat compact little territory in the interior of the island; but here also the Greek language is encroaching on its domain.

(4) *The Tungusian Group*

Comprises three distinct branches: the *Mandchu*, the *Lamutic*, and the *Tungusian* proper.

The *Tunguses*, numbering about 70,000, are situated about the centre of Siberia; the *Lamuts* stretch more to the north-east, and are connected with the *Mandchus*, who occupy the north-east corner of the Chinese empire.

The Mandchus possess a curious graphic system, of Syriac origin, and consisting of twenty-nine letters, each with a triple form, as in Arabic, according as they are initial, medial, or final, though the change at times is but slight.* To these are added some complex signs derived from the Chinese, and serving, apparently, for the transcription of foreign words. The letters mostly consist of a stroke ending in various curves, and are written in vertical lines from left to right, in which arrangement Chinese influence may be recognised. The Tungus has no special graphic system.

On the Mandchu vowels there is not much to be said, but the consonantal system is somewhat complex, rendering its classification rather difficult. There are two kinds of k, g, h, t, and d, one of

---

* Besides these there is the full, unconnected form, of which the others are obvious curtailments, always showing more or less conspicuously the essential part of the letter.—*Note by Translator.*

which is joined to the strong vowels *a, o, ó*, only, the other to the so-called *neutral* vowels *i, u*, and to the *weak e*—a distinction we shall have again to refer to in speaking of vowel harmony. A curious point, occurring also in the Dravidian languages, is that words cannot begin with the soft explosives *g, d, b*. In Mandchu there are several (two) kinds of *n*, the sounds *ch* and *j*, and various sibilants.* In the Siberian dialects, which allow of the soft consonants, initial, there is a much greater number of sounds, including a series of liquid consonants, analogous, for instance, to the Magyar *gy, ty, ly*. The accent falls on the last syllable.

In Mandchu the noun has neither gender nor number, but the Tungus dialects have retained a plural sign. The so-called declension, as in all agglutinating tongues, is effected by means of suffixes answering to our prepositions. The adjective is naturally invariable, being nothing but a noun placed before another to qualify it (as in the English *wine-merchant, house-top*). The conjugation presents the same peculiarities as the Turkish and other agglutinating idioms, and comprises a large number of secondary forms. The root *to drink*, for instance, gives such derivative forms as "to cease to drink," "to come from drinking," "to go to drink," "to drink together," and so on. In all this the Siberian dialects resemble the Mandchu, but possess greater wealth of forms, especially in their derived voices.

The Mandchu-Tungus vocabulary, as might be supposed, is far from copious. Properly speaking, it does not possess the verb *to have*, a common feature of the first two types of speech; and it has borrowed largely from Chinese, more or less modifying the forms of the words.

The question of priority has been decided by M. Lucien Adam in favour of Tungusic over Mandchu, on the ground that it possesses the sign of number, the possessive pronouns affixed, and other important elements unknown to its congener. In other respects they are both closely allied, as shown by the constant

---

* L. Adam, "Grammaire de la Langue Mandchoue." Paris, 1872. By the same writer, "Grammaire de la Langue Tongouse." Paris, 1874.

identity of the principal pronouns, of the numerals, the most important suffixes, and the great bulk of their vocabularies. They clearly come of one source, and must have been separated only after a long period of grammatical development in common.

(5) *The Mongolian Group*

Comprises three dialects: *Eastern* (or *Sharra*) *Mongolian*, spoken in Mongolia proper, that is, in the centre of the northern portion of the Chinese empire, and west of Mandchuria; *Kalmuk*, or *Western Mongolian*, reaching westwards into Russia as far as the Caspian, towards the mouth of the Volga, between the two Turkic tribes of the Kirghiz and Nogair; the *Buryetic* or *Northern Mongolian*, spoken by a tribe numbering about 200,000, near Lake Baikal, in Southern Siberia, thus verging on the Eastern Mongolian spoken still farther south; lastly, some other Mongolian varieties occur in the neighbourhood of Cabul.

Although quite as interesting as the foregoing group, these idioms need not detain us long, as their main features are very analogous to those of the others noticed in this chapter; the chief differences between Tungus and Mongolian being found in their vocabularies, and in their greater or less grammatical development.

Mongol has an alphabet closely related to the Mandchu, embracing seven vowels, *a, e, i, o, u, eu* French, *ü* (French *u*), and seventeen consonants, amongst which *ts* and *ds*. The letters, as in Mandchu, vary in form according as they are initial, medial, or final; and each consonant, as in Devanāgari, has always an inherent vowel, except when it is final.

The progressive vowel harmony characterising the Uralo-Altaïc group forms a feature of the Mongolian also, but with some peculiarities, amongst which are, in *Buryetic*, the elision of final vowels, and certain modifications experienced by the consonants in contact with each other. As to conjugation, it may be remarked that in Mongol the direct pronominal object is not incorporated with the verb. Thus, the forms " I see it," " I eat it," which in Turkish are expressed by one word, appear as two in Mongolian.

The little-known Buryetic occupies a very important place in the Mongolian group, its grammatical development, according to M. Adam, being all the more instructive, that in it there occur the intermediate forms through which the pronouns have passed in becoming suffixes. But this phenomenon of the superiority of a comparatively rude dialect over literary and cultivated tongues, such as Mongol and Mandchu, is by no means of rare occurrence.

(6) *Vowel Harmony.*

The phenomenon of vowel harmony, in the Altaïc tongues, is all the more important, that it forms one of the main arguments generally relied upon to establish the affinity of the Samoyede, Finnic, Turkic, Tungus, and Mongol groups. In what then consists this quality ? what is its origin, its value ? and what conclusions are to be drawn from its simultaneous prevalence in these various idioms ?

This progressive vocal assimilation may be described as a sort of progressive *umlaut*, and is practically reduced to this : the vowels being divided into two classes, all those in a word that follow the vowel of the primary root must be of the same class as that root-vowel. In certain Uralo-Altaïc tongues, however, there are what are called the "neutral" vowels, occurring indifferently with either class. The vowels, in some of the leading members of this family, are thus classified :*

	Gutturals, or hard.	Palatals, or weak.	Neutrals.
Suomi ...	u, o, a	ü, ö, ä	e, i
Magyar ...	u, o, a	ü, ö	e, i
Mordvinian	u, o, a	ä, i	—
Syrenian ...	ô, a	ä, i, e	—
Turkish ...	u, o, a, e	ü, ö, e, i	—
Mongolian ...	u, o, a	ü, ö, ä	i
Buryetic ...	n, o, a	ü, ö, ä	e, i
Mandchu ...	ô, o, a	e	u, i

In this table u stands for the French *ou*; $ö =$ French *eu*; $ü =$ French *u*. The classification is much the same everywhere of the

---

* L. Adam, "De l'Harmonie des Voyelles dans les Langues Uralo-Altaïque." Paris, 1874.

three primitives *a*, *u*, *i*, the first two being, in principle, guttural, the third neutral. In the same way the intermediate are in principle weak or palatal. But great differences prevail in practice. Thus, the harmony may extend to the whole word, or be restricted to the suffixes; it may apply to all the words or to the simple ones only; that is, to those that are not composed. For instance, in Turkish, the whole word must be harmonised, as is the case also in Mandchu, Mongol, Suomi, and Magyar; while in Mordvinian and Siryenian, the final vowels alone are affected. In Magyar, again, compounds retain the vowels of the simple word.*

But whence arises this phenomenon? is it primitive or recent? M. Adam, who has devoted himself specially to this subject, finds little difficulty in refuting the opinion of those who, with Bœhtlingk, see in it nothing but the result of local physiological circumstances, or who, with Pott, look on it as merely a mechanical accident. But Schleicher and, after him, Riedl have found the true solution of the problem. Schleicher had turned his attention only to the most general and most remarkable case, that of the harmony of the suffixed vowels, presenting each of them a double form, hard or soft, according to the nature of the suffix. He was struck by the way in which the terminal vowels were affected by the root; and he concluded that it was the necessary result of agglutination, and of the

* With this singular law of vowel harmony may be compared the Irish rule of "broad to broad," and "slender to slender;" which is also, in fact, a species of progressive assimilation. The Irish broad vowels *a*, *o*, *u*, answer to the Uralo-Altaïc *u*, *o*, *a*, as above; the corresponding slenders being *e*, *i*. According to this law, Irish grammarians tell us that a broad vowel must be followed by a broad in the next succeeding syllable, and a slender vowel in the same way by a slender. To this are also analogous the peculiar modifications of the Latin root-vowels, produced by prefixes, whether these be due to composition or reduplication, as in *cado*, *cecidi*; *ars*, *iners*; *lego*, *diligo*; *annus*, *perennus*, &c. But here it is the root-vowel that is modified by prefixes, whereas in the Uralo-Altaïc system, there being no prefixes, the root-vowel remains unchanged, the progressive harmony affecting some or all of the following syllables, as the case may be. But the principle is probably the same in all these linguistic groups, being simply more consistently carried out, or more highly developed in some than in others: in Turkish for instance, than in Latin.—*Note by Translator.*

tendency in speech to bring into the closest possible juxtaposition the idea and its relations so intimately associated in the mind. Riedl has shown that such was really the case, for the study of the old Magyar documents revealed in this respect a very marked development from the twelfth century to the present time. In the oldest texts, anti-harmonic forms abound; thus, *halál-nek*, at death, which would now have to be *halál-nak*; *tiszta-seg* for *tiszta-ság*, purity, and so on.

M. Adam rightly concludes that previous to the twelfth century the number of harmonised derivatives was still more restricted, being replaced by real inharmonic compounds. " Take," he says, " two radicals, *fa*, tree, and *vel* (*veli*), companion; where *fa-vel* will be the unharmonised compound of these two nominal elements. But when *vel* has come to be successively suffixed to a certain number of roots it will begin sensibly to lose its original meaning of *companion*, gradually assuming the sense of the relational *with* in connection with the root to which it is added."*

We have here, therefore, a case of phonetic decay, arising from forgetfulness of the primitive sense of the formative element. But the process was very slow, nor at all uniform in the various Uralo-Altaïc idioms, many of which, such as the highland Cheremissian and Wotyak, even now betray but the merest traces of rudimentary vowel harmony. M. Adam, however, believes that these two dialects have lost the principle of progressive assimilation under the pressure of powerful foreign influences. According to him, they would seem still to possess sufficient traces of it to enable us to conclude that at some epoch all the Uralo-Altaïc family was subject to vowel harmony. We certainly look upon the principle as a feature of great importance, though, after all, but a relatively recent historic fact. This is not the place to seek for the causes and conditions of its development; but we do not believe that of itself alone it would suffice to prove the common descent of the five groups that have here been described.

Meanwhile, we may say that if their original parentage is highly

* *Op. cit.*, p. 67.

probable, it has not yet been definitely established. There is room to hope that it may be, some day or other; but many preparatory studies of details will have, doubtless, to precede such a result. In any case, progressive vowel harmony connects the members of the Uralo-Altaïc family, in their morphological aspect, in such a way as to render it extremely undesirable to separate them from each other in the general series of agglutinating tongues.

§ 15.—*Basque.*

This remarkable and interesting language is at present spoken by scarcely more than 450,000 persons, possessed of no great social originality or separate political existence. About three-fourths of this number belong to Spanish nationality, and the rest, approximately 140,000, to France. There are also about 200,000 Basques settled on the shores of the river Plate.

We are, of course, here speaking only of the individuals using the Basque *language*, without at all considering the special question of the Basque *race*. In truth, thanks to the excellent treatises of M. Broca, we now know that there are Basques and Basques; that, for instance, the Spanish Basques are of much purer blood than the French.*

The attempt has frequently been made to fix the limits of the Basque language, but not till lately have any results been arrived at which, without being altogether unassailable, are nevertheless entitled to be considered as really trustworthy. The chart recently drawn up by M. Broca, and published by him in "La Revue d'Anthropologie," seems to us more particularly reliable.†

Let us endeavour to give some more or less accurate idea of its outlines. Starting from a point on the coast a little to the south

---

* "Sur les Crânes Basques de Saint Jean de Luz," in the "Bulletins de la Soc. d'Anthropologie de Paris," 1868, p. 48; with which compare "Revue d'Anthropologie," iv. p. 29, Paris, 1875.

† "Sur l'Origine et la Répartition de la Langue Basque," *op. cit.*, iv. p. 1 et suiv., planche iii. Paris, 1875. The larger chart of Prince L. L. Bonaparte does not materially differ from this. It places Puente la Reina in the zone where Basque is still spoken.

of Biarritz, the border line passes to the south-east of Bayonne, follows the course of the Adour somewhat closely, and by a brusque movement southwards encloses the territory of Bastide-Clairence. It then by an equally sharp turn returns towards the Adour, and, passing below Bidache, Sauveterre, and Navarreins, advances in the direction without reaching the town of Oloron. It returns almost horizontally westward to Tardets, whence it gains the Pic d'Anie, and enters Spanish territory. It then proceeds towards Navascues, surrounding the northern environs of Pamplona, redescends towards Puente la Reina, passes a little above Estella and Vitoria, reaches Orduna on the north-west, and reascends towards Portugalete, here terminating at the coast. Its greatest length (from Orduna to about five kilometers to the west of Oloron) would therefore be approximately 190 kilometers, its breadth varying from 50 to 80.

Information drawn from an independent but not less reliable source agrees on all points with these data. According to it the frontier line leaving the Gulf of Gascony a little above Biarritz strikes the Adour below Saint-Pierre d'Irube, two kilometers south of Bayonne, follows this river to a point beyond Urcuit, then quits it so as to enclose Briscous and Bardos (to the exclusion of Bastide-Clairence), then Saint-Palais and Esquiule, near Oloron, thus reaching the Pic d'Anie. In Spain its limits reach beyond the valley of Roncal in the direction of Aragon. After passing Burgui it bends to the left towards Pamplona, which it skirts, thence redescending till it gets beyond Puente la Reina, returning in an almost straight line to Vitoria, whence it ascends towards the sea, which it reaches a little to the west of Portugalete.

The Basque district therefore comprises in Spain nearly the whole of the Spanish province of Biscaya, Guipuzcoa, the northern portion of Alava, and nearly half of Navarre; in France, one commune of the arrondissement of Oloron, and nearly the whole of those of Mauléon and Bayonne, corresponding to the ancient local divisions of La Soule, Basse-Navarre, and Labourd.

There exists no really historic proof that in former times Basque occupied a wider geographical area than this. We shall revert in another place to the *Iberian* question, meantime remarking that in France it is quite impossible to show with any certainty that Basque was at any time spoken in any of the hamlets where Gascon is now exclusively current. On the other hand, it is undeniable that in Spain it has been losing ground for some centuries past. Thus Pamplona, formerly Basque, is now altogether Spanish; and in our own days it is easy to show a perceptible shifting in the more important localities subject to the influence of modern life and to greater contact with strangers. The dialects of San Sebastian and of Saint-Jean de Luz, for instance, are very incorrect, having appropriated a great number of Spanish and French words.

Another very important fact should be noted. M. Broca's chart comprises not only the three zones—*Gascon* (Bayonne, Orthez, Oloron); *Basque* (Tolosa, Saint-Jean de Luz, Mauléon; *Spanish* (Vitoria, Estella, Pamplona)—but also a fourth, or mixed Basque and Spanish zone, in some places from 15 to 20 kilometers wide, in others extremely narrow, and containing besides other towns those of Bilbao, Orduna, Agiz, and Roncal. In his memoir on the distribution of the Basque language, M. Broca has offered an ingenious explanation of the absence of an analogous zone between Basque and Gascon. "In Spain," he says, "Basque comes into collision with Spanish on its border under conditions of such inferiority as to render inevitable the gradual encroachment of the latter. But in France the dialect hemming in the Basque is not, like the Spanish, an official, administrative, political and literary, language. It is merely a local idiom, an old *patois*, without any expansive power, but, on the contrary, actually dying out. There is no good reason why such a dialect should supplant the Basque, or the Basque encroach upon it. The two idioms, therefore, remain stationary, both equally weak and alike threatened to be sooner or later absorbed by the French, which language alone the Basques have any interest in learning. All those that have received any instruction are already familiar with it, and all the inhabitants of towns of any importance speak or understand it. Thus, every town and market-place becomes a focus for the spread of French, and a time must come when Basque will cease to be spoken, except in the most secluded hamlets and least accessible valleys, and will ultimately fall into abeyance even there. It will therefore perish under influences that doubtless will not be felt on all points to the same extent, but which will everywhere be felt simultaneously. Thus it will not retire, step by step, as in Spain, before the ever-forward march of Spanish, because in France it is not pressed more on the frontier than in the rest of its domain. We do not say, however, that it will maintain itself to the last in its actual limits. It is very probable that the Béarn *patois* encircling it will first disappear, and that French, thus coming to press on the Basque frontier, will drive it gradually southwards towards the Pyrenees, whose upper villages will probably be the last refuge of the oldest language in Europe." *

The proper and original name of the Basque is *Escuara, Euscara, Useara*, according to the various dialectic forms, whence the French *Euscarien*, synonymous with *Basque*. The Spaniards call it *Vascuence*, and those who speak it *Vascongados*. On the origin of these terms it is not easy to pronounce definitely. The most likely, though not fully established etymology of *escuara*, is no doubt that of M. Mahn, who explains it as " manner of speech," " language." The explanations given by the people themselves are, as might be expected, extremely fantastic. When they compare their language with those of their neighbours, they find themselves so completely at sea that they forthwith fall into ecstasies of admiration for their mother-tongue. One of them, the Jesuit Larramendi, whose work bears the grandiloquent title of " El Imposible Vencido," ("The Impossible Overcome") makes it pretty well the common source of all other languages. Another, Astarloa, asserts that each of the Escuara letters possesses a hidden virtue. A third, the Abbé Darrigol, proves, with the aid of Beauzée, the everlasting perfection of Basque. Chaho invents his ingenious theory of the Basque " seers," whose precocious civilisation was extinguished by the Kelto-Scythian barbarians; and the Abbé d'Iharce de Bidassouet makes Escuara the language in which the Eternal Father conversed with the first of the Jews.

* *Op. cit.*

But there is no absurdity to which this precious relic of the primeval languages of Europe has not given occasion. In truth, Escuar presented insurmountable difficulties to those who were accustomed to nothing but commenting on Greek and Latin texts by means of empiric processes. Accordingly, the learned in medieval times looked on Basque as an indecipherable puzzle, an utterly insoluble problem. A proverb preserved in the north of Spain pretends that the devil himself spent seven long years amongst the Basques without succeeding in understanding a single word of the language. We are thus enabled to explain the following remarkable definition in a Spanish dictionary: "*Vascuence*: *Lo que está tan confuso y oscuro que no se puede entender*;" that is, *Basque*: anything so confused and obscure as to be unintelligible.

Unfortunately the problem has been taken in hand by many learned men unacquainted with philological principles, and by many foreign amateurs, without special preparation for such studies. Hence their bootless efforts have merely had the effect of increasing the infatuation by which the Basques had already been inspired by so many previous abortive attempts in the same direction. The study of Basque may, without much exaggeration, be said to have led to downright insanity. But things have greatly changed since the discovery of the true philological method. The sphinx, more skilfully attacked, has been made to yield up her secret, and although a number of points still remain to be settled, it may be presumed that, at no distant day, we shall be able to congratulate ourselves on having mastered the numerous and intricate laws of the Basque language. There were undoubtedly many excellent things in the writings of Oihenart, of Chaho, and, above all, of Lécluse; but the quite recent works of Prince L. L. Bonaparte, W. Van Eys, and Julien Vinson[*] have more decidedly tended towards a solution of the difficulty.

[*] Prince L. L. Bonaparte has issued many texts and a valuable treatise on the verb. To Van Eys we owe the first Basque-French dictionary ever printed, and the first elementary grammar: "Essai de Grammaire de la Langue Basque," 2nd edition, Amsterdam, 1867. The numerous writings, with which M. Vinson has enriched the "Revue de Linguistique," are, in our opinion, amongst the best modern contributions to the study of

Basque, for a stranger, is in a completely isolated condition, offering no point of contact with the surrounding tongues, either in the formation of its words or its morphology; and the Magyar, which most resembles it in some general features, is geographically widely separated from it. Besides, we have some knowledge of the history of the Hungarian language, while that of the Basque is utterly unknown. No unequivocal traces of the Basque tongue are to be met with in any authentic documents older than the tenth century. And even to this epoch nothing can be referred except a Latin chart, dated 980, limiting the episcopal diocese of Bayonne, and giving the names of some Basque districts in a more or less modified form. It is now well established that the pretended Basque warsongs, attributed to a period many centuries older than the tenth century, are purely apocryphal. Even from the tenth to the sixteenth century we meet with nothing beyond some few names of places in sundry charters, letters patent, pontifical bulls, and the like. The first to speak of the Escuara tongue, and to give some of its words, is Lucius Marinæus Siculus, in his "Cosas Memorables de España," Alcala, 1530. The oldest printed text known to us is the short discourse of Panurge, in the famous ninth chapter of the tenth book of Rabelais, published in 1542. The first printed book, however, is dated 1545. It consists of poems, partly religious and partly erotic, by Bernard Dechepare, curé of Saint-Michel-le-vieux, in Lower Navarre, and has recently been correctly reissued.* The changes the language has undergone since that time, though doubtless perceptible enough, cannot be said to be very important.

Even now, more serious divergences are ascertained to exist between the various dialects. In fact its varieties are, so to say, innumerable, every hamlet presenting some local forms peculiar to itself. Of course there is nothing abnormal in this; but while, side by side with their spoken and local forms, most languages have a general or conventional standard, the result of education, and often closely resembling the written form, in Basque there is no such

philology, based on sound knowledge and scientific method. To them we are ourselves largely indebted.

* Édition Cazals. Bayonne, 1874.

CHAP. IV.] SECOND FORM OF SPEECH—AGGLUTINATION. 115

general standard, each writer forming one to suit his own fancy. Some writers have reckoned as many as eight dialects, yielding no less than twenty-five principal varieties—in Spain, the *Biscayan*, *Guipuzcoan*, *Upper Navarrese*, north, *Upper Navarrese*, south; in France, the *Labourdin* (in the south-west of the arrondissement of Bayonne); the *Souletin*, in the two cantons south-east of the arrondissement of Mauléon (old Navarre), the *Lower Navarrese*, east, and *Lower Navarrese*, west, spoken in French Navarre, that is in the rest of these two arrondissements.

But these eight dialects are easily reducible to three principal groups. The first of these, comprising *Biscayan* alone, is especially remarkable for the originality of its verb. The second, including the *Souletin* and the *Lower Navarrese*, is marked by frequent aspirates and the interchange of *u* with *i*. The third, embracing the four remaining dialects, *Guipuzcoan*, *Labourdin*, and *Upper Navarrese*, north and south, presents fuller and generally less modified forms than the second group.

Without attempting to indicate the more or less striking differences by which these dialects are distinguished from each other, it may be stated in a general way that the four French dialects possess the aspirate, which is utterly unknown to those of Spain. As to the special interest that they may present, it may be remarked that the Souletin, the Labourdin, the Guipuzcoan, and the Biscayan have alone been seriously studied, because they alone possess a literature, such as it is. The central dialects, Guipuzcoan and Labourdin, seem to have undergone the least changes, while the others have all of them been more or less deeply modified. M. Vinson places Labourdin even before Guipuzcoan in this respect.

It is, of course, only by the simultaneous and comparative study of all its eight dialects, that it becomes possible to determine the general character of the Basque language, by restoring, as far as may be, its common forms. Their phonetics, which alone can accomplish this result, must now briefly engage our attention.

There are five simple vowels, *a, e, i, o, u*; six diphthongs, *ai, ei, oi, ui, au, eu*; the two semi-vowels, *y* and *w*; and twenty-two consonants, which may be thus classified: *k, y, gh; ch, ts; t, d, th;*

p, *b*, *ph* ; *n* of the Greek αγγελος ; *n mouillé* of the French *agneau* ; *n dental* ; *m* ; the fricatives *h*, *sh*, *z*, *s* ; *r hard*, nearly *rr* ; *r soft* (very near to *l*) ; lastly, *l*. But were the sounds peculiar to the various dialects to be included in this list, it would have to be more than doubled, so as to embrace the French *u* (for Souletin), the French *j*, the Spanish *jota*, and the liquids *g*, *t*, *d*, *l*.

Some of the more important phonetic laws, which are somewhat numerous, may here be described. In the case of two vowels coming together, the first is elided, if it be at the end of a word. But if they occur in the body of the word, a hiatus is the general rule, with a change, such as *e* to *i*, *o* to *u*, &c., *a* always remaining unmodified.

The consonantal changes are much more remarkable. Thus a final *sharp*, when followed by an initial *soft*, disappears, the soft then becoming sharp. Thus *hunat goiti*, here above, is pronounced *hunakoiti*. Again, sharp explosives, *k*, *t*, &c., disappear before nasals; after sibilants the explosives must be sharp, but after a nasal they must be soft. Double consonants, *tt*, *gg*, &c., are unallowable; sharp explosives, initial, readily become soft; between two vowels, *g*, *d*, *b*, *n*, and *r* are entirely suppressed; foreign words take an initial vowel, the French *raison* thus becoming *arrazoin*.

The orthography now mostly in use is somewhat recent, and in any case is merely a reform of former systems. Not having preserved any special graphic signs, if it ever possessed them, in transcribing the Basque sounds, recourse was necessarily had to the Latin alphabet, as current amongst the Gallo-Romans or Hispano-Romans of the Pyrenees districts. Thus, two orthographic systems perceptibly different, the Spanish and the French, were brought into use, each possessing the capital defect of representing the same sound by different letters. Thus they wrote *z*, *c*, and *ç* for *s* and *c*, *qu* and *k* for *k*. The reformed orthography was based more on the Spanish than the French system; *z*, however, is pronounced as *s*.

Coming to the formation of words, declension and conjugation must first claim our attention.

The Basque declension is simple enough, consisting in postpositions attached to the noun. Thus, they do not say to the man, but, man the to (as in the Urdu: *admi-ko*), employing post instead of pre-positions; that is, suffixes more or less agglutinated to the noun or article. The principal suffixes are *en*, of (possessive); *i*, to (dative); *ko*, of, for, *tik*, from (ablative); *n*, in, *z*, by, *kin* or *gaz*, with, *ra*, towards, *ik*, some (partitive); *no*, till, into; *gabe*, without; *gatik*, on account of; *tzat*, for, &c.

Besides the definite declension, which takes the article, grammarians distinguish the declension of rational beings from that of irrational ones. The first would seem to be characterised by the insertion of the syllable *baith* between the article and the suffix, a syllable which has not been yet explained, but which etymologists have naturally compared confidently with the Hebrew *beth*, a house, on the ground that it is inserted only after local suffixes, in, towards, &c.

The indefinite declension is so far unique that it has positively neither a singular nor a plural number. This arises from the fact that Basque nouns cannot take a plural sign unless they are determined; hence it cannot say men, but the men. It follows that the plural sign, which is *k*, is added as a suffix to the article *a* only, which was itself an old demonstrative pronoun, still preserved in Biscayan. Thanks, therefore, to this article, the definite declension has both a singular and a plural.

Great irregularities result from the addition of the suffixes to the noun, as, for instance, the occasional disappearance of the article and of the sign of plurality. But in a sketch of this sort it is impossible to enter into such details.

From the foregoing remarks we readily see how inconsistent it would be to speak of cases, nominative, genitive, &c., in connection with Basque nouns. At times these expressions are used, but they should not deceive us, as they are simply a conventional way of speaking. In Basque there can be no such thing as a nominative, accusative, or other suffix, such as the *s* and *m* of the Latin *dominu-s*, *dominu-m*. The theme alone is used in its simple state; but when it is the subject of an active verb it takes the suffix *k*, of unknown origin. Thus: *gizonak eman du*, the man has given it; *gizonak yo dute*, the men have struck him: where *gizon* man, *a* = the article, *k* = sign of the subject just mentioned.

A feature, though not a very exceptional one, of the Basque language, is the large number of words, often reduced to one syllable, attached to others to denote enlargement, diminutives, plenty, bad qualities, excesses, want, attachment, repugnance, and the like. But many modern and other languages also possess, to a greater or less degree, this power of forming diminutives, augmentatives, &c.

The adjective, which never changes, is placed invariably after the noun. The expression, "the fine house of the little man," would run in Basque: "man little the of house fine the," where we see the adjective inserted between the article and its noun, while the genitive "of the man" precedes the noun "house" on which it depends (as in the alternative English form: the little man's fine house).

The personal pronouns are: *ni*, I; *gu*, we; *hi*, thou; *zu*, you. The present language uses the second plural for a polite singular, as in French; hence another *real* plural, *zuek* = ye, has been developed on the previous. There are no relative pronouns, the interrogatives, in imitation of French and Spanish, being now often used relatively; but this is utterly opposed to the essential genius of the language.

As regards number, there is no original word for a thousand, and everything points at a vigesimal system. Thus thirty-nine becomes twenty + nineteen; sixty is three score, and so on.

The verb is either simple or periphrastic. In the simple conjugation derivative elements attached to the root denote tense, mood, and person; in the periphrastic, the two simple auxiliaries *dut*, to have, and *naiz*, to be, are joined to a noun of action subject to inflection. The whole question of the Basque verb is of great importance. It is the feature of the language which causes most trouble to those accustomed to Greek and Latin grammars, nor can it be said to be yet settled, even after the labours of Van Eys, Prince L. L. Bonaparte, and M. Vinson.* One of the first points that have been discussed turns on the relative priority of these two conjugations. In the opinion of Mahn, Van Eys, and Vinson, the

---

* "Le Verbe Basque," "Revue de Linguistique," vi. p. 238. Paris, 1874.

simple conjugation alone is primitive, and the other developed within the historic life of the language. Without entering into the special arguments which, in our opinion, indisputably confirm this view, we need but remark that the opposite theory, maintaining the existence of a radical with a verbal sense in the forms of the auxiliaries, has a metaphysical stamp about it, which amounts to a *primâ facie* argument against it.

The periphrastic conjugation has the advantage of allowing to each verb a double expression, answering to a transitive and an intransitive sense. The intransitive voice is a noun of action, accompanied by *naiz*, to be; the transitive is a noun also of action, accompanied by *dut*, to have. Like the Semitic verb, which incorporates the direct object, or rather expresses it by a pronominal sign attached to the verb; like a similar process in Magyar, Wogulic, and Mordvinian (though the pronominal sign is not here put in the same place as in the Semitic tongues), the Basque verb proceeds somewhat similarly, but with the disadvantage, when compared with these languages, that it is unable to separate its direct object from the active verb. For instance, it cannot say *I love a woman*, but only *I her love a woman*. But in its verb the Basque expresses the indirect object, saying in one word *I give it to him*; here also, however, it cannot omit the direct object, and say simply, *I give to him*.

Each of these complex forms is subject to four modifications, according as they speak familiarly to a man or to a woman, to a person they wish to honour, or, lastly, when no account is taken of such considerations. Grammarians describe these modifications under the names of masculine, feminine, respectful, and indefinite treatment.

Certain features of the Basque language, as has often been remarked, are met also in the American idioms. The Basque verb has, no doubt, certain analogies with the conjugation in those tongues; but to conclude from this, as some writers do not hesitate to do, that Basque is intimately related to Chippeway and Lenapé, is stretching the argument very far indeed. Before asserting that Basque, like these idioms, is polysynthetic or incorporative, it would be desirable, in the first place, to determine the exact meaning of these terms. We shall endeavour to do so in the section devoted to the American languages, meanwhile resting satisfied with indicating a feature of the idioms of the New World, which is met with in Basque also. This is composition by syncope, which, however, is not quite unknown to modern European tongues. From *ortz*, cloud, and *azantz*, noise, Basque forms *ortzanz*, thunder, *cloud-noise*. But compounds of this sort are not very numerous, being more usually met with in the names of localities, those precious but too often inexplicable relics of a primeval epoch.

Such names of places may possibly some day enable us to restore many words that have become obsolete, and at length forgotten. In its present imperfectly-known condition the Escuara vocabulary may be described as somewhat poor. Excluding the many Gascon, French, Spanish, and Latin words it contains, besides others that can be referred to some other foreign sources, it is probable that the genuine Basque words express no abstract ideas. Thus there is no simple Basque word answering to the wide sense of *tree*, *animal*. Thus also in Basque *God* is "the Lord on high;" and if they have a term answering to our *will*, it means also *thought*, *desire*, *fancy*, indifferently.

In order, as far as possible, to restore the common Basque vocabulary, it will be necessary to collect all the words current in the several dialects, and of course not even then admit them as original until they have been also shown to belong to no foreign tongue. History tells us that the region occupied by the Basque language has been at different times traversed by Keltic, Teutonic, Arabic, and especially Romance speaking peoples. The influence of Latin must have been all the greater for having been felt during a period of nearly two thousand years, and more actively than any of the others. In order, therefore, to properly understand Basque it is necessary to know Latin thoroughly, as well as the history of its two modern forms, French and Spanish, and to be as familiar with their *patois* in the Pyrenees regions as with their literary standards.

Unfortunately no help can be derived from written documents, such is the singular poverty of Basque literature, which is composed almost exclusively of translations of devotional works, absolutely without interest in themselves. There is little inducement to spend one's time poring over "meditations," "hymns," "spiritual guides," and other such-like "moral" and "moralising" productions. No doubt some collections of popular songs have been published, but nearly all of indifferent merit. No tales have yet appeared, nor any of those interminable "pastorals," that the Basques of La Soule delight in on their local feast-days. These are so far curious, from the fact that they have been evidently inspired by the "chansons de geste," the "soties," and the epic poems of medieval times. There are scarcely a thousand Basque books altogether, including even all the works on the language, the country, the manners, and the origin of the Basque people, written in French, Spanish, Latin, Italian, German, and even Hungarian.

This last subject of their origin has given rise to numerous writings; but, in our opinion, the problem remains yet to be solved. We persist especially in holding that if Escuara was the language of the ancient Iberians, or at least one of the dialects of their language, the fact has not yet been scientifically proved. According to some very old traditions, the Iberians, before the arrival of the Aryans, occupied the whole of the Spanish peninsula, as well as all that part of Gaul known afterwards as Gallia Narbonensis. Their first known relations with any foreign race date back to the times of the Phœnician expeditions mentioned in history. Then came the Keltic invasion. The Keltiberians bravely resisted the Roman legionaries, and after submitting to the sway of the Visi-Goths, still held out against the Moslem.

Kept alive in the region occupied by the Iberians, Escuara, being neither Semitic nor Aryan, began naturally to be looked upon as one of the direct representatives of the old Iberian language. In support of this opinion three different kinds of arguments are usually urged—those based on the customs, on the type, and on the language itself.

The argument based on customs is limited to a legal disposition prevailing in the French Pyrenees, even beyond the Basque district, establishing in inheritance an absolute right of primogeniture, without distinction of sex; and Strabo tells us that amongst the Cantabrians, seemingly an Iberian people, daughters inherited property. But M. J. Balasque, a Bayonne jurisconsult, has shown that the right of primogeniture is derived from the essentially Gallic or Keltic principle, requiring patrimony to be preserved entire.

The Basque type is now well known. We possess the characteristics of the true Basque skull, that of Spain. But however widely it may have been spread throughout the whole of the Peninsula (and it is undoubtedly met with in Corsica also and the north of Africa), it would never prove that this one race may not have spoken several distinct languages, as is even now very frequently the case.

The linguistic proofs turn upon attempts to explain Iberian words through the Basque. The monuments of the Iberian language that have reached us are of two kinds, medals and inscriptions on the one hand, on the other, proper names, and especially topographical ones, transcribed by classical writers. The medals and the inscriptions offer the elements of an alphabet derived from the Phœnician; but it would be idle to deceive ourselves on their pretended interpretation, than which nothing can be more problematical. We agree with M. Vinson in seeing in the various readings hitherto proposed nothing but hazardous and strained renderings.

The form of names collected by Strabo, Pliny, and other ancient writers, on the other hand, presents a certain basis; which, however, the etymologists have, as usual, recklessly perverted to their purposes. The explanations proposed by Humboldt, and after him by a number of etymologists without sound principles or method, are, to say the least, very doubtful. It may be remarked that the only two philologists deserving our full confidence in this department, Van Eys and Vinson, entirely agree on the point.* We adopt their view, and we hold that the name of Humboldt is not of itself sufficient to settle the matter conclusively. His conjectures may have been just—it is possible, it is even probable, that the ancient

* Van Eys, "La Langue Ibérienne et la Langue Basque," "Revue de Linguistique," vii. p. 1, Paris, 1874; Vinson, "La Question Ibérienne," "Mémoires du Congrès Scientifique de France," ii. p. 357, Paris, 1874.

inhabitants of Iberia spoke a language akin to the Basque, if not even an older form of this tongue. But it cannot be allowed that this has yet been proved, nor is it possible to establish it in the actual state of our knowledge without compromising the strict scientific method.

To resume, this assumed identity is quite possible, but the facts quoted in its support have merely rendered it a plausible hypothesis still awaiting definite settlement.

§ 16.—*The American Languages.*

In no part of the globe, says Frederic Müller, do so many languages exist as in America, whose resemblance is so striking, but whose constituent elements are so different. This is the reason why their study has as yet been scarcely commenced, and why it is so very difficult to form even some general and definite notion of them. There are, no doubt, a great number of grammars, vocabularies, devotional books, such as catechisms and versions of Scripture, calculated to facilitate the study of many of them. But most of these works have been composed for objects so purely unscientific, or in so defective a manner, that but very little help is, as a rule, to be obtained from them.

Amongst the most instructive of these writings may be mentioned John Pickering's " Remarks on the Indian Languages of North America," which has been long before the public; Duponceau's " Système Grammatical des Langues de quelques Nations de l'Amérique du Nord," crowned by the Institute in 1836; sundry notices by Mahn, Frederic Müller, and Charencey, that have appeared mostly in special periodicals. We have also consulted the " Études sur quelques Langues Sauvages de l'Amérique," by N. O., an ex-missionary. This work contains an interesting and seemingly trustworthy sketch of the Algonquin and of the Iroquois, but the author shows himself far too ignorant of the most elementary scientific methods.

According to Fr. Müller, there would be in the whole continent, from Cape Horn to the regions of the Eskimos, twenty-six languages, or rather groups of different languages; a large number, when we remember that the native population bears no comparison with that of the Old World.

Müller's classification we here subjoin:

1. *Kenaï* group, north-east of North America.
2. *Athapasque* group, east of the Kenaï, stretching from the Yukon, and the Mackenzie, to the mouth of the Churchill in Hudson's Bay. Much farther south, and separated from the bulk of this group, are other dialects belonging to it. Such are the Qualihoqua, north of the Columbia river; the Umpqua, south of it; Apache, still farther south, in Nevada and Upper California.
3. *Algonquin* group, south of Hudson's Bay, and stretching eastwards to the Atlantic. It includes the Mikmak, on the east coast of the Canadian Dominion and in Newfoundland; the Leni-Lenapé or Delaware dialects (Narraganset, Mohican, &c.); Kree, Ojibway, Ottawa, and others.
4. *Iroquois* group: Onondago, Seneca, Oneida, Cayuga, Tuskarora.
5. *Dakotah* group, in the centre of North America, including the Sioux and others.
6. *Pawnee* group.
7. *Appalache* group, including, amongst others, the Cherokee, Kataba, Chacta, Krik, Natchez.
8. *Koloche*, in the extreme west of British North America.
9. *Oregon* group, farther south.
10. *Californian* group: Periku; Monki; Cochimi.
11. *Yuma* group, in Lower Colorado.
12. The independent idioms of the Pueblos de la Sonora and of Texas (Zuni, Tegua, and others).
13. The independent Mexican idioms: Totonak, Othomi, Taraska, Mixtek, Zapotek, Mazahua, Mame, and others.
14. *Aztek* group, and the languages of Sonora,* including, on the one hand, Nahuatl or Aztek, and on the other Kahita, Kora, Tarahumara, Tepeguana; Opata, Tubar; Pima, Papago; Kizh, Netela, Kahuillo; Chochoni, Komanche, Moki, Utah, Pah-Utah, &c.
15. *Maya* group, in Yucatan, including Maya, in the north, Quiché, Huastek, in the north-east of Mexico.
16. The independent idioms of Central America and of the West Indies, such as Kueva, towards the Isthmus of Panama, Cibuney in the Antilles.
17. *Carib* and *Arevaque*; the former (called also Galibi) in Venezuela and French Guiana, the latter in British and Dutch Guiana.
18. *Tupi, Guarani,* and *Omagua,* of which the two first form a special

---

* Buschmann, "Grammatik der Sonorischen Sprachen," "Memoirs of the Academy of Sciences." Berlin, 1863.

group, including the dialects spoken in the regions watered by the Parana, the Paraguay, and the Uruguay rivers. Here, also, are certain idioms, such as that of the Botocudos, east of the San Francisco river, which do not seem to belong to this group.

19. The independent languages of the region of the Andes.
20. *Araucanian.*
21. *Guaykuru*, spoken between the Paraguay and the Pilcomayo; *Abipon*, in the valley of the Salado (Argentine Republic).
22. *Puelche*, in the Pampas, west of Buenos Ayres.
23. *Tehuelche*, the language of the Patagonians.
24. The various idioms of Tierra del Fuego, and neighbouring islands.
25. *Chibcha*, west of the Andes, in New Granada, as far as the vicinity of Santa Fé de Bogota.
26. *Quichua* group, farther south, from the frontiers of New Granada and Equador to the northern parts of Chilé. Related to the Quichuas are the *Aymaras*, on the borders of Peru and Bolivia.

All these idioms are generally assumed to resemble each other, and to possess some salient features in common. We shall now have to see in what the common character consists.

It may first of all be asked whether their forms and functions are so very discrepant and peculiar, as to prevent us from classifying them in any one of the three great categories—isolating, agglutinating, and inflectional—which embrace all the languages of the Old World? This is the opinion of many writers, who suppose that the American tongues have a special property, requiring them to be classed apart, or in a fourth category, called by them the *incorporating* or *polysynthetic* system.

Whilst endeavouring to avoid any needless, dry details, let us examine the nature of the phenomena on which this doctrine of a distinct classification is based. We shall conclude with a brief notice of the Algonquin and Iroquois groups, spoken in large tracts of North America, and undoubtedly the best known of all the American tongues.

The meaning of the terms *isolating* and *agglutinating* has already been explained more than once. The former is characterised by the constant and exclusive use of independent and invariable roots, while in the latter the primary idea alone is expressed by an independent root, those of relationship being dependent upon and attached to them. We shall see, later on, that true *inflection* occurs only where the various relations of time and space can be expressed by an organic modification of the radical vowel. It becomes impossible to be mistaken as to the position to be assigned to any given language, if it can be ascertained to possess one or other of these three characters—isolation, agglutination, inflection. Thus the Semitic group is eminently inflectional, although agglutination occurs, for instance, in the pronominal prefixes and suffixes of the verb, and even in the development of the derivative voices. Hence M. Chavée was, to a certain extent, right in treating as defective the name that has been given to the intermediate class. In truth, however far the formative elements may become fused, the moment that there are as many distinct roots as there are principal and relational ideas, agglutination is established. From this point of view Sanskrit in no way differs from Magyar. In our sixth and concluding chapter we shall speak of the encroachments of one class on another, and of the absolute certainty of the progressive order of succession from the monosyllabic, through the agglutinative, to the inflectional state.

The number of agglutinating idioms is vast, but in them agglutination assumes every possible phase and variety. If, therefore, we have to establish a secondary morphological division, it cannot be based exclusively on the intensity, or greater or less amount of agglutination in these tongues. Account must also be carefully taken of the usual order in which the formative elements occur, that is, of their more or less marked tendency to be placed in the beginning, at the end, or even in the body of the primary word. Such, doubtless, was Schleicher's view, when he refused to recognise a fourth category, formed by the American idioms.

What, then, is this *polysynthesis*, or *incorporation*, which we are asked to accept as constituting a fourth type of human speech? Here is what Fr. Müller says on the subject, in his " Allgemeine Ethnographic : " " The American tongues, taken as a whole, rest on the principle of polysynthesis, or incorporation. While, in our languages, the isolated conceptions bound together in the sentence are represented by separate words, they are, on the contrary, in the

American idioms, joined together in one indivisible whole; consequently, here word and sentence are confused (or become convertible terms)."

The polysynthetic theorists give, as special features of these languages, the following peculiarities: Fusion of the pronouns, and even of the direct object with the verb; nominal possessive conjugation; verbal modification to express a change of object or greater emphasis in the action of the verb; lastly, indefinite composition by means of syncope and contraction.

The first and second of these pretended characteristics will not stand the test of a moment's criticism. In truth, the nominal possessive conjugation is common to the Semitic group and to many agglutinating tongues in the Old World. The Algonquin *nirdawema*, my sister, and the Iroquois *onkiasita*, the foot of us two, are formed on the same principle as the Hebrew *el-i*, my God, and the Magyar *atya-nk*, our father; although here the formative elements are not placed quite in the same way. As to the verbal modifications, intended to vary the meaning of the action, Duponceau quotes, after Molina, the Chilian *eluu*, to give; *eluguen*, to give more; *eluduamen*, to wish to give; *eluzquen*, to seem to give; *eluvalen*, to be able to give, &c. But does not this very example resemble exactly analogous Turkish forms? Besides, in many agglutinating idioms, we find traces of similar derivatives closely resembling the voices of the Semitic verb. Instances have already been given from the Dravidian languages and from the Basque.

More weight might, perhaps, be attached to the third characteristic; that is, the fact that the verb varies with its object. In Cherokee, for example, *kutuwo* means, "I wash myself;" *kukūsquō*, "I wash my face;" *tsĕkūsquō*, "I wash another's face;" *takungkulā*, "I wash my clothes;" *takuteyi*, "I wash dishes," &c. In Tamacan, *jucurù* is "to eat bread;" *jemeri*, "to eat fruit, honey;" *janeri*, "to eat cooked food," &c. In Lenapé, and Chippeway, there are different verbs for "to eat soup," and "to eat pap." But are these not cases of composition by syncope? If so, they present a feature that we shall have presently to examine. If not, we can see nothing in this phenomenon beyond that repugnance to abstraction, that absence of general ideas already observed in many of the agglutinating tongues.

The objective pronouns are joined to the verb by processes analogous to that of nominal conjugation. Hence this feature prevails also amongst those idioms that blend the possessive affixes with the noun. Here Basque presents a striking exception, as it rejects nominal affixes altogether. On the other hand, its "objective" conjugation is richer than that of any other European or Asiatic language. In fact, it incorporates with the verb not only the direct pronominal object—me, thee, him—but the indirect also, whilst Mordvinian (Uralo-Altaïc group) is able to express the three persons as direct objects only. Wogulic, of the same group, but less wealthy in forms, incorporates the second and third persons only, and Magyar, showing still greater poverty, can, in principle, render the third person only in this way. But these different languages have what the Basque has not, that is the verb by itself, and independent of its object. In the Semitic group the conjugations "by pronouns affixed" are in any case real objective conjugations. The Hebrew *sabagtani* = thou hast forsaken me ; the Magyar *latlak* = I see him ; the Basque *demogu* = we give it to him ; and the Iroquois *kheiawis* = I give to them, so far as concerns their formation, differ only in the order of the elements composing the word.

As to the incorporation of nouns with the verb, said to be an ordinary feature of the American idioms, we cannot at the moment quote a more pregnant example than the Algonquin *naulholineen* = bring us the canoe, made up of *naten* = to bring, *amochol* = canoe, *i* euphonic, and *neen* = to us ; or the Chippeway word *sogininjiniti-zoyan* = if I do not take the hand, in which *sogenat* = to take, and *oninjina* = hand, are components. Formations of this sort are but simple extensions of the principle by which the verb incorporates its object. It has been justly remarked that certain locutions in the modern Romance languages are genuine instances of rudimentary incorporation. When the Italian says *portandovi* = taking to you, *portandovelo* = taking it to you, and the Gascon *deche-m droumi* = let me sleep, the process recalls the incorporating method of the Basque and the American idioms.*

We hold, in fact, with Mr. Sayce, that polysynthesis must be distinguished from incorporation, which last should be reserved for the phenomena that we have just examined, and which, as we have seen, are neither peculiar to the American tongues nor important enough to justify the creation of a fourth great morphological category. Mr. Sayce is even of opinion that there is much greater difference between incorporation and polysynthesis than between incorporation and inflection.

We shall therefore express by polysynthesis the last feature appealed to as peculiar to the American idioms, that is the indefinite composition of words by syncope and ellipsis. This is certainly the most important character, and is that which Fr. Müller describes in the above-quoted passage. Duponceau, who does not confuse incorporation with polysynthesis, gives this last as the distinctive mark of the languages of the New World, and he assures us that he has met with it in all the idioms known to him from Greenland to Chili. They all blend together a great number of ideas under the form of one and the same word. This word, generally of considerable length, is an agglomeration of diverse others, often reduced to a single intercalated letter. Thus the Greenland *aulisariartorasuarpok*, he hastened to go fishing, is formed of *aulisar*, to fish, *peartor*, to be engaged in anything, *pinnesuarpok*,

---

* But there is a wide difference between the two. The former incorporate the *pronominal* element only, while the latter incorporate the *nominal* object also. Hence the one is limited to the few possible combinations of verb and pronoun, while the other is practically *unlimited*, the number of possible nouns capable of being blended with the verb being numberless. If the Italian could melt down into one word the phrase *portandovi il bastone*, fetching the stick to you, and say, for instance, *portandovilstone*, the analogy would be so far complete between it and the American process. But even then only so far, because in point of fact the American tongues fuse together whole sentences, including verb, nominal object, pronominal subject, and indirect object, conjunctions, conditional, honorific, euphonic, and other formative elements. It is this *universality* of the process that seems to constitute the real distinction between the polysynthetic and the agglutinating systems.—*Note by Translator.*

K

he hastens. The Algonquin *amangamachquiminchi*, broad-leaved oaks, is formed of *amangi*, great, large, *nachk*, hand, *quim*, ending of names of shell-fruit, and *achpansi*, trunk of a tree. The Mexican *notlazomahuizteopixcatātzin*, my beloved, honoured, revered, priestly father, is made up of *no*, my, *tlazotli*, beloved, *mahuitztic*, honoured, *teopixqui* (from *Teotl*, God, and *piu*, to keep guard), priestly, *tatli*, father, and *tzin*, a reverential ending.* The Chippeway *totochabo*, wine, is formed of *toto*, milk, and *chominaibo*, bunch of grapes.

Polysynthesis, therefore, consists of composition by contraction; some of the components losing their first, others their last syllables. Consequently there is this difference between incorporation and polysynthesis, that the process of the latter is essentially syntactical. Incorporation belongs to the period of development, while polysynthesis took its rise during the historic life of the language.

Hence polysynthesis is not a primitive feature, but an expansion, or, if you will, a second phase of agglutination, offering insufficient grounds for constituting the American idioms in a separate class. They will simply be placed last in the ascending order of the agglutinating series. For instance, we shall have, in the first place, the Dravidian group, with its scanty grammatical forms; then the somewhat more developed Mandchu, the Turkish already incorporating; after which the Finnic tongues in this order: Suomi, Magyar, Wogulic, Mordvinian, all incorporating; then the Basque, of which more farther on, and which is incorporating with polysynthetic tendencies; lastly, the American languages, which are incorporating and polysynthetic. But this progressive arrangement no more proves the original parentage of these different tongues, than do certain common features that of the amentacea and the conifera.

Besides, the historic stage once reached, all languages might become polysynthetic, and in a great many of them there are forms

---

* Hervas, "Idea dell' Universo," xviii.; also the Translator's "English Language," p. 49 of enlarged edition, 1875.

of expression quite analogous to the contractions of the American tongues. Thus in German, *beim* = *bei dem*, in or by the; *zur* = *zu der*, at or to the; in current French *mamzelle* for *ma demoiselle*. [But see Translator's note at p. 129.]

As Duponceau has well observed, these contractions are readily produced in compound words in current use, which have gradually become simple words, whose original complex nature has been forgotten. In Europe the Basque seems to have made the greatest use of this process, and it is on this account that, in a progressive morphological arrangement of the agglutinating languages, it may be placed between the Uralo-Altaïc and the American idioms.

It is impossible to notice, even in the most summary way, all the different languages above enumerated. While, therefore, occasionally alluding to the others, we shall confine ourselves to a general sketch of the two more important groups in North America —the Algonquin and the Iroquois. These are not related to each other, offering noteworthy differences both as regards their phonetic and formative systems.

Algonquin, spoken in Canada and in the north of the United States, is subdivided into some thirty dialects, the principal of which are the *Mikmak*, in Canada, Nova Scotia, and neighbouring regions; *Abenaki*, in Maine and Massachusetts; *Narragansets* in Rhode Island; and *Mohican*, in Connecticut. The languages of Canada proper: *Algonquin*, properly so called; *Chippeway* or *Ojibway*; *Ottawa*, *Menomeni*, and *Cree*.

The Iroquois tribes occupy the western portion of the state of New York, and generally the southern shores of the great lakes. They may be subdivided into the *Onondago*, *Seneca*, *Oneida*, *Cayuga*, and *Tuscarora*.

The Algonquin phonetic system is poor, and the Iroquois poorer still. They have our vowels, *a, e, i, o,* some dialects adding *u*; also the two semi-vowels, *y* and *w*, the second changing to a sort of labial sibilant. This is the sound that the missionaries transcribe by the cipher 8, under the pretext that this sign resembles the Greek *8*, while the French *huit* expresses the sound in question.

But the use of this 8 gives the strangest appearance to the American texts in which it occurs.*

Algonquin possesses the two gutturals k, g, whilst Iroquois has one only, sometimes transcribed by g, sometimes by k. Both have the palatal *ch*, and some Algonquin dialects *j* also. Algonquin employs t and d, Iroquois t only, and it has no labials, while Algonquin has p and b. Both have the nasals belonging to their respective explosives, and l and r, always interchangeable and often indistinct. In Algonquin there are numerous sibilants, h, *ch* hard (German), *s*, *z*, and French *j*. But in Iroquois, h and s alone occur, f being restricted to some dialectic varieties. Both have three nasal vowels: *an*, *en*, *on*. The only sound presenting any difficulty to Europeans seems to be the *w* placed before a consonant. On this, Duponceau remarks: "It is like *ou* in the French *oui*, but followed immediately by a consonant, and uttered without any intermediate rest, for which reason it is called sibilant *ou* or *w*, because, in fact, we must pronounce it with a whistle. The same utterance exists in Abenaki, but, instead of being labial, as in Lenapé, it is guttural, being pronounced from the depths of the throat . . . . It occurs neither in Algonquin proper nor in Chippeway, and in Ottawa *on* takes its place. Thus, whilst a Lenapé says *w'danis*, his daughter (with a whistle), the Ottawa will say *oudanis*."

He further observes that the Algonquins articulate very distinctly, pronouncing the vowels very openly, the short with the sharp, the long with the grave accent, the last syllable of the phrase being uttered with great energy. The South American pronunciation is rougher than that of the North.

Many American tongues, notably Algonquin and Iroquois, do not distinguish the verb from the noun, the verb being nothing but

---

* The names of a team of Iroquois Indians, who played the Canadian game of "La Crosse," before the Queen at Windsor, during last summer, appeared in the periodicals at the time in this wise: Aton8a Tekanennao-Siheu (Hickory Wood Split); Sha8atis Anasotako (Pick the Feather); Sha-8atis Aientonni (Hole in the Sky); 8ishe Taiennontii (Flying Name); Aton8a Teronko8a (The Loon); 8ishe Ononsanoron (Deer House), &c.—*Note by Translator.*

a noun accompanied by suffixes denoting possession. This seems to us somewhat the case with the agglutinating languages generally, and we have shown how the Dravidian verb may take nominal suffixes, just as the noun itself is declined by means of pronominal suffixes.

The article, which some writers do not recognise, Duponceau detects at least in Algonquin. It is, as is usually the case, a demonstrative pronoun, *monko* (in Massachusetts), reduced to *m* prefixed. But its presence is now so little felt, that it is retained concurrently with the possessive affixes. Thus the Chippeway says *mittig*, tree, and *ki mittig*, thy tree; and the Lenapé *hittuk*, tree; *m'hittuk*, the tree; and *k'hittuk*, his tree. The article occurs in other idioms also, as in Iroquois *ue*, and in Othomi *na*, but it has often been overlooked, owing to the tendency of those languages towards determinating forms, causing the nouns to be always accompanied by a possessive affix.

In Algonquin there is no distinction of gender, while in Iroquois there are two genders, called by the grammarians *noble* and *ignoble*; the first being applied to divinities and to the male of the human race, the second to everything else. But in the declension there are particles or different affixes for animate and inanimate beings.

The nominal conjugation, or rather, as above explained, the possessive derivative, is formed by the addition of the pronominal elements to the beginning of the noun, the adjective being always invariable, and placed, in Algonquin, before the qualified word. Thus, *kuligatchis*, thy pretty little paw, is formed of *ki*, thy, *walit*, pretty, *wichgat*, paw, and the diminutive *chis*; and *Kitanittowit*, the Great Spirit, of *kita*, great, *manitu*, spirit, and the adjectival ending *wit*.

The Algonquin verb may be either absolute, that is, without an object; transitive, that is, with a direct object; or passive. A great number of moods have been wrongly ascribed to it, there being, in reality, none at all, or at most a conditional, formed by the insertion of a particle. The Iroquois verb is also absolute, reflective, reciprocal, passive, and transitive, with direct and indirect object. There would also seem to be in some idioms traces of a so-called sexual conjugation. Thus, in Abenaki, a man would say *nenanan-*

busanbai, where a woman would say *nenananbuseskonai*, I am not very intelligent. Thanks to such numerous variations, one begins to see how the English missionary, Edwin James, came to credit the Chippeway verb with six or eight thousand forms.

Algonquin and Iroquois are no more able than are the Dravidian tongues to express the absolute sense of *to be* and *to have*. Thus the sentence, I am a man, in Narragansets will be *ninin* = I man ; and in Lenapé, *lenno n' hackey* = a man my body. The question, Whose is this canoe ? is in Ottowa *watchimānet* = to whom canoe ? In Menomeni, *wahotosoyāwik* = who owns canoe ?

Altogether the vocabulary of these idioms is very poor, lacking, as might be supposed, nearly all the abstract terms, which are replaced either by words from English, French, Spanish, and even German, or else by developed periphrases, often spoken of by grammarians as words of ten or twelve syllables.

In the Algonquin dialects the five first numerals are simple words, and these alone seem to be primitive. "Ten" seems to be "five more" (than five) ; a hundred, "ten times ten ;" and a thousand "the great ten of tens." Iroquois, on the contrary, seems to have reckoned as far as ten.

Many curious remarks might be made on the terms of relationship, which in Iroquis, for instance, are very numerous. They have been arranged in categories—superior consanguinity, as father, mother ; inferior, as son, younger brother ; superior affinity, as father-in-law ; inferior, as daughter-in-law. Collateral connections, as brother-in-law, &c.

The Dravidian group is also remarkably rich in words of this sort, distinguishing, for instance, the elder from the junior brothers, just as in Basque a woman's sister is distinguished from a man's. The cause of these intricacies is, we have no doubt, the lack of general expressions, which is a usual feature of inferior languages, though not unfrequently mistaken for wealth by writers on ethnography and geography.

Notwithstanding the length of these remarks, we should have liked, did our space afford it, to give some further illustrations, and analyse some complete sentences. The American languages continue to give occasion to such unscientific writings that their connection with the other agglutinating tongues cannot be too much insisted upon. We trust, however, that the distinction has been made perfectly clear between the terms *polysynthesis* and *incorporation*, the misunderstanding of which may and does give rise to many serious errors.

§ 17.—*The Sub-Arctic Languages.*

Under this geographic designation are comprised all the idioms spoken in the Arctic regions.

Yukagiric, the speech of about 1,000 persons in the north-east of Siberia, immediately east of Yakutic, which belongs to the Turkish group.

Chukchik (Asiatic), and *Koryak*, still further east, in the extreme north-east of Siberia. These two idioms are nearly akin to each other.

Kamchadale, in the south of the peninsula;* still farther south, in the Kuriles and northern islands of the Japanese Archipelego, the language of the *Ainos*.†

Ghiliak, on the mainland opposite.

Ostyak-Yenisei and *Kotte*, in the heart of Siberia.

Innuit dialects, spoken by the Eskimos along the northern coast of America. Related to them is the American *Chukchik*, on the north-west coast, and not to be confounded with the Asiatic Chukchik above mentioned.

Aleutian dialects, essentially different from the Innuit.

But although grouped under one common designation, we cannot, on that account, form any conclusion as to the greater or less affinity of these languages, either amongst themselves or with any other idioms. On this subject there is still room for many hypotheses;

---

* See "The Ethnographic Chart of Kamchatka," by C. de Dittmar, "Bulletins of the Historical, Philological, and Political Section of the St. Petersburg Academy," viii. p. 107. St. Petersburg, 1856.

† Pfizmaier, " Ueber den Bau der Aino-Sprache," " Bulletins of the Vienna Academy," vii. p. 382. Vienna, 1851.

but it is probable that some of them will permanently resist any attempts that may be made to classify them with any other better-known groups.

§ 18.—*Languages of the Caucasus*.

Frequent futile attempts have been made to identify these idioms both with the Aryan and the Semitic system. We agree with Fr. Müller in regarding them as an entirely distinct group, different even from the Uralo-Altaïc. They are divided into two branches—the Northern and the Southern.

The Northern Division extends along the northern slopes of the Caucasus, between the Caspian and the northern shores of the Black Sea, as far as the Straits of Yenicale, and comprises three distinct sub-branches: the *Lesgian* in Daghestan, bordering on the Caspian, and numbering about 400,000 souls; the *Kistian*, central, and much less considerable than the previous; the *Cherkessian*, or *Circassian*, occupying nearly half of the entire north-west of the Caucasus, and nearly as numerous as the two foregoing groups.

In the Lesgian are included the *Avare*, *Khasia-Kumuk* or *Lak*, *Akusha*, *Kurine*, *Udi*, and other dialects.

The Kistian group comprises the *Ingush* or *Lamur*, *Karabulak*, *Cheehenze*, *Tush* or *Mosok*, which last, though belonging to the Northern Division, is spoken south of the Caucasus towards the source of the Alasan. The various Kistian idioms are spoken altogether by about 140,000 individuals. Formerly the Circassians numbered about 500,000, but large numbers of them have in recent times migrated to European Turkey.

The *Southern Divison* comprises *Georgian*, *Suanian*, *Mingrelian*, and *Lazian*. The Suanian lies north-east of the Georgian, and the Mingrelian lies south of the Suanian and west of the Georgian. Lazian is spoken still farther to the south, in Lazistan, a province of Asiatic Turkey, on the south-east coast of the Black Sea.

These last four languages would seem to derive from a common source, but their affinity with the Northern Division is far from having been established. Nor has the relationship of the idioms of this division itself been even yet made clear, although several of the Caucasian tongues have been carefully studied, notably by Schiefner, in the "Memoirs of the St. Petersburg Academy."

They are all of them obviously agglutinating, the idea of case being expressed in the usual way by suffixes, between which and the root is inserted the element denoting number. Occasionally, however, the derivative element precedes the root, as from *bustani* = garden, *mebustani* = gardener, *puri* = bread, *mepuri* = baker.

§ 19.—*On some little-known Idioms classified with the Agglutinating Languages.*

We have just mentioned those sub-Arctic idioms which have no known connection with any other group, which seem to differ even from each other in the most decided manner, but which, by their structure, belong all of them to the agglutinating class.

We have now to say a few words on those sorts of languages that have been also classed amongst the agglutinating, but concerning which we possess such unsatisfactory and contradictory information that they must be spoken of with the greatest reserve. Some of these are still spoken, such as the Brahui; whilst others are extinct, such as that of the second column of the trilingual cuneiform inscriptions, and the so-called Sumerian or Accadian tongue.

(1) *Sinhalese or Elu.*

Sinhalese, spoken by the indigenous population in the southern districts of Ceylon, is an agglutinating language—by some writers, on insufficient grounds, connected with the Dravidian group, and with still less probability, by R. C. Childers, with the Sanskrit; though it cannot be denied that it has borrowed largely from that source.

The Elu consonantal system is tolerably rich; possessing, besides the ordinary explosives, the lingual explosives ṭ, ḍ, and the fricatives *ch, j*.

Number is expressed by the addition of sundry particles, *val, hu, lá*, and others, some being reserved for animate, others for inanimate beings. The cases also are denoted by suffixes: *geval* = the houses, *gehi* = in the house, *gevalhi* = in the houses.

Amongst the numerous Sanskrit elements in Sinhalese, that of the numerals is one of the most striking. Sanskritists will readily recognise Sanskrit or Pali forms in the Sinhalese *éka* = one, *deka* = two, *tuna* = three, *hatara* = four, *paha* = five.

The Sinhalese writing system is of Dravidian origin.

(2) *Munda*.

The language of the Kols, or Kolhs (south-west of Calcutta), would seem, like Sinhalese, to be independent of the Dravidian group.

(3) *Brahui*,

Spoken in the neighbourhood of Kelat, in the north-east corner of Beluchistan. Although largely imbued with Sanskrit and Arabic terms, it would seem to be related to the Dravidian family.

(4) *The Pretended Scythian Language*.

The term *Scythian* has been used in two different ways, having been applied both to a particular people and to a collection of tribes more or less related together. In the first case some one definite Scythian language and people is implied; in the second will be understood not one, but many Scythian races and languages. The first opinion has found but few defenders, while the second has contrived to seduce even such competent authorities, for instance, as Whitney, who has given to the Uralo-Altaïc group the name of Scythian, a term applied by the Greeks if not to all, at least to many of the nomad tribes dwelling on the north-east.*

But this appellation seems to us much too vague. It is, doubtless, very likely that the ancients included in it more than one tribe belonging to the Uralo-Altaïc group, although no direct

* "Language and the Study of Language," third edition, p. 309. London, 1870.

proof can be advanced in support of the statement.* But, on the other hand, it seems quite certain that they also gave the name of Scythians to races speaking Aryan tongues; as, for instance, the Scythians of Pontus, whose language, as Müllenhoff has endeavoured to show, seems to have been Iranian.

Several writers have, with some probability, considered that a section of the Scythians spoke an idiom akin to the Slavonic group.† In a word, we agree with Frederick Müller‡ that Scythian is merely a geographical expression, answering to no definite idea of race or language. Scythia is simply the north of Europe and of Asia, and the Scythian races are the nomad tribes inhabiting those regions. Hence it seems to us at least somewhat rash to speak of a Scythian language, or even of a Scythian group, and give this name, whose origin is otherwise very obscure, to the collective body of the Uralo-Altaïc tongues.

(5) *The Language of the Second Column of the Cuneiform Inscriptions.*

The first column of the triglott inscriptions of the time of the Achæmenides, as is well known, is composed in Old Persian; and this was the first to be deciphered. The third column, which was not interpreted for a long time after the first, is in Assyrian, a Semitic dialect.

To the language of the second column various names have been given; amongst others, those of Median and Scythian. This last, proposed and employed by Rawlinson§ and Norris,‖ is far too vague to be applied to any definite idiom, as explained in the

* Schiefner, " Sprachliche Bedenken gegen das Mongolenthum der Skythen," " Mélanges Asiatiques," ii. p. 531. 1856.

† See Gr. Krek, " Einleitung in die Slavische Literaturgeschichte und Darstellung ihrer älteren Period," i. p. 36, Graz, 1874; also Fr. Spiegel, " Eranische Alterthumskunde," i. p. 333 and following, Leipzig, 1873.

‡ " Allgemeine Ethnographie," p. 351. Vienna, 1873.

§ "Notes on the Early History of Babylonia," in " Journal of the Royal Asiatic Society," xv. p. 215.

‖ " Memoir on the Scythic Version of the Behistun Inscription," " Journal of the Royal Asiatic Society," xv. p. 1. London, 1853.

foregoing paragraph. That of Median seems more suitable; and in its favour is urged the fact that certain inscriptions composed in the language of the second column of these monuments have also been found in the regions of Ancient Media, unaccompanied by Iranian or Assyrian versions. The three languages of these rock inscriptions, it is added, must have been those of the three principal nations of the empire. But the first being Persian and the third Assyrian, the second could have been no other than Medic.*

Norris held this so-called Median as a member of the Uralo-Altaïc group, closely allied to Magyar, Ostyak, Permian, and others of the same family. Mordtmann also made it an Uralo-Altaïc language, grouping it, however, with the Turkish or Tatar branch,† and assuming the intrusion at different epochs of a certain number of Aryan elements. He gave it the name of the language of Susiana.

Oppert also has discussed this matter,‡ and, after adopting the term *Scythic*, has finally decided in favour of *Medic*, regarding it as the language of the Median dynasty, which seems to have reigned from 788 to 560 B.C., and to have differed both in language and religion from the dynasty of the Achæmenides. However, Oppert prudently avoids connecting the language in question either with the Uralo-Altaïc or with the Sumerian.

But the question ultimately hangs on these two points: Does the language of the second column belong to the Uralo-Altaïc group? Is this language that of the Medes? On the first we can unhesitatingly answer with Spiegel§ that the language in question has not yet been deciphered. The above-mentioned writers, to whom may be added some others, such as Westergaard, are far from having induced all competent judges to accept their opinion on the

---

* Benfey, " Geschichte der Sprachwissenschaft und Orientalischen Philologie in Deutschland," p. 633. Munich, 1869.
† " Ueber die Keilinschriften zweiter Gattung, Zeitschrift der Deutschen Morgenländischen Gesellschaft," xxiv. p. 76. Leipzig, 1870.
‡ *Ibid.*
§ " Eränische Alterthumskunde," i. p. 381. Leipzig, 1871.

Finnic or Tatar character of this tongue, nor has Caldwell been more successful with his assumed Dravidian affinity. In the present state of the question it therefore seems wise to await the results of further research.

Besides, it seems somewhat rash to look on the ancient Medes as a people of Uralo-Altaïc origin. Spiegel is unable to adopt this view, and it must be confessed that his arguments are very formidable against it. The evidence of Herodotus is explicit, and that of Strabo no less so; and they both regard the Medes as Aryans. Moreover, their proper names and geographical terms can all be interpreted, not by the Finnic or Turkic, but by the Iranian tongues.*

It seems, therefore, reasonable, pending further information, to abstain from at all classifying or giving any special name to the language of the second column of the cuneiform rock inscriptions.

(6) *The so-called Sumerian or Accadian Language.*

Some twenty years ago it was supposed that a race speaking an agglutinating idiom had occupied the Babylonian plains before the Assyrians, and that Semitic civilisation had gained a footing in the country by grafting itself on to this anterior civilisation. To this language Hincks gave the name of *Accadian*, which, though proposed by him with all reserve, seems now to enjoy a certain amount of favour. Oppert, however, takes Accadian to be absolutely synonymous with Assyrian, both simply implying the Semitic speech of Nineveh and Babylon, the language of the third column of the Achaemenidian cuneiform inscriptions. To the race that is assumed to have preceded the Semites in Assyria, and to have transmitted to them their cuneiform letters and their civilisation, Oppert gives the name of *Kasdo-Scythic*, or *Sumerian*, and calls their language *Sumerian*. We shall not attempt to decide the point at issue.

The champions of the Sumerian, or of the Accadian theory, as the case may be, assume that this language disappeared at a certain

* Spiegel, *Op. cit.*, i. p. 384.

crisis, but that the so-called "Turanian" priests carefully preserved it in the practice of their religion. From this there was needed but one step to set about restoring the language in question, by means of monuments, where this pretended "Turanian" text, written in Assyrian cuneiform characters, was supposed to be accompanied by an interlinear Assyrian version. The step was taken, and the doctrine was proclaimed that the forerunners of the Assyrian Semites on Babylonian soil had spoken an Uralo-Altaïc tongue, more specially allied to the Finnic group; that they had reached a high state of culture; that they had communicated to the Assyrian immigrants their cuneiform graphic system; lastly, that before losing their own language they had initiated the new comers into a civilisation which these latter had not, therefore, arrived at independently.

This Sumerian theory was not of a nature to be accepted off-hand, and after twenty round years since its announcement it can scarcely be said to have yet hopelessly routed the objections of its opponents. On the contrary, not satisfied with merely assailing it, M. Joseph Halévy * has recently attempted an interpretation of the texts totally different from that of the "Accadians." He first of all set himself to show that the language in question has nothing in common with those of the Uralo-Altaïc family, from which its phonetic system differs widely, while its roots have neither the same form nor the same use. Moreover, the manner of forming words is quite different—the pronouns have nothing in common, the conjugation is constructed on essentially different conditions, and, lastly, the two vocabularies do not bear serious comparison. There are scarcely a dozen so-called Accadian words that can be at all made to answer to a corresponding number brought together from the various Finnic tongues. Halévy, therefore, holds that the presence of an Uralo-Altaïc speaking people on Mesopotamian soil has been proved neither by the monuments, which all belong to Semitic art, nor by the geographical names (also Semitic), nor yet by the evidence of writers.

* " Observations Critiques sur les prétendus Touraniens de la Babylonie," " Journal Asiatique." June, 1874.

In fact, the Accadian texts would seem to be Assyrian, pure and simple, no longer written with a phonetic system, but by means of monograms artificially combined. In other words, we would have, in both cases, nothing but Assyrian, the so-called Sumerian texts being merely written in an ideographic instead of a phonetic graphic system.

Let us, however, hasten to say that M. Halévy's theory, especially in its positive statements, does not seem to us at all convincing. We do not, of course, say that it is absolutely improbable, but we cannot admit as conclusive the proofs on which it relies. But we do not on that account accept the Sumerian or Accadian theory, on which, till better informed, we shall continue to hold the same views that M. Renan does.*

There can be no doubt that before the arrival of the Assyrians and of the Iranians, Babylonia had already been the field of a true civilisation, which, adds M. Renan, very probably possessed, and even invented the cuneiform manner of writing. But to convert their speech into an Uralo-Altaïc language passes all reasonable bounds. There were good grounds to feel surprised at seeing "this ancient underlying Babylonish culture credited to the Turkish, Finnic, or Hungarian races—races that have scarcely ever been able to do aught but destroy, and who have never created a civilisation of their own. Truth, however, may at times seem unlikely, and if they can prove to us that Turks, Finns, and Hungarians really were the founders of the most powerful and the most intelligent of the ante-Semitic and ante-Aryan civilisations, we shall believe—for all *à priori* considerations must yield to *à posteriori* arguments. But the strength of such proofs must be in proportion to the unlikelihood of the issue." Let us add, that whatever may be constantly said to the contrary, these proofs have not yet been supplied. We are quite ready to accept the Sumerian, and class it with the agglutinating idioms, and even attach it to the Finnic group; but we await conclusive arguments, a genuine grammar—not a series of etymologies which cannot

* "Journal Asiatique," p. 42. July, 1873.

advance the question a single step. Much—too much, perhaps—is already written on the Accadian theory, whereas a short but methodic work might suffice to cause it to be accepted. Such a demonstration may be near at hand, but so far it has not appeared. The defenders of the Sumerian theory must, above all, be perfectly familiar with the phonetics, the structure, and the special vocabulary of the Uralo-Altaïc idioms, which can scarcely be said to be the case with all those that have written upon the subject.

§ 20.—*The Theory of the Turanian Languages.*

During the formative stage of new sciences, while the chief object still is to group and classify the first secured results, there often arise some of those general theories alluring to minds fond of the simple and the easy, but which are doomed, soon or late, to collapse hopelessly before the onward march of sound criticism.

Philology has not escaped from such theories, amongst the most eccentric of which may be included that of a *Turanian Family*, which, notwithstanding its improbability, still continues to enjoy a certain credit. This theory may be said to have two essential qualities. It is at once indefensible and pretentious. Before speaking of its origin and its name, let us see wherein it consists.

And in the first place it is necessary to distinguish between two varieties of the Turanian school—the absolute and the moderate party.

The first, or the orthodox, school holds that all languages that are neither Aryan, Semitic, nor Hamitic, constitute a "Turanian" group. The idioms of this group would have in common not only a certain amount of structural processes, but also a large number of roots. There would therefore thus be a common language, a Turanian mother-tongue. In some indefinite and unexplained way, there are admitted into this group two great divisions, a Northern and a Southern; the first comprising the already-described Uralo-Altaïc idioms, the second not only all the other agglutinating tongues, but also the monosyllabic languages of the extreme East.

The second, or heterodox, party may be divided into two varieties. The first, strictly speaking, no longer believes in the Turanian theory proper, but by a sort of conservative instinct would like to preserve at least the name of the thing. This they apply to our Uralo-Altaïc family, including all its five groups, as above explained.

The second variety, less daring than the previous one, makes the Turanian group consist not only of the Uralo-Altaïc tongues, but also of the Dravidian, the Malayo-Polynesian, the Tibetan, and the Siamese. We are simply stating the case, without criticising, hence are not called upon to ask why Chinese is excluded, together with the Annamese, the Burman, the Caucasian tongues, the Basque, the Nubian and Fula groups, the Corean, the Japanese, the American, the sub-Arctic, Australian, African, Hottentot, and New Guinea languages.

This theory, we have said, is essentially deceptive, calculated to mislead the credulous, or those who lack time and the means of testing for themselves the statements advanced in the name of science itself. Some venerable patriarch, "Tur," is assumed to have given birth to a race, whose speech would thus be the common mother-tongue of the various so-called Turanian idioms. A Persian legend was skilfully grafted on to this invention, nor did Iudaico-Christian orthodoxy fail to discount a theory which, though utterly unsupported by any serious argument, did not on that account seem the less acceptable, since it readily accommodated itself to the teachings of Holy Writ.

If there is one fact better verified than another it is that which Schleicher, Whitney, and so many others with them have clearly shown, namely, that these pretended Turanian languages have but one thing in common—the whimsical name conferred on them. The general structure of Basque, Japanese, and Magyar, is doubtless the same. They all suffix to the noun perfectly analogous elements, that is, they are all, in a word, agglutinating. But the elements constituting the common stock of each are different, and their roots incapable of being reduced to unity. It is in vain boldly to proclaim their common origin or identity, while we are unable even remotely to reduce them to a common form.

L.

The Turanian theory cannot therefore be taken seriously. Begot of much assumption, it vanishes before a very little criticism. Hence it is to be regretted that, while condemning it, certain authors should do the name of Turanian the honour of looking on it as a thing that can be no longer got rid of. It is by this very condescension that it may acquire fresh vitality, and possibly succeed in establishing itself permanently. The best means of combating it is therefore, perhaps, to pass it over in silence. The unlucky term "Semitic" answers at least to a well-defined collection of definite facts, and can be accepted without any reserve. But that of "Turanian" and "Turanian tongues" is only calculated to perpetuate serious misconceptions.*

CHAPTER V.

THIRD FORM OF SPEECH—INFLECTION.

WE have now reached the third and last form of articulate speech—inflection. We have seen that during the monosyllabic period root and word were one, the sentence being a mere series of monosyllabic roots isolated one from the other. In the second phase we saw that certain roots, passing from the position of independent words to that of mere suffixes or prefixes, serve henceforth to express the relations only, whether active or passive, of the roots that have retained their full meaning.

In the first stage, the formula of the word, as already explained, is simply R, and that of the sentence R + R + R, &c., R standing for the root. If we represent by r those roots whose sense has

---

* The term "Turanian" continues to hold its ground in popular English works on ethnology, as in Dr. R. Brown's "Races of Mankind," the fourth and last volume of which has recently appeared. In it the human race is divided into the following groups, an arrangement which, it need scarcely be remarked, is utterly irreconcilable with any intelligible philological distribution: 1. American; 2. Oceanic; 3. Turanian; 4. Persian; 5. Indian; 6. African; 7. Caucasian; 8. European.—*Note by Translator.*

become obscured, and which thus pass to the state of prefixes and suffixes, we shall have as formulæ of the words in the second period, RR, RRR, RR, RRR, and such like analogous combinations.

Two systems of languages, the Semito-Hamitic and the Aryan, after passing through the monosyllabic and the agglutinating phases successively, arrived at last, and independently of each other, at the third or inflecting state.

§ 1.—*What is Inflection?*

Its essence consists in the power of the root to express, by a modification of its own form, its various relations to other roots. In an inflecting language, however, *the roots of all words are not necessarily modified*, remaining at times such as they were in the agglutinating stage, but *they may be modified*. Languages in which relations may thus be expressed, not only by suffixes and prefixes, but also by a modification of the form of the roots, are inflectional languages.

Representing this power of the root by the index ^{x}, the agglutinating formula RR may become R^{x}R in the inflecting stage. Nay, more; not only may the "full" root—as the Chinese call it—receive this index, as in the foregoing formula, but even the relational root, or suffix, may be similarly modified. An example taken from the Aryan system will make this clear. The Sanskrit *êti*, he goes, the Latin *it* (old form *eit*), and the Lithuanian *eiti* flow all from one common form AITI = he goes. The two roots of which this word is composed are I = to go, and TA = the demonstrative pronoun met with in the Greek το = *the* (neuter), and in the Latin *iste*. These two roots have been subjected to inflection in the word in question, though we do not know the real cause that has brought about the modification of the radical I to AI. We do know, however, that the element TA has been changed to TI in passing from the passive to the active state. Thus we find this pronoun with a passive sense wherever it retains its pure form, as in the Latin *scrip-tu-s*, written, *rup-tu-s*, broken; in the Greek θε-το-ς, placed, γνω-το-ς, known. In its modified form, on the contrary, it imparts an active sense to the root to which it is suffixed, as in the Latin *res-ti-s*, and the Greek μαν-τι-s, a seer. This same suffix *ti* has produced in the Aryan tongues a number of active nouns, as opposed to the passive and older forms in *ta*. Thus, in Sanskrit, *pati* = master, lord = the Latin *poti* (nominative *potis* or *pos*, as in *compos, impos*) = the Lithuanian *pati* (nominative *páts*).

In an inflecting idiom the formula of the word may therefore also be R^xR^x, RR^x, RRR^x, besides many other combinations that cannot here be enumerated.

§ 2.—*Aryan and Semitic Inflection.*

We shall presently notice in more or less detail the two systems of inflecting languages—the Aryan (Sanskrit, Persian, Greek, Latin, Slave, Keltic, &c.) and the Semitic (Hebrew, Arabic, &c.). But a very important fact of a general nature must be first placed in a clear light. It is that the Aryan and the Semitic languages differ altogether from each other, not only in their roots, but also in their structure itself. Both are unquestionably inflecting tongues, but the inflection of the one is not that of the other. Schleicher* and Whitney † have examined this question carefully, in the safe and methodical way that characterises all their writings, and we cannot do better than here reproduce what they say on the subject.

Before breaking up into distinct languages, says Schleicher, the Semitic system had no roots to which a sonant form of any sort can be given, as in the case of the Aryan system. The general sense of the root rested in simple consonants, this general sense receiving its various relational meanings by the addition of vowels to the consonants. Thus the three consonants *q, t, l*, constitute the root of the Hebrew *qâtal* and of the Arabic *qatala* = he killed, of *qutila* = he was killed, of the Hebrew *hiqtil* = he caused to kill, and of the Arabic *muqtâlun* = killed. The case is altogether different in the

---

* "Die Deutsche Sprache," 2nd edition, p. 21, Stuttgart, 1869; "Semitisch und Indo-Germanisch, Beiträge zur Vergleichenden Sprachforschung," ii. p. 236, Berlin, 1861.

† "Language and the Study of Language," 3rd edition, p. 300. London, 1870.

Aryan system, where the sense and the full utterance of the syllable are coincident.

Further, the Semitic root admits of all the vowels capable of modifying its sense, while the Aryan root possesses one organic vowel, as in the root of the Sanskrit *manvê* = I mind or think; of the Greek μενος = the mind; of the Latin *mens, moneo*; of the Gothic *gamunan* = to mind, where the organic vowel of the root is not *a, e, o, u*, indifferently, but, necessarily, *a* alone. Besides, this organic vowel can be changed into certain others, only under certain conditions and according to laws recognised and determined by philological analysis.

A third difference consists in the triliteral character of the Semitic root: *qtl* = to kill, *ktb* = to write, *dbr* = to speak, derived no doubt from simpler primeval forms, but which are now thus reconstituted. On the other hand, the Aryan root is much more varied in form, as in *i* = to go, *su* = to pour, to shed, though always monosyllabic.

The Semitic system had three cases and two tenses only, while the Aryan has eight cases and at least five tenses.

All Aryan words have one and the same form, that of the root (modified or not) accompanied by the derivative suffix. This form occurs in Semitic also, as in the Arabic *qatalta* = thou man, thou hast killed; but it also possesses the form in which the derivative element is prefixed, where the root comes between two derivative elements, and others also.

Semitic inflection, observes Whitney in his turn, is wholly different from the Aryan, so that the two systems cannot be derived one from the other any more than from one common system. The fundamental character of the Semitic resides in the triliteral form of its roots, which are composed of three consonants, to which are joined various vowels in their formative capacity—that is, as formative elements indicating the various relations of the root. Thus in Arabic the root *qtl* presents the idea of to kill, and *qatala* means he killed, *qutila* = he was killed, *qatl* = murderer, *qitl* = enemy, &c. Jointly with this inflection, due to the use made of various vowels, the Semitic also forms its words by means of

150   THIRD FORM OF SPEECH—INFLECTION.   [Chap. v.

suffixes and prefixes, and occasionally with infixes. But it does not pile up affixes on affixes, or derivatives on derivatives—whence the almost complete uniformity of the Semitic tongues.

The structure of the Semitic verb differs profoundly from that of the Indo-European. In the second and third persons it distinguishes the gender (masculine or feminine) of the subject: *qatalat* = she killed, *qatala* = he killed—which is not the case in the Aryan tongues: *bharati* = he or she bears.* The contrast between past, present, and future—so fundamental in Aryan—does not exist in Semitic, which has two tenses only, answering, the one to the action done, and the other to the action not done.

We thus see how serious are the structural differences between the two systems, and how discrepant is their method of inflection. To what has been said must be added the other characteristic fact, that the Aryan system alone has the power of augmenting its vowels. This feature consists in prefixing an *a* to an *u*, an *i*, or a

* But it may be doubted whether the process by which gender is or is not distinguished in the personal endings, constitutes a *fundamental* difference between the Aryan and Semitic families, or whether the fact that the organic Aryan does not so distinguish gender is due to more than an accidental line of development taken by it at a certain stage. It is at least certain that Hindī, without at all ceasing to be Aryan in its structure, has also come in the course of time to distinguish gender in its conjugation, not only in the second and third, but in all three persons, singular and plural; and not only in tenses that may be looked upon merely as declined participles, but in the future, which is based on an organic aorist. Hence it is that this tense is, so to say, both conjugated and declined, as thus:

            Masculine form.   Feminine form.
   Sing. 1.   jălūngā   jălūngī ⎫
        2. 3. jălēgā   jălēgī   ⎬ Shall or will
   Pl. 1. 3. jălēngē   jălēngīn ⎨   burn.
        2. jălōgē   jălōgīn ⎭

There are even cases in Hindī where the verb so agrees, not with the subject but with the object, as in *ŭs-nē lărkyān mārīn* = he struck the girls; here *mārīn* = struck, being feminine plural in agreement with the object *lărkyān* = girls. Thus it is that features which would at first sight seem to constitute radical differences between two distinct families of speech may be found to exist in both, showing that their presence or absence is often the result of some particular tendencies worked out while the languages were being developed either in a synthetic or an analytic direction.—*Note by Translator.*

u radical. In the Aryan form ΛΙμι = I go (Sanskrit *émi*, Greek ειμι, Lithuanian *eimi*) the radical *I* = to go, is augmented in this particular tense, mood, and person, and in Semitic there is nothing resembling this.

These two languages have therefore emerged from the agglutinating state by different ways, and are accordingly as independent of each other in their structure as in their roots, the assumed possibility of reducing which to older forms common to both no longer calls for special refutation.*

We shall now proceed to speak in their turn, under three main divisions, of the Semitic, Hamitic, and Aryan languages.

(A) *The Semitic Languages.*

It is needless to say how entirely conventional are the terms *Semite* and *Semitic* tongues. They do not even agree with the biblical account, which treats as descendants of Shem races whose idioms cannot be classed amongst those that we call Semitic, and which, on the other hand, does not regard him as the father of peoples whose speech is undoubtedly Semitic. But however this be, the words have now acquired such currency, that it would be hopeless to attempt to supplant them by others of a more acceptable nature. The more rational expression, *Syro-Arabic*, is sometimes used, but it can scarcely be expected to take the place of the now generally received nomenclature. As remarked by M. Renant† in his now classical work, to which we are largely indebted, its use can occasion no inconvenience, once it is taken as merely a conventional name, its utter inadequacy being otherwise thoroughly understood.

§ 3.—*The Semite and the Semitic Languages collectively.*

In spite of the labours of Gesenius (1786-1842) and of Ewald, we still lack a comparative grammar of these tongues, and even any really comprehensive work on their main features. Such a

---

* Th. Nœdleke, " Orient und Occident," ii. p. 375. Göttingen, 1863.

† " Histoire Générale et Système Comparée des Langues Sémitiques," première partie, " Histoire Générale des Langues Sémitiques."

work once successfully carried out, the so-called Hamite group should be taken in hand, and the general Hamite forms should then be compared with the primitive Semitic forms, and an effort be thus made at last to restore the broad outlines of a rudimentary Hamitico-Semitic grammar. Such a grammar might doubtless be contained in a very few pages, but the possibility of composing it can scarcely be questioned. A deeper insight may even yet be had into the secrets of the evolution of inflecting idioms, so as to attempt the reconstruction of the main features they must have presented while still in the agglutinating stage.

Efforts have already been made to reduce to a biliteral form the triliteral, or rather triconsonantal, Semitic roots, and it is not too much to hope that this undertaking will prove successful.* Benfey rightly thinks that it will be greatly promoted by a knowledge of the Hamitic roots.† The Semitic quadriliteral roots, no one now doubts, will be all, without exception, ultimately restored to an older triliteral form.

In the Semitic system the noun is formed, in the first instance, by the addition of certain vowels to the triconsonantal root.

It will be the duty of a comparative Semitic Grammar to determine the use made of the various vowels that impart such and such a character to the noun thus formed. This method of nominal formation is elementary enough; but there is another, that of derivation, in which certain syllables are prefixed or even suffixed to the root, the latter process being more recent than that in which they are prefixed.

In the common Semite speech, the noun would seem to have had the three genders,‡ the neuter disappearing at a very remote period. The masculine was expressed by no special element,

---

* Chavée, "Les Langues et les Races," p. 44, Paris, 1862; Renan, *op. cit.*, i. ch. 3; "Rapport Annuel Journal Asiatique," vii. série iv. p. 27, Paris, 1874; Schleicher, "Die Unterscheidung von Nomen und Verbum in der Lautlichen Form," p. 18.

† "Geschichte der Sprachwissenschaft und Orientalischen Philologie in Deutschland," p. 691. Munich, 1869.

‡ Ewald, "Ausführliches Lehrbuch der Hebräischen Sprache," 8th ed. p. 445. Göttingen, 1870.

whereas the feminine was in all likelihood denoted by the ending *at*.* The organic plural ending was probably *mân*,† possibly *umâ* or *unâ*,‡ or even some other form, and it seems to have been anterior to the dual.

In the declension there were three cases, a number much inferior to that of the Aryan noun. They were the nominative, genitive, and accusative, but they have disappeared, to a large extent, from all the idioms of the Semitic group except the Arabic, as will be seen when we come to treat each of them separately. According to some writers the vowel *u* was the sign of the nominative, *i* of the genitive (in principle) and *a* of the accusative.§ The case-endings, according to Fr. Müller were: *â* for *hû*, third personal pronoun; *i* relational suffix, and the demonstrative *an*.‖

The common Semite tongue had two tenses only, as above stated —a *past* tense denoting finished action, and an *imperfect* expressing incomplete action. They are distinguished from each other by the position of the pronominal suffix in regard to the theme. Thus the suffix TA of the second person masculine singular, if placed after the theme marks complete action, or the past tense: *katabata* = thou hast written, in Arabic *katabta*; if placed before the root it denotes unfinished action, or the imperfect tense, as in the Arabic *takataba*.

According to Fr. Müller, the organic Semite verb was capable of being conjugated on fifteen themes (or modifications of the root): the simple form *kataba* = he wrote, and a strengthened theme *kattaba*, followed by a series of secondary ones, formed by the help of sundry reflective and causative prefixes. However, none of the members of the group have retained these fifteen forms, all having lost some, and several a great many of them. The same

---

* Ewald, "Ausführliches Lehrbuch der Hebräischen Sprache," 8th ed. p. 416. Gottingen, 1870.

† *Ibid.*, p. 165.

‡ Fr. Müller, "Der Verbalausdruck in Semitischen Sprachkreise," "Sitzungsberichte der Phil. Hist. Classe der K. Akademie der Wissenschaften," lx. p. 520. Vienna, 1868.

§ Olshausen, *op. cit.*, p. 25. Cf. Ewald, *op. cit.*, p. 523 and following.

‖ *Op. cit.*, p. 519.

writer thinks that the passive was merely a reflective form, constructed by the aid of the pronominal element *hu*. The restored form *kutaba* = it has been written—in Arabic *kŭtiba*—would represent an older *hakatiba*. Comparative Semitic grammar is so little advanced that it is well to record the sound and methodical essays in this direction, although still in a very incomplete state.

The Semitic alphabet, in its main features, would seem to have been developed out of the Egyptian hieroglyphics,* not exactly by the Phœnicians, says Ewald, but by some Semitic people intimately associated with Egypt. Anyhow the name of the people is now unknown to whom civilisation is indebted for the immense service of having converted the old hieroglyphics into an alphabetic system. This alphabet consists of twenty-two consonants, each of which must have expressed the sound answering to the initial sound of the being or object represented by the sign itself. Thus the old picture of the camel stood for a *g* in the Semite alphabet, because the name of the camel began with a *g* in their language: Chaldee, *gimel*; Syriac, *gomal*. It is needless to observe that these new alphabetical signs were diversely modified by the various peoples adopting them.

The Semitic graphic system is generally divided into three distinct groups. The western comprised the Phœnician and the old Hebrew, which latter was still current in the second century before our era. The eastern branch embraced the regions of the Euphrates and the Tigris. Being of a rounder form than the western type, it was soon changed into a cursive style, which was diffused over the countries to the west and north of Arabia. In the south of Arabia itself the third or Himyaro-Ethiopic system had been developed. We shall say a few words on each of these three varieties, when treating of the several idioms of the Semitic group.

To the Assyrian cuneiform writing of the third text of inscriptions of the Achæmenides must be assigned a totally different origin, as will be seen in its proper place.

* E. de Rougé, "Mémoire sur l'Origine Egyptienne de l'Alphabet Phénicien." Paris, 1874.

The classification of the Semitic idioms is now fairly determined, though at first far from being so easy to settle as that of the Aryan family. In truth they do not present amongst themselves such marked features as those, for instance, that distinguish the Keltic from the Iranian, the Italic from the Slavonic branches. It has been justly remarked that all the various Semitic idioms do not differ more widely from each other, than do the different members of one single branch of the Aryan family; as, for instance, Russian, Bohemian, and Croatian (in the Slavonic); English, Flemish, and Danish (in the Teutonic branch).

Still we may reckon three sufficiently distinct groups in the Semitic family:

The *Aramæo-Assyrian Group*, comprising the two Aramaic dialects *Chaldee* and *Syriac*, together with the *Assyrian*.

The *Canaanitic Group*, embracing *Hebrew* and *Phœnician*.

The *Arabic Group*, including Arabic proper and the idioms of South Arabia (and Abyssinia)—*Himyaratic* and *Ehkili; Gheez* and *Tigré; Amharic, Harrari*.

Some writers reduce this classification to two groups, including the first two in one single branch, which they call the *northern*, in contrast with the *southern*, composed of the two varieties of the Arabic group.

We shall now briefly notice these various idioms, and endeavour, in conclusion, to ascertain whether it might not be possible to form some conjecture as to their original home and common primeval type.

§ 4.—*The Aramæo-Assyrian Group.*

(1) *Chaldee and Syriac.*

The name of Aramean is given to two closely related varieties of this group: the *Chaldee*, or eastern, and the *Syriac*, or western dialect. The first is spread over the greater part, if not the whole, of Babylonia and Assyria, the second over Mesopotamia and Syria.

Its general character, compared with the cognate tongues, consists in the greater loss it has sustained of the old Semitic vowels, which relative inferiority may be attributed to its earlier development. Though, as stated, differing little from each other, their accentual system is quite distinct. While the accent in Chaldee falls in principle on the last syllable, affecting the penultimate in certain special cases only, in Syriac, on the contrary, it falls regularly on the penultimate, in exceptional cases alone affecting the final syllable.

Of the primitive Aramean tongue no documents have survived, such as we possess of the Assyrian, which we shall presently speak of. The oldest Aramean texts are contained in the sacred writings of the Jews. They are generally spoken of as biblical Chaldee, and may date from the fifth or sixth century before our era. Other Aramean passages in Holy Writ are still more recent, and about the Christian era there appear the Targums, translations and paraphrases of the Jewish writings. The language of the Talmuds, some four or five centuries older, is much more affected by foreign elements, borrowed from the surrounding languages.

In his history of the Semitic tongues, M. Renan treats successively of the Pagan and Christian Aramean—specimens of the first of which we have in the *Mendean* and *Nabatean*. This last name is equivalent to that of Chaldee, and of its important literature we now possess nothing but the treatise on Nabatean agriculture, of unknown date, but translated into Arabic in the tenth century. The *Sabean*—or, more correctly, the language of the Mendeans—produced nothing at all so important or practical as the Nabatean literature seems to have possessed. What we do possess, including the "Book of Adam," a mass of extravagant ravings, seems posterior to Islamism. M. Renan mentions, as peculiar features of Mendean, the confusion and frequent elision of the gutturals, the interchange of sharps and flats, and numerous contractions.

The Christian Aramean is represented by the Syriac; which shows nothing really national older than the first centuries of our era, although it seems certain that a literature of this sort had been developed at an earlier period. The Palmyrene inscriptions date from the first three centuries, and the Syriac writings from the latter half of the second century. The "Peshito" version of the Bible is the oldest Syriac work, and is referred to the second century. In the fourth there flourished a very important Christian Aramean literature, though strongly impressed with Hellenic influences. It served in a way as an intermediary between Greek and Arabic science, bringing about the transition from the former to the latter. Nearly all the Arabic translations from the Greek, says M. Renan, would seem to have been made by Syrian writers* and on Syriac versions.* Syrian letters began to decline about the tenth century, when the ascendancy of Moslem culture was finally established, and Syriac sank to the condition of a liturgical language. It is now no longer spoken, except in a very few places in the neighbourhood of Lake Urumiah; and even these last vestiges must ere long disappear before the advance of the Arabic.

In our fifth paragraph we shall speak of the *Samaritan* dialect, which, though frequently grouped with the Chaldee and Syriac, is really more akin to the Hebrew; thus belonging, not to the Aramean, but to the Canaanitic group.

(2) *Assyrian*.

Side by side with the Aramean, the second language of the north-eastern Semitic group, is that of the third text of the cuneiform rock-inscriptions, to which has been given the name of Assyrian. According to Oppert we might just as well call it Accadian, the name given by Hincks to the still contested agglutinating tongue, that Oppert calls Sumerian, and here spoken of at p. 141.

The Assyrian was not admitted without a long and lively struggle into the Semitic family, its right to membership with which can now no longer be seriously called in question. However, the opposition it met with has been of singular advantage to the studies connected with the subject, and it may be asserted that we already know nearly as much of its grammar as we are ever likely to do. The important writings of Rawlinson definitely brought to

* Renan, *op. cit.*, iii. ch. 3, § 2.

a close the series of works whose object was to settle the nature itself of the Assyrian language. The objections fell one after the other; that first of all, which consisted in denying its Semitic character, based on the difference of its alphabet from the ordinary Semitic graphic system.

The various Assyrian writings, whether Ninevite or Babylonian, are composed of wedge (or clove) shaped signs, of diverse length, and differing in their disposition from those of the Persian system, which will be described when we come to the Iranian tongues. These cuneiform (literally wedge-shaped) letters derive from ancient hieroglyphics, whose forms may still be easily recognised in some of them. Though differing from the Persian, the Assyrian cuneiforms are pretty much the same as those of the second text of the rock inscriptions. Their common origin is obvious, and may be detected at the first glance. Their number is considerable, and they denote either ideas or sounds. The latter—that is the phonetic signs—stand for full syllables, and for such and such vowels or consonants—a fact pointed out by Hincks as far back as 1849.

They are easily transcribed in Roman letters, which, of course, is not the case with the ideographic signs. In fact, the phonetic value of these can be ascertained only by secondary considerations, and to meet the difficulty the ideograms are conventionally transcribed precisely as if they were phonetic, but in Roman capitals.

The Assyrian texts already collected and preserved in the various museums of Europe are very numerous, and it is certain that they will be still greatly increased. In the country itself there are vast numbers of inscribed monuments, including some of considerable length. Thus the third text of the inscriptions of the Achæmenides is, as stated, in Assyrian. The language of the second column has already been referred to at p. 139, and we shall in its proper place speak of the Persian, which is that of the first column.

Oppert, who has contributed greatly to the elucidation of the Assyrian cuneiforms,* may be justly considered the founder of

---

* "Expédition scientifique en Mésopotamie," ii. Paris, 1859.

Assyrian grammar,* his writings marking a new period in Assyriology. Other grammars have subsequently appeared, and the study of Assyrian no longer presents any serious difficulty.†

We subjoin a few notes on Assyrian Grammar:

Its phonetics seem less changed than those of the other two Aramean dialects, the sibilants especially having undergone but little modification.

The element *at* (at times *it*) in Assyrian, as in the other Semitic tongues, denotes the feminine gender: *sar* = king, *sarrat* = queen; *ilu* = god, *ilat* or *ilit* = goddess; *rabu* = great (masculine), *rabit* = great (feminine).

The masculine plural is *i*, answering to the Aramean *in* and Hebrew *im*: *yum* = day, *yumi* = days. The feminine plural is properly *ât* (in Hebrew *ôt*), but also *ut* and *it*. The dual occurs but rarely.

The old case-endings have disappeared, though not without leaving clear traces of their former presence. They were *um*, nom., *am* and *im* for the two other cases. According to Oppert, this "mimmation" would seem to answer to the "nunnation," to be referred to further on in Arabic. In course of time the final *m* gradually disappeared, causing the preceding vowel itself to be diversely affected.

In Assyrian there is no article, but, as in the other Semitic tongues, the possessive pronoun is expressed by a suffixed element: *bitya* = my house; *babiya* = my gates; *sumya* = my name; *sumiya* = my names. For the second person singular *ka* masculine and *ki* feminine: *sumka* = thy name (speaking of a man); *sumiki* = thy names (speaking of a woman).

No trace of the organic Semitic perfect tense has been discovered, there being nothing but the imperfect, expressing unfinished action, and formed by the theme preceded by the personal suffixes.

---

* "Éléments de la Grammaire Assyrienne," 2nd edition. Paris, 1868.

† Ménant, "Exposé des Éléments de la Grammaire Assyrienne," Paris, 1868; "Le Syllabaire Assyrien," Paris, 1869-74; "Leçons d'Épigraphie Assyrienne," Paris, 1873; Sayce, "An Assyrian Grammar," London, 1872; Schrader, "Die Assyrisch-Babylonischen Keilinschriften," "Zeitschr. der Deutschen Morgenländischen Gesellschaft," xxi. p. 1-392, Leipzig, 1872.

The direct pronominal object is attached to the verb, as in the Semitic system generally. Thus the phrase, "I have-subdued-them," is expressed in one word, by adding the pronoun *sunut* = them, to the form "I have subdued."

We may remark, in conclusion, that Assyrian was spoken down almost to the Christian era, when it was at length supplanted by Aramean; which, in its turn, had to yield to the spread of Arabic.

§ 5.—*The Canaanitic Group.*

The languages of this group have been, on the whole, much better preserved than the Aramean, as is clearly shown by the forms of old or classic Hebrew.

(1) *Hebrew*

Has passed through three successive phases, thus described by Ewald.* The fragments, dating from the time of Moses, show Hebrew already formed, and essentially the same as that of more recent times. It must, therefore, even then have been already very old. In the second period, dating from the Kings, it shows symptoms of diverging into two styles, an ordinary and a more artistic style. The third period begins with the seventh century before our era; it is a period of decay, during which it is continually encroached upon by the Aramean tongues.

However, the differences are but slight between each of these periods. "The important point," says Renan, "is to insist on the grammatical unity of Hebrew, on the fact of the great uniformity of records of such diverse times and sources as have entered into the Jewish archives. It would doubtless be rash to assert, with M. Movers, that one hand had retouched all the writings of the Hebrew canon, in order to reduce them to a uniform language. Still it must be allowed that few literatures present such an impersonal character, or one so free from the particular stamp of any individual writer or definite epoch."†

* "Ausführliches Lehrbuch der Hebräischen Sprache," 8th ed. p. 23. Göttingen, 1870.
† *Op. cit.*, ii. ch. 1.

Not till the eleventh century before our era do we meet with any Hebrew writings that have not been subsequently retouched. Three or four centuries later on, the Hebrew language enters on its golden age, and towards the sixth century begins to disappear as a national form of speech. Long before the epoch of the Maccabees Aramean had assumed the ascendant in Palestine. Nevertheless, works continued to be still written in Hebrew, till within about a hundred years of our era. Renan divides into two distinct periods the history of modern or post-biblical Hebrew. The first extends to the twelfth century, its principal monument being the Mishna, a collection of Rabbinical traditions, or a sort of second Bible. In it occur a certain number of Aramean, as well as some Greek and Latin words. After having adopted Arabic culture in the tenth century, the Jews saw a revival of their literature, when their fellow-countrymen, banished from Mussulman Spain, found a refuge in the south of France. The language of this epoch is still the literary idiom of the Jews.

The Hebrew vowel system, like the Aramean, is of the simplest, but the consonantal, as in all the Semitic family, is rich in sibilants and aspirates. The sibilants are four in number, answering to our *sh*, *s*, *z*, and *ts*. These letters play a much more prominent part in Hebrew than in the cognate tongues. There are also four aspirates, two soft and two guttural, *hheth* and *oyin*, which last interchange occasionally with *k* and *g*. Besides the three pairs of explosives: *k*, *g*; *t*, *d*; and *p*, *b*, there is a *q*, stronger (that is, uttered lower down in the throat) than the simple *k*, and a *th*, as transcribed by some authors, stronger (or thicker) than the *t*; also a labial explosive distinct from the *p*, and often represented by an *f*. It should, however, be observed that those consonants naturally susceptible of being aspirated really are aspirated in pronunciation when preceded by a vowel. Lastly, there are the *l* and *r*, the nasals *n* and *m*, the semi-vowels *w* and *y*.

In nouns the feminine is formed, as a rule, by adding the element *at*, subject to certain modifications, the *t* sometimes changing to a simple aspirate, and the *a* disappearing at others.

Masculines form their plural, in principle, by the addition of *im*,

M

occasionally replaced by the Aramean *in*, and the general feminine plural ending is *ôt*. The Hebrew dual, less general than in Arabic, but better preserved than in Aramean, is formed by the ending *aim*.

The nominative is no longer marked by any special ending. Whatever is to be said of the attempts made to restore the primitive forms of the Semitic cases, there remain in Hebrew but very doubtful traces of the old nominative suffix; and the same is true of the accusative and genitive.

Apart from the nominative, which is expressed by the theme itself, the Hebrew cases are now indicated either by prepositions or by what is called the state of the noun in government. A noun in this state, opposed to the "noun absolute," assumes a really dependent position, from which we see that the principal function of this state is to express the idea of the genitive. In the singular masculine nouns in this state remain in principle unchanged, immediately preceding the noun they govern. In the plural they lose, in principle, their final *m*, at times the preceding vowel also. It has been above stated that the final *t* feminine is sometimes changed to an aspirate; but in government the organic *t* of these feminine nouns remains in full vigour, while in the plural they retain the ending *ôt*. These, of course, are but the general laws, subject to many exceptions that cannot here be noticed. We may add, however, that the noun in construction may be followed, not only by another noun, but also by a pronoun: *gham-ô* = his people; *ben-î* = my son.

By employing prepositions, as it does, instead of case-endings, Hebrew exhibits so far a perfectly analytic character. It is, in fact, incorrect to speak with grammarians of a dative, a locative, or an ablative, the forms thus described being nothing but nouns or pronouns combined with prepositions. The more frequently recurring of these prepositions consist of a single consonant only: *l* = to, towards; *b* = in. The origin of nearly all of these particles is unknown, but they derive, in principle, from verbal roots, whereas the corresponding Aryan prepositions are mostly of pronominal origin.

Inflection plays an important part in the formation of nouns. It consists, as already remarked, in the variation of the radical vowels.

Besides the prepositions, Hebrew possesses an article, closely united to the noun, its exclusive function being that of a simple determinative.

It is diversely modified by euphonic laws, but its primitive form seems to have been *hal*. The consonant *l* assimilates always to the initial letter of the following noun, and the vowel *a* is sometimes lengthened. Thus, from *máqôm* = place, we get *hammáqôm* = the place. After certain prepositions the *h* disappears.

We have already stated that the Semitic system has two tenses only—one denoting complete, the other denoting incomplete action. Hebrew remains faithful to this simple conception. The two tenses, as stated, are distinguished by the position of the personal suffix, which in the past is placed after, and in the imperfect before the theme.

Thus in *záquanti* = I am old, I have grown old, in *hálakti* = I have gone, we recognise perfect forms; because here the pronominal element *ti* is suffixed. But in *nâsub* = we will return, the action is not yet completed, because the personal element is prefixed.

The verbal forms themselves are now five only, whereas we have seen that there were reckoned fifteen in the primitive Semitic type. Even now Aramean possesses one more than the Hebrew, while Arabic is still more wealthy. The five Hebrew forms consist of the simple and four derivative ones.

Until the last few centuries of the old era the rude and angular Phœnician alphabet was that of the Jews also. It was then advantageously replaced by the rounder and more flowing Chaldean letters. The old alphabet is still found on the coins of the epoch of the Maccabees, and on some others apparently struck later on during the war with the Romans. Nevertheless, at the time of the Maccabees the Jews were already in possession of a more recent alphabet, that continued in use amongst the Samaritans.*

The new, or Chaldean, alphabet no more distinguished the vowels

---

* Olshausen, *op. cit.*, p. 52.

than did the old one. This was a serious defect, which was attempted to be partly remedied by employing consonants to represent vowel sounds; but the device, though applied with some judgment, could produce but partial and unsatisfactory results. To the Massoretes is attributed the invention of the vowel points, dating seemingly from the beginning of the sixth century of our era. A certain number of useful modifications was also introduced in the character of the consonants. Thus, those meant to be uttered strongly were distinguished from the others by a point (*dagesh*) in the body of the letter. The sound of *s* and *sh*, hitherto represented by the same sign, were now distinguished by a diacritical point over this sign to the right or the left, as the case might be. (Thus ש = s; שׁ = sh).

A word on *Samaritan*, by some writers grouped with the Aramean branch. Others seem, more correctly to classify it with the Canaanitic division, while still admitting that it has been profoundly influenced by Aramean.

(2) *Phœnician.**

Very little is known of the races occupying Palestine before the arrival of the Semitic tribes, probably from the south-east, who called themselves Canaanites. These tribes themselves, amongst which must be included the Phœnicians, were obliged to give way before the *Beni-Israel*, who, under the leadership of Joshua, overran the greater part of Palestine about 1,300 years before our era. The Canaanites were now driven westwards towards the coast, and it may be supposed that this event contributed greatly to develop their relations with the lands watered by the Mediterranean. The Israelites, from whom civilisation has otherwise suffered so much, may have thus, though indirectly, rendered it for the nonce a most important service.

This is not the place to discuss the question whether the Israelites originally spoke an Aramean dialect, afterwards adopting a Canaanitic

---

* Schrœder, "Die Phœnizische Sprache." Halle, 1869. One of the best essays on Phœnician, to which we are indebted for much of these details. Renan, *op. cit.*, ii. ch. 2.

form of speech. The only fact we are concerned with is the present identity of Hebrew with Phœnician. It may be unhesitatingly asserted that there existed a common Canaanitic language that in due course gave birth to both of these varieties, which are sister-tongues standing on the same level; and it is therefore incorrect to represent Phœnician, as is often done, as a dialect of the Hebrew. The error dates from the time when the first attempts were made to interpret the Phœnician documents. Comparative grammar was still unknown at that period, and the linguists, who came across Phœnician texts, naturally derived this language from Hebrew, which they found it so strongly resembling. But there is now no longer room for any doubt on the subject; the two idioms, as stated, are cognate, descending both in parallel lines from a common mother-tongue. Once severed from one another, they followed each its own destiny, "developing themselves independently, amongst peoples of different character and manners, and thus diverging in course of time, not so much in their grammar, as in the general features of their composition."—(Renan.) It has justly been said that their differences were mere provincial varieties.

Amongst their more marked differences is mentioned the Phœnician peculiarity of employing in the current speech a certain number of forms and expressions that in Hebrew are looked on as archaic, occurring in the more lofty style only. Many Phœnician terms have a different meaning from the corresponding Hebrew words, being sometimes taken in a wider, sometimes in a narrower, sense. On the other hand, Phœnician possesses a relative pronominal form more primitive than the Hebrew form, and is otherwise distinguished by some further peculiarities, now well enough understood, but which need not be here dwelt upon.

Phœnician, as it appears in its inscriptions, which are not of very great antiquity, betrays important marks of Aramean elements, more, perhaps, than Hebrew does. The Phœnician of the colonies settled on the north coast of Africa also shows these same Aramaic traces; though the fact is not surprising, when we consider the extreme antiquity of Aramean influences, and the constant relations maintained by the African settlements with the mother-country.

Punic, or African Phœnician, which was of course the language of the Carthaginians, is very clearly divided into two dialects—an ancient and a more recent; the first being identical with the Phœnician of Palestine. Neo-Punic is more corrupt, and its orthography often very defective. Its chief monuments are met with in Tunis and Eastern Algeria. The neo-Punic alphabet differs materially from the old Phœnician, of which, however, it is but a variety. Its letters have been generally simplified, some of them being reduced to a single stroke, and being often almost confused with each other.*

Of Phœnician literature there survive only a few fragments of Sanchoniathon's Phœnician history, and the "Periplous of Hanno," translated into Greek; further, some words occurring in the classics, a passage in Plautus, and a series of coins and inscriptions. These last monuments have been mostly discovered on various points along the shores of the Mediterranean, at Marseilles, in Spain, on the north coast of Africa, and in the islands of Cyprus, Sardinia, and Malta—Phœnicia itself so far supplying but a limited number of inscriptions.

Phœnician disappeared from Palestine even before Punic had been, like it, absorbed by more fortunate tongues. We may believe, with Renan, that Punic was spoken down to the Mohammedan invasion, and that the ease with which Arabic spread over certain regions of northern Africa, was precisely due to this persistence of the Semitic Phœnician, from which Arabic itself did not greatly differ, although belonging to another branch of the family.

§ 6.—*The Arabic Group.*

It is only for want of a better term that the name of Arabic is given to the southern branch of the Semitic tongues. The word is, properly speaking, applicable only to the Ishmaelitic, which is but one of the two sub-divisions of the Arabic group. The Himyaritic, Gheez, and other Semitic idioms of southern Arabia (and Abys-

---

* Judas, "Étude démonstrative de la Langue Phénicienne et de la Langue Libyque," Paris, 1847; also by the same writer, "Nouvelles Études sur une Série d'Inscriptions Numidico-Puniques," Paris, 1857.

sinia) were not known for a long time after the Arabic, and it was in consequence of their close affinity to this language that the generic term of Arabic came to be somewhat incorrectly extended to them also.

(1) *Arabic.*

The astonishing stability peculiar to the Semitic idioms is nowhere more conspicuous than in the Arabic, nor is there anything more singular, not to say strange, than the almost absolute uniformity of this language, throughout the ages it has lasted and the vast domain it has occupied.

Since the epoch of Mohammed (end of sixth and beginning of seventh century), and even in the poems anterior to Islamism, Arabic appears such as the literary language is at the present day, that is, in full possession of all its forms, of its copious vocabulary, and, one might say, perfect as ever.

The original form of the Koran was that of a sort of narrative composition. According to Renan's expression, it is, so to say, a collection of Mohammed's " orders of the day." It was not entirely composed in the lifetime of the Prophet, certain portions being subsequent to his death. In any case his followers scraped together all the shreds and fragments of his utterances, forming of them a sort of typical or standard work, the copies of which were, in their turn, revised by the Caliph Othman, in the middle of the seventh century (644–656). The preponderance of the Koreish dialect, spoken in the heart of Arabia, was thus definitely established. The style of the Koran itself is of two kinds, the first a sort of poetic prose, the second rhythmical.

The older poems, above referred to, were certainly not much anterior to Islamism, and the language of the Mollakâts, referred to the beginning of the sixth century, is pure literary Arabic, not an ancient or older form of the language.

The Semites of central Arabia were unacquainted with the art of writing, properly so-called, previous to the beginning of the sixth century. From the first very defective, and leading to the confusion of certain consonants represented by one and the same character, the Arabic alphabet was reformed at an early date, in fact, during the first century of the hegira, as is supposed, though the reform was not accomplished all at once. It was effected gradually, reducing the alphabet to its present form, with its vowel points and with certain diacritical marks, distinguishing several of the characters whose primitive form was the same. (Thus: ح = *hh*; خ = *kh*; ج = *j*.)

Not without good reason has Arabic been called the Sanskrit of the Semitic race. In truth it plays the same part amongst its cognate tongues that Sanskrit does amongst the Aryan languages, regard being always had to the far more intimate resemblance of the Semitic idioms to each other.

We have already remarked that Arabic has retained the three cases of the primitive Semitic tongue—the nominative, accusative, and genitive—faint traces only of which are to be detected in the northern groups. These cases are formed, as already stated, by the three vowels, *u, i, a*, with which the word ends when preceded by the article; but when this is not the case, they are followed by a nasal.

Thus the noun ends in *un, an, in*, as the case may be, when unaccompanied by the article, but in *u*, nominative; *a*, accusative; and *i*, genitive, when joined with the article. The state of government exists in Arabic as well as in Hebrew.

Number is denoted in two ways. One is the usual Semitic process, *ûna* for the nominative, and *îna* for the oblique case masculine; *âton* and *âtin* for the corresponding feminine, with which compare the Aramean *în* and *ôt*, and the Hebrew *îm, ôt*. This plural form is called *sound, perfect, external*, or *regular*.

The second process is described as *broken, imperfect, internal, irregular*. Here plurality is expressed by a modification of the root: "*Frangitur forma singularis vel mutata una alterave vocalium, vel aliqua literarum transposita aut abjecta, vel nova litera inserta.*"*

---

* Zschokke, "Institutiones Fundament. Ling. Ar.," Vienna, 1869; H. Derenbourg, "Essai sur les Formes de Pluriels en Arabe," "Journal Asiatique," 1867; S. Guyard, "Nouvel Essai sur la Formation du Pluriel Brisé en Arabe," Paris, 1870.

At times the body of the word is lengthened, and *a* prefixed: *tifl* = child, *atfâl* = children. Other processes may be seen in special works on the subject.*

The dual endings are *âni* nominative, *aini* oblique: yadâni = the two hands.

Arabic retains the two organic Semitic tenses, the present being expressed sometimes by one and sometimes by the other. Thus the perfect is used if the present action has already been previously accomplished, and if it is a continued action, as in the formula: *dixerunt dicuntque*. But the other tense is used, if the present action is connected with some other action presently to be spoken of. The future is treated in the same way.

Both tenses are formed as in the other Semitic tongues. The personal element is prefixed to express imperfect, and suffixed to express perfect action.

It may be added that of the fifteen primitive forms, Arabic has retained nine, which is considerably more than the Hebrew.

It would be a mistake to look on vulgar Arabic as anything more than the literary language simplified. The main difference between the two is, that the vernacular has allowed the cases to drop out of current use, thus arriving at a state of analysis analogous to the Aramean and Hebrew. It has also entirely lost the process of the noun in government. In any case, as Renan observes,† a number of facts show that the main features of the literary language existed also in the ancient Arabic tongue. Thus, the inflections peculiar to the former are absolutely necessary to explain the metrical system of the old poetry. It is even supposed that certain tribes of central Arabia still retain in ordinary speech the inflections peculiar to the written form,‡ and which would elsewhere seem pretentious and pedantic.

In the literary style there can be no question of dialects. It is a language fixed once for all, and which must die out such as it is, without leaving any varieties behind it. But the same cannot be

* Derenbourg, "Note Sur la Grammaire Arabe," première partie, Théorie des Formes. Paris, 1869.
† *Op. cit.*, iv. ch. 2. ‡ *Ibid.*

said of the spoken tongue, which, however little differing from the other, differs from it precisely by one of those changes that constitute the very life of so many languages—that is, the transition from the synthetic to the analytic state. Vulgar Arabic grows, no doubt, very slowly, but still it grows; whence its present dialectic varieties, which are mainly four, those of Barbary, Arabia, Syria, and Egypt. The last three are allowed to differ but slightly, each possessing a number of local terms and peculiar expressions, but the divergence goes no farther. The Barbary dialect presents some grammatical differences, though not serious enough to prevent it from being readily understood throughout the whole domain occupied by the Arabic language.

Maltese is of Arabic origin, but is now nothing but a rude jargon full of real barbarisms and foreign elements. The same was the case with the *Mosarabic* of the south of Spain, which seems not to have quite died out till the last century.*

Arabic has supplied a large number of words to certain European and Asiatic languages. This is particularly true of the Iranian idioms, including the present Persian, of the Turkish, and of some modern Indian dialects, which swarm with Arabic words. Amongst the neo-Latin tongues Spanish and Portuguese have borrowed both directly and indirectly from it, and amongst the Arabic words in English and French may be mentioned the following: cotton, zero, cipher, algebra, crimson, magazine, nadir, chemistry, &c. (See Translator's "English Language," p. 164.)

(2) *Languages of South Arabia and Abyssinia.*

The second branch of the Arabic group, known also as the "Yoktanide," is composed of two branches, which it took some time to classify not merely with the Arabic, but even with the Semitic at all. It occupies on the east the south of Arabia, and on the west at least a portion of Abyssinia.

The primitive Semitic language of the south of Arabia was the *Himyaritic*, now known by a large number of inscriptions. It possesses, like the Arabic, the peculiar form of "broken," plurals

* Renan, *op. cit.*

already spoken of. Its alphabet has given occasion to some interesting researches. It is now known to derive from the primitive Semitic writing, from which, as we have seen, have also sprung the Chaldean, Arabic, and, in fact, all the Semitic alphabets except the Assyrian cuneiforms.

The Mohammedan conquest overthrew the Himyaritic civilisation, and Arabic spread gradually throughout the south of the peninsula, as far as the shores of the Indian Ocean and the Gulf of Aden. Still the Himyaritic language did not perish without leaving some traces behind. In the extreme south of Arabia, and more particularly in the Mahrah district, about 50° long. and 20° lat., some forty years ago there was discovered the *Ehkili* language, which, if not a lineal descendant of the old Himyaritic, is at least closely allied to it.

From a very remote period the Semites of South Arabia had known and colonised the south-west coast of the Red Sea. Many centuries before our era, though at what particular date it is now impossible to say, they brought thither, together with their civilisation, the language known as the *Gheez*, sometimes also called by the vague and misleading name of *Ethiopian*, whose forms are intimately related to those of the Himyaritic. The Gheez is now no longer spoken, and exists only as a learned and liturgical language. Christianity is known to have spread over Ethiopia towards the fourth century, to which period must also in all probability be referred the Gheez version of the Bible, besides which, Ethiopian literature is enriched by translations of a number of Jewish, Christian, Greek, and Arabic works. With the arrival of the Jesuits in Abyssinia set in the period of decay. Those formidable apostles, whom the Abyssinians got rid of only too late, "by attracting to themselves all the instruction and opposing the native teaching, left the country in a state of profound barbarism, from which it has not yet recovered."*

Gheez was a highly-developed language, possessing, like the Arabic, the "broken" plurals, and retaining certain endings that Hebrew and Aramean have lost. Of the fifteen primitive forms of

* Renan, *op. cit.*, iv. ch. 1.

the Semitic verb it preserved thirteen (Fr. Müller, *op. cit.*, p. 529), that is, far more than any of the cognate tongues. The Gheez alphabet, though written from left to right, and not from right to left, like the other Semitic alphabets, is now known to have derived from the same source as the Himyaritic.

Besides the Gheez, which, as stated, is now a dead language, there are still spoken in Abyssinia a number of Semitic idioms belonging to the same group, and which, if they do not derive directly from it, are at least closely related to Gheez. Of these there are three leading languages: the *Amharic*, in the south-west of Abyssinia; the *Tigré*, in the north; and the *Harari*, in the south-east, at about 40° long. and 10° lat. These have, perhaps, been grafted on to older languages belonging to other families, but their grammar is unquestionably Semitic, so that they must necessarily be grouped with the Gheez.*

§ 7.—*Individuality of the Semitic Idioms.*

Their Primeval Home.

Much greater pains have been, and still are, taken to find a common link between the Aryan and the Semitic families, than to compare the various members of this last group together, and thus restore, at least in its general outlines, the common mother-tongue of all the Semitic languages. It may be presumed that, considering the slight differences that exist between them, this task may, in the present state of our knowledge, not prove too formidable. In any case it must prove far less so than the analogous undertaking on behalf of the Aryan tongues, which has so far been attended with so little success.

It need scarcely be observed that the writers who have been most zealous in their endeavours to compare the Semitic with the Aryan group have never thought of the obvious objection, that they should not compare Hebrew or Arabic with Zend, Sanskrit, or Greek, but rather the common Semitic with the common Aryan mother-tongue. All the points of resemblance they have sought

* Fr. Müller, "Ueber die Harari-Sprache im östlichen Africa." Vienna, 1864.

to establish may be said always to rely on etymologies, and never on grammar: and this alone at once and hopelessly condemns them. Etymology, as shown in our first chapter, is in no sense a science. By means of it we might easily derive the most irreconcilable languages one from the other—not only Basque from Irish, Etruscan from Tibetan, but even Hebrew from Sanskrit, or Sanskrit from Hebrew, at pleasure. It is grammar, as Renan has well said, that constitutes the individuality of a language; hence "the attempt must be abandoned to establish a connecting link between the Aryan and Semitic grammatical systems, which are two distinct creations, absolutely separated from each other."—(*Op. cit.*, v. ch. 2.)

When speaking of inflection in general (p. 147), we remarked upon the deep and radical difference that existed between the Semitic and Aryan grammar. Here it will be enough to repeat that the pretended relations sought to be established between them are reduced to some futile etymologies, lacking all scientific character. All such facts, past, present, and future, would be at once outweighed by one single argument drawn from the formation of the words themselves.

Two principal causes seem to have been at the bottom of the unscientific conception of the common origin of the Aryan and Semitic tongues. The first of these lies in the nationality, or rather in the race itself, of a certain class of writers that have upheld this opinion. Without quoting names, the fact is known well enough that a great many of them are Jews; which will account for much of the spirit pervading their writings. The second cause lies in the biblical, or clerical feeling, the spirit of infatuation and medieval darkness, which sees nothing true except in theology, and which begins by denouncing free and secular inquiry, while ever ready at the last moment to turn round and cry out that all knowledge proceeds from it, and from it alone. But with this second cause we need not trouble ourselves, for discussion is out of place with people who proclaim themselves inspired and above reason. The motive, however, is easily understood that induces these champions of Holy Writ to attribute to all the languages of the universe one common source, and more particularly to associate them directly or indirectly with the assumed speech of the father of the Jewish race. But, as Scripture itself says, we must let the dead bury their dead.

It is difficult to pronounce dogmatically on the question of the region in which was spoken the common mother-tongue of all the Semitic idioms. The Aramæans and Canaanites are generally allowed to have entered Palestine from the south-east, but it would, perhaps, be wise to venture on nothing further. Some more daring writers assume that this common speech—whence sprang the Aramæan, Canaanite, and Arabic—was spoken in the north of Arabia, or, perhaps, in central Arabia. The fact, of course, is possible, but so far utterly unsupported by any sort of positive proof.*

Questions of this sort must always remain obscure, nor can they be solved by philology alone without the aid of anthropology and archeology.

(B) *The Hamitic Languages.*

It is needless to say that the expression *Hamitic* is quite as defective as *Semitic*. But it seems now consecrated by use, and we have been fain to adopt it for lack of a better. The term "Libyan" has indeed been proposed, but it says too little, and is applicable to one division only of the Hamitic family.

However probable in itself, it is difficult to assert positively that the Hamitic tongues, spread over most of Egypt and along the southern shores of the Mediterranean, did at any time occupy the regions of the Euphrates and Tigris, thence making their way through Syria, Palestine, and Arabia Petræa into Africa.

Still less, if possible, is known as to the country in which the Hamitic broke away from the Semitic family. All that can be said on the subject is that the separation must have taken place at a very remote epoch. The stability of the Semitic idioms in their old forms throughout the historic period speaks at once for the

---

* The whole question has been fully discussed by Schrader in "Die Abstammung der Chaldäer und die Ursitze der Semiten," "Zeitschr. der Deutschen Morgenländ. Gesellschaft," xxxvii. Leipzig, 1873.

great antiquity of the time when Semitic and Hamitic were yet to be, but when a now forever lost language did exist, whence both would some day spring.

In his "Allgemeine Ethnographie" (p. 445) Fr. Müller well describes the relations that existed between the two. Their affinity, he justly remarks, is rather in the identity of the organism than in the coincidence of fully-developed forms. The two families must have separated at a time when their common mother-tongue was still in a very backward state of development. Moreover, the Hamitic group seems at a very early date to have split into two branches, the various idioms of which are far less allied to each other than is the case with the different members of the Semitic group.

The pronominal system of the two families has been mainly instrumental in establishing their affinity, the roots of their pronouns and the process of forming the plural by means of an ending being identical in both;* a fact which has now been thoroughly ascertained.

In the philological section of "The Voyage of the Novara round the World" (Vienna, 1867), Fr. Müller has essayed to draw a somewhat summary outline of the general Hamitic grammar. In the nouns the feminine is characterised by the element *ti, t*; the plural sign is, in principle, *an*, sometimes *ut*, and occasionally *u*, which may be merely a secondary form of *an*. There is in this group no trace of nominal inflection properly so called, its place being supplied by particles placed either before or after the noun, to express the usual relations of the noun to the rest of the phrase.

Verbal forms are numerous, as in the Semitic group, and the tense system is equally elementary, as will presently be seen.

The three Hamitic groups, as stated, are: the *Egyptian*, the *Libyan*, and the *Ethiopian*. And first—

§ 1.—*The Egyptian Group.*

It was at the beginning of the present century that the ancient

* Maspero, "Des Pronoms Personnels en Égyptien et dans les Langues Sémitiques." Paris, 1872.

Egyptian hieroglyphics were again deciphered, after having remained a dead letter for many hundreds of years. Their interpretation has shed a lustre on the name of Champollion, who, if not the only expounder of these precious texts (having, in fact, been anticipated by Young), has undoubtedly done more than any other for their rapid elucidation.

Here let us premise a few words on the nature of these hieroglyphics.*

The number of these characters is considerable, some being phonetic, others figurative. The phonetic signs are easily transcribed in Roman letters, though the Egyptians themselves often wrote the consonants only, omitting the vowels of the word. Still these may generally be easily restored, either from the context or by comparing the word in question with the word answering to it in the Coptic language, of which we shall have presently to speak. Let us add that the phonetic signs may be either simply alphabetical—that is, expressing, for instance, one consonant only—or else syllabic—that is, denoting a full syllable. But in either case their transcription is, of course, equally easy.

The figurative signs are true images, or pictures, and are placed at the end of words written in phonetic letters, their object being to determine more precisely the sense of these words. At times, however, the text contains none but figurative characters, and then they present a serious difficulty to the reader, who, in such cases, must have recourse to any possible duplicates of such texts.

In Egyptian there are two genders, the masculine and the feminine, the latter being denoted by the characteristic suffix *t*. Thus *son* = brother; *sont* = sister. Observe, however, that this *t* may also be placed before the noun.

The dual endings are: *ui* masculine, *ti* feminine; *sonui* = two brothers.

The plural is *u* for both genders: *sonu* = brothers, *teju* = fathers, from *son* and *tef*.

Of declension properly so-called there is no trace.

The article is occasionally used, especially in the more recent

* Brugsch, "Grammaire Hiéroglyphique." Leipzig, 1872.

language. It is *pa* or *pe* for the singular masculine, *ta* or *te* for the feminine. Thus *nuter* = god; *nutert* = goddess; *pa nuter* = the god; *ta nutert* = the goddess. In the plural *na* or *ne* for both genders: *na nuteru* = the gods.

The adjective, as a rule, immediately follows its noun, agreeing with it in gender and number: *sat urt* = elder daughter; *amu nru* = great masters, where in the first example *t* marks the feminine singular, in the second *u* denotes the plural.

The subject is placed sometimes before the verb, but the usual order is—verb, subject, direct object, indirect object, adverb.

In the verbal forms the personal element is suffixed:

> Uonk = thou art (masculine).
> Uont = thou art (feminine).
> Uouf = he is.
> Uons = she is.
> Uouten = you are.
> Uouu = they are.

At the opening of this paragraph we spoke of the *hieroglyphic* writing only. But it will be easily imagined that this system must have been simplified in course of time, becoming considerably modified in order to adapt itself to the wants of every-day life. Thus arose the two cursive writing systems known as the *hieratic* and *demotic*. In his second book Herodotus speaks of the twofold Egyptian writing—the sacred and the popular. The hieratic, running from right to left, is merely a cursive and often much shortened form of the old hieroglyphics. It is seldom met with on the granite monuments, and occurs mostly on the papyrus documents. It was the learned and religious writing, of which the demotic itself was in its turn a more curtailed form, though still containing a number of real ideographic signs. This was the popular style, employed in transcribing the language in current use,[*] a language which helps to explain many differences between the old Egyptian and the Coptic.

Coptic derives directly from the ancient Egyptian, its literary period extending from the second to the seventh century of our

---

[*] Brugsch, "Grammaire Démotique." Berlin, 1855.

era. It is a purely Christian, though somewhat copious, literature, brought to a sudden close by Islamism, which ruined the Coptic language, supplanting it by the Arabic wherever it was still vernacular. It continued, however, for some time to eke out a precarious existence in some few monasteries, but is now quite extinct.

Coptic phonology was richer than the old Egyptian, though its grammar did not greatly differ from it. Any one familiar with Coptic may easily learn Egyptian, or *vice versâ*, though the Coptic vocabulary includes rather a large number of Greek words. As in Egyptian, Coptic marks the feminine by prefixing *t* to the noun; and we have seen that the old language could use this element as a prefix as well as a suffix. The plural sign is *u*, also as in Egyptian; but there is a second form, *i*, which may combine with the first: *sbô* = teaching; *sbôui* = teachings. Of cases there are no traces, their want being supplied by prepositions.

The Coptic verb possesses the twofold formation of prefixes and suffixes, which may easily be compared with the double Semitic formation above spoken of. But to the two Coptic forms no special value can be attributed, such as can be to the Semitic.*
Thus the masculine pronoun *k* = thou, is sometimes prefixed to the verbal theme, and sometimes suffixed, without any apparent difference of meaning. The different tenses, past, future, &c., are distinguished by means of auxiliary verbs placed before the verbal theme.

The Coptic alphabet is nothing but the Greek, written somewhat in a fuller and rounder form, and occasionally slightly inclined backwards to the left. To this alphabet, however, have been added some characters to denote sounds peculiar to the Coptic, and unknown to the Greek, such as the *sh* of *she*.

In Coptic there are distinguished three dialects—the *Memphitic*, which possessed the aspirates *kh*, *th*, *ph*; the *Theban* in the south, and a northern dialect.

---

* Fr. Müller, "Reise der Oesterr. Fregatte Novara, Linguistischer Theil," p. 63. Vienna, 1867.

§ 2.—*The Libyan Group*.

The ancient Libya occupied the north of Africa west of Egypt, and it was in this region that the Punic, or Phœnician of Africa, found a home. The grammar of the ancient Libyan has not yet been compiled, but it is beginning to be known through its inscriptions. Of these, General Faidherbe has recently published an important collection, about 200 altogether, including several bilingual ones, one accompanied by a Phœnician text, and others by a Latin.*

The present Libyan is known by no generally received name, though that of *Berber* may perhaps become ultimately adopted. Those of *Kabyle*, *Ta-masheq*, and many others are merely the names of particular dialects, which cannot therefore be applied to the whole group.†

It is difficult to define the limits of the *Berber* language. It seems to occupy the whole country to the south of Tripoli, Tunis, Algeria, and Morocco, at certain points reaching even to the coast, as in Algeria, from Dellys to Bugi, and even farther east (Kabyl), between Tenes and Shershel.‡

The phonetic system of the various Berber dialects is tolerably rich in consonants. As in the other Hamitic tongues, *t* is the sign of the feminine, placed occasionally at the beginning only, but more usually both prefixed and suffixed at once. Thus, *akli* = negro; *ekahi* = cock; but *taklit* = negress; *tekahit* = hen; *amaher* = a Tuareg; *tamaher* = a Tuareg woman. The Berber verb has one form only, a sort of aorist to which a present or future idea is imparted by purely accessory processes.

A number of Arabic words have crept into the Berber dialects,

---

* "Collection Complète des Inscriptions Numidiques," "Mémoires de la Soc. des Sciences . . . de Lille," 3rd series, viii. p. 361. Paris, Lille, 1870.

† Yet these terms are constantly so misapplied by English philologists. Thus, a writer in a recent number of *The Saturday Review*, otherwise usually so correct, speaks of "the Berbers, or Amazighs," as convertible terms. June 17, 1876, p. 767.—*Note by Translator*.

‡ Hanoteau, "Essai de Grammaire de la Langue Tamachek," in fine. Paris, 1869.

and, with the exception of the Ta-masheq, they have all lost whatever special graphic systems they may have ever possessed. The Ta-masheq, composed of tolerably regular characters, is difficult to read, the vowels not being expressed nor the words separated in writing. To decipher it one must therefore, in the first place, be acquainted with the language itself.

M. Hanoteau estimates the Berbers of Algeria at upwards of 855,000, of which 500,000 are in the Government of Constantine alone. How many there may be in the regions stretching south from Algeria it is impossible to say.

It may be stated in conclusion that the language of the Guanches, the aboriginals of the Canaries, was connected with the Libyan group.*

§ 3.—*The Ethiopian Group.*

The idioms composing this group, which has not yet been very well defined, are not to be confused with the Semitic tongues of Abyssinia, such as the Tigré, Amharic, and others above spoken of. These latter have sometimes been called Ethiopian, whence the confusion; to avoid which we reserve this name, as is now generally done, for the Hamitic branch of the languages of Central Africa spoken towards the south of Egypt.

Of this group there are six principal members:

Somáli, in the extreme eastern point of the continent, stretching south from the Straits of Bab-el-Mandeb nearly to the Equator.

Galla, west of Somáli, south of Abyssinia, and north of the Bantu system.

Beja, spoken by the Hadendoas, and by some of the Beni-Amer, between the Nile and the Red Sea, north of Abyssinia.

Saho, *Dankáli* and *Agáü*, in western Abyssinia.

The classification, however, of these idioms is not yet settled, and all that can for the present be done is to group them together in connection with the Hamitic family, to which they clearly belong.

* Sabin Berthelot, "Mémoire sur les Guanches," deuxième partie, "Mémoires de la Soc. Ethnologique," ii. p. 77. Paris, 1845.

Thus in *Beja* the feminine element is *t*, which, as in Egyptian, may be placed either before or after the noun. Thus the masculine suffix *b* is replaced by *t* in the forms *erab* = albus ; *erat* = alba. At times the feminine element occurs both at the beginning and end of the word.

In Ta-masheq the verbal causative sign is *s*: *erhin* = to be ill ; *serhin* = to make ill. In Beja it is *es*: *edlüb* = to sell ; *esdelüb* = to cause to sell. In *Galla*, *za*: *gua* = to be dry ; *guaza* = to make dry.

So with conjugation itself, where in *Saho*, as in Coptic, we have a form in which the personal element precedes, and another in which it follows the root. It precedes it in *nekke* = we were, and follows it in *kino* = we are (*ne-kke*, *ki-no*). So with the Galla: *gigna* = we went, and *nefdeg* = we lost (*gig-na*, *ne-fdeg*), where the first is a perfect, the second an aorist, or indefinite form. The process is analogous to that employed by the Semitic tongues in like circumstances.

(C) *The Aryan Languages.*

We shall have to enter into fuller details concerning this important family than we have given of any others, and the reason must be obvious enough. Their importance is immense from every point of view. They serve nowadays as the instruments of modern culture after having been the interpreters of most of the older civilisations. No forms of speech have lived so much, if not as regards the actual term of their existence, at least in respect of the manifold periods that they have passed through.

Another consideration interests us in a special manner. The Aryan tongues alone possess a real comparative grammar. While the grammar of the Semitic family has still to be compiled, that of the Aryan is already nearly complete, not merely in its grand outlines and general features, but in a vast number of minor details.

A man of genius, Bopp, was the first to demonstrate the identity of the great bulk of the Aryan tongues. He did not live definitely to codify their phonetic laws, their processes of word-formation, and his "Comparative Grammar" is now merely a historical monument, though his name is not the less permanently associated with one of the discoveries that do honour to the nineteenth century.

In all his writings Bopp had aimed at establishing the close affinity of Sanskrit, Zend, Persian, Greek, Latin, the Keltic, Teutonic, Slavonic, and Lithuanian groups. This great truth once thoroughly secured, the science of the Aryan tongues made new and rapid strides. From the affinity of all these idioms some older form was assumed, whence they all sprang; a form, doubtless, extremely remote, and lost for ever, but which might possibly be restored. And here it is but just to mention two names, those of Schleicher and Chavée, which the science of language never can overlook without ingratitude. To them we owe the first realisation of the fruitful conception of a common primeval Aryan mother-tongue. In the introduction to an important work published nearly thirty years ago, Chavée was able to write: "These languages are for the philologist merely varieties of some one primeval form of speech formerly spoken in central Asia. Convinced of this truth, we have undertaken to restore the words of this primitive language organically, by everywhere re-establishing the original type by means of its better preserved varieties."* This contains the very essence of the modern science of language. Schleicher, in his turn, produced that admirable manual, which may doubtless be revised, supplemented, improved, but which must still ever remain the foundation of Aryan philological studies.†

§ 1.—*The Common Aryan Mother-Tongue.*

Before speaking of the various members of this family, and inquiring into the degree of affinity that knits them together, we must sketch a general outline of the common mother-tongue that gave birth to these different idioms. It is sufficiently known in its main features to enable us to reproduce its general characteristics, and at times to go even still farther. It is, indeed, merely a language

* "Lexicologie Indo-Européenne." Paris, 1849.
† "Compendium der Vergleichenden Grammatik der Indo-Germanischen Sprachen," 3rd edition (posthumous). Weimar, 1871.

that has been restored, and of which there remains no written record. But the comparison of the various idioms sprung from it shows clearly enough wherein consist the organic and primitive elements of each, what they still possess of the common inheritance, and what we are to think of their phonetic variations and diverse forms, much in the same way as a classical scholar is enabled to restore the original form of a lost manuscript, of which there may exist only a certain number of defective or imperfect copies.

The common Aryan speech possessed the three vowels, *a, i, u*, with their corresponding long sounds, *ā, ī, ū*. Sanskrit, and certain Slavonic tongues, such as Croatian, have a lingual *r* vowel-sound, which is usually considered as quite secondary. But some writers, with whom we agree, believe that the common tongue also possessed a vowel *r*,* though the matter being still controverted, it need not further detain us here.

An important fact to be noted is the variation of the radical vowel, which occurs in two ways. The first is what is called the "gradation" of the vowel, consisting in the introduction of a short *a* before the radical vowel, the radical *i* thus becoming *ai*. *u* becoming *au*, and *a* becoming *ā*, that is *aa*. Thus the root *I* to go, gives in the indicative present the organic form *aiti* = he goes, whence the Sanskrit *éti*, the Latin *it* for *eit*, the Lithuanian *eiti*. It is now difficult to say whether this first variation of the radical vowel was the only one known to the common Aryan tongue, or whether it had also another, consisting in a fresh insertion of the vowel *a*, whence *āi, āu*, for *aai, aau*.

It is no less difficult to understand in what way this modification of the radical vowel effects certain changes in the sense of the word itself. Have we here a real inflection in the strict sense, an internal modification of the root, such as has been above described? It may be so, but it has not yet been clearly proved.

There can, however, be no doubt that the second process of vowel change is a true inflection. It consists in the change of the

* "Mémoire sur la Prononciation et la Primordialité du 'R' Vocal Sanskrit." Paris, 1872.

vowel *a* of the pronominal elements *ta, ma,* to *i, u*; these elements, which were previously passive, thus acquiring an active force. This will be made clear by an example. Take the root *ma* = to think, to which may be suffixed the demonstrative *ta,* as a derivative element, producing *mata* = thought, the thing thought of. Now, if the vowel of the derivative pronoun become *i*, the sense becomes active, *mati* meaning the act of thinking. These are the Sanskrit forms *mata-, mati-*. No more striking instance could be given of true inflection, that is of the process of changing the relational sense of a root by means of an internal modification of the root itself.

The common Aryan consonantal system was extremely simple, consisting of the three explosives *k, t, p,* of their corresponding softs *g, d, b,* and of the aspirates *gh, dh, bh,* making altogether nine explosives. Besides these the two nasals *n, m,* one dental, the other labial, the liquid *r*, the dental sibilant *s*, and a *r*, uttered doubtless as is our *r* (and not as *w*, as has been supposed). Had it been so pronounced it would have been a semi-vowel, and not a consonant. The system, however, did possess the semi-vowel *y*.

Here then was a system simple enough in itself, and to which the various Aryan tongues have added more or less. The Indian, Iranian, and Slavonic groups developed the so-called palatal sibilants *sh, j,* and various kinds of sibilants. The Hellenic changed the soft aspirates *gh, dh, bh,* to the corresponding sharps, *kh, th, ph*; while the Teutonic, Latin, and Keltic groups remained more faithful to the original consonantal system, though these also produced some new sounds, as, for instance, *f*. The liquid *l* was unknown to the common Aryan speech, this sound developing itself more or less rapidly out of the old liquid *r* throughout all the branches of the family.

We shall not dwell at any length on the Aryan process of word-formation, which is extremely simple, being effected generally by suffixing an element of pronominal origin to one of verbal origin, as in *mata-, mati-*, above quoted. The hyphen attached to this word denotes that it represents a radical form only, or, in other words, that it constitutes merely a simple theme. We shall presently see how the case and personal suffixes are added to the theme, thus making it a true word—that is, either a declined noun or a conjugated verb. Derivation is said to be on a verbal basis, when the element to which the derivative element is attached is a verbal root. In the same way it is said to rest on a pronominal basis when the derived element is itself a pronominal root; a case which, though less frequent than the other, is far from rare. An instance is the theme AIKA, whence the Sanskrit *ēka* = one, one alone, one and the same, and the Latin *æquo-*, in the nominative singular masculine *æquus* = equal, united. Here the derivative element is the pronoun KA = who, and the derived element is the determining pronoun I (the Latin *is, id*), which has become *ai* by "gradation," that is by *a* being prefixed, as above explained.

Let us add, that derivation may also be effected by means of a verbal instead of a pronominal element, though this is of much rarer occurrence. But it should be carefully noted that in all cases derivation always takes place in the Aryan tongues by means of suffixes, and never by prefixes, and this is a characteristic feature of the family.

The common Aryan declension included the three genders—masculine, feminine, and neuter; the three numbers—singular, dual, and plural; and eight cases—thus being in every respect more complex than the Semitic system of declension.

The gender is denoted, in principle, by the case-ending itself. Thus, in themes ending in *a*, the element of the nominative case singular is *s*, which in the neuter is *m*, the same as the accusative. Thus AKVAS = horse (Sanskrit, *açvas*; Latin, *equus*); YUGAM = yoke (Sanskrit, *yugam*; Latin, *jugum*). The plural sign follows, in principle, that of the case; but this sign is not always the same, and it is often very difficult to discover its primitive form. In many cases it is simply the consonant *s*, the remnant of an element formerly seen in its integral form.

It must not be forgotten that these suffixes—some indicating case, others number—were originally independent forms, which in course of time became merely secondary elements, adapted to indicate the relations and manner of being of other roots. But the numerous attempts to discover the primitive form of these elements have hitherto remained without any definite results. Many more or less probable conjectures have been proposed, but the problem remains still to be solved.

The common Aryan noun had, as stated, eight cases—two direct, the nominative and accusative; and six indirect, the locative, dative, ablative, genitive, and a twofold instrumental. The organic form of these suffixes was in the singular, as follows: Nominative, s, generally persisting, but in the derived languages occasionally disappearing, in virtue of certain euphonic laws; accusative of themes ending in a consonant, AM, of those ending in a vowel, M, as in the Latin *sororem*, where the theme is *soror*, and in *sitim*, where the theme is *siti*; locative singular, I, which we shall see has passed in Greek to the dative, and in Latin has not been quite lost; dative singular, AI, strictly retained by Zend and the Indian languages only; ablative, sometimes AT, sometimes T; genitive, usually AS, occasionally S, and when the theme ends in A, SYA. The first instrumental *ā*, the second *bhi*.

These various endings are applied to all nouns substantive, adjective, and participial, which threefold division has nothing to do with the form itself of the word, with which we are now concerned. The vocative is not, strictly speaking, a case at all, being in principle the same in form as the theme itself: AKVA = O horse; AVI = O sheep; AGNI = O fire. But in course of time certain Aryan tongues have sometimes assimilated it to the nominative, or, to speak more correctly, have sometimes used the nominative in a vocative sense.

The Aryan verb has two voices, one transitive—I hear, I strike; the other intransitive—I hear myself, I strike myself; both, however, being active. These different senses are expressed by the pronominal element placed at the end of the verbal theme. In other words, there are two kinds of personal suffixes—transitive and intransitive. Thus, in the third person singular, for instance, the suffix of the transitive voice is TI, and of the intransitive TAI, where we recognise the Greek form ται of the voice spoken of by the grammarians as passive, which in Greek really has this sense, but the primitive meaning of which was simply intransitive or reflective. There is no doubt that the personal suffixes of the intransitive voice derive from those of the transitive, that of the first person evidently meaning *I myself*; that of the second, *thou thyself*; and that of the third, *he himself*, in Latin *ego me*, *tu te, ille se*. This point has not yet been definitely settled, but it is hard to believe that it will not be sooner or later.

While the Semitic system possessed two tenses only, one expressing complete, the other incomplete action, the common Aryan tongue had six, four simple and two compound tenses.

The simplest form of the *present* is the theme itself, followed by the personal suffix. At times the root vowel has been augmented in the manner already explained, as when the root I = to go, becomes AI: AITI = he goes (Sanskrit *êti*, Lithuanian *eiti*). At times the verbal root itself is derived. Thus, in the case of a complex form, such as *bhara*, where *bhar* is radical and *a* derivative, we shall get the present *bharati* = he bears. But in any case the present is always a simple tense, whether the root itself or some derivative form of it is to be conjugated.

The *imperfect* is formed by prefixing the augment A to the present theme, whether it be simple or derived, the personal endings being further shortened, *ti* of the third, to *t*, and *mi* of the first, to *m*. Thus from the present BHARATI = he bears, we get the imperfect ABHARAT = he was bearing.

The *simple aorist*, like the imperfect, is denoted by the augment and the personal endings contracted, being distinguished from the imperfect by its departure from the form of the present. In Greek, for instance, the root, θε = to put, is doubled in the present, giving τιθετε = you put; to this reduplicate form the imperfect prefixes the augment, making ετιθετε = you were putting. But the simple aorist disregards the reduplication, making εθετε.

The *perfect* is characterised by reduplication of the root. To these four tenses there are added, as stated, two compound ones, of which one is the *future*, which is composed of the verbal root and an element ASYA, SYA, whose primitive sense seems to have been that of "aiming at," whence the Sanskrit *dâsyati* = he will give.

The compound aorist, preserved by Sanskrit, Zend, the Slavonic tongues, and Greek (this last under the name of first aorist), is characterised by the element SA.

In the common Aryan tongue these six tenses are completed by three moods—the indicative, conjunctive, and optative. The indicative has no characteristic, here the tenses remaining in their simple form. The conjunctive is marked by an A placed between the theme and the personal suffix; thus the indicative present being ASTI = he is, the conjunctive will be ASATI. The optative, sometimes called potential, is formed by inserting the element YA, YÂ, between the verbal theme and the contracted personal suffix: ASYÂT = may he be!

The table here presented of the different organic forms of the primitive Aryan system is doubtless but little developed. We trust, however, that it may suffice to convey some idea of the general spirit of this system. When we come to speak of the different members of the Aryan family, it will be impossible for us to do more than point out, in a summary way, what each of them has preserved or lost of the common inheritance; but enough has already been stated to show, at least in a general way, the nature and the wealth of this inheritance.*

The Aryan family is divided into eight great branches: The *Indic*, *Iranic*, *Hellenic*, *Italic*, *Keltic*, *Teutonic*, *Slavonic*, and *Lettic*. These we shall now pass in successive review, noticing their special features, the sub-divisions of each, their history and their literature. We shall have also to inquire into the degree of affinity by which certain branches of this great family may be more closely related to each other, and shall, in conclusion, devote a few words to the region where in all probability the Aryan mother-tongue was spoken.

* Here follow some remarks on the terms "Indo-Germanic," "Indo-European," and "Aryan," by which this family has been variously known. The writer, on very insufficient grounds, rejects "Aryan," and retains "Indo-European" for want of a better. But, the question having been practically settled in Germany and England, and, indeed, in France itself, in favour of "Aryan," the passage has been omitted, and Aryan everywhere substituted for Indo-European in this translation.—*Note by Translator.*

§ 2.—*The Indic Branch.*

As early as the sixteenth century, an Italian named Filippo Sassetti drew attention to Sanskrit, the old and sacred language of the Hindus, going so far as to compare certain words of his own mother-tongue with it.* Two hundred years thereafter, towards the end of the eighteenth century, the friar Paulinus a Sancto Bartholomaeo published at Rome the first Sanskrit grammar composed in a European language. Some years previously, the Frenchmen Cœurdoux and Barthélemy, had communicated to the Academy their views on the affinity of Sanskrit with Latin and Greek. Lastly, the works of a great number of Englishmen, amongst whom, Sir William Jones, Colebrooke, Carey, Wilkins, prepared the way for and rendered possible the really fundamental work of Bopp.

It was on Sanskrit that the whole structure of Aryan comparative grammar was now based. Not that this old language could be regarded, even in its most ancient monuments, as the common mother of the Iranian, Greek, Latin, Slave, and other members of the same family; but it departed, on the whole, far less than any of them from the now lost tongue, from which they all equally sprang. Greek, Latin, and their congeners, no more derive from Sanskrit than do Hebrew and Phœnician from Arabic. Hence the term "Sanskritic," as sometimes applied to the Aryan tongues, is altogether out of place. Doubtless the Sanskrit forms are often more correct and better preserved than those of the cognate tongues, but these last, in their turn, often surpass the Sanskrit in these respects, approaching more closely to the common type whence all derive. And what is here stated is quite as applicable to the Sanskrit of the Vedas as it is to the classic Sanskrit (of a later period).

The Indic branch embraces, after all, one class only of idioms, but of these some are very old, while others are still spoken; hence we shall discuss them under two separate headings.

* "Lettere," p. 415 and following. Florence, 1855.

(1) *The Ancient Hindu Languages.*

The word *Sanskrta* means "perfect, finished;" hence the Sanskrit is the perfect, the finished language. This name was given to it in contrast with the term *prākrta*, which means "natural," and is applied to the old vernacular, or, to speak more correctly, to the various dialects of the vulgar tongue. Sanskrit had become the language of religion, law, and letters, while Prākrit was the current popular form of speech, which was not at first a written language at all.

Sanskrit possessed the vowels a, i, u, long and short, the lingual vowels r, l, the first of these also long, $\bar{e}$ and $\bar{o}$ representing the old diphthongs ai and au; lastly, the diphthongs $\bar{a}i$ and $\bar{a}u$. Its consonantal system was rich; besides the explosives k, t, p, g, d, b, comprising the palatal explosives ch and j, and some linguo-dental explosives, borrowed seemingly from the Dravidian family, and usually transcribed by a t and a d, with a dot underneath. Moreover, while the only aspirates known to the common Aryan tongue were gh, dh, bh, Sanskrit possessed, side by side with each simple explosive, its corresponding aspirate, as, for instance, kh, th, ph, making altogether twenty explosives, of which ten were simple and ten aspirate. The common Aryan tongue had only two nasals, m and n, while Sanskrit had one for each order of its consonants, a labial, a linguo-dental, &c., five altogether. Instead of a simple sibilant, s, it had four, besides an aspirate h, and lastly y and v.

The Sanskrit euphonic laws are very intricate, and can be mastered only by long practice. They are exceedingly strict, and while depending in general on perfectly intelligible acoustic principles, they may be said to be characterised at times by an almost excessive nicety of utterance, which it is somewhat difficult to understand.* The euphony of the Slavonic tongues, with all its delicacy, is far from being so nice as that of the Sanskrit, in comparison with which, that of Latin and Greek is no more than an essay of a very rudimentary nature.

* In our "Euphonic Sanskrite," we have endeavoured to draw up as simple a scheme of them as possible. Paris, 1872.

On the other hand, the formation of the words offers no very great difficulty, owing to the high state of preservation in which the language still exists. The elements entering into the derivation of the words are far more easily detected in Sanskrit than in any of the cognate tongues, the (old) Iranic idioms alone perhaps excepted.

The Sanskrit declension may be said, on the whole, to represent the common Aryan system very closely. The greatest discrepancy between the scheme of a Sanskrit declension and that of the corresponding organic form would be connected with the euphonic modifications to which Sanskrit is subject. Not however that, apart from this, its declension can be said to be perfectly organic. Thus, it preserves the true form of the ablative singular in those nouns only whose theme ends in *a*; hence the old Latin form *senatud*, *navaled*, and others, have nothing analogous to them in Sanskrit. But this, on the whole, is but an exceptional case, and Sanskrit declension may, speaking generally, be said to reflect faithfully enough that of the common mother-tongue whence it flows. In this respect it unquestionably surpasses the ancient Iranian declension, though this also is fairly well preserved.

Sanskrit retains the six organic Aryan tenses, present, imperfect, simple aorist, perfect, future, compound aorist, to which it has added the conditional, a new creation of its own. This conditional is nothing but the future with the augment prefixed, and its personal suffixes contracted. Thus, from *bhôtsyati* = he will know, we get *abhôtsyat* = he might or would know. The Sanskrit conditional is therefore to the future what the imperfect is to the present.

The ancient Vedic language differs relatively but little from the classic tongue; that is, the Sanskrit of the Hindu epics, the points of divergence in no way affecting the essence or constitution of the language, so that it would be impossible to dwell on this subject without entering into a series of needless details.

The Hindu graphic system, known as the *Devanāgari*, or "divine writing," is composed of some fifty simple characters, read from left to right, and of a multiplicity of complex signs, containing two or three simple letters blended together. It has the great advantage of being able to be transcribed in Roman letters, furnished with the necessary diacritical marks. A consonant in principle is never read alone, being always followed by an inherent vowel *a*, unless some secondary sign denote that the vowel thus following is other than *a*. If a word end in a consonant and the next begin with a vowel, the two words are connected in writing; a difficulty which, with some others equally serious, renders the *Devanāgari* of little practical use.

The oldest Hindu inscriptions were cut on rock surfaces, about the third century before our era. The origin of these characters seems now fairly established, and it is generally connected with the old Phœnician alphabet above explained.* The Hindu alphabet did not remain confined to a corner of India, but is now, under various forms, employed by nearly all the modern dialects of the peninsula. The Tibetan also is derived from it, as well as the Javanese, besides a number of other alphabets.

Amongst the Prākrit, or vulgar forms, that were current side by side with the sacred and literary language, there was one which was reserved for quite a special career. This was the *Pāli*, the instrument of Buddhist propagandism, the special language of a religion endowed with an enormous power of expansion. Hence the importance of the literature of Pāli, which seems to have been no other than the vulgar speech of the district of Magadha, in north-eastern India; a language itself extremely ancient, and in some respects showing a marked superiority even over the old Prākrit documents embodied in ancient Hindu dramatical literature. Thus, it does not, for instance, change *y* to *j*, as we shall see is the case with the neo-Sanskrit idioms. It has, moreover, retained certain forms of the old declension lost in the other tongues, and its conjugation also is more highly synthetic than theirs. The Sanskrit vowel *r* has disappeared from Pāli, being mostly replaced by *a*; the long vowels also become short in certain positions; the three sibilants are confused in a single *s*; the assimilation of the con-

* A. Weber, "Indische Skizzen," p. 125, Berlin, 1857; Fr. Müller, "Reise der Oesterr. Fregatte Novara, Linguistischer Theil," p. 219, Vienna, 1867.

sonants is more and more developed, and all words must end either in a simple vowel or a nasal vowel. In the declension the dual is entirely lost, and the dative is absorbed in the genitive. Such are some of the leading peculiarities of Pāli.

Of all Aryan tongues there are but few whose literature can compare with that of ancient India. Hindu literature was distinguished not only by its wealth and variety, but also by the excellence of a great number of its productions. A. Weber has given a rapid but very accurate sketch of it.* The ancient Vedic literature comprised, in the first place, the Rig-Veda, the Sāma-Veda, the two collections of the Yajur-Veda, and the Atharva-Veda. The first of these Vedas is a collection of songs and religious hymns; the second and the third contain prayers and formulas to be recited at the sacrifices; the fourth is much more recent than the others, especially than the Rig-Veda. Besides the collections of hymns, Vedic literature also includes the "Brāhmanas," writings that contain a great number of religious ordinances, traditions, expositions, and the "Soutras," a sort of appendix to the preceding compilations.

The classic period is much more varied. It is illustrated at the outset by its grand national epics, then by the drama, lyric poetry, fables, narratives, and proverbs. Lastly, it produced important works on grammar, rhetoric, philosophy, astronomy, medicine, and a number of technical works. Then follows the Buddhist literature, of which Pāli, as above stated, was the principal instrument.

(2) *Modern Indian Languages*

Are spoken by about 140 millions of people in the north of India, and occupying approximately about two-thirds of the entire peninsula.

They do not derive directly from Sanskrit, but from the old Prākrits, or vulgar forms of speech, spoken (for a time) side by side with Sanskrit itself. They are generally said to have been

* "Akademische Vorlesungen über Indische Literaturgeschichte." Berlin 1852.

O

formed towards the tenth century of our era, possibly a little earlier. But by this we are merely to understand that their present form may date from somewhere about that period. They are, of course, otherwise much older, being after all nothing but the ancient vulgar Prākrits continuously spoken (though here and there more or less affected by Persian, Arabic, and other foreign elements).

Of these neo-Hindu idioms there are a considerable number, some possessing but few written records, while others boast of a highly-developed literature. Amongst the principal are the *Bengali*, which retains many features of the ancient literary language; *Assam*, differing little from the foregoing; *Uriyā*, spoken with the two previous in the north-east. In the north-west, towards the mouth of the Indus, the *Sindhi*, *Multani*, *Gujarati*. In the north the *Nepāli* and *Kashmīrī*. In the centre, *Hindī* and *Hindustani*, called also *Urdū*, and a little more to the south the *Marāthi*.

The name of *Hindūī* is given to a language which, during the mediæval life of the Indian idioms, had a great literary expansion, and is now represented by certain dialects in the north-western provinces. It has been rightly remarked that *Hindī* is nothing but the modern form of *Hindūī*. As to *Hindustani* or *Urdū*, that is the "Camp" language, it was formed about the eleventh century under Mussulman influences. Its vocabulary teems with Arabic and Persian words, and, unlike the other neo-Sanskrit tongues, whose alphabets derive from the Devanāgari, it employs the Persian, that is the Arabic (slightly modified and) increased by a few additional letters. [But it would be more correct to say that Urdū is so written by the Mussulman population, the Hindus still using a slightly modified form of Devanāgari. The former also affect an Arabo-Persian vocabulary, while the latter remain more faithful to the Sanskrit and Hindī elements, both in writing and speaking. It is as if an English writer, affecting a Norman or Book-Latin style, should prefer *royal* or *regal* in all cases to the Saxon or Old English *kingly*.]

There is a considerable contemporary neo-Prākrit and Hindī

literature, and Hindustani especially gives daily proofs of an activity that promises it a protracted future.*

The general character of the phonetics of these idioms is a strong tendency to assimilation, the substitution of the sound *j* for an older *y*, the rather frequent change of *r* to *d*, the simplification of the classic system of sibilants, the substitution, also frequent enough, of the simple aspirate *h* for the older aspirated explosives *kh*, *gh*, *dh*, &c. The neuter gender has disappeared in nearly all the neo-Hindu tongues, and themes ending originally in vowels often reject these vowels, thus terminating now with a consonant. The plural, again, and the cases are expressed by particular suffixes, giving these idioms a very modern air, and clearly marking their transition from an older synthetic to an analytic state. [Thus in Urdū all real cases have entirely disappeared, their place being taken by postpositions attached to the theme, either modified or slightly changed in the singular, and in the plural increased by the nasal *on*, as in *larka* = the boy ; *larke-ko* = to the boy ; *larkon-ko* = to the boys.] Conjugation also has become analytical, the old Prākrit forms having disappeared, and the actual changes being now (mostly) restricted to present participial or past participial forms.

(3) Gipsy Dialects.

The language of the Gipsies is nothing but a neo-Hindu dialect. It is difficult to determine precisely the time of their emigration and of their first incursions westwards through Asia into Europe. Still their arrival here would not seem to have taken place much later than the twelfth or thirteenth century of our era.

Their speech is essentially *Hindu*—a corrupt and often very disfigured Prākrit. The vocabulary, however, is full of foreign elements borrowed from the various peoples met with in their passage westwards, or with whom they may have resided for a longer or shorter period.

* Garcin de Tassy, "Histoire de la Littérature Hindoui et Hindoustani." 2 vols. Paris, 1839-47.

Miklosich has availed himself precisely of the state of the vocabulary of the different Gipsy tribes in order to endeavour to determine their line of march from India to Europe. The Persian and Armenian elements occurring in it would seem to point at a former residence in those Asiatic regions where the Iranian tongues are spoken. When they reached Europe they found themselves first of all in a Greek-speaking country, as shown by the fact that amongst all the Gipsy tribes of Europe, without exception, the presence of elements borrowed from the Greek has been certified. From Greece they proceeded towards Rumania, Hungary, Bohemia, Moravia, Germany, Poland, and Lithuania, Russia, Scandinavia, Italy, the Basque districts, England, Scotland, and Spain.* This refers of course to the European Gipsies only. On those of Asia, and on the amount of foreign elements introduced into their dialects, our information is much more limited.

§ 3.—*The Iranic Branch.*

To the Sanskritist the study of Zend and Old Persian, the two oldest members of this group, presents but little difficulty. Indeed of all the Aryan tongues the Iranian are most closely related to Sanskrit. As a rule, their phonetic system is less complex and less delicate than the Hindu, though on many points allowing of comparison with it. The Zend and the old Persian of Darius and Xerxes may even be said in some respects to surpass the Sanskrit itself, approaching more nearly to the common Aryan mother-tongue. One or two examples will suffice to establish this truth. Whilst Sanskrit changes to a simple $\bar{o}$ the organic diphthong *au*, Persian preserves it intact, and Zend only modifies it to *ao*. Sanskrit again substitutes the genitive for the old ablative in *at* (except in the case of themes ending in the vowel *a*), whereas Zend always retains the old ablative ending. On the whole, however, Sanskrit is nearer to the common Aryan type than is the Zend. For

---

* Miklosich, "Ueber die Mundarten und die Wanderungen der Zigeuner Europa's," 2nd part. Vienna, 1873.

instance, it does not possess the great wealth of sibilants occurring in the Iranian tongues.*

The classification of the Iranic tongues has not yet been thoroughly established. A very few of them may possibly not be directly related to each other, and it is at least certain that not any one of them can boast of having been the common mother-tongue of all the rest. Old Persian in some respects surpassed the Zend, while in others surpassed by it. Altogether the only possible classification of the members of this group must for the present be purely chronological, depending on the epochs when they were spoken. Thus, amongst the older tongues will be grouped the *Zend, old Persian,* and *old Armenian.* To the Medieval period will belong the *Huzváresh, Parsi, and classical Armenian;* and amongst the modern idioms must be included the *Persian, neo-Armenian, Afghan, Beluchi,* &c., and this order will here be followed.

(1) *Zend.*

Towards the middle of the last century a Frenchman named Anquetil-Duperron, in his twenty-third year, embarked as a simple soldier for India, being unable in any other way to undertake the distant journey that he wished to make. The object of this brave man, whose name science can never forget, was to study the languages of the country on the spot. Disappointed in his hope of being able to learn Sanskrit at Chandernagor, he made his way to Pondicherry, alone and without means, and exhausted by a march of a hundred days. From the shores of the Bay of Bengal he directed his steps towards the coast of Malabar, reached Mahé, and thence pushed on to Surat. It was here that, gaining the confidence of some Parsee priests, he was by them initiated into a knowledge of Zend and Huzváresh. He returned to France

---

* Here again the writer has a remark on the Term *Iranian,* for which he would substitute the older form Eranian. But, for the reason stated in the note at p. 188, the form Iranian is retained in this translation.—*Note by Translator.*

in 1762 in possession, not of a fortune, but of over a hundred precious manuscripts.

Zend is the language in which was composed the old text of the "Avesta," the sacred book of the Zoroastrian religion. We cannot here discuss the question of Zoroaster's personality, nor of the contents of the sacred writings attributed either to him or to his disciples. It will be enough to remark that, of the books of the "Avesta" a small portion only has reached us—the *Vendidad*, the *Vispered*, the *Yaçna*, and a number of devotional pieces, private meditations, and the like, known as the "Little Avesta."

Anquetil's translation of this work was very faulty, having been executed on the uncritical data supplied to him by the Parsee priests. But when consigning his manuscripts to the Royal Library, he furnished his successors with the sole means of revising, correcting, and prosecuting his labours. This task devolved on another Frenchman, Eugène Burnouf, who has been equally distinguished by his studies on ancient Persian, a sister language to the Zend. Burnouf was not only the real founder of Zend grammar, but was also the head of the traditional school of interpretation of the Zend writings—a school at present represented chiefly by Spiegel.

It seems now settled that Zend was the language current in the eastern Iranian regions, limited, according to Burnouf, on the north by Sogdiana, by Hyrcania on the north-west, and on the south by Arachosia. It was owing to the general adoption of this opinion that Zend came to be called the Baktrian language—a name in itself otherwise perfectly justifiable. The term Zend, applied even to the language of the old texts of the "Avesta," is purely conventional, the primitive meaning of which has not yet perhaps been quite satisfactorily determined, but which it would now be difficult to dispense with, in the new sense it has acquired.

The Zend alphabet is purely alphabetical, that is to say, each of its letters denotes either a vowel or a consonant. There are very few ligatures, and its reading, which is from right to left, presents little difficulty. It is certainly of Semitic origin, but does not seem to be very ancient; nor is it now known what graphic system was in use amongst the eastern Iranians at the period when their Persian neighbours on the west were employing the cuneiform characters.

Zend comprises two varieties—the ordinary dialect and the language of the "Gâthâs," the term applied to a number of pieces in the Yaçna, whose interpretation still presents the greatest difficulties. The two dialects are closely related, that of the "Gâthâs" being generally considered the most ancient, and supposed to have been spoken in the highland regions of the country, though the point is not yet settled.

The Zend vowel system is not very complex. Besides a, i, u, long and short, there is a long e, and another which seems to have been very short, besides two other e's, and two kinds of o, of which the quantity varies; also a nasal a and a strong labial $â$. We have stated that Zend, herein more primitive than Sanskrit, had not reduced to one single vowel the old diphthongs of the common Aryan tongue. The first of these it represented by $aê$, the second by ao; the Persian, in this respect still purer, preserving the primitive diphthongs unchanged.

Passing to the consonants, we may observe that the sibilants readily interchange with each other; a change, however, which is common to the whole Iranian group. On the other hand, the consonants of different orders interchange to a very limited degree—herein contrasting strikingly with the Sanskrit.

The Zend declension is, on the whole, well preserved; retaining, as already remarked, the old ablative singular in at—which has fared so ill in nearly all the other Aryan tongues. Conjugation also is very perfect, reflecting with tolerable fidelity the primitive system whence it sprang.

The question of the antiquity of the Zend language can be settled, as we believe, with some approach to accuracy. It is no doubt difficult to pronounce definitely on its first and remote origin, or even on the time when it ceased to be spoken; but it may well be supposed to have been at some given period contemporary of the ancient Persian. This last we are doubtless acquainted with only through the monuments of the Achæmenides, ranging over the sixth, fifth, and fourth centuries before our era, but it is possible, and even probable that it had been spoken long previous to this epoch. On the other hand the language of the "Avesta," and the very contents of its various texts, do not permit of their being removed from the time of the Persian monuments. Hence, as stated, the two languages must have been contemporaneous at that particular point of time—Zend in Eastern, Persian in Western Iran.

(2) *Old Persian.*

The triglot inscriptions in cuneiform characters discovered in Persia on the ruins of the ancient palaces and on the surface of the rocks were composed in Persian, Assyrian, and a third language, of which but very little is still known. We have spoken higher up of the various attempts at interpreting the text of the middle column composed in this unknown tongue (p. 139), and we have seen that Assyrian, the language of the third column, was a Semitic idiom.

It was in the year 1802 that the learned Hanoverian, Grotefend, attempted to decipher the first column, composed in Persian, or as it is often called, in old Persian. His starting-point was simple and ingenious. Setting out with the idea that inscriptions, some of which must have cost considerable labour, naturally referred to historical events, and could scarcely be other than royal records, he first of all noted the frequent recurrence of a certain group of characters, to which he assigned the meaning of "king." This group was often followed by the same group, increased by some additional signs. Grotefend concluded that this last was but the genitive plural of the first, and he interpreted the two together as meaning "king of kings." The name preceding these two groups was necessarily a proper name, and the constant repetition of these same groups made it clear enough that we had here to do with a series of genealogies: "Such a king, king of kings, son of such a one, king."

The researches of Grotefend were the starting-point for the deciphering of the Persian inscriptions, though they went no farther. Rask, the Dane, added a little, but it was reserved for Eugène Burnouf and Chr. Lassen to give a real version of these inscriptions and to construct their grammar. Their essays appeared simultaneously in France and Germany, in the year 1836, and from that time the structure of old Persian was finally established. It had been systematically compared with that of the Sanskrit and Zend, and the way was opened for those who have carried its study to the state it has now reached in the hands of Rawlinson, Spiegel,* Oppert, and Kossowicz.

The inscriptions of the Achæmenides comprise but a small number of words, some four hundred altogether, including a great many proper names. Still there is enough for the grammarian: and the phonetics, declension and conjugation of old Persian now no longer present any mystery. Some writers have fancied that this language is older than Zend, whilst others hold, on the contrary, that Zend comes nearer to the common Aryan type. But we think a third view might be taken, namely, that Persian, as already remarked, surpasses Zend in some respects, and in others is surpassed by it. Both have in principle changed the original Aryan sibilant *s* to *h*, but Persian, herein less correct than Zend, often drops this aspirate where the sister-tongue preserves it. Thus the Sanskrit *asmi* = I am, in Lithuanian *esmi*, becomes *ahmi* in Zend, and *amiy* in Persian. On the other hand, old Persian retains the common Aryan diphthongs *ai*, *au*; which in Zend are modified to *aê* and *ao*. Thus each in its turn might claim the superiority in these examples, which it would be easy, though needless, to multiply.

The cuneiform characters of the first of the trilingual texts are far from being as numerous as those of the two other columns. There are about sixty, all alphabetic, that is, representing not syllables but vowels and consonants. Their number is greatly increased by the fact that some of the consonants are sometimes represented by a different sign, according as they precede or follow certain vowels. Each word is separated by an oblique wedge, which circumstance has greatly facilitated the reading of the Persian

* "Die Altpersischen Keilinschriften." Leipzig, 1862.

texts. The question of the origin of this alphabet has not yet been clearly settled; still the Persian cuneiforms may be regarded as merely a particular variety of the general system of this graphic method, and it is most assuredly by far the simplest, or rather the most simplified of any of them.

(3) *Armenian.*

Armenian seems to have detached itself at a very remote period from the other Iranian tongues. Anyhow a special and somewhat independent place must be assigned to it in the Iranic family. Of its primitive state we know little beyond the few allusions occurring in the classic writers. Its first period closed with the opening of the fifth century of our era, when the classic epoch begins with the formation of the Armenian alphabet by Mesrobius. Both it and Georgian, Fr. Müller* thinks, are based on a Semitic form, and more particularly on the Aramean variety of it. The golden age of Armenian letters lasted about seven hundred years, between the fifth and the beginning of the twelfth centuries. Its literature was copious, its dialects somewhat numerous, and one of these, that of the province of Ararat, soon acquired the position of the standard literary language. There are still spoken a considerable number of Armenian dialects, that it would be a mistake to look upon as mere *patois* of the literary form, which seems to have acquired a certain fixedness, whereas the actual varieties are but modern forms of the older dialects. As early as the eleventh century they were employed for literary purposes, to the detriment of the classic tongue. They seem now to be divided into two tolerably distinct groups— the eastern, embracing the dialects of Armenia, Georgia, southeastern Russia, Persia, and India; and the western, comprising those of Hungary, Poland, and the Crimea.

One of the leading features of modern, or at least of western, Armenian is the change of the old sharp explosives to soft, and of the old soft to sharp ones. Thus k, t, p, become g, d, b, and g, d, b, become k, t, p. The vowel and consonantal system is

* "Ueber den Ursprung der Armenischen Schrift." Vienna, 1865.

fairly developed, including, besides the explosives just mentioned, a considerable number of sibilants, and two sorts of r. The Armenian declension is much fuller than the (modern) Persian, of which we shall have to speak presently, and it still to some extent retains the old case-endings. Its conjugation is still more wealthy, in fact retaining all the old tenses except the perfect, while it has created three new ones—a perfect, a pluperfect, and a future—by employing participial forms in conjugating the verb. Thus of all the neo-Iranian idioms still spoken Armenian has preserved most of the common stock of the original mother-tongue.

Its vocabulary, like that of all the cognate Iranian languages, contains a considerable number of foreign words, some derived from the Greek in medieval times, others, in still greater numbers, borrowed at an earlier period from the Aramean. But the essence of its vocabulary, as well as the whole of its grammar, is still Iranian.

At a very early period Armenian was written, if not constantly, at least in certain documents, with cuneiform letters. Inscriptions of this sort have been found, more particularly in the ruins of Armavir, not far from Mount Ararat. The Armenian cuneiform writing is not alphabetic, like the Persian, but syllabic, each sign denoting, not a vowel or a consonant, but a full syllable.

(4) *Huzváresh*.

The "Avesta," or rather those books of the "Avesta" that were still extant in the Middle Ages, were at that period translated into a language which we know not only by this translation, but also by a number of numismatic legends, and a very important cosmogony, called the "Bundehesh." At first this language received the name of *Pehlei* [also *Pehlevi* and *Pahlavi*, this last form by E. W. West, who has been recently collecting fresh materials for the study of Pahlavi literature, and is altogether one of the greatest authorities on the subject], but this term seems somewhat too vague. That of *Huzváresh*, as has been shown by Joseph Müller and Spiegel,* is

---

* "Grammatik der Huzváreschsprache," p. 21. Vienna, 1856.

its proper name, and the only one it has borne. It is now generally admitted that this language was spoken in the western district of Sevâd. Nothing very definite is known as to its origin, but the Huzvâresh coins of the dynasty of the Sassanides show that it was still current in the middle of the seventh century of our era.

Huzvâresh deserves to be mentioned as one of those languages that have been most affected by foreign influences. It has been, so to say, penetrated by Aramean on all sides, of which it betrays the most unmistakable proofs in its vocabulary, its grammar, and phonetic system; so that if such a thing could exist as a mixed language, Huzvâresh would be one of the most striking examples of such a phenomenon. But hybrids of this sort cannot be [a statement to be received with some reserve], and Huzvâresh is in truth an Iranian tongue, quite as much as English is a Teutonic. [But the comparison does not hold, because English *grammar* is purely Teutonic, and wholly unaffected by French, Latin, or any other foreign element.]

Besides the Aramean elements present in the language of the time of the Sassanides, that of the "Bundehesh" includes some Arabic forms, betraying its more recent composition, probably by some learned Persian intimately acquainted with the language into which the sacred books were translated.*

The Huzvâresh grammar shows a great falling off from the correctness and fidelity to the older forms that characterise the Zend and old Persian. Gender is no longer distinguishable by the ending of the nouns, and the dual has disappeared; the accusative has no more special ending than has the nominative; the genitive, or rather the idea answering to that expressed by the old genitive, is rendered by an element *i*, the remnant of an old relative pronoun; while the conception corresponding to the old dative is expressed by means of particles, that is of true prepositions. Conjugation is equally fragmentary, but in any case the language has still remained essentially Iranian. This appears clearly from the fact that Huzvâresh possesses compound verbs, formed not only by

---

* F. Justi, "Der Bundehesch," preface, p. viii. Leipzig, 1868.

Iranian root and preposition, but also by Iranian root and Semitic prefix, by Semitic root and Iranian prefix, and, what is much more remarkable, by both Semitic root and prefix. And yet Semitic itself, unlike the Aryan, possesses no compound verbs at all, no forms, for instance, answering to our *ap-prehend, com-prehend, re-prehend, under-take, over-take, par(t)-take*, and the like.

There are few alphabets more defective than the Huzvâresh. One and the same sign often denotes several different senses, and there are a great many ligatures, or agglomerations of several characters all blended together (like so many monograms). Hence in philological treatises Huzvâresh words are seldom quoted in their own characters, but are mostly transcribed in Roman, or even in Hebrew or Arabic letters.

(5) *Parsi*.

Parsi has occasionally been incorrectly named *Pazend*. Modern orientalists look on Zend and Pazend as the titles of books, not the names of languages, and their opinion on this matter seems perfectly reasonable. No doubt Zend has supplanted all other names as applied to the language of the "Avesta;" but Pazend has not met with such general acceptance that it may not be set aside for the much more appropriate term *Parsi*, that is, language of the Parsees.

Parsi was undoubtedly contemporary of the Huzvâresh, but survived it by several hundred years, and was at once the current and the literary language. It was, moreover, spoken in a more eastern region of Iran, so that we do not meet in it that abundance of Aramean elements possessed by the Huzvâresh.

Its grammar, however, has equally diverged from the ancient standard by which Zend and old Persian are marked. Without being in this respect much removed from the Huzvâresh, it approaches much nearer to the Persian, while still considerably surpassing it in the fulness of its forms. Thus it preserves much more of the old pronominal elements, and retains a great many verbs that have disappeared from the Persian. Burnouf and Spiegel believe that Parsi may have been spoken till the time of the poet Firdousi, that is, till the beginning of the eleventh century.

Parsi has no peculiar writing system, employing sometimes the Zend and sometimes the Arabic characters. The Parsees are settled chiefly in Bombay, Surat, Baroda, Gujerat, and are variously estimated at 50,000, 80,000, and 150,000.

(6) *Persian.*

Of all the modern Iranian tongues *Persian*, or neo-Persian, is the most diffused and the best known. It is an Iranian dialect that became a literary language about the year A.D. 1000. Its literature, with which we are not here concerned, has been one of great importance, simultaneously embracing poetry, history, and the sciences. The "Book of Kings" (Shāh-Nāma) of Firdousi ("the Homer of Persia"), who flourished at the close of the tenth and the beginning of the eleventh century, is a national epic that may well rival the chief productions of many other literatures.*

Persian has adopted the Arabic alphabet, increased by the four letters, *p*, *ch*, *j* (French), and *g* hard.

Declension has disappeared, the dative and accusative being expressed simply by prepositions joined to the noun. The idea of the genitive is denoted, as in Huzvâresh and Parsi, by inserting (between the two words) the element *i*, a remnant of an old relative pronoun: *dast-i-pusar* = the child's hand; *pusar-i-man* = my child. As much as to say: the hand which (is that of) the child; the child which (is) mine. (So also *Koh-i-nūr* = the mountain of light). So that we have here a purely syntactical process (supplanting inflection).

Conjugation has been equally simplified. The personal suffixes have been fairly well preserved: *m* for the first person singular and plural, *d* (for an older *t*) for the third person. But the tenses have shared the fate of the case-endings, being now expressed by modern processes; in other words, Persian has become an analytical language. Its vocabulary contains a large number of Arabic words.

* Mohl, "Firdousi: Le Livre des Rois," publié en Persan, avec une traduction Française en regard. Paris, 1838.

Besides the literary Persian tongue, there are a number of current varieties, such, for instance, as the *Mazandaran*, each of them presenting certain peculiarities, either lexical, phonetic, or even occasionally grammatical.

(7) *Ossetian, Kurdic, Beluchi, Afghan, &c.*

Although here grouped together under one heading, these various idioms are no more closely related to each other in the Iranian family than are some of the other members of the same family above spoken of.

The *Ossetian* declension is fuller than the Persian, while its conjugation is somewhat analogous to it; so that, on the whole, it approaches more to the older Iranian forms such as they still exist in Armenian, Huzvâresh, and Parsi. Ossetian is spoken both north and south of the Caucasus, in the neighbourhood of Dariel, and is split up into a number of local varieties.

Kurdic may, in a general way, be said to be allied to Persian, though perhaps rather to the popular dialects than to its literary form. Its phonetic system seems more changed than the Persian. There are several dialects, of which the principal is the *Kurmanji*, in the west between Mossul and Asia Minor. The *Zaza*[*] is in some respects less, in others more, corrupt than its congeners.

Beluchi resembles Kurdic; it contains a considerable number of foreign elements, especially of words borrowed from the Arabic.

Some writers would seem inclined not to look on the *Afghan* or *Pakkhto*[†] as a pure Iranian language, considering it as an independent idiom, forming a class by itself, and related to the Hindu

---

[*] One of the questions discussed at the last meeting of the International Congress of Orientalists, held at St. Petersburg in the month of September, 1876, was the connection of this Zaza dialect with the other Kurdish idioms. But no very definite result seems to have been arrived at.—*Note by Translator.*

[†] Here the form *Pakkhto* has been substituted for the more usual, but certainly less correct *Pushtu*, or, as the author writes it, "pachto ou pouchtou." The form Pakkhto at once connects this people with the πάκτυες of Herodotus, whom he places in the region at present occupied by the Afghans, and from whom there can be little doubt that they are descended. Their own popular belief of their descent from the lost tribes of Israel—

quite as much as to the Iranian family. But Fr. Müller thinks otherwise, regarding it as an eastern Iranian dialect, the direct descendant of some old Bactrian idiom. Its conjugation is inferior to that of the Persian, having entirely lost certain ancient forms of the present tense retained in Persian, and usually employing the verbal theme for that tense. Its vocabulary includes a number of Persian and Arabic words.

This is far from comprising the whole of the modern Iranian idioms. Besides those here spoken of, and which may be considered the most important and the best known, there are some others, such as that of the *Lurs* (Bachiari and Feïli) related to the Kurdic, but concerning which we have but few particulars, and that of the Tâts, in the south-east of the Caucasus, and not unlike Persian.

It is, moreover, quite certain that many other Iranian tongues have perished during the course of ages. It is quite possible that amongst the races spoken of by the ancients, and especially by the Greeks, under the name of Scythians, there may have been some Iranians. For this opinion there is some presumptive evidence, but the documents so far available are too limited to enable us to pronounce definitely on the subject. Certain languages of Asia Minor have also been included in the Iranian family, as for instance the Phrygian, which has been grouped more particularly with the Armenian, Lycian, Carian, and some others, though this classification is, perhaps, somewhat premature; but our remarks on these idioms must be reserved till we come to speak of certain languages which are evidently Aryan, but whose true position in this family has not yet been definitely settled.

§ 4.—*The Hellenic Branch.*

Of all the Aryan languages spoken in Europe, Greek is most

a belief still shared in by many English writers, who ought to know better —no longer calls for any special refutation. With those who persist in believing that an Aryan race could possibly be "Baní-Isráíl," that is, "Sons of Israel," and therefore Semites, there is no reasoning. "Non ragionam di loro, ma guarda e passa."—*Note by Translator.*

closely allied to Sanskrit and the Iranian group. A better knowledge of the Aryan idioms of Asia Minor—Phrygian, Lycian, and others—may possibly, and even probably, some day, show that the relationship is even closer than is generally supposed. We shall revert farther on to this question of the various degrees of affinity of the several Aryan groups, and it will be enough here to guard the reader against the idea, at one time very generally adopted, and still common enough, that Greek and the Italic tongues form together a separate branch of the great linguistic family of which they are members. Greek has doubtless many intimate relations with Latin; but it has others, quite as intimate, with Sanskrit and Zend. Latin, on the other hand, is in many respects more closely allied to the Keltic idioms than it is to the Hellenic.

Greek has much better preserved the vowel than the consonantal system of the common Aryan mother-tongue, in this respect closely resembling Zend and old Persian. For instance, it retains the old diphthongs, reduced in Latin as well as in Sanskrit to a long vowel. With regard to the consonants, which it has less faithfully preserved, one of its most striking changes is that of the (soft) aspirates *gh*, *dh*, *bh*, to the corresponding (sharp) aspirates, *kh*, *th*, *ph*. It would be difficult to say how this modification was occasioned, but the fact is certain and constant. Thus the Sanskrit *dirghas* = long, *bharâmi* = I bear, appear in Greek as *dolikhos* (δολιχος), and *pherō* (φερω). Far from retaining, as Latin does, the primitive κ in all cases, it frequently changes it to *p* and even to *t*. Thus the Latin *quis*, *quinque*, are in Greek τις, πεμπε and πεντε. But it is in the letters *s*, *y*, *v* that it departs most widely from the common primitive type, here showing itself inferior to all the other Aryan tongues of Europe, without any exception. Words beginning with *s* are usually changed to the rough (breathing or) aspirate (') generally transcribed by *h*. Thus *hêdus* (ἡδυς) corresponds to the Sanskrit *svâdus* = sweet; *hepta* (ἑπτα) is the Latin septem = seven; and *hekuros* (ἑκυρος) is *socer* = father-in-law. This sibilant occasionally disappears altogether, especially when occurring between two vowels, which is also the case with the primitive *y* in the same position. But at the beginning of words *y* becomes either *z* (pro-

P

nounced *dz*) or the rough breathing. Thus *zugon* (ζυγον) and *hagios* (ἅγιος) correspond to the Sanskrit *yugam* = yoke, and *yajyas* = holy. The primitive *v* initial also disappears, or becomes *u* in classic Greek. Thus the original Aryan *kvans* = hound, becomes in Sanskrit *çvá*, and in Greek *kuón* (κυων), where *v* has changed to *u* (which *u* was very probably pronounced as the German ü or the French *u*). In the words *neos* (νεος), *oíkos* (οικος), and *ois* (οις) corresponding to the Sanskrit *navas* = ship, *veças* = house [or *wick*, *wich*, as in *Greenwich*], *avis* = ewe, the *v* has disappeared altogether, though, as we shall presently see, preserved in certain dialects under the form of the digamma: νεϝος, ϝοικος, οϝις. This digamma, however, was not retained in the Attic dialect, which, owing to political [and other] circumstances, became the preponderating and classical language of Greece.

Though less complex than the Sanskrit, still the phonetic laws of Greek are important enough in themselves, and are mainly based on a strong tendency to assimilate consonants of different orders when thrown together. "Zetacismus" also plays an important part in all the Greek dialects, resulting in the organic combinations $y + y$, $d + y$ changing to z. Thus Zeus (Zευς) answers to the Sanskrit *dyáus*. Greek admits of no final consonants except *s* and *n* (also *k*, as in εκ). Hence the *m* of the accusative singular everywhere becomes *n*, or is dropped, as in φεροντα, ναυν, which in Sanskrit are *bharantam*, *navam* (and in Latin *ferentem*, *navem*).

The Greek declension is well preserved, for, if it has lost the ablative singular, it has retained the old locative, both in the singular and plural. This locative serves also as a dative, μητρι = to the mother; νεκυι = to the dead; ποιμενι = to the shepherd; but its form has otherwise nothing to do with that of the organic dative, the sense of which it has merely acquired in course of time.

The plural locative is in *si* (σι): ναυσι = in the ships; Αθηνησι, Ολυμπιασι, which classic grammars wrongly treat as so many datives. Greek possesses also under the single form of φι, the instrumental singular *bhi*, and the instrumental plural *bhis*, which so many other Aryan tongues have lost. The grammarians treat this syllable φι as a mere addition, but it is really a true case [which appears in the

Latin *ibi, ubi, sibi*, and the plural *ibus*]. The dual is only partly retained, the genitive and locative having disappeared. But, speaking generally, the Greek declension may be said to be the best preserved, next to the Sanskrit and ancient Iranian types.

Passing to its conjugation, we find that it retains the old intransitive voice (λυομαι, λυεται) which has disappeared from the Italic, Keltic, Slavonic, and Lettic groups. It also preserves fairly well the six organic tenses, besides creating some new ones, amongst which, a pluperfect, built on the reduplicated perfect. Altogether, Greek has remained tolerably faithful to the common Aryan type in all that regards its accidence, while departing greatly from it in many points of its phonetic system.

Its dialectic varieties are mainly of a phonetic character. The numerous dialects may all be easily grouped under four special forms, the Æolic, Doric, Ionic, and Attic, which are themselves sometimes reduced to two main divisions, one comprising the Æolic and Doric, the other the Ionic and Attic.

The Æolic, properly so called,* was spoken in Asia Minor, in the Lesbos variety of which Alcæus and Sappho wrote. It possesses the digamma corresponding to the organic *r*, and is fond of doubling the liquid consonants, as in εμμι (for ειμι) = I am; it also frequently retains the primitive *á*, which in Ionic becomes *é*. Another of its characteristics is the greater abundance of verbs in μι, as in φιλημι (for the ordinary φιλῶ) = I love. Bœotian, belonging to the same group, retains the digamma, contracts the diphthongs into one long vowel; keeps the old *á* for the Ionic *ē*, and often substitutes *d* for the ordinary *z*, the Attic Ζευς, ζυγον thus appearing in Bœotian as *Deus, dugon*. It has left but few literary remains.

Thessalian also was included in the Æolic group; it was considered at Athens as rather a rude dialect, but has left scarcely anything whereby to judge of its true character.

Doric was spoken in nearly the whole of the Peloponnesus, in Crete, and in the Greek colonies in Sicily, Libya, and Southern Italy. Pindar wrote in Doric, which was also the language of

---

* Ahrens, "De Græcæ Linguæ Dialectis." 2 vols. Göttingen, 1839-43.

pastoral poetry. It is subdivided into two branches, of which one is more severe than the other. It retained the digamma, as well as the organic *t*, which in the classic language becomes ς; hence διδωτι (for διδωσι) and ϝικατι, ϝεικατι (for εικοσι) = twenty.

Of the *Ionic* there were two periods—the old, or epic, embracing the language of Homer and Hesiod, and the new period, represented by Herodotus. It was spoken in certain districts of Asia Minor, in Attica, and in a great many of the islands.

Many writers connect *Attic* with Ionic, from which indeed it differs so little, that it may be considered an Ionic dialect. It was the language of Athens, the mother-tongue of Æschylus, Sophocles, Euripides, Aristophanes, Thucydides, and Demosthenes; it was the dialect that ultimately prevailed over all the others, and that the reformers of the Greek language ever look to as their standard.*

Each dialect, as stated, had its own literature; still the Attic dialect gradually gained the ascendant, thus becoming the common written language, ἡ κοινη διαλεκτος, of all Greek-speaking races. But this somewhat unnatural expansion was precisely the cause of its decay and corruption. As spoken by Greeks outside Attica, and more especially by the "barbarians," the "common dialect" was no longer what it had been in Athens; it gradually became "Byzantine," the Byzantine language of medieval times.

Out of this grew the *Modern Greek*, to which has been given the name of *Romaic*, a reminiscence of the eastern empire of Rome. But it is an unfortunate misnomer, apt to lead to confusion, and which we have therefore discarded.

The position of modern in relation to ancient Greek can scarcely be compared with that of the Romance tongues in relation to Latin. These have, in truth, departed far more from their common source than the Greek of the present day has from that of antiquity. Modern Greek, however, includes a great many dialects, differing perceptibly from each other; and these are met with not only in

---

* Thus Dr. Donaldson remarks that a Greek scholar should aim, not at being a Hellenist merely, but at being an Atticist, as the highest type of Hellenic literature. "Greek Grammar," p. 4.—*Note by Translator.*

the islands but also in the mainland, as, for instance, the *Zaconic*, spoken in the heart of the Morea. But the literary, or common form, is really but little removed from the Hellenic as written 2,000 years ago. It is this very resemblance that has suggested to some Greeks the idea of a reformation, based on a return to the forms, and even the very expressions, of the language of Thucydides. But nothing could be less practical, and any such attempt must end in failure. The present Greek differs doubtless but little from the classic; still the difference is very marked and clearly defined. Thus, it has lost both the dual and the dative, this last being employed only in the more elevated style, and could not be used in conversation, or even in current literature, without affectation. The old infinitive in ειν (ελθειν = to come) has also disappeared everywhere except from the pseudo-classic literature. It is usually replaced by a conjunctive form, as in θελω να ελθω = I wish to come; literally, " I wish that I come." The future has also become analytical, being expressed, amongst other ways, by the present preceded by a conjunction. The Greek conjugation presents many other instances of a decided transition to the analytic state, which need not here be dwelt upon.

It is further distinguished from the old Greek by a feature which, though not affecting accidence itself, is not the less important. Accent has here taken the place of quantity. In other words, it is the accented syllable in modern Greek that is long, and the unaccented one short. This phenomenon is not peculiar to Greek, and in the chapter devoted to the Teutonic tongues we shall see that it also constitutes one of the features of modern German. In Middle High German (twelfth to fifteenth century), the radical syllable was sometimes long, sometimes short; while in the present language, being accented, it is always long— all which is quite a modern tendency.

Greek is spoken not only in Greece, but also in many parts of Turkey, as in Thessaly, where it comes in contact with Albanian to the west and Bulgarian towards the north. It is spread over all the northern coast of the Ægean, and makes the complete circuit of the Sea of Marmora, reaching at some points far inland, as, for instance, to Adrianople in Rumelia. In Candia it reigns everywhere supreme, except in a single central district occupied by Turkish. Altogether the Greeks in the Ottoman Empire are estimated at about 1,000,000. In Russia also Greek is spoken, on the north coast of the Sea of Azov, at two points between Taurida and the Don Cossacks. It further occupies the three shores of Asia Minor, from a point opposite Cyprus as far as the mouth of the Kizilirmak in the Black Sea (a little to the east of Sinope).

We come now to a secondary, though not uninteresting, question —that of the pronunciation of ancient and modern Greek.

No less than six characters—three simple and three compound— answer in modern Greek to the sound of i (ee). These are η, ι, υ; ει, οι, υι, the other vowels being pronounced as written. On the other hand, the groups αυ, ευ, ηυ, ου, are pronounced av, ev, iv, ov. In the consonants, θ answers to the English th hard, as in $three$; δ to the English th soft, as in the; φ sounds as f; χ, as the ch of the German words $noch$, $nach$, $buch$, or as that of ich, $fechten$, according to the accompanying vowels; γ before ε or ι as the French or English y.

There is obviously a great difference between this pronunciation and the so-called classic, attributed to Erasmus; yet there is a wide school of Hellenists who consider that the modern Greek pronunciation should be applied to the ancient language, and who are zealously agitating for this change, absolutely unscientific though it be. To read Greek in this modern fashion is a mistake, as Schleicher very justly remarks, due to complete ignorance of the laws of phonetics and of the life of human speech. And, in truth, the theory is utterly indefensible by any *à priori* or *à posteriori* arguments.

A mere comparison of ancient Greek with the cognate Aryan tongues shows that the sounds $\bar{e}$, i, u, answered to the vowels $\bar{a}$, i, u, and were accordingly from the first perfectly distinct, having only gradually become ultimately all three confused in the single sound of i. The mutual transcription of the Greek η by the Latin e, and of the Latin e by the Greek η clearly shows that the sound of the old Greek η was not that of *i*. Thus we find κηνσωρ, Αυρηλιους for *censor*, *Aurelius*. Nor can it be doubted that the vowel *u* was anciently in Greek pronounced like the Latin *u* (or English *oo*); during the classic period it answered to the French *u*,* while the diphthong ου (that is *o* + *u*) was reduced during the same epoch to the simple vowel *u* (or *oo*). Thus the Latin words *Titius*, *tuum*, *circuitum* are translated in Greek as Τιτιους, τουομ, κιρκουιτουμ. It is no less certain that originally the Greek β was uttered like our *b*, and not like *v*, as it now is. In the classic Greek writings the bleating of sheep is denoted by βη, βη, which it would be ridiculous to pronounce *vi*, *vi*. At a certain period no doubt the Greeks took to transcribing the Latin *v* by their β; but they had previously denoted it by ου, as in Ουαρρω, Ουαλεριος, Ουεργιλιος, for Varro, Valerius, Virgilius, &c. The change of *b* to *v* took place probably at an early period, at least in some dialects, but originally *b* had everywhere its true and proper sound. When the Greeks began to transcribe Latin names, their β was far from having always and everywhere its present value, for at this very time it is still regularly used to transcribe the Latin *b*, and it is only in connection with ου or *o* that it is at this period employed to represent the Latin *v*.†

Lastly, there can be no question as to the utterance of the old aspirates φ, θ, χ, which had the sound of *p*, *t*, *k* aspirated, that is: *p* + *h*, *t* + *h*, *k* + *h* (as in the English *shep-herd*, *hit-him*, *hack-him*, or better still, in the Urdu *phūl* = blossom, *thōrā* = little, and *khānā* = to eat), so that these letters in no way answered to the English *th hard*, to *f*, or to either of the two *ch* sounds in German. These consonants are now no doubt fricatives, but they were originally true aspirates, which might be easily proved in many ways.‡ One proof may be drawn from the shifting nature of the aspirates accompanying the simple explosives *p*, *t*, *k*. Thus the

---

* This is also the opinion of Mr. A. J. Ellis, for which see a lecture by him on Greek Pronunciation, delivered at the College of Preceptors, in 1875, and published in the "Educational Times" of January, 1876.—*Note by Translator*.

† G. Curtius, "Grundzüge der Griechischen Etymologie," 4th ed. p. 571. Leipzig, 1873.

‡ *Ibid.*, p. 416.

reduplication of the theme θε gives τιθεμεν (not θιθεμεν): and so with the reduplication of φ and χ by π and κ. In the same way the Sanskrit reduplicates *dh*, *bh* by the simple unaspirated explosives *d*, *b*, as in *dadhâmi* = I put, *babhûu* = I have shone. In forms like τρεφω, I nourish, and θρεψω, I will nourish, the shifting nature of the aspirate is equally obvious. Here, as in the preceding case, the φ and θ are evidently not fricatives, but real aspirated explosives; and to this the Sanskrit forms *bandhâmi*, I bind, and *bhatsyâmi*, I will bind, are perfectly analogous. It may also be remarked that certain dialects readily displace the aspirate in the body of the word, the ordinary Greek ενταυθα, χιτων becoming ενθαυτα, κιθων. The Barbarians introduced on the stage by Aristophanes are made to replace the Greek aspirates φ, θ, χ by the simple unaspirated *p*, *t*, *k*, which is again conclusive as to the real sound of these letters. Another similar argument is deduced from the way in which the old current Latin renders these same Greek aspirates, which it does by simply dropping their aspirates; and even in the fourth century Gothic represents the Greek χ by a *k*.

Lastly, many modern Greek dialects have a pure unaspirated explosive instead of the aspirated consonant of the literary language. There can be no doubt that these dialects in this reflect a very ancient period, which, for the rest, is often enough the case with dialects. In a word, the old Greek aspirates had unquestionably the force of $p+h$, $t+h$, $k+h$, passing in later times only to the fricative order of letters.*

It would, however, be idle to attempt to fix the epoch when the change in the pronunciation of Greek was brought about. Speaking generally, two principles were at work in effecting these various changes—time and place. Some modifications occurred at one time

* At the same time it is not easy to understand how these aspirates could have been so pronounced when found in juxtaposition, as in ελεχθην = *elekhthēn*, or when followed by σ, ρ, or other consonants, as in χριμφθεις *khrimphtheis*. Nor is the difficulty at all diminished if recourse be had to the archaic spelling, as in επιφσεφιο, εδοχσεν, occurring on the recently-discovered treaty-stone between Athens and Chalkis in Euboea, and which would have to be somehow pronounced *epip-hsep-hio*, *edokhsen*, which seems intolerably harsh.—*Note by Translator.*

in one place, which were not effected in others till long after, and which in yet another place may have been already long previously established. Hence, in studying the old Greek pronunciation, special details only can be taken into account. Later on the results of these special investigations may perhaps be collected, and some general deductions drawn from them. Meanwhile, however, it will be wise to keep to the so-called Erasmian pronunciation, faulty though it be, in preference to the still more defective modern system.

§ 5.—*The Italic Branch.*

Until the bases of comparative Aryan grammar were definitely settled, Latin and the other ancient Italic idioms allied to it may well have been supposed to derive from the Greek language. One of the results of the great work of Bopp was precisely to show that Latin no more derived from Greek than did Greek from Sanskrit; and that all three flowed from a common source, from the mother-tongue, whence also sprang the Iranic, Slavonic, Lettic, Teutonic, and Keltic groups. Comparative grammar, in fact, teaches us that Latin teems with forms more ancient than the corresponding Greek ones. In its phonetics, for instance, Latin retains the initial *s*, which Greek changes to a rough breathing, as in *septem*, *sex*, *socer* compared with ἑπτα, ἑξ, ἑκυρος. It retains also the old semi-vowel *y* (represented by *j*), where Greek changes it either to ζ (sounded *dz*) or to the rough breathing: *jecur*, *jugum*, contrasting favourably with ἥπαρ, ζυγον. In the same way the primitive *k*, in Greek often changed to *p* and *t*: *quinque*, *quis* being thus older than πεμπε, τις.

It is of course by systematic comparison alone with the other Aryan tongues that we can ascertain the purity of these different Latin forms, and the corrupt state of their Greek equivalents.

In its declension also we find that Latin has preserved the ablative singular, no longer known to the Greek, while in its conjugation the second person plural suffix is more correct than the Greek: *estis* = you are, coming nearer to the organic *astasi* than do either the Greek εστε, the Lithuanian *este*, or the Sanskrit *stha*.

On the other hand, it is often surpassed by Greek, especially in the conjugation, where the latter has better preserved the primitive tenses. Thus both have their strong and weak points; so that, after all, neither of them can boast of being more correct, purer, or older than its congener.

In this section we shall have to treat successively of the old Italic tongues—Latin, Umbrian, &c.—and of the Romance or neo-Latin languages, now spoken in the south-west of Europe, and on the Lower Danube.

(1) *Primitive Italic Languages.*

Latin is the great representative member of this group. Compared with it the *Oscan* and *Umbrian* play but an insignificant part, though they cannot be altogether overlooked. A number of other idioms belonging to this same family were also spoken in Italy, but being still almost unknown we shall have to pass them over unnoticed. Nor shall we here speak of the Etruscan language, which may possibly have been a member of this group, and sister to the Latin, Oscan, and Umbrian. But in our opinion this relationship is not yet sufficiently established to allow of its being unreservedly accepted. We shall refer to it, however, after concluding our survey of the different Aryan groups, and shall then include it amongst the Aryan tongues, whose classification has not yet been finally settled.

The *old Latin* forms, occurring down to the middle of the third century before our era, that is, before the time of the first Punic war, and known to us by a number of inscriptions, do not differ essentially from the classical Latin forms. The differences that do occur are mainly phonetical, and affecting more particularly the vowel system.

Classical Latin may at once be said to differ from the older tongue by a very marked tendency to reduce the ancient diphthongs to simple vowels; in fact it is more than a tendency, it is a decided and very prominent feature, from which the diphthong *au* almost alone has escaped, the others nearly everywhere becoming long vowels. Thus the old Latin forms: *loumen, jous, oinus, oitile, ploeres, ceivis,* *leiber, veicus,* become in classic Latin : *lumen, jus, unus, utile, plures, civis, liber, vicus.* At the time of the Gracchi, a hundred and thirty years before our era, the old diphthong *ai* had definitely become *ae,* which *ae* in its turn changes to *e,* at first in the popular speech before the Christian era, and then in the written some three or four centuries later on.*

Certain changes of the simple vowels effected during the transition from old to classic Latin, though relatively of less consequence, must still be regarded as characteristic. Thus *o* occasionally becomes *e,* as in *verto, vester,* for the older *vorto, voster;* *u* becomes *i* as in *optimus, decimus, mancipium,* replacing *optumus, decumus, mancupium;* *i* becomes *e,* as in *navem* for *navim.* These various changes, besides a considerable number of analogous variations, are doubtless not regulated by special laws, nor are they as uniform as the contraction of the primitive diphthongs into simple vowels; still they produce a certain general effect which cannot be mistaken by those at all accustomed to the ordinary classic forms.

The euphonic laws affecting the Latin vowels are far from numerous. An organic *a* changes readily to *e* before a nasal in final syllables, as in *septem, nomen, patrem;* after *v* it usually becomes *o,* as in *vomo, vos, volvere, colo,* and at times even before *v,* as in *novus, ovis.* A comparison with the other Aryan tongues shows that here the *o* replaces *a* in the primitive Aryan tongue. In other respects the Latin vowel scheme is of the simplest, closely resembling the Greek, which differs mainly from it by its more general retention of the ancient diphthongs.

On the other hand, the Latin consonantal system is more faithful than the Greek to the primitive type. Lithuanian alone, of all the Aryan tongues, has better than Latin preserved the organic *s* of the common mother-tongue. In Latin it at times becomes *r* between two vowels, as in *generis,* genitive of *genus,* or at the end of words, as in *arbor* for the older *arbos.* But this solitary modification is of

* Corssen, "Ueber Aussprache, Vokalismus und Betonung der Lateinischen Sprache," 2nd ed., i. p. 695. Leipzig, 1868.

far less consequence than the development of so many new fricatives peculiar to Greek, Slavonic, Iranic, and Sanskrit.

While Greek changed to the sharp aspirates *ph, th, kh*, the soft *bh, dh, gh*, of the common Aryan tongue, Latin, especially in the middle of the word, rendered them in principle by the corresponding unaspirated explosives *b, d, g*, as in *nubes, lingo*, compared with the Greek νεφος, λειχω. But it modified these primitive aspirates in two other ways, especially at the beginning of words, where they become sometimes *h* and sometimes *f*. Thus *fero* = I bear, answers to the Greek φερω and the Sanskrit *bharami*. At times both forms occur, as in *hordeum* and *fordeum* = barley; *horda* and *forda*. This change of the primitive aspirates to *h* and *f* has been variously explained, but the point is not yet quite cleared up.

Another peculiarity of Latin phonetics is the change of *d* to *l*: *lacrima* = tear, *levir* = brother-in-law, *lingua* = tongue, *olere* = to smell, for the older *dacrima, devir*, &c. This explains a number of double forms, such as *impelimenta* and *impedimenta*; *delicare* and *dedicare, olere* and *odor*.

The Latin consonants are readily affected by the niceties of at least a rudimentary system of assimilation. This is often partial only, as in *actus*, where *c* stands for *g*, as seen in *ago*; but it is sometimes complete, as in *summus*, where the *mm* stand for *pm*, as shown by *super, supremus*. Again, if a word begin with two consonants, the first of these often disappears. Thus *notus, nomen* were formerly preceded by a *g*, as shown by the compounds *cognosco, cognomen*. At the beginning of words also the group *dv* may change to *b*, as in *bis* and *bonus*, for the older forms *dvis, dvonus*, while *bellum* and *dvellum* coexist.

With regard to the pronunciation of Latin, we may remark that it is a question many have essayed to solve without even so much as suspecting the nature of the conditions on which its solution depended. Now, however, it may be said to be settled, at least in a general way. The work of Corssen, quoted higher up, has collected all the results hitherto arrived at, and which may be safely looked on as conclusive. On the pronunciation of a good many consonants, *p, b, f, d, m, n, r, l*, &c., there is no diversity of opinion, so that we need not dwell on these, and our remarks will be restricted to such points as may still seem to present any doubt.

It is generally admitted that before the vowels *a*, *o*, *u*, and before consonants, the Latin *c* had the same sound as *k*; but what was its pronunciation before *e* and *i*? Did it sound like *ch*, as in Italy, or like *ts*, as in Germany, or like *s*, as in France [and England]? Did the Latins say Chichero, Tsitsero, or Sisero? We are now in possession of more than sufficient materials to decide this point, and the transcription of foreign words in Latin, and of Latin words in foreign languages, ought alone to remove all doubt. The Goths, for instance, when borrowing from Latin the terms *lucerna*, *carcer*, *acetum*, changed them to *lukarn*, *karkara*, *aikeits*, while the Greeks wrote πριγγκιπια πατρικιους, κηνσωρ, κεντυρια, for *principia*, &c. On the other hand the Latins at all times represented by *c* the κ Greek, as in the forms *Cerasus*, *Cimon*, *Cecrops*, and Corssen justly concludes that down to the sixth or even seventh century of our era the Latin *c* had the force of *k* before all the vowels.* Besides the old Latin grammarians† never say that the sound of *c* differs according to the vowel by which it may be followed, and we may feel satisfied that if it was at all changed to *s* before *e* and *i* previous to the seventh century, this took place in the vulgar speech or in the provincial *patois* alone.

Before *i* pure, that is followed by another vowel, as in *justitia*, *servitium*; *t* also remained hard, not till much later on becoming a fricative, at least in Latin. In Oscan and Umbrian the change occurred at an earlier period, but was not regularly adopted in good Latin pronunciation till the fifth century, although traces of it occur so early as the third.

The letter *g* also, before the vowels *e*, *i*, may with equal certainty be said to have had the same sound as before *a*, *o*, *u*. Later on it often became *i*, but only in the vulgar speech.

* *Op. cit.*, tom. i. p. 48.
† Amongst others Quintilian, whose language is conclusive of the contrary: Nam *k* quidem in nullis verbis utendum puto, nisi quae significat, etiam ut sola ponatur: hoc eo non omisi, quod quidem eam, quoties a sequatur, necessariam credunt, cum sit *c* littera, quae ad omnes vocales vim suam perferat. "Institutiones," i. 7.—*Note by Translator.*

The aspirate *h* was perhaps distinctly heard at a certain epoch, but it gradually lost its force, and was omitted altogether in a number of words, such as *anser*, whose root is the same as that of the Greek χην [and the English *goose*].

The sound of *j* is not at all doubtful, being always like our *y* in *you*. On this point the evidence of Priscian (sixth century) leaves no room for equivocation.

Altogether a reformation in Latin pronunciation is perfectly feasible, and we may add desirable, though we cannot hope that it ever will be realised.* It is well, however, that in any case the pronunciation of the classic period should be known, and especially that no attempt should be made to cause the adoption of any of the systems current in Italy, France, Germany, or elsewhere, which are all alike defective.

Besides, any reform of the kind should be based on a strict observance of the laws of quantity. In Latin there successively prevailed two systems of accentuation. The second, which was that of classic times, was regulated by quantity, and may be said to have been extremely simple. The fundamental principle was that the accent should fall invariably on the penultimate syllable when long, as in *canímus*, but on the antepenultimate when the penultimate is short, as in *cánimus*. This, of course, in case the word has three or more syllables, for in words of two syllables the accent falls necessarily on the penultimate whatever be its length. Thus: *fécit*, *nóbis*, where it is long; *déus*, *téner*, where it is short.

Hence the accent may shift its place in the declension and conjugation according to the number of the syllables, as in *amabímur* = we shall be loved, where it falls on a long antepenultimate, and in *amabímini* = you will be loved, where it falls on a short antepenultimate. In fact, in these two examples the penultimate is short, and it is the quantity of this syllable, as

---

* In England such a reform has already made a good beginning, and has received a certain stimulus from the advocacy of Mr. A. J. Ellis, who has embodied his views in a valuable little work entitled "Practical Hints on the Quantitative Pronunciation of Latin." London, 1874.—*Note by Translator.*

stated, that decides as to the position of the accent, independently altogether of the quantity of the other syllables.

Hence, in order to settle the position of the accent, we must be first acquainted with the laws of quantity, which, however, are neither difficult nor numerous. And herein precisely lies the advantage of the practice of Latin verse in schools, as the only means of ascertaining whether the learner is acquainted or not with quantity. If he knows it, he can also place the accent, which we shall see plays a chief part in the formation of the Romance tongues, and especially of French, in which the very form itself that the word has assumed depends on the position of the Latin accent.

Returning to the subject of grammar, we find that Latin has lost the dual, which Greek has at least to some extent preserved, and is therefore so far superior to its congener. In respect of the case-endings, they are each of them superior in some points and inferior in others. We have stated that Greek has lost the old ablative retained in Latin. Here the organic ending was *t* for themes ending in a vowel, and in Latin this *t* has become *d*, whence the forms: *sententiad, praivatod, magistratud, marid*. However, this *d* disappeared at an early period. The organic form of the dative singular was *ai*, reduced in Sanskrit to *ê*, whence in Latin the old forms *populoi, Romanoi*, which subsequently became *populo, Romano*. The organic form of the old locative was *i*, which is not always lost in Latin; where, however, it becomes long *i*, owing to a secondary cause that we are not here concerned with. Anyhow, *domi, humi, belli*, are true locatives, wrongly treated in grammars as genitives. In the plural we may notice the total disappearance of the locative, still retained in Greek.

Coming to conjugation we find that the personal endings are tolerably well preserved, though of the old *mi* = I, of the present tense, the only traces now left are the two forms *sum* and *inquam*. Of the six primitive tenses Latin has retained the present, a few reduplicate perfects, such as *cecinimus* = we have sung, and perhaps some traces of the simple aorist. But this was at best but little, and recourse was necessarily had to fresh formations. The perfect in *si* (luxi, dixi), the perfect in *ni* or *vi* (monui, amavi), as well as the imperfect in *bam* (amabam), the future in *bo* (amabo), and a number of other analogous formations, were all amongst those subsequently developed. But we cannot dwell upon this subject, and will merely add, that of the old Aryan tongues Latin is one of those that have given birth to the greatest number of such new forms, some of which may doubtless seem even superfluous.

There is one of them, however—that of the middle, or passive, voice—which cannot be passed over in silence. In the Italic, as in the Keltic tongues, there was created a middle voice, which later on acquired a passive sense, and which was formed by adding to the verb the reflective pronoun. Thus, *amor* stands for an older form *amos*, which again stands for *amo-se*. Lithuanian also has developed a middle voice by an analogous process.

Of all the Italic tongues, sisters to the Latin, and destined gradually to disappear before it, the *Oscan* and the *Umbrian* are the most important. Umbrian was spoken in the north-east of the peninsula, and the *Volscian* dialect is generally believed to have been allied to it. Oscan was spoken in the south, and was related more to the *Sabellian* [or Samnite]. But all three, Umbrian, Oscan, and Latin, sprang from one source; and although neither preceded any of the others, still a comparison of their phonetics and of their forms shows that of the three Oscan came nearest to the common type, from which Umbrian departed more even than Latin.

Oscan was spoken in Samnium, in Campania, and in the neighbouring districts,* and is known to us through some important inscriptions, the bronze tablets of Agnone and Bantia and the Abella Stone. Oscan is particularly distinguished from Latin and Umbrian by its careful preservation of the ancient diphthongs, and by its retention of the organic *a* often replaced by an *i* in Latin. Thus the Oscan *anter* represents the Latin *inter*. These are not the only primitive features of its vowel system, but they may be mentioned as the most striking. With regard to its consonants, while in some respects inferior, it is also often superior to the

* Rabasté, "De la Langue Osque." Rennes, 1865.

Latin. Its inferiority is shown especially in the substitution of *p* for the primitive *k*, as in *pam* for the Latin *quam*. Before a *t* it replaces *k* by *h*, as in *Ohtavis* for the Latin *Octavius*. But in many cases its superiority is very marked. Thus it does not, as a rule, change the *s* to *r*. as Latin does; and it also avoids a number of assimilations, writing *kenstur* where the Latin has *censor* for *censtor*. A phonetic peculiarity distinguishing it from Latin consists in its frequent change of the organic aspirates to *f* in the body of the word, a change which in Latin scarcely occurs except with initial letters. Thus the Oscan *sifei* stands for the Latin *sibi*.

Umbrian we are acquainted with through a very important monument, the bronze tables known as the "Eugubine Tables," from Gubbio, the ancient Eugubium, where they were discovered in the middle of the fifteenth century (1446). These tables for a long time taxed the ingenuity and sagacity of the old linguists, but it was reserved for Aufrecht and Kirchhoff to satisfactorily decipher them, reducing their grammar to a scientific basis, in a work on the Umbrian language, to which all subsequent essays on the subject are largely indebted.*

The Umbrian vowel system is more closely related to the Latin than is the Oscan, while showing a still greater tendency than the former to reduce the ancient diphthongs to a single vowel; and, what is still more remarkable, it frequently omits many vowels altogether. Thus it has *nomne* for the Latin *nomini*. Like the Oscan it sometimes changes the primitive *k* to *p*, whence *pis* for the Latin *quis*. As in Oscan also it substitutes *f* for the organic aspirates, which in Latin become simple explosives, whence the Umbrian *tefe*, *ife*, answering to the Latin *tibi*, *ibi*. As in Oscan also it changes the group *kt*, to *ht*, *rehte*, corresponding to the Latin *recte*. In certain cases the primitive *d* becomes *r*, which seems to have had a somewhat peculiar utterance, and which is usually denoted by a dot underneath: *areeita*, *rere*, *ranum* thus answering to the Latin *adeehita*, *dedit*, *donum*.

* "Die Umbrischen Sprachdenkmäler," Berlin, 1849-51; André Lefèvre, "Les Dialectes Italiques: L'Ombrien," Paris, 1874.

Q

But these few remarks will probably be sufficient on the two Italic tongues, sisters to the Latin, from which they do not in fact differ essentially, not more perhaps than do the various Greek dialects from each other, and certainly much less than the neo-Latin or the Keltic languages do amongst themselves.

Let us conclude with a few words on the old Italic characters, which, according to Corssen, derive all of them from two Greek alphabets. (*Op. cit.*, i. p. 1.) One of these, the old Doric, or some allied system, would seem to have been the parent of the Samnite, of three Etruscan systems, of the Umbrian, of the Eugubine Tables, and of the Oscan of the Abella Stone. All these varieties, except the last, possess two signs to denote the *s*, that is, the Greek capital sigma, represented either in the usual way, or else inclined one fourth to the right, so as to look like a sort of M.

A more recent Doric alphabet seemed to form the basis of the Faliscan and the Latin, the oldest documents of which last date from the end of the third century before our era. The old *k* had already disappeared except in certain words, the *c* having long denoted as well the sound of *g* as of *k*, and being at last replaced for the first of these functions by the new letter *g*, itself derived by a slight modification from *c*. From about the middle of the second to the middle of the first century before our era, that is for about a hundred years, the practice seems to have prevailed of denoting the long vowel by doubling it, thus *aara, ree, Muucius* [for *āra*, &c.]. About a century before our era the long *i* was denoted by giving it a longer or higher form than that of the other letters of the same word: ɒlvo, vlcus; at times also this sign was employed to denote the semi-vowel *j* (our *y* in sound), as in lus, MAIOR.

In the middle of the first century after our era the Emperor Claudius essayed to enrich the Latin alphabet with three new letters. In order to distinguish the consonant *v* from the vowel *u* he proposed to denote the first by the Greek digamma reversed. For the combinations *ps, bs* he suggested an inverted *c*, and lastly the sign ⊢ for the sound of the French *u*, that had been introduced into certain words. But none of these innovations took root, and the Roman alphabet remained in the same state as heretofore.

(2) *The Neo-Latin Languages.*

At the beginning of the present century a strong belief prevailed, still shared in by many, that French came of a *Romance* tongue, which towards the end of the [Western] Empire and during the first centuries of medieval times, had succeeded to its direct progenitor, Latin. The writings of the illustrious linguist Raynouard contributed not a little to the spread of this theory. It was readily adopted; much was written on the Romance tongue; its texts were commented on, and many still persist in looking on the present Provençal as this Romance idiom. Raynouard had unfortunately trespassed beyond the field of his proper linguistic studies, intruding somewhat rashly and without method on the domain of philology; hence his theory of a Romance language was fated to disappear soon after its author.

In truth, no such language ever existed, nor did Latin give birth so much to a single Romance form as to several neo-Latin tongues.

At the same time we must avoid the mistake of supposing that these new idioms are merely a sort of corrupt Latin. They are, on the contrary, the vulgar or popular Latin, as spoken in Spain, Portugal, France, the Grisons, Italy, and on the Lower Danube. In fact, by the side of the literary standard there co-existed an ordinary current Latin, diffused by the legionaries and the settlers throughout Iberia, Gaul, and Dacia. It was this vulgar speech that became gradually modified, reappearing in one place as Spanish, in another as French, elsewhere as Rumanian, just as in Italy itself it became Italian. Meantime the literary Latin, becoming less and less intelligible to the vulgar, passed at last to the condition of an ancient, classic, or dead language.

"When Latin," says M. Littré, "had finally caused the indigenous tongues of Italy, Spain, and Gaul to disappear, there was but one literary standard for these three great countries, but the vulgar speech (that is, of course, the Latin vulgar speech, scarcely any other having survived) was everywhere respectively different. This, at least, is what the Romance tongues bear witness to by their very existence. Had Latin not been spoken somewhat differently in each place, the languages flowing from it would

possess no distinctive features, and would be confused together.
But these Italians, Spaniards, and Gauls, having all alike been
brought, by the force of circumstances, to speak Latin, spoke it
each of them with their own peculiar accent and sense of euphony.
. . . . Those great regions that we call Italy, Spain, Provence,
and France, stamped their special character on this language, just
as those smaller districts did which we call provinces. And these
discrepancies were themselves governed by laws from which there
was no escape. These laws lie in the geographical position,
involving essential and characteristic differences amongst the inhabitants. French, the farthest removed from the Latin centre,
was that which modified it the most; I speak of the form only,
for the common Latin groundwork is as pure in French as in the
other idioms. Provençal, placed by the lofty Alpine barrier in
the Gaulish zone, but on its verge, is intermediate; nearer than
French, somewhat less so than Spanish, to the Latin form. Spain,
again, skirting the Mediterranean, and so closely resembling Italy
in its soil and climate, resembles it also in its speech. Lastly
Italian, being placed in the very centre of Latinity, reproduces it
with the least change. And there is for this theory of the formation of Romance, a negative proof, which, like all the others, is
conclusive. In truth, were such not the law that regulated the
geographical distribution of the Romance tongues, we should here
and there light upon some break in the type peculiar to each region,
some evidences of types peculiar to other districts. Thus, for instance, in the French domain, in the remote parts of Neustria, or of
Picardy, we should meet with Provençal, Italian, or Spanish formations; in the heart of Spain we should come across French,
Provençal, or Italian forms; in the extremity of Italy we should
encounter Spanish, Provençal, or French peculiarities. But it is
not so. The local type once established, undergoes no further
deviation, no return to the type of any other locality; everything
takes place regularly under the local influences, which may be
considered partial, when contrasted with those of the larger
regions."*

* "Dictionnaire de la Langue Française," t. i. p. xlvii. Paris, 1863.

This Latin origin of the Romance tongues is now a firmly-established fact, that can no longer be called in question. The grammar of Frederick Diez, first published some forty years ago,* has once for all disposed of those Iberian, Keltic, or other theories, which nevertheless still crop up from time to time. French may no doubt be derived from Keltic, but so might Latin, in the same way, from Hebrew. This Keltomania is in fact a thing beyond discussion, for it rides over French, Latin, the Keltic languages themselves; and perhaps this is its only excuse.

But we do not, at the same time, deny the existence of a tolerably important foreign element in the neo-Latin tongues. French, for instance, possesses a certain number of words of Keltic origin: *arpent, lieue, dune, alouette*; but even this element is far from being as extensive as might be supposed, and it may be well to remark that all such terms, before becoming French, were first latinised; that, in a word, they passed through the Latin into the French language. The invasion of the barbarians, again, introduced some four hundred words of Teutonic origin, while contact with the East also contributed its share; but the grammar remained essentially Latin.

There are reckoned altogether seven neo-Latin tongues: Portuguese, Spanish, French, Provençal, Italian, Ladin, and Rumanian. Before speaking of the geographical distribution and special features of each of these idioms, it will be necessary to draw attention to two leading facts which form the groundwork of the whole subject. One of these is the play of the tonic accent in the formation of the neo-Latin words; the other is the transition from Latin declension to the analytic state of these idioms.

Of all the members of this group it may be said in a general way, that the formation of their words is based on the persistence of the tonic accent.† The accented syllable in Latin is still the accented syllable in French and Italian. This is the fundamental

---

* "Grammatik der Romanischen Sprachen," 2nd ed. Bonn, 1856-60.

† Littré, "Histoire de la Langue Française," 6th ed., t. i. p. 212, Paris, 1873; G. Paris, "Étude sur le Rôle de l'Accent Latin dans la Langue Française," Paris, 1862.

principle which remains unaffected by secondary laws. Let us illustrate it by what occurs in the French language.

Side by side with the continuance of the Latin accent, French discloses two secondary principles. One is the suppression of short unaccented vowels preceding the toned syllable; the other is the disappearance of certain consonants in the body of the word.* Thus the accent is on the vowel *a* in the words *bonitátem*, *liberáre*, *sanitátem*, and it remains on the corresponding vowel in the French *bonté*, *livrer*, *santé*, and we see that in these three examples the unaccented vowel *i* or *e* has disappeared. So also in *lier*, *douer*, the middle consonants *g* and *t* of *ligare*, and *dotare* have dropped.

Observe, also, that French sacrifices everything that follows the accented syllable. Its masculine final syllables, as in *essaim*, *peuplé*, *hôtel*, are always the toned syllables, while in the so-called feminine endings, as in *meuble*, *esclandre*, the accent is still on the last syllable (here *eu* and *a*), because the final is now silent, possessing merely an artificial existence in poetry. Practically *esclandre*, *semaine* are dissyllables, whose last, that is *an* and *ai*, are toned.

But a time came in the history of the French language, when the vocabulary flowing continuously from the old Latin vulgar tongue was found to be no longer sufficient, and then such terms as were needed began to be taken bodily from classic Latin. But this fresh supply could not of course be subjected to the fundamental principle regulating the play of the tonic accent, any more than to the secondary laws affecting medial consonants and untoned vowels. To this new stock the name of "learned words" was given, as might almost seem by a sort of irony, while that of "popular words" was applied to the really natural and genuine French element. Nor was the fabrication of such book-Latin terms limited to those the want of which really existed, but a crowd of others was introduced, which had already assumed a popular, correct, and genuine French form. Thus the accent, for instance, is on the first syllable in the Latin *debitum*, *cancer*, and in French these two

* Brachet, " Gram. Historique de la Langue Française," introduction, sect. ii. Paris.

words were regularly modified to *dette, chancre*; but the "learned" formation again adopted them, and, neglecting the tonic accent, fabricated the really barbarous forms *débit, cancer* (where the tone falls on the last, thus violating the fundamental principle regulating the formation of French words). The terms *opérer, cumuler, séparer*, and numbers of others have no doubt the accent on the same syllable as their Latin prototypes *operare, cumulare, separare*; but they are, nevertheless, mere pedantic and secondary forms when compared with the genuine *serrer, combler, ouvrer*, which (not only preserve the accent but also) omit, as they ought to do, the untoned vowel preceding the accented syllable. So also *lier, douer*, answer exactly to the Latin *ligare, dotare*, of which the coined forms *liguer, doter*, retaining the middle consonant, are merely arbitrary imitations.

We come now to the second, and no less interesting main feature of the neo-Latin tongues, the already-mentioned transition from the synthetic Latin, with its declensions and case-endings, to the analytical state, in which every trace of declension has vanished.

In the oldest Spanish and Italian records we meet with languages already reduced to complete analysis (that is, as regards nominal and adjectival declension, the verb still remaining largely synthetic). But this is the case neither with the old French nor with the old Provençal, which at a certain period show not merely the traces of case-endings, but two genuine cases—the nominative and the accusative. "At the time," writes M. Littré, "when a modern speech was being formed in Gaul, Latin, as still spoken, was in a peculiar state in respect of its rich declension. It employed the nominative correctly enough; but it confused the remaining cases, using them indifferently for each other. This at least is what we find in the monuments of the period, which teem with solecisms.*

---

* As in the following, where we have the accusative for the ablative, the masculine genitive for the feminine genitive, the ablative for the accusative, and the accusative plural in *is* for the genitive plural, besides *d* for *t*, *c* for *t*, *u* for *o*, *e* for *i*, &c. "In jure adque domenacionem Sancti Maria et sponsarum Christi in praedicto locum consestentis," which should be "In jus atque

The new language, then budding, with a sort of instinct infused regularity into all this chaos by retaining the nominative, and of all the rest making one single case—the objective. Hence, in its primitive state, French was not an analytical tongue, like modern French, or like Spanish and Italian in their oldest records. It had a synthetic, consequently, an older character, expressing the relations of the nouns to each other and to the verb, not by prepositions, but by true cases. . . . . It is, as we see, a sort of half Latin syntax, which French has in common with Provençal, so that these two languages of Gaul, possessing each of them two cases, resemble each other more closely than they do either Spanish or Italian, while these two in their turn are more nearly akin to each other than they are to the *Langue d'oïl* or the *Langue d'oc*.

"This inheritance of two cases, and of a half synthetic syntax, was no passing feature of the French tongue, leaving behind it no traces except for the curiosity of the learned. It continued in this state for three centuries, from the eleventh to the thirteenth, during which this syntax formed the rule of the written and the spoken language. Latin, which for us is a classic tongue, is much praised for the way in which its declension directs the thought. I am not discussing the relative superiority of languages with and without cases, but a portion of this praise should fall to the share of old French, whose declension, though curtailed, is still a reality, and which on this account ranks so far with Latin."—(*Op. cit. ibid.*)

The old French declension is very simple. In the case of forms answering to the Latin declension in *us*, such as *dominus*, the nominative singular retains the *s* of this ending *us*; the objective plural also ends in *s*, which again corresponds to the *s* of the Latin accusative plural *dominos*. The two other forms, that is the nominative plural and the accusative singular, remain in the simple state (the corresponding Latin endings of *domini* and *dominum* here simply disappearing in virtue of the accessory laws above explained in connection with the tonic accent).

dominationem Sanctæ Mariæ et sponsarum Christi in prædicto loco consistentium." M. J. D'Arbois de Jubainville's "Déclinaison Latine en Gaule à l'Époque Mérovingienne," Paris, 1872, p. 109.—*Note by Translator*.

We thus get the subjoined table of old French declension :

 Singular—Nominative : li chevals = caballus.
     Accusative : le cheval = caballum.
 Plural—Nominative : li cheval = caballi.
    Accusative : les chevals = caballos.

We should exceed our limits were we to dwell further on this subject, nor is it possible here to give a complete history of the declension of the Langue d'oïl or of that of the Langue d'oc. It is enough to establish the fact that these two languages had a period of true declension, which cannot be detected in the oldest texts of the other Romance tongues. Hence, as M. Littré remarks, we cannot speak of an old Spanish or an old Italian language in the same sense as we can of an old French and an old Provençal tongue.

This point settled, we may now pass in rapid review each of the seven branches of the neo-Latin family.

(a) *French.*

The indigenous Keltic idioms had in the first century of our era been already supplanted in Gaul by the vulgar Latin (that is by the *sermo plebeius*, as opposed to the classic standard). This result was brought about by numerous and irresistible causes, foremost amongst which was the strong interest the Gauls had in assimilating themselves to their masters. The literary language also was soon introduced, and the Gaulish schools, developed under Latin culture, acquired a well-earned reputation. Nevertheless, vulgar Latin alone contributed to the development of the popular speech, which derived exclusively from it. The classic language, for instance, wrote *urbs, iter, osculari, os, hebdomas*; but it is the popular forms, *villa, viaticum, basiare, bucca, septimana*, that reappear in the modern *ville, voyage, baiser, bouche, semaine*. The name of the French language, that is of the Langue d'oïl, at that time was *lingua romana rustica*, and in the eighth century the clergy preached in this "lingua rustica," which was the French of the period. The glosses lately discovered at Reichenau,* and which date from this epoch, are the oldest French texts yet discovered (being anterior even to the famous "Serment des fils de Louis le Débonnaire," which bears the date of 842).

But the eleventh, twelfth, and thirteenth centuries were the golden age of the Langue d'oïl. "Then was developed," says Brachet, "an absolutely original poetic literature, a graceful or sparkling lyrical, and a grand epic poetry, of which the 'Chanson de Roland' remains the most perfect example. Italy, Germany, Spain, adopt our poetry and our romances, translating or imitating them, &c."— (*Op. cit. ibid.*)

The declension with two cases, as above described, died out in the fourteenth century, after which period the French becomes decidedly a modern and analytic tongue, like Italian and Spanish.

From the moment that we are able to observe it, French conjugation seems to have become entirely analytic.† Side by side with the tenses flowing from the Latin, tenses such as the present *j'aime*, it developes others by the modern process : *j'ai aimé, j'aurais aimé*. Such also is the origin of the future : *aimerai = aimer ai*, as is placed beyond all doubt by the corresponding old Spanish and Provençal forms. Besides, classic Latin itself recognised this analytical future form, expressions such as *dicere habeo* occurring even in good writers. The conditional *j'aimerais* also is merely an artificial formation, based in some way on the future.

* Found in 1863 by Holtzmann, in a MS. in the library of this place. It is referred to the year 768, and it contains many contemporary forms explaining the difficult words of the vulgate. These words are written in two columns, thus :

Latin.	French of 8th century.
tugurium	cabanna
sindones	linciolo
minas	manatces, &c.

(*Note by Translator*).

† This is certainly an extraordinary statement. Analytical forms have doubtless been added to the French verbal system, and the old future has perished. But enough remains to render French conjugation still highly synthetic. Thus, it retains both participles, the infinitive, both presents, both pasts, and the imperfect indicative—all purely synthetic forms.—*Note by Translator.*

In medieval times a number of French dialects existed, independent of each other, and all possessing a special literature. It could scarcely have been otherwise under the feudal system. Still these various dialects differed mainly in their phonetics. Those of Burgundy, Picardy, and Normandy, were in any case compelled to give place to that of the Isle of France after the family of the Capets had finally chosen Paris as the centre of the kingdom. They gradually sank to the position of mere *patois*, "in which a careful study still detects the features of the old dialects as they existed previous to the literary productions of the Middle Ages. Hence those *patois* are not, as is generally supposed, the literary French corrupted in the mouth of the peasantry; they are the remains of the old provincial dialects, reduced by political circumstances from the position of official and literary to that of merely spoken tongues."—(Brachet, *op. cit.*, p. 47.)

The *Wallon* dialect maintained its independence for a long time. It had two varieties, that of *Liége* and that of *Namur*,* which have been wrongly grouped with the Picardy dialect, from which the Wallon is quite distinct. It is now merely a *patois*, having yielded in common with the other medieval dialects to the literary standard.

We have had several times to refer incidentally to the actual limits of the French language. On the north it meets the Flemish a little above Calais, whence it stretches through Saint-Omer, Armentières, Tourcoing, and Ath, to Liége and Verviers. On the east it is inclosed by the German, by a line including Verviers, Longwy, Metz, Dieuze, Saint-Dié, Belfort, Delémont, Friburg, and Sion, and farther south by the Italian. In the centre it now occupies the whole domain of the Provençal dialects, of which we shall presently speak.

In Switzerland French is the native speech of about 600,000 people, in the Cantons of Neufchâtel, Geneva, Vaud, the greater part of Friburg and of the Valais, and a fifth of Berne. In Belgium it is spoken by about 2,000,000, occupying the whole south-eastern portion of the kingdom, and in Germany by over 200,000 about

* Chavée, "Français et Wallon." Paris, 1857.

Malmédy, Metz, and Château-Salins. It is also still spoken in the English colonies of Mauritius and [parts of] Canada.

(β) *Provençal.*

The opinion of some writers that both the Langue d'oïl and the Langue d'oc, or Provençal, derive indirectly only from vulgar Latin, through an intermediate form common to both, rests so far on nothing but empty and utterly ungrounded statements, and we may add that in itself it is highly improbable. The current Latin speech cannot have modified itself uniformly throughout the whole of Gaul. It would be even surprising if in this vast region it assumed no more than two distinct types, those of the Langue d'oïl and the Langue d'oc. Anyhow, in the absence of all proof it will be prudent to doubt whether there can have at any time existed a common Franco-Provençal speech. The northern and the southern dialects, no doubt, resemble each other the more closely the more ancient are their texts, but this is simply because the older they are the more closely do they approach their common (vulgar Latin) origin.

Provençal, as already observed, had, like the Langue d'oïl, its semi-synthetic period, during which it possessed the declension with two cases, the nominative and the accusative. Its conjugation is quite as analytic as that of the Langue d'oïl, and it is in Provençal that we meet with the old form of the future *dir vos ai=je vous dirai*, which so clearly shows the mechanism of the modern tense.

The meaning in which the term Provençal is used is now thoroughly understood. Here a part is taken for the whole, for the language of Provence proper was and is one dialect only of the Langue d'oc, which includes also those of Languedoc, Limousin, Auvergne, Gascony, and part of Dauphiny. The question has often been asked whether it should not also comprise the Catalonian, at present spoken in Catalonia, Valencia, and the Balearic Isles, and formerly diffused thoughout the territory of Aragon, or whether this variety should not rather constitute a distinct neo-Latin group by itself. The point is not yet settled, nor can the view be altogether condemned which includes Catalonian amongst the Provençal dialects.

Provençal literature flourished mainly in the twelfth and thirteenth centuries, but its oldest records are anterior to this period. It received a fatal blow with the defeat of the Albigenses, after which French gradually encroached upon the whole country as far as the Pyrenees, and the southern dialects have now fallen to the position of mere *patois*, unconnected with any literary language.

The actual limits of the northern and southern *patois* have not been very carefully determined. The last information on the subject fixes the extreme frontier of the Langue d'oïl on the west at Blaye, Angoulême, Confolens, Montluçon, and Saint-Étienne. Towards the east the frontier is more difficult to settle, but it seems to reach the Alps a little above Grenoble.

(γ) *Italian*.

As known to us even in its oldest records, Italian is unquestionably the best preserved of all the neo-Latin tongues, both in its structure and vocabulary. Diez calculates that not a tenth part of its vocabulary can be referred to other than Latin sources. If so, this would certainly be not a little remarkable; but in any case Italian certainly contains far less German terms than does the French.

In the tenth century what we now understand by Italian was already spoken—that is to say, the vulgar Latin had already at this epoch been sufficiently modified in Italy to be entitled to this name. But its written monuments do not date farther back than the twelfth century, nor was it till the following century that the language of literature was developed in Tuscany—a purely literary language that never was spoken.* Anyhow, the Italian of this period had the same general features of the Italian of the present

---

* This expression is too strong. Amongst the educated classes, especially in Rome and Florence, the current speech does not materially, if at all, differ from the ordinary language of literature; and certainly all educated foreigners speaking Italian adhere very closely to the literary forms.—*Note by Translator*.

day; so that there was no old Italian in the sense that there was an old French and an old Provençal tongue.

In Italy there are a great number of dialects—a circumstance readily explained by the configuration of the country. These dialects have always been clearly distinguished from each other, and in his treatise "De Vulgari Eloquio," Dante reckons fourteen altogether, which he divides into eastern and western, or else into cis-Apennine and trans-Apennine dialects. This division, however, has been advantageously replaced by that of upper, central, and lower Italian dialects, the last class comprising the Neapolitan, Calabrian, Sicilian, and Sardinian. In the second are included the Tuscan, Roman, and Corsican; while the northern division embraces the Genoese, Piedmontese, Venetian, Emilian, and Lombard varieties. Each of these dialects possesses a copious literature, and many of them have monuments dating from the period of the Renaissance, while some, such as the Neapolitan and Sardinian, are still older.

Towards the north Italian crosses the political frontier, being spoken by a population of about 140,000 in the Canton of Ticino, and in the south-eastern portion of the Grisons in Switzerland. In Austria also, in a portion of Southern Tyrol, as well as in a narrow strip along the west coast of Istria, Italian is current.

(δ) *Ladin*,

Known also as the language of the Grisons, the Rheto-Romance, the Rumonsh, and Rumansh. But it seems best to call it simply *Ladin*, with Ascoli, who has recently devoted an important work to its elucidation.* According to this writer it comprises three distinct groups: on the east that of Friuli, spoken by upwards of 400,000 people in Italy on the banks of the Tagliamento, and in Austria as far as Goritz; in the centre, two tracts in Austrian Tyrol, at some distance from either bank of the Adige, by upwards of 90,000 persons; on the west, under the name of Rumansh, it

* "Archivio Glottologico Italiano," vol. i. Saggi Ladini. Rome, Turin, Florence, 1873.

stretches across the greater part of the Swiss canton of the Grisons, being there spoken by about 40,000; making altogether 580,000— a number which, though inconsiderable, cannot deprive the Ladin of its claim to be regarded as a true language. Its central and eastern groups have been wrongly connected with the Italian system, from which they differ altogether both in their substance and phonetics, while closely allied to each other in those respects.

The literature of the western branch, that of the Grisons, is but little developed. Its oldest document is a version of the New Testament dating from the sixteenth century, while those of the Friuli dialect are referred to the twelfth century, consisting, no doubt, of rather short inscriptions, but long enough to enable us to characterise the language of that period.

(ε) *Spanish*.

Spanish departs most from Latin in its phonetics and vocabulary, which latter, amongst other foreign elements, contains a considerable number of Arabic words; but in the formation of its words it remains very faithful to its prototype. Its oldest texts belong to the middle of the twelfth century, still somewhat scanty at that period, but growing more and more abundant in the following century. But there exist older traces still of the Spanish language consisting mostly of words occurring in the writings of S. Isidore of Seville, who flourished in the seventh century.

Spanish is at present confined on the west by the Portuguese, on the north by the Basque, whose limits are given at p. 109, and in the east it is spread throughout Catalonia and Valencia, but as the literary standard only, the current speech here being the Catalonian, referred to in our notice of the Provençal. On the other hand, Spanish has occupied Aragon, where Catalonian was formerly spoken, and it is also encroaching on the southern frontier of the Basque, which it has already driven from Vitoria, Estella, Pampluna, and Navascues, while Bilbao and Agiz already occupy a mixed zone. Thus Basque is losing ground much more rapidly on the south than on the north of the Pyrenees; because, as already explained, it finds itself in Spain directly opposed by an official language, while in France it comes more directly in contact with Gascon, a Langue d'oc dialect, whose own existence is already imminently threatened by French.

(ζ) *Portuguese.*

Though nearly allied to Spanish, Portuguese cannot be looked upon as a Spanish dialect. With Galician, spoken in the northwest corner of the peninsula, it rather forms an entirely independent branch of the Romance family. Its oldest records are more recent than the Spanish, dating apparently only from the last years of the twelfth century. The stock of Arabic words occurring in Spanish is much the same as that found in Portuguese, which, however, also contains a number of French terms foreign to Spanish. They are supposed to have been introduced during the rule of Henry of Burgundy, at the end of the eleventh century.

(η) *Rumanian*

Derives from the vulgar Latin, introduced into Dacia by the Roman legionaries settled there by Trajan, during the first years of the second century of our era. "The Roman soldiers released from further service," says Picot, "together with the *honesta missio*, obtained the *jus connubii* and the *jus commercii*, that is the right of trading and intermarrying with the barbarians. Thus forever cut off from their native land, and stationed for five-and-twenty years in the same outposts, the legionaries became attached to the country where they had lived and fought, and availed themselves of the opportunities afforded them by the law, to settle down there permanently. It was thus that were formed on the banks of the Danube the first centres of a Roman population, and these veteran settlers were soon joined by other colonists from all quarters of the empire, and especially by the barbarians attracted thither by the allurements of trade. The military colonies were very numerous in Dacia, at the period when the Romans were compelled to withdraw from that province. The purely Roman population may be supposed to have followed the legions to the right bank of the Danube, whilst the issue of the unions of the veterans and the barbarians, remained in the country of their birth, retaining the language they had adopted from their masters, and from these doubtless are sprung the modern Rumanians."

We shall have to speak farther on of the old Dacian tongue, whose position in the Aryan family is far from being yet settled. Rumanian very probably retains in its vocabulary some remains of this ancient language, though what they are, it might be somewhat difficult to determine. To do so, it would be necessary in the first place to know more of the old Dacian idiom than we now do, or than we are ever likely to do. However, a list, not without importance, has been made of the elements borrowed by the Rumanian from the Slavonic tongues, in historic times; and besides these there are a number of words derived from the Greek and other sources.

Rumanian was long supposed to be a Slavonic dialect; an error due not only to the Slavonic words existing in it, but also to the circumstance that it was till recently written in Cyrillic letters, that is, with the same alphabet employed by the Russian, Serbe, and Bulgarian. In certain cases this alphabet offered considerable advantages, but was in other respects very inconvenient, so that it has been at last finally abandoned for the Roman letters. When it was found necessary to make a selection of the diacritical signs needed to supplement the Roman alphabet, there were several systems of transcription to choose from. Hence no complete agreement was arrived at, though this much-to-be-desired result will doubtless, some day be achieved.*

The Latin vowels, as shown by Mussafia, have undergone two main modifications in the mouth of the Dacian populations. On the one hand, the vowels *e* and *o*, when toned, have in certain cases been changed to *ea* and *oa*, that is, they have become diphthongs; on the other, many vowels have acquired a very deep and almost nasal sound. This double phenomenon constitutes one of the leading features of the Rumanian tongue.†

* Picot, "La Société Littéraire de Bucarest et l'Orthographie de la Langue Roumaine." Paris, 1867.
† "Zur Rumaenischen Vocalisation." Vienna, 1868.

It possesses an article which, however, as in Bulgarian and Albanian, it suffixes instead of prefixing: *omul = man-the*. This agreement of three perfectly distinct idioms, but spoken in the same geographical zone, is not a little remarkable. But whether it is to be looked upon as a relic of some common speech, such as the old Dacian, which may have left this inheritance to the various tongues supplanting it in these regions, is still a moot question.

Rumanian is very homogeneous, more so than any other neo-Latin speech. The meaning of certain terms may vary from place to place, but this is not enough to constitute distinct dialectic varieties. There is scarcely any true dialect except the Macedo-Rumanian spoken in Rumelia, Thessaly, and Albania.

With the exception of this detached subdivision, Rumanian is singularly uniform and compact, forming a sort of irregular circle of over a hundred leagues in length, from the Dniester to the Danube, and about the same in width from Arad to the mouth of the Danube. Besides Wallachia and Moldavia, that is Rumania proper, it comprises the north-east of the principality of Servia, the banat of Temesvar, a great part of eastern Hungary, the greater portion of Transylvania, South Bukovina, Bessarabia, and the Danubian delta. It is at present spoken by perhaps 9,000,000 of people, about half of whom are in Rumania proper. The name of Wallachians (that is Walsch = Welsh = foreign) given to them by the Germans, they naturally repudiate, calling themselves *Rumanians*, and their speech *Rumanian*, herein anxious above all to perpetuate the memory of their origin.

§ 6.—*The Keltic Languages.*

Few words have given occasion to more anthropological, ethnographical, and archæological misconceptions than this of *Kelt* and *Keltic*. Amidst all this confusion erroneous theories of language and races have played a larger part than elsewhere, but the matter seems at last fairly set at rest. Cæsar's tripartite division of Gaul (at the opening of the "Commentaries") into Aquitania on the south, Keltica in the centre, and Belgium on the north, was quite correct. Building upon this classification, which is moreover confirmed by a great number of other passages, anthropology has shown that the present people of Auvergne and the Low Bretons are the principal French representatives of the small and swarthy Keltic race, which neither had nor has any connection with the tall, fair, blue-eyed and soft-complexioned neighbouring race that we may call by the name of Galats, Wallon, Belgian, or Kymric. This latter people has often but wrongly been spoken of as a Keltic race, and, as M. Broca has conclusively shown in an excellent essay on the subject, it never had any claim to this title.*

The confusion that has too long obscured the subject was largely due to the name itself of "Keltic languages," applied in too general a way to the Kelts and the Galats of the north-east. From the fact that these last spoke a language called "Keltic," they were converted into "Kelts," whose languages and races were again confused. It would have been just as reasonable to apply the term Galat to the Keltic tongues, and that this has not been done is undoubtedly due to the fact that the Kelts, a small, dark, brachycephalous race, had invaded the region known afterwards as Gaul, long before the Galats, allied to them in speech but not in race, also arrived there.

To explain this now ascertained fact of two very dissimilar races speaking closely connected varieties of the same language, it must be admitted that they both at some period lived in close intimacy. But this is nothing more than what is taking place everywhere at the present moment. Thus, for instance, there is no such thing as a French race, but rather many races speaking French; no Italian race, but rather many races speaking Italian; no Germanic race, but rather many races speaking German.

It would be impossible accurately to determine the region where the Galats and Kelts, living almost in community, spoke idioms known afterwards as "Keltic;" but all the anthropological

* "La Race Celtique Ancienne et Moderne, Arvernes et Armoricans, Auvergnats et Bas-Bretons," "Revue d'Anthropologie," ii. p. 577; and by the same author, "Nouvelles Recherches sur l'Anthropologie de la France en général et de la Basse-Bretagne en particulier," "Mémoires de la Soc. d'Anthropologie de Paris," iii. p. 147.

arguments point at a country situated towards the south-east of Europe, and we have elsewhere suggested that it may very well have been the region of the Dnieper and the Lower Danube.*

Without, however, dwelling on this side of the "Keltic question," without even inquiring as to which of the two branches of the Keltic tongues is to be referred to the Galats and which to the Kelts, we shall at once deal with the purely philological question, with which we are here alone directly concerned.

The Keltic tongues are divided into two distinct and clearly defined branches. One of these has received the names of *Hibernian*, *Gaedhelic* or *Gaelic*, the other those of *Breton* (*Welsh*) and *Kymric*. Following the usual practice, and for the purpose of avoiding any misunderstandings, we shall speak of them under the names of *Gaelic* and *Kymric*. Nor do we pretend to assert that there may not formerly have been other branches of the Keltic family besides these two. The fact is even probable, if we admit the wide diffusion of these idioms in very remote times. It does not seem quite impossible that documents may yet be brought to light in central Europe, perhaps in the region of the Danube, tending to confirm this supposition. But pending the discovery of such documents, our remarks must be limited to the two groups above mentioned.

The *Gaelic Branch* comprises three languages, *Irish*, *Erse*, and *Manx*, all three closely allied to each other.

Owing to its better preservation and to the wealth of its literature, the importance of Irish for the study of the Keltic tongues is very considerable. Its literary wealth is doubtless relative only, that of the cognate languages having been so little developed. The oldest Irish documents consist more particularly of more or less lengthy glosses occurring either in the margin or between the lines of Latin manuscripts as old as the eighth century. The old Irish inscriptions in the so-called "Ogham" characters cannot be more recent than the fifth century, that is the epoch when Latin writing spread among the Irish and Bretons. But the

* "Bulletins de la Soc. d'Anthropologie de Paris," 1874.

origin of these characters is as yet far from being cleared up, and we cannot therefore further occupy ourselves with them here.

Irish letters reached their greatest height in the Middle Ages, and of this period there remain a number of chronicles and tales, besides translations of foreign works. At the time of the Renaissance the language entered on the period of decay and ultimate extinction. At present there are at the utmost not more than 950,000 speaking both Irish and English, and not more than 160,000 speaking Irish exclusively, all restricted to the west [and south-west] part of the island.

Its geographical position has better preserved the *Erse*, or *Scotch Gaelic*, from the encroachments of the English language. Still, it is now spoken by scarcely more than 400,000 individuals, many of whom also speak English. And it would be rather difficult to say how many are acquainted with Gaelic alone. It occupies all the north of Scotland, except a small tract on the extreme north-east, besides the west and [a portion of] the centre, say, approximately, the south of Caithness, Sutherlandshire, Invernessshire, Argyleshire, and the west of Perthshire. It also extends over the neighbouring Hebrides, but is unknown in the Orkney and Shetland Islands.

Though less ancient than the Irish, the Gaelic literature of Scotland has the great advantage of having more faithfully preserved the memory of the old traditions (a statement which would probably be warmly contested by Irish writers). The apocryphal poems of Ossian, which gave rise to so much controversy about a hundred years ago, had unquestionably a groundwork of truth; and even now the Scotch Highlanders are far from having forgotten all the legends of their forefathers.

The dialect of the Isle of Man is of but secondary interest, and is now spoken by scarcely a fourth, if even so many, of the inhabitants.

The *Kymric Branch* comprises *Welsh*, *Cornish*, *Low Breton*, and *Gaulish*, of which two only still survive (the Welsh and Breton).

Of all the Keltic literatures that of Wales shows at present the greatest symptoms of vitality. Welsh glosses occur as early as the eighth century,* consequently as old as the Irish glosses above alluded to; though otherwise in every respect of far less importance. The flourishing period of Welsh literature extends from the eleventh to the thirteenth century, during which time were produced a number of chronicles and poems. The Renaissance seemed at first to threaten Welsh letters with extinction, but they subsequently recovered to some extent, and Welsh is still a written language.

Cornish, on the contrary, became extinct in the last century. Its most ancient monument is a glossary with the title of " Vocabula Brittanica," dating from the thirteenth or (more probably) from the twelfth century. [It is marked Vesp. A 14 in the Cotton Collection in the British Museum, and has been carefully arranged alphabetically, and printed by Mr. Edwin Norris in his " Cornish Drama," vol. ii., and also by Zeuss in his "Grammatica Celtica," less correctly.] Some other Cornish writings may be referred to the period of the Renaissance, more particularly a sort of Christian mystery on the Passion, into which a number of English words have already found their way. [Of this poem there are four copies extant, and it has been more than once printed. But the corrected edition by Whitley Stokes in the " Transactions of the Philological Society of London," 1862, supersedes all the others, which were almost worthless. It is accompanied by a translation.]

Breton or *Armorican* possesses no documents of any great antiquity, and those referred to a period anterior to the fourteenth century are doubtless not so old. [Yet the chartularies of the monasteries of Rhedon and Landevin belong partly to the tenth and partly to the eleventh century. Some of them have been printed by Courson in his " Histoire des Peuples Bretons," Paris, 1846.] The best known Breton work is the life of St. Nonna

---

* The oldest Welsh records of this sort probably are the vellum MSS. in the Bodleian—Auct. F. 4—32, in Wanley's Catalogue of Anglo-Saxon MSS. 2. 63. It includes accounts of weights and measures in Welsh, intermixed with Latin, the alphabet of Nemnivus giving the forms of the letters and their names in Welsh, the grammar of Eutychius with interlined Welsh glosses, &c. These glosses Zeuss refers to the eighth or ninth century.—*Note by Translator.*

(or Nonita) and her son (referred by Zeuss to the fourteenth century, and published under the title of "Buhez Santez Nonn, on vie de Sainte Nonne et de son fils Saint Devy," &c., with a French translation by M. Legonidec, in 1837). Breton literature, however, may now be said to be entirely extinct. All that survives of the old songs and traditions is being rescued from oblivion, though the publication of some more or less apocryphal pieces ought not to be allowed to cast a doubt on the genuine nature of many others.

Breton is spoken in the department of Finistère and in the western parts of the Côtes-du-Nord and of Morbihan. It comprises four dialects, that of Léon being the best known and seemingly the most important.

The twenty-four inscriptions we possess in the old *Gaulish* language were mostly discovered in the region of the Middle Sâone, though some come from the Lower Rhone, from eastern Normandy, and from other places. Written in Latin characters, and occasionally in Greek, as, for instance, that of Nîmes, these Gaulish records still remain undeciphered, though they have given occasion to some really valuable essays, such as that of Pictet[*] and others. But we have moreover the names of localities and of other proper names occurring in the classic writers, all of which together is more than enough to allow of the old Gaulish being classed with the Kymric branch of the Keltic tongues; but we shall again revert to this subject a little farther on.

The incursion of the Galatians into Asia Minor, where they settled, is an historical event. But their speech, which, according to the old authorities, resembled that of the inhabitants of Treves (Lower Moselle), disappeared during the first centuries of our era, certainly not later than the fourth.

The Keltic tongues doubtless lack what the Teutonic possess, some leading feature such as the (regular) interchange of consonants. But whilst showing strong affinities as well to the Teutonic tongues on the one hand, as to the Italic on the other,

[*] "Revue Archéologique," 1867, p. 272; *Ibid.*, Alfred Maury, 1866, p. 8; Whitley Stokes, "Gaulish Inscriptions;" also in the "Beiträge zur Vergleichenden Sprachforschung," ii. p. 100.

they do not the less present a very striking character of their own. It would be impossible, perhaps, to define this character very exactly, but it is the result of a perfectly definite aggregate. All the Keltic tongues in the matter of word-formation may be said to have shown a strong tendency towards contraction. We saw higher up how French, resting mainly on the Latin toned syllable, often disregarded the unaccented ones, as in *porche* from *pórticus*, *livrer* from *liberáre*, *règle* from *régula*, *leur* from *illórum*. It may possibly have inherited this tendency from the Keltic-speaking inhabitants of Gaul, before the vulgar Latin had there become (what we now call) French. Hence the contracted and condensed state of the Keltic words themselves might be supposed due also to an analogous tendency. But what was the law regulating the play of accent in the prehistoric or primitive Aryan Keltic? Unfortunately this is a point that it is now impossible to settle, and it consequently leaves a wide scope for conjecture.

A glance at the vocalismus of the old Irish readily shows that it is closely akin to that of the Latin language. Thus the vowel *a* of the common Aryan speech frequently becomes *e*, as in Irish *ech* = Latin *equus* = primitive Aryan *akva-s* = horse. The diphthongs also are contracted, as in Irish *fich* = Latin *vicus* for *veicos* = Aryan *vaika-s*. The final vowels are, moreover, usually sacrificed, as may be seen by these two examples. What we have said of the old Irish is equally applicable, not only to the other Gaelic dialects, but also to those of the Kymric branch. Both of these branches resemble each other very closely in their consonantal systems also. Thus each in certain cases aspirates the common Aryan consonants *k t p*. But this is less common in Kymric than in Gaelic: thus Breton and Welsh have *dec* for the old Irish *deich* (the *ch* = χ) = ten, which in modern Irish becomes *déag*, the aspirates being again corrupted to simple explosives.

The Kymric and the Gaelic phonology, again, are distinguished from each other by a very general and striking characteristic. The organic *k* of the common Aryan continues in the Gaelic group (except its occasional change to an aspirate as above), whereas in the Kymric it becomes *p* as a rule. Here are a few examples of this important fact: Welsh *pedwuar*, *pedwar* = four; Breton *peuar*, *pevar*, where the primitive *k* has become *p*, in the Gaelic branch continuing, as in the Irish *cethir* (*c* = *k*) compared with the Latin *quatuor* and the Lithuanian *keturi*. So with the Welsh *pimp*, *pump* and Breton *pemp*, compared with the old Irish *cóic*, modern Irish *cúig* and Latin *quinque*.

This change of *k* to *p* is clearly seen in the old Gaulish, and is one of the reasons for grouping this language with the Kymric. We know, for instance, that the Latin *quinquefolium* = cinquefoil or "five-fingered grass," was named *pempedula*, which compare with the Welsh *pump* and Breton *pemp* = five, as above; nor is this an isolated instance.

Irish declension has suffered much, the primitive case-endings having generally been very seriously corrupted, and occasionally disappearing altogether, rendering it difficult to determine at a glance the case of the noun. [This corruption of the *auslaut* had already affected the oldest historical forms of the Irish to such an extent as to render their comparison with the primitive Aryan almost impossible without assuming two or three intervening stages, as thus :

	Primitive Form.	Prehistoric Form.	Oldest Historic Form.
Singular—Nom.	ballas	balls	ball
Acc.	ballan	ballu	ball
Dat.	ballni or ballú	ballu	baul
Plural—Dat.	ballabis	ball (a) bis	ball (a) ib, &c.]

Old pronominal forms, assuming the force of true articles or prepositions, came to be employed as a remedy for the confusion thence arising. Thus the form *athir* = father, has, as it stands, the force of no particular case, but *intathir* becomes the nominative *pater*, and *sinnathir* the accusative *patrem*. Declension may be said to fare still worse in the Kymric group, all trace of case-endings having well-nigh disappeared, whilst the article itself has lost its distinctive force. Thus in Breton *roen* = king, means at once *rex*, *regem*, *regis*, &c., the article *an* always preceding it: *an roen* = rex; *an roen* = regis, &c. Hence the relational value of the noun is determined solely by the accompanying prepositions, just as in the English: *to the man, of the man, from the man, for the man,* beyond which analysis cannot go.

The Gaelic and Kymric conjugation follow essentially the same system, which is one that presents great difficulties to the learner, in fact constituting the real obstacle to the acquisition of the Keltic tongues. And here again, as might be expected, the Kymric group is much more corrupt than the Gaelic.

It would be an endless task to attempt to specify all the monstrous absurdities that have been written concerning the Keltic languages. Even now, it is by no means rare to hear of Phœnician and Etruscan being interpreted by Keltic roots, and still less rare to hear of the Basque being explained by Kymric or Irish words. But of even more frequent occurrence are those theories, cropping up almost intermittently, which, in spite of all that has been said, written, and proved, over and over again, respecting the origin of the Romance tongues, still insist upon deriving them from Keltic sources.* This obstinacy of the Keltomanian school is solely due to its utterly ignoring three essential elements in the calculation— that is the Keltic, the Latin and the neo-Latin tongues themselves. All the adherents of this school are etymologists, and etymology is the essential condition of Keltomania.

Thus the French *un* looks more akin in appearance to the Welsh and Cornish *un*, and the Breton *eun* than to the Latin *unus*, hence the irresistible conclusion of the etymologist that the French *un* comes from the Keltic *un*. But nothing can be further from the point, two important factors being here entirely overlooked. One is the old form of the French *un*, the nominative of which in the eleventh century (when there were two cases) was *uns*, where the Keltic *un* utterly fails to account for the final sibilant *s*, explained at once by the Latin *unus*. Again, before speaking of a Keltic *un* the Keltomanian has forgotten to compare the Welsh and Cornish *un* itself with the Gaelic *óin*, and thus reduce them both to some

---

* But even these visionaries are outdone by Charles Mackay, who has in some recent numbers of the *Athenæum* been amusing the public by his ingenious attempts to explain Shakespeare by means of Irish and the cognate tongues.—*Note by Translator.*

common form. But he does not concern himself with the scientific method, he is a pure etymologist, and were he not one, he would not be a member of the Keltomanian school.

At the same time, no one pretends to say that the Keltic tongues have not furnished a certain number of words to the vocabulary of the neo-Latin languages, though even this is by no means considerable, consisting mainly of geographical terms, such as the names of the Danube, Alps, and Ardennes. The words *lieue*, *dune*, *alouette*, and others, are also of Keltic origin, but only indirectly, that is, as already explained, by filtering through the Latin.

[The progress of Keltic philology, in the scientific sense, is marked by the names of Dr. Prichard: "The Eastern Origin of the Celtic Nations," 1832, in which he, for the first time, sought to prove the true affinities of the Keltic tongues, with the cognate Sanskrit, Greek, Latin, Gothic, and Slavonic branches of the Aryan family; Adolph Pictet, "De l'Affinité des Langues Celtiques avec le Sanskrit," 1837, a study based mainly on the Irish, and still valuable; Bopp, "Die Celtischen Sprachen," 1839, containing many important discoveries, and forming a sort of supplement to his Aryan "Comparative Grammar," in which Keltic had not been included; J. Kaspar Zeuss, "Grammatica Celtica," 1853, a fundamental work on Keltic philology, and an imperishable monument of the author's genius and industry; Dr. Hermann Ebel, a disciple of Zeuss, several important contributions to the study of the Keltic tongues, contributed to the "Beiträge Zur Vergleichenden Sprachforschung, vols. i. and ii., *passim*; Dr. Lottner, "Celtisch-Italisch," also in the "Beiträge," ii. 309; Whitley Stokes, "Irish Glosses, a Mediaeval Tract on Irish Declension," including the "Lorica" of Gildas, Glosses from the "Book of Armagh," &c., edited for the Irish Archaeological Society; Dr. W. K. Sullivan, papers in the "Atlantis," based on Ebel, and resumed, with valuable additions, in his "Celtic Studies," 1863; Rev. U. Burke, of Tuam, several works, not always sound; and Thomas Stephens, "The Literature of the Kymry," 1849 and 1876.

In Keltic archaeology, the most distinguished names are Dr. Petrie, "The Round Towers;" Eugene O'Curry, "The Brehon

Laws;" O'Donovan, Todd, Stokes, Reeves, &c. But in spite of the labours of all these and other scholars, the race still flourishes of the Valleneeys, Pinkertons, Vans, Kennedys, Bethams, Mackays, and other "Milesians," who continue to identify the Kymric and Gaedhelic tongues, not only with Phœnician, Etruscan, Basque, and Romance, but even with the Leni Lenapé Indians of North America, with the Lappish of the sub-arctic regions, the Ostyaks and Tungus of Siberia, with the Jaloffs of northern, and the Hottentots of south Africa, and with the English of Shake-speare. Such is the vitality of national prejudice when fostered by ignorance!]

§ 7.—*The Teutonic Tongues.*

The terms German, Germany, *Germanic*, to explain which several unsuccessful attempts have been made, do not appear to be of Teutonic origin, and ought, doubtless, to be replaced by the word Tudesk (or Teutonic), representing the modern German *Deutsch*, the old High German *diutisc*, and answering to a still older *thiudisks*, an adjective primarily meaning *popular*, *national*. Still the name of Germanic has become too general now to be replaced by any other: and the Germans themselves, while protesting against this term, still speak, somewhat inconsistently, not of the Indo-Teutonic, but of the Indo-Germanic languages. [But English philologists having long ago very properly rejected the term Indo-Germanic for Indo-European, and this latter now mostly for the simple word Aryan, they are not affected by this argument; as they have, moreover, shown a preference for the more correct Teutonic over the foreign Germanic, Teutonic is retained in this translation, as the *generic* term of the race. It would be hopeless to attempt to revive its modern form *Dutch*, restricted as this now exclusively is to one little section of the race, occupying mainly the delta of the Rhine; though there are writers who affect to speak of High Dutch and Low Dutch, instead of High German and Low German. From these examples it will be seen that while Teuton and Teutonic are by English use reserved for the whole people, in the widest sense, German and Germanic are conveniently employed in speaking of any section or subdivision of them. Hence we say the Teutonic branch of the Aryan family, but the High German or Low German subdivision of that branch, and so on. When, as is here the case, convenience and accuracy can be reconciled, we should be slow to forego the corresponding advantages, out of deference for foreign usage.]

The Teutonic system is divided into four distinct groups: the *Gothic*, *Norse*, *Low German*, and *High German*. But before treating of these in detail, let us cast a glance at the general system of all the Teutonic tongues.

Its main feature consists in its peculiar treatment of the organic Aryan explosives: k, t, p; g, d, b; gh, dh, bh, which it always strengthens. The aspirated Aryan explosive thus becomes unaspirated, and the soft becomes a strong explosive, while the strong Aryan explosives become fricatives, k changing to h, p to f, and t to the English *th* hard, as in *three*, *thank*. Hence where the Sanskrit, faithful to the organic explosives, says *bhrátá*, the Gothic has *bróthar*, changing the aspirate to a non-aspirate, and the strong to a fricative. So also the Sanskrit *ajras* = the Greek αγρος and Latin *ager*, in Gothic becomes *akrs* = acre, the weak explosive changing to a strong one.

Nothing is simpler or more uniform than this law, being always constant except when interrupted by some physiological impediment, as when an *s* precedes the explosive that would have to be made strong, in which case it remains unchanged. Thus the Sanskrit *asti* and Lithuanian *esti* answer to the Gothic *ist* = is.

This leading characteristic of the Teutonic system, in its broad outlines, was in the course of ages further developed and completed, but it still remained the very groundwork of the whole system.

Besides the new fricatives, f, h, th, hard and soft, and z, the old Teutonic tongues added little to the common stock of the organic Aryan consonants. On the other hand they lost the three aspirated explosives gh, dh, bh, which, as explained, have been converted into three simple explosives.

In their vocalismus the Teutonic tongues are less pure, having greatly modified the original Aryan system, and developed a great wealth of diphthongs. Their old declension, though not so well preserved as that of most of the other Aryan groups, is still organic enough in many respects; but the conjugation has suffered considerable losses, including nearly all the organic tenses.

(1) *Gothic.*

But for the generally received practice, we should be tempted to discard the *h* and spell this word more correctly as *Gotic*, and as the Goths themselves wrote it. The difference is material, because, as already remarked, the *th* of the old Teutonic tongues was a true fricative, and not a more or less aspirated explosive. The Romans wrote correctly *Goticus*, and the Greek historians alone are responsible for the vicious spelling *Gothic*.

Gothic was long supposed to be the common progenitor of all the Germanic tongues. But this was not the case; and though as a whole more correct and more akin to the common Aryan than any one of them individually, it is still in some respects inferior to its congeners. It must, in fact, be placed by the side of the old Icelandic and of the two Low German idioms, also often on the same level as the old High German, though this last, on one special point, is far inferior to all the kindred tongues. Doubtless many High and Low German forms are explained by the Gothic, but none of them derive directly from it. In a word, Gothic, Norse, High and Low German, all descend from one common source, which none of them now adequately represents.

When this common Teutonic mother-tongue was spoken is a question that will scarcely ever be settled. The Gothic we are acquainted with in the form it had assumed in the fourth century of our era, in the version of the Old and New Testaments, due to Wulfila (A.D. 318-388), the Ulphilas of Greek writers, bishop of the Goths, settled in Mœsia. It continued to be spoken for five hundred years thereafter, finally dying out in the ninth century.

Its vocalismus is the least complex of all those of the old Teutonic tongues. We will merely observe that it usually changes the organic *â* to *ê* or *ô*, herein often inferior to the High German idioms.

The old diphthongs *ai*, *au*, also changes it as a rule into *ei* and *iu* respectively.

We have spoken of the general tendency of the Teutonic tongues to strengthen the explosives of the common Aryan. After rigorously applying this law, Gothic afterwards further modified the fricatives thus obtained. Thus at times *h*, representing an older *k*, becomes *g*; *th*, from an older *t*, changes to *d*; and *f*, from an older *p*, passes into *b*. This phenomenon is very remarkable, and the numerous examples of its occurrence have frequently been wrongly cited as so many exceptions to the general principle of strengthening the organic explosives. M. Chavée has given it the title of "law of polarity," and we shall see how the expression may be justified, when speaking of the Low German tongues, in which this secondary law may be detected in actual operation. Meanwhile it will be enough to have noticed its effects on the Gothic language, where, though less general, it still exists.

The laws of Gothic phonology are important enough without being very numerous. One of the most characteristic is that in words of more than one syllable the vowels *a* and *i* preceding a final consonant disappear. Another important phonetic law peculiar to Gothic is that which as a rule changes *i* to *ai* and *u* to *au* before *r* and *h*.

In the nominal declension Gothic has lost all the dual forms, and the ablative, while nearly all the datives are borrowed from the vocative. Of the organic conjugation it has retained the present and the old reduplicate past only. the latter at least for a portion of its verbs; but no vestige remains of the two aorists, the imperfect, and future. It expresses the future by present forms, and for the bulk of derivative verbs it has developed a sort of past tense.

Gothic disappeared without leaving any issue, as was the case with so many other Teutonic tongues spoken about the same period— those, for instance, of the Vandals, Heruli, and Burgundians, of whom no records have survived.

(2) *The Norse Tongues.*

The old Norse speech was transplanted to Iceland by the

Norwegian settlers; and in consequence of the slow development of civilisation in this remote and inaccessible island, it was here able to maintain itself much more easily than in the other Scandinavian countries. In fact the modern Icelandic differs little from that old tongue: and its superiority over all its European congeners, not only of the Teutonic, but also of the Slavonic, Keltic, and neo-Latin groups, would be uncontested but for the existence of the Lithuanian. The weak point in modern Icelandic is its subjection to the already described law affecting the organic explosives, a law, however, common to all the Teutonic family, and from which it could not therefore escape.

The old Norse phonology is much more delicate than the Gothic, embracing some twenty different vowels, long and short, besides several diphthongs. There are also twenty consonants, including, besides the sharp and soft explosives, the two fricatives f, h, and the English *th*, hard and soft. Norse is, moreover, distinguished from the other cognate Germanic tongues by a greater tendency to assimilate its consonants. Its declension, as a rule, is as well preserved as in Gothic, and its conjugation has suffered the same losses. It has developed a future, a conditional, and a new past tense by analytical processes.

In Iceland were composed the noblest monuments of old Norse literature—the two "Eddas," consisting of a collection of old mythical tales. The first, which is in verse, dates from the eleventh century; the second, which is in prose, is more recent, forming a sort of supplement to the first.

There are four modern Scandinavian tongues: *Icelandic*, *Norwegian*, *Swedish*, and *Danish*. According to some writers, Icelandic alone derives directly from old Norse, the three other Scandinavian tongues coming from different though nearly related varieties of that old language. Others, on the contrary, hold that old Norse is the common parent of all four. In any case the greater affinity of Icelandic with Norwegian, and of Swedish with Danish is unquestioned. They may thus be divided into two tolerably distinct groups.* Icelandic and Norwegian, for instance, retain the old

---

* M. Möbius, "Dänische Formenlehre," p. 2. Kiel, 1871.

diphthongs, which Swedish and Danish change to long vowels; these last again preserve certain initial consonantal combinations, lost or only partly pronounced in Icelandic and Norwegian.

Norwegian, whose literature is purely popular, has lost much ground, to the advantage of Swedish, which possesses a genuine literature. Swedish not only occupies a large part of the Scandinavian peninsula, but is also spread over two tracts of the Finland coast, one on the Gulf of Bothnia, with Vaza as its central point, about fifty leagues in length, but very narrow. The other, which is more important, occupies the western portion of the northern shores of the Gulf of Finland, with Helsingfors for its central point. Landwards both of these territories are encircled by Suomi or Finnish-speaking races.

Swedish may, in a general way, be said to have preserved the main features of old Norse better than has the Danish. The consonants, k, t, p, for instance, when final, are weakened to g, d, b, in Danish, while they remain unchanged in Swedish. In fact, of all the Norse tongues actually spoken, Danish is the most modern in its forms. It is not only spoken in Denmark but currently written in Norway, and spoken there by the educated classes, Norwegian having sunk to the position of a purely vulgar tongue. Danish is also diffused over the northern portion of Slesvig, including the city of Flensborg. However, there are several varieties. Its oldest records date from the thirteenth century, but its present form seems to have grown out of the Zeeland dialect in the sixteenth century. Its vocabulary includes a number of foreign words, borrowed from Latin, Swedish, French, and especially German.

(3) *The Low German Group.*

This branch of the Teutonic tongues is split up into a considerable number of offshoots. It would seem to have first of all given birth to two distinct varieties, the Saxon and the Frisic, the former again giving rise directly or indirectly to some half-dozen languages, the

s

whole being usually comprised in some such scheme as the subjoined:

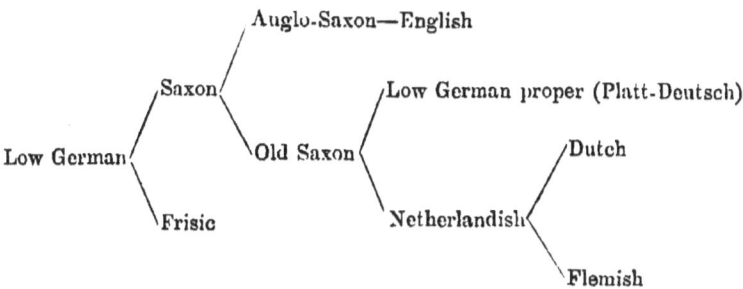

We have no direct knowledge of the common primitive Low German form of speech, any more than of the common primitive Saxon tongue, whence came the Anglo-Saxon and the old (or Continental) Saxon. These two last, however, are historic languages, thoroughly well known.

The *Old Saxon* was spoken from the Rhine to the Elbe, to the south of the Frisic, which occupied the extreme north (western) districts of Germany. Of this old Saxon tongue we possess an important record in the Christian poem of the *Héliand = Healer = Saviour*, extant in two manuscripts of the ninth century.* Anglo-Saxon (literature) dates from the seventh century, at least in England, to which period is referred its great epic "The Beowulf." [But the MS. of this poem in British Museum, Cott. Vitellius, A 15, is referred by Grein to the tenth century, though it probably represents the West-Saxon speech of the seventh.] The forms of these two old Low German languages did not greatly differ, though presenting certain strongly marked divergences, especially in their phonology. The old Saxon vowel system is much simpler than that of the Anglo-Saxon, which is very complex, and its vocalismus remarkably complete.

Anglo-Saxon is divided into two periods, the first, the Anglo-

---

* "Héliand: Poema Saxonicum Sæculi noni," Edidit I. Andreas Schmeller, Monachii, Stuttgartiæ, Tubingæ, 1830; also, "Glossarium Saxonicum e poomate Héliand," 1840.—*Note by Translator.*

Saxon period proper, reaching to the beginning of the twelfth century; the second, a semi-Saxon, to the middle of the thirteenth. [The term semi-Saxon is now mostly discarded by English philologists, though they have scarcely yet hit upon a convenient substitute for this transition period. In his history of the English language, 1861-75, the translator has used the term Broken Saxon for lack of a better.] The first stage of early English is about equally long, extending from 1250 to about 1350, and with it there begins a rapid decay of forms (and endings, which, however, had set in long before). Of the old cases there now remains the genitive only, which is itself often replaced by relational particles. In the middle of the fourteenth century begins the middle English period, which lasts for two hundred years, and during which the process of disintegration goes on with accelerated speed, so that when the new era, or modern English period, sets in, about the middle of the sixteenth century, the language is found to have become almost entirely analytical.*

* It is scarcely necessary to remind the reader that no two authors are quite of accord as to the proper distribution of the various stages of the English language. Some learned and noisy pedants will even insist upon rejecting the nomenclature by which the old or synthetic is clearly distinguished from the modern or analytic state of the language. They will not hear of the convenient, and in fact almost indispensable, terms Saxon and Anglo-Saxon, and will have nothing but English and old English for all the stages of a language that differs much more at its two extremes than does the modern Italian from classic Latin. The grounds of their violent opposition to the terms Saxon and Anglo-Saxon are based partly upon a mistaken national sentiment, partly upon the practice of Alfred, and partly upon the supposed danger of destroying the historic continuity of our tongue by speaking of its different stages under different names. This last argument being the weakest of all, is that which, as usual, is most insisted upon. It is as if an Italian should object to his speech being called *lingua Toscana* or *lingua Italiana*, lest its lineal descent from Latin might be thereby obscured. And yet the Italian has really far more right to speak of his tongue as Latin than we have to confound the languages of Alfred and of Shakespeare under one nomenclature, the difference between the first two being so much less than that existing between the latter. Or, to push the argument a step farther, it is as if a French philologist gone mad should object to his speech being described as French or Romance, or even neo-Latin, and insist upon its being called Indo-European, to show its

The English dialects are numerous, but they may all be said to have reached the same state of grammatical simplicity. They, however, all of them, in common with the literary standard, retain enough grammar to show the essentially Teutonic character of the language. The introduction of a large number of French (and book-Latin) words into its vocabulary in no way affects its grammar, as has been supposed and asserted. English is not a mixed tongue, but thoroughly Teutonic (in its structure), though its accidence has suffered more than that of any other cognate language.

Returning to the second, or old Saxon branch, we have already remarked that its vowel system was much simpler than the Anglo-

---

historical connection with the Aryan inflectional system, and lest it might be mistaken for some agglutinating or polysynthetic form of speech. Let it be borne in mind that the two extremes of our language differ materially in two essential points—their structure and their vocabulary—the one being largely synthetic and homogeneous, the other being of all non-isolating languages the most analytical, and of all cultivated tongues the most heterogeneous in its vocabulary, the Persian, perhaps, alone excepted. Hence the inconvenience of speaking of the whole historic period under one name is so great that if two terms did not exist it would be desirable to invent a second. Alfred's practice is nothing to the point. Whatever he called it, the language he spoke and wrote in was Southern—that is, a West-Saxon dialect, and nothing else—and hence is now properly called Saxon. If the term "Englisc" began in his time to be spread southwards, it was simply due to imitation mainly of Bede, who, being a Northerner and writing in Latin, properly spoke of his people as *Angli*, though also in many places using the term Saxon, even when speaking of all the Teuton inhabitants of Britain collectively, just as the Englishman Boniface in the middle of the eighth century spoke of his country as *Saxonia transmarina*, in a letter to Pope Zachary. It should be also remembered that the Northern, or Anglian, dialect was the first to be cultivated, whence the term *Englisc*, correctly used by the northern writers, came readily to be adopted in the south when the southern dialect began to be written. But, however called, the fact remains that nearly the whole of extant Anglo-Saxon literature is composed in this Southern or West-Saxon dialect, and is therefore scientifically not English, or Anglian, at all, but Saxon in the strictest sense of the word. Thus, then, this term is in every way justified, and will doubtless hold its ground in spite of all the empty clamour to the contrary. It has national *instinct* on its side, which is a more potent factor than false sentiment, and often quite as correct as the soundest scholarship.—*Note by Translator.*

Saxon, possessing far less vowel sounds. The same holds true of its modern representatives, whose vocalismus is also far less complex than the English. Of these there are two divisions—the Low German proper and the Netherlandish.

The *Low German* proper, or *Platt Deutsch*, is the current speech of the lowlands of north Germany. Eastwards it has encroached considerably on the regions where were formerly spoken Slavonic, and even Lettic idioms, such as old Prussian and Lithuanian. But it has never risen to the position of a cultivated tongue, all essays made in this direction having been rendered for ever fruitless by the preponderance of High German.

The *Netherlandish*, or second branch of the Old Saxon, is divided into two varieties, closely akin, if not almost identical—the *Dutch* and *Flemish*. The latter is often wrongly regarded as a dialect of the former. They stand both on the same level, being so nearly related that they have justly been said to differ in pronunciation alone. Flemish is still spoken by about 2,500,000 people, and Dutch approximately by 3,500,000, making altogether about 6,000,000, including the French Flemings of the Département du Nord.

The frontier line between French and Flemish passes in the north below Gravelines, Hazebrouck, Courtrai, Halle, Brussels, Louvain, and Tongres; in the south above Calais, Saint-Omer, Armentières, Tourcoing, Ath, Nivelles, Liége, and Verviers.

We have so far spoken of one branch only of Low German, that is the Saxon. The other is immeasurably less important, comprising the *Frisic* only, a somewhat ancient variety spoken on the coast of the North Sea, as well on the mainland as in the islands facing it. The Frisians seem to have shrunk from taking part in the migrations that the other Low German tribes undertook, preferring to remain in their native homes, where their speech retained certain very old characteristics, in spite of the influence exercised on it by the neighbouring Dutch, Danish, and Platt Deutsch dialects. [This statement about the "stay-at-home" character of the Frisians must be received with great reserve, there being good grounds for suspecting the existence of a good deal of Frisian blood in almost every part of England and the Scotch Lowlands.] Frisic has long ceased to be cultivated, having been, like the Platt Deutsch, completely overshadowed by the High German literary standard.*

When speaking higher up of the Gothic tongue, allusion was made to a Teutonic phonetic principle secondary to the general law by which the organic explosives are strengthened, and which prevails throughout the four branches of this family. And we remarked at the time that this new phenomenon is nowhere more easily to be detected in active operation, than in the various members of the Low German branch. This statement we shall now proceed to illustrate.

We know that in virtue of the general principle already explained, the organic explosives k, t, p, became in the Teutonic system true fricatives, h, th, f. The new phenomenon we now come to, consists in a further modification of these letters, which at times became g, d, b, and this in all the Germanic tongues. But this change was not effected abruptly, there having been an intermediate stage between h and g, th and d, f, and b. And it is here that the Low German idioms are of such extreme importance, often, in fact, showing the simultaneous existence of these various terms of the series. Thanks to them we know that the intermediate between the sharp fricative and soft explosive was the corresponding soft fricative. Thus the transition from f to b is effected by v; from h to g hard by a soft h; from the English th hard to the soft

* The oldest Frisian records extant are some legal documents referred to about the middle of the thirteenth century. There has recently appeared an extraordinary work under the title of "The Oera Linda Book, from a MS. of the thirteenth century. The original Frisian text, accompanied by an English version of Dr. Ottema's Dutch translation, by W. R. Sandbach," London: Trübner and Co., 1876. This MS., its Dutch editor asks us to believe, is but a copy of an older one still, that being in its turn a copy of another, and so on back to the original, composed mainly in the year B.C. 559. It purports to give an account of the wanderings and earliest settlements of the Frisian people, but teems with such gross absurdities and glaring anachronisms, both philological and chronological, that it is not likely to deceive anyone at all competent to form an opinion as to its authenticity. As literary forgeries the poems of "The Monk Rowley" were triumphs of genius compared with this clumsy and impudent fraud.—*Note by Translator.*

d by the English *th* soft, making altogether three successive stages, which will be made clear by one or two examples. The organic pronoun *ta*, by passing from a strong explosive to a sharp fricative, appears in Gothic as *tha* (*th* hard), while in the English article *the*, this sharp fricative has become soft, and in the Dutch and Flemish *de* we see the evolution fully carried out. Thus also the Dutch *doorn* answers to the Gothic *thaurnus* = *thorn*, *voor* to *fuur* = for, *vol* = *fulls* = *full*. At the same time the English does not always stop at the intermediate letter on the one hand, nor does it on the other always pass over to that letter, but the frequent occurrence of *th* hard showing it still in the first period; the word just quoted, *thorn*, for instance, standing with the Gothic in the first stage, as compared with the Dutch *doorn* in the third. But this in no way affects the principle, and a time may be confidently anticipated when every *th* in English will have become *d*, as is already the case in Dutch and Flemish. A number of English dialects have already arrived at this third period, as shown by *dey* for *they*, *de* for *the*, in Kent and Sussex, and *vor* for *for* in the Isle of Wight, *f* becoming *v* in the same way in Dorsetshire, Devonshire, and Somersetshire. The literary standard will, in its turn, have eventually to suffer the successive modifications that its dialects are now passing through. [On the other hand, the literary standard itself, and the spread of education, are meantime acting as a most powerful check against this very tendency, so that the modifications above spoken of, instead of being further developed, are actually dying out in many parts of the country, where a corresponding reaction has set in in favour of the older pronunciation. Thus, in the Isle of Wight, where even the hard *th* had in some cases passed over to the soft *d*, such expressions as "*dree* or *vour* years ago," common enough some years back, are now rarely heard, except among the extremely old and extremely young. The School Board here, as elsewhere, shows itself the implacable enemy of all dialectic variety, and is everywhere effecting changes in the *Conservative* interest, that is, running counter to the tendency spoken of above.]

(4) *The High German Group.*

New High German occupies a wide domain in the very heart of Europe. In the northern lowlands it is the literary and cultivated language of countries where Low German proper is spoken, and as such it reaches as far as Flensborg, in South Sleswig. Towards the north-east it extends almost to the Russian frontier, where, however, a narrow Lithuanian strip maintains itself, below Memel and Tilsit. A more extensive Polish tract shuts it off from the frontiers of Poland; but even here it at least occupies all the chief places, such as Graudenz, Thorn, Posen, and Oppeln. Inclosing east and west the Tzech or Bohemian territory, and coming southward by the neighbourhood of Pilsen and Budweis, towards Brünn, in Moravia, the German frontier reaches Presburg, for some forty leagues skirting the Magyar territory, and takes in north Styria (Gratz), north Carinthia (Klagenfurt), the greater part of Tyrol, and three-fourths of Switzerland. Leaving Belfort on the west, it returns northwards by the Vosges, as far as Strasburg, then turns obliquely towards the north-west so as to inclose Thionville and Arlon. Thence extending to Aix-la-Chapelle, it henceforth follows very closely the Netherlandish frontier. In the Austrian Empire it is spoken by about 9,000,000, and in Switzerland by nearly 2,000,000.

New High German dates from the sixteenth century. The Teutonic branch, which it represents, had previously passed through two stages—the old High German and the middle High German. With these our survey of the Teutonic tongues must conclude.

Of High German there are two kinds, the strict grammatical language, and the current speech that has not conformed to the common law. These, however, are not two distinct languages, but one and the same substantially, each containing about equal parts of the two elements. This, as we shall see, is owing to the fact that German was developed in the atmosphere of the courts, and does not therefore represent any particular dialect that has passed from the vulgar to the literary state.

The fundamental but extremely simple principle of this grammatical style consists in a further strengthening of the organic explosives. We have seen that the primitive Aryan *gh, dh, bh* had become *g, d, b,* in Gothic, Low German, and Norse. They are now further strengthened to *k, t, p,* in High German. Again, the organic *g, d, b,* having become *k, t, p* in the Low German group, they are in the same way further strengthened in High German, *k* changing to *h* (also written *hh* and *ch*), *p* to *f* (also written *pf* or *ph*), while *t*, instead of becoming *th* fricative, changes to *ts* written as *z*. The organic explosives, *k, t, p,* having become *h, th, f,* in the Low German idioms, High German retains the *h* and *f*, which were incapable of being further strengthened, while to the *th* soft it applies the law of "polarity," this third series thus reappearing in High German as *h, d, f*.

This is the reason why a German *d* answers to the English *th*, *der, dorn, drei, dünn,* standing for *the, thorn, three, thin*. And here again, as in all the other cases, English is thus one degree (sometimes two) purer than German, *zähmer, zähre, zu, zwei* being in this respect less pure than *tame, tear, to, two*. Hence the absurdity of deriving English from High German, from which it would be just as reasonable to derive the Gothic itself. They are two parallel branches, the phenomenon of a further strengthening of certain consonants rendering German unquestionably inferior to English.

All the High German dialects have changed to *t, z, d,* the *d, th, t* of the Low German group; and on this account they so far belong to the strict High German division. But the case is different with the two other orders of consonants, some only of these idioms having changed *k* and *g* of the first stage to *h, k,* and *p, b,* to *f, p*. That is to say, some only of them have worked out the principle to its fullest extent. Whilst Gothic, for instance, says *brinnan* = to burn, some High German dialects say, *prinnan,* and these consequently belong to the strict division; but others have not strengthened the *b,* and the present literary German writes *brennen.* The Gothic *galeiks* = like, appears in the strict old High German as *kilih,* but the literary language again writes *gleich*. So also the

Gothic *kunnan* = to ken, to know, becomes in the strict High German *chunnan* (where *ch* = *h*), and in literary German *kennen*. But, as stated, the evolution has been completely worked out in the case of the dental series.

Old High German comprises three principal dialects, themselves subdivided into a number of less important varieties. The three main divisions are: The *Frankish*, *Alamanno-Swabian*, and *Austro-Bavarian*, their literary remains ranging from the seventh to the eleventh century. The leading feature of these idioms is their retention of the old vowel endings: *nimu* = I take; *nimit* = he takes; *nëmat* = you take. With the twelfth century we shall see that these vowels began to change to *e* or disappear altogether. Old High German had, properly speaking, no national literature; it possesses a number of versions of religious works and some Christian poems, but no genuine Teutonic records.

Middle High German sets in with the twelfth century, when its literature returns to the old traditions and legends neglected by the old High German; but these national subjects are now contemplated through the medium of Christian thoughts and conceptions. This period, which lasts about four hundred years, is the age of the renowned Minnesingers, Walther von der Vogelweide, Wolfram von Eschenbach, Nithart, Heinrich von Morungen, Tanhûser.

The chief characteristic of the language of this period is the absorption in *e* of the different vowels of the final grammatical syllables. Thus the old High German *gibu* now becomes *gibe* = I give. The various old High German dialects were also subjected to this law, whilst continuing each to preserve its own individuality and special character. There was, however, formed a literary and Court standard, based on the Swabian dialect,* which had no precedent in the foregoing period.

Two striking facts, says Schleicher, distinguish *middle* from *modern* High German. In the first the radical syllable is sometimes long and sometimes short; in the second it is always long and accented. Hence accent in modern German determines the

* Schleicher, "Die Deutsche Sprache," 2nd ed. p. 103 and following. Stuttgart, 1869.

length of the syllable it falls on, that is the radical. The other point he thus explains : " In old High German we have to do only with the dialect of whoever happened to be writing. There was no literary standard in general use, and claiming superiority over the other dialects. During the period of middle High German a more general language was developed, that of the Courts. Modern German is still less a particular dialect than was the middle High German of the Courts. It is not the speech of any particular locality, having never been spoken by any community. This is the reason why German is so artificial, and why in its phonology and formations it is often so unnatural. But on the other hand, from the very fact of its unprovincial character, it acquires the power of serving as a bond of union between the various Germanic branches."—(*Op. cit. ibid.*)

German can be traced step by step from the time of Luther down to the present day. During this period of three hundred years it has doubtless undergone many modifications, but it is, in substance, always one and the same language. We see it taking its rise in the Chancelleries in the sixteenth century ; we see the diplomatic documents borrowing arbitrarily from the various current forms of speech, so that German, in a sense, is born on paper. Thanks to the influence of these official deeds, thanks above all to the spread of Lutheranism, it gradually makes its way, penetrating into the sanctuary, into the schoolroom, into the courts of justice. The vulgar idioms yield slowly before it, until at last they find themselves banished to the rural districts.

It must, however, be confessed that the eccentric orthography with which it was handicapped was not at all calculated to speed its literary diffusion. There is nothing more arbitrary [except the French and English systems] than this orthography. To lengthen vowels an *h* is sometimes placed after them, a letter answering to absolutely nothing in the past life of the word thus disfigured ; long vowels are also denoted by doubling them, and as their length is on other occasions denoted by no expedient at all, it follows that a long *a* may be rendered in three different ways—by a simple *a*, by *ah*, and by *aa*, as is the case with the three words *zwar, wahr, haar.* Again, instead of a simple *i*, we often meet with *ie*, while *i* alone frequently occurs where historical etymology would require *ie*. Lastly, what is no less whimsical, *t* is often replaced by *th*. Many efforts have been made at effecting at least a partial reform of modern German spelling, and these efforts will no doubt be renewed, but we can hardly believe they will ever prove successful.

§ 8.—*The Slavonic Languages.*

The Slavonic tongues during Medieval times (seventh, eighth, and ninth centuries) occupied extensive tracts where German alone is now spoken. Such were Pomerania, Mecklenburg, Brandenburg, Saxony, West Bohemia, Lower Austria, the greater part of Upper Austria, North Styria, and North Carinthia. Slavonic tongues were thus spoken in the localities now occupied by Kiel, Lubeck, Magdeburg, Halle, Leipzig, Baireuth, Linz, Saltzburg, Gratz, and Vienna.

The Slavonic tongues are generally divided into two principal groups. But before specifying them, or attempting a general classification of all the members of this family, it will be first necessary to broach the subject of the old ecclesiastical Slavonic language.

In the seventh century the Slave races had reached their extreme western limits, where they found themselves exposed to the influences of Christianity on the east and south, from the two central points Constantinople and Rome.* The Bulgarians, Serbes, and Russians were visited by the missionaries from Constantinople, whose triumphs were extremely rapid. With Christianity a regular liturgy was introduced into the Slavonic language.

The apostleship of the brothers Constantine (Cyrillus) and Methodius gave a decisive impulse to this movement. Towards the middle of the ninth century Cyrillus remodelled the Greek alphabet for the use of the Slaves and Bulgarians, and translated the Gospels and a number of liturgical pieces, thereafter proceeding with his

---

* Schafarik, "Geschichte der Südslavischen Litteratur," iii. Prague, 1865.

brother to the Slaves of Moravia. Methodius, Bishop of Moravia and Pannonia, outlived his brother, dying in A.D. 885. The gospel of Ostromir, dating from A.D. 1056, is the oldest manuscript of the language used by Cyrillus and Methodius, and which, on account of its being employed in the church service, is known as Church Slavonic, besides being called by some other titles, as we shall presently see.

The modification of the Greek alphabet effected by Cyrillus came to be called *Cyrillian* or *Cyrillic*, and is still in use in an almost identical form amongst the Russians, Bulgarians, and Serbes [or at least such of the latter as belong to the "orthodox" Greek Church—that is, the Church independent of Rome.] The Rumanians, though speaking a neo-Latin tongue, had also adopted this alphabet, but have fortunately since discarded it and returned to the Roman system, adding a number of more or less conventional symbols for sounds peculiar to their language.

It is to be hoped that a day may come when Russian literature also may in its turn give up its traditional alphabet. Without anticipating the circumstances that may bring about this great and fruitful change, we may believe that they will not be long deferred, advantageous as the reform would prove to the civilisation of both extremities of Europe.

The Slaves of the Latin rite made use of another alphabet, also known as the *Glagolitic*, the origin of which is still obscure. Some have thought that it was the older of the two, but the most received and likely opinion now is that it is nothing but a perversion of the Cyrillian. It is supposed to date from the end of the eleventh century, owing its origin to the desire of the south-western Slaves to preserve, by means of incomprehensible characters, a liturgy that had been condemned by a council. But however this be, to us it seems all but proven that the Glagolitic alphabet has no other origin than the Cyrillian system.*

* This view would not seem to be quite so generally accepted as is here implied. It is certainly not entertained by Miklosich, a great authority on the subject, and in his "Standard Alphabet," Dr. Lepsius remarks that "the Glagolitic is based on an old national alphabet which originally was

It is impossible now accurately to determine the geographical limits of Church Slavonic in the ninth century, and those who have essayed to clear up this obscure point have not arrived at the same conclusion. Some think it was spoken in the southwest of the present Russia; others in Moravia, and others again in the regions of the present Carinthia, Croatia, Slavonia, and Servia; while some suppose that it spread over the whole territory between the Black Sea and the Adriatic. According to Dobrovsky, whose opinion must always carry great weight in all questions of Slavonic philology, it was spoken northwards on the right bank of the Danube, from the Adriatic to the Black Sea, passing through Belgrade and southwards as far as Salonika—that is in Servia, Bulgaria, and Macedonia.

Church Slavonic has entirely disappeared as a spoken idiom, but survives, as stated, as a liturgical language; not, however, without having undergone some slight changes, due especially to the influence of the living tongues, in the midst of which it was employed as a dead language. These changes have been investigated and are well understood, now forming the basis of the two-fold division into old and modern Church Slavonic. It is the first, of course, that philologists so frequently avail themselves of in the study of the Slavonic tongues, although it should not be looked on as the common source of all of them.

The Slavonic idioms now spoken are the *Russian*, *Ruthenian*, *Polish*, *Tsech*, *Slovakian*, the two *Sorbian* dialects, *Bulgarian*, *Servo-Croatian*, and *Slovenian*.

The limits of *Russian*, northwards and eastwards, are difficult to determine, as it here comes in contact with the numerous *Uralo-Altaic* idioms (Samoyede, Wogul, &c.), which it is gradually encroaching on. Towards the Baltic it scarcely touches the coast-line occupied by the Finnic idioms (Suomi and Esthonian), the

taken from the Greek, but was remodelled in the ninth century and adapted to Christian literature by the two Slavonic apostles, Cyrillus and Methodius, brothers:" 2nd ed. p. 143. The Cyrillian Dr. Lepsius attributes to St. Clemens, who introduced it soon after the other, about A.D. 900. *Ibid.*, p. 147. —*Note by Translator.*

Swedish (at Helsingfors), and the Lettic (Riga, Mitau); a little farther south it comes in contact with Lithuanian. From Grodno to about a hundred leagues southwards, and in nearly a straight line, it is flanked on the west by Polish; and lastly, on the south it meets the Ruthenian, of which presently.

These limits, however, comprise the so-called "White Russian" dialect, spoken by about 3,000,000, to the north of Ruthenian, to the west of Russian, and east of Lithuanian and Polish, at Vitebsk, Minsk, Mohilev, but whose literature is insignificant.

Great Russian, or simply *Russian*, as written, is not quite the same as the spoken form, the literary style having borrowed largely from the Church Slavonic. The oldest Russian monuments, whose records can be traced to the eleventh century, consist of tales and narrative poems. During the eighteenth century the language was reduced to uniformity, thanks partly to the famous scholar and man of letters Lomonosov (1711-66), after which epoch it has shown signs of an originality and literary vitality that is too seldom appreciated.

Russian grammar, unfortunately, presents serious difficulties to the student familiar with the Romance and Teutonic tongues alone. Its phonology is somewhat complex, nor is the sound of the vowels always the same. Thus, *a*, in untoned syllables, is somewhat like *e*, while *e* itself is sometimes open and sometimes shut. In untoned syllables *o* is uttered like *a*, as in *kolokol* = bell, where the accent being on the first, the first *o* alone retains its force, the others becoming *a*: *kolakal*. Moreover, Russian accent itself, like that of some cognate tongues, is not at all easy; though well enough known, its laws are far from all being yet determined.

Russian declension is much the same as that of its congeners, the only point to be noticed being the phonetic laws more or less peculiar to it. In its conjugation, it is distinguished by the complete loss of two of the old tenses—the aorist and the imperfect—lost also in Ruthenian, but retained in Servian and Bulgarian, and traces of which are to be detected in the oldest Polish and Tsech monuments. They are replaced in Russian by a participle: *on dal* = he has given (mas.), *dala* fem., *dalo* neuter, *dali* plural of all genders, a periphrasis which has somewhat the sense of " I am having given, we are having given."

Ruthenian, called also *Rusniak* and *Little-Russian* [and even *Small-Russian*], is not a Russian dialect, though nearer akin to it than any of the other cognate tongues. It occupies approximately one-fourth of European Russian, south of a nearly straight line, passing above Vladimir in Volhynia, Kiev, and Kharkov. In Austria it is spread over the greater part of Galicia, skirting Hungary on the north-east, above the Magyar and Rumanian. The Russian Ruthenians, including the Cossacks, are about 11,500,000 and those of Austria upwards of 3,000,000, making a total of over 14,500,000 speaking Little-Russian.

Their literature, like that of the southern Slaves, and like that of the Russians themselves, is above all national and traditional. A great number of compositions in Ruthenian have within the last fifty years been published under the titles of popular songs of Ukrania, national songs of southern Russia, of Galicia, and Volhynia.

Though diverging little from Russian, Ruthenian still distinctly differs from it. Thus, it does not convert into liquids all the consonants that may be so treated in Russian, amongst others the labials *p, b, v, m*. It changes the older *k* and *g* to *ch* and French *j* oftener than Russian does; its accent often differs; it has lost the present participle passive retained in Russian, and it possesses infinitive forms with diminutive meanings. These, with some other more or less noteworthy peculiarities, have sufficed to cause it to be treated as a distinct and clearly-marked idiom.

Polish comprises a number of dialects, the whole covering a vast extent of territory, divided between Russia, Austria, and Prussia. Its eastern frontier extends from Grodno to Jaroslav, partly following the course of the *Bûg*; but its western limits are less distinct, being daily encroached on in this direction by German, which has already occupied all the more important localities. In Austria Polish is restricted to western Galicia, a tract much less in size than the eastern portion of the same region, occupied, as above stated, by the Ruthenians. German has gained considerably on the Polish domain, its whole eastern territory, even in Russia, being interspersed with German-speaking communities, some reaching almost to the gates of Warsaw; nor has Galicia escaped this invasion, due mainly to the spread eastwards of the German Jews.

The number of Poles in Russia is set down at 4,700,000, in Prussia at 2,450,000, and in Austria and Hungary at 2,465,000, making an approximate total of 9,615,000 still speaking Polish.

Its phonology is simple enough, and the alphabet employed by it may be looked on as one of the most defective. Thus the sound of *ch* (as in *church*), instead of being denoted by a single symbol, such as the *č* Tsech and Croatian, is expressed by the combination *cz*, while *sz* is made to do duty for the Tsech and Croatian *s* answering to our *sh*, and instead of the Croatian or English *v* it uses *w* in the German fashion. Nor are these the only shortcomings of its method of transcription, so that should the present efforts at reform prove successful, there will be good grounds for congratulation.

Besides the vowels *a, e, i, o, u, y* (somewhat like French *u*), *é* (very like *i* in sound), *ó* (resembling the English *oo*), there are two nasal vowels, answering to some extent to the French *an* and *in*, but in certain cases, especially at the end of words, being uttered as *o* and *e*. In short they correspond to two nasal vowels of the old Church Slavonic, which seemed to have answered to the French *on* and *in*. The variations of the Polish consonants, according to their juxtaposition with certain other consonants, are somewhat important, as in the case of the fricatives, which often undergo such permutations as to render the origin of the word very obscure. Accent is very simple, falling always on the penultimate, except in foreign words, whereas in Russian and Ruthenian, as already remarked, it may fall on any syllable, and we shall see that the same is the case in Slovenian and Croato-Servian, while in Tsech and Sorabian it affects the first syllable. Hence Polish is in this respect clearly distinguished from its congeners.

Polish literature is at once important and original, dating from the end of the tenth century, and including a great number of chroniclers and poets, some of them as old as the twelfth. It

T

continues still to flourish, and a statement published in connection with the last Exhibition of Vienna gives three thousand and upwards as the number of works either printed in Polish or published by Poles in foreign tongues during the single year 1871.

The actual limits of *Tsech* and of *Slovakian*, which is closely allied to it, are not easy to determine. The region occupied by them, comprising all Bohemia, except a strip on the west and north, the greater part of Moravia, and the tract to the south of the Polish domain, stretches from Pilsen to the Carpathians, for a distance of about one hundred and fifty leagues, varying in breadth from twenty-five to fifty. The last official returns estimate the number of Tsechs, Moravians, and Slovakians at about 6,500,000.

From the time of its earliest records, dating from the eighth century, the Tsech language has undergone serious modifications, a fact to be attributed to the important political movements of which Bohemia has been the scene. Nor do we refer merely to orthographic differences, due to the fact that in the oldest Tsech documents the Roman letters were used in their simple state, without being supplemented by the necessary diacritical signs; the changes alluded to affect the structure itself of the language. The reform of the Tsech orthographic system, begun some centuries back, was completed in 1830, by the substitution of the ordinary Roman for the medieval Gothic characters, and the finishing stroke was given to it some twenty years ago, by discarding the Polish and German *w* for the Latin *v*. This reform, so urgently needed in itself, was of the greatest consequence for the language also, and for its development and diffusion. Nothing was more uncertain than the old Tsech writing system, in which one and the same sound was often denoted in three, four, five, and six different ways. Thus *s* was transcribed by *z*, *s*, *sz*, *szs*, *ʐ*, and *ss* indifferently, *k* by *c*, *k*, *q*, *ch*, *ks*, *ck*, and so on. On the other hand, a single Roman letter often stood for three or four totally different sounds, so that the difficulty of correctly settling the old Tsech texts may easily be conceived, with such a system, or rather utter want of system, as this.

The Tsech vowels, *a*, *e*, *i*, *o*, *u*, *y* (usually pronounced as *i*) have all their corresponding long vowels now marked with an oblique stroke: *á*, *é*, &c. Another Tsech vowel, pronounced *yé*, has no diacritical sign to denote its long sound. Tsech also possesses the vowels *r* and *l*, always short in the ordinary dialect, but which may be long in Slovakian. But the Polish nasal vowels are unknown, nor have any traces of them been discovered in the oldest texts. The Tsech vowels are somewhat shifting, being especially affected by contact with a *j* (pronounced *y*), which changes, for instance, *a* and *i* the following *a* and *e*, and to *e* the preceding *a*. The consonantal system is rich, including some liquid dentals, a peculiar *r* answering to the Polish *rz*, and with the force of the French *rj*, besides some fricatives readily affected by contact with certain other sounds. It has been above stated that in Tsech, the accent falls on the first syllable of every word. Let us observe, in conclusion, that the old Tsech conjugation was in a good state of preservation, but that the modern language, like most of the cognate tongues, has lost the old imperfect and aorist.

Tsech literature dates, as already stated, from the eighth century, its first records being the celebrated manuscripts of Královdor (Königenhof) and of Zelenohora (Grünberg), discovered in 1817, and the genuineness of which is now established. They belong to the transition period from heathendom to Christianity, and are as important philologically as they are for the study of the old Bohemian religious myths. There are also several fragments dating from the tenth century. Down to the epoch of the Hussite war, Bohemia, which had struck the first note of religious freedom, possessed the most important of all the Slavonic literatures. When it fell under German rule, its national speech was rigorously proscribed, whoever attempted to restore it to its pristine honour, becoming the victims of the Jesuits. [There seems here to be a trifling anachronism, Bohemia having been finally brought within the German political system on the conclusion of the Hussite struggle, in 1437; that is to say, about a century before the foundation of the order of the Jesuits, by Loyola, 1491-1556.] It was not till towards the end of the last century that Bohemian letters were again revived.

The *Sorbian*, or *Sorabian*, called also *Wendic*, or *Lusatian* comprises two distinct varieties, *High* and *Low Sorbian* [or, according to some Sorbian writers, High Lusatian and Wendic]. Its whole territory is now reduced to about twenty-five leagues by twelve, watered by the Spree, two-thirds in Prussia, and the rest on the south in Saxony, its most important points (Kottbus, Bautzen) being already absorbed by the surrounding German. A tract of about twelve leagues separates the Sorbian frontier southwards from the northern Tsech frontier. About the middle of the sixteenth century the Lusatian territory was twice as extensive as at present, and it is being still constantly encroached on from the north, west, and east by the German, so that it now contains scarcely more than a population of 130,000 speaking Slave dialects.

The oldest printed Wendic document is a book of Catholic devotion, published in 1512. During the seventeenth century there were a number of works written in Sorbian, but at the beginning of the ninteenth this literature was almost entirely extinct. Attempts were later on made to revive it, and in 1845 a society was formed, around which the literary life of the country has rallied.

The *Serrian*, or *Croatian*, or better still, the *Servo-Croatian*, with its two great intellectual centres, Belgrade and Agram, or Zagreb, occupies a considerable position not only amongst the south Slavonic, but amongst the Slavonic tongues generally, a position it is entitled to on the threefold ground of its history, philology, and geography. It is spread over the principality of Servia, Bosnia, Herzegovina, Montenegro, a portion of south Hungary (Zombor), Slavonia, Croatia, nearly the whole of Istria and Dalmatia, a region embracing altogether a population of about 6,000,000. In such a wide domain the dialectic varieties are naturally somewhat numerous; they may, however, be grouped in three main divisions— the western, less cultivated than the others; the southern, mostly in Dalmatia; and the eastern, in Servia and south Hungary, on the banks of the Danube. The leading feature of these three varieties is the different pronunciation of a vowel, which was originally undoubtedly an *é*. In Belgrade, south Hungary, and Sirmia it still retains this sound, but in the western dialect it becomes *i*, and in the southern *je* or *ije* (pronounced *yé* or *iyé*). But whether you say *vera*, *vira*, or *vijera* = belief; *reka*, *rika*, or *rijeka* = river, you will be readily understood from the Adriatic to the Rumanian frontier. The Croato-Servian language is unfortunately burdened with a twofold writing system, in the east the Cyrillian, in the west the Latin alphabet, supplemented with some accessory symbols. This much-to-be-regretted discrepancy is the result of the old religious schism, and must for a long time delay the union that European civilisation has so much interest in seeing effected between the Serbes of Turkey and the triple Dalmato-Croato-Slavonian territory. Not that an important step had not already been made in this direction at the beginning of this century, notably by the sort of unification and codification effected by the celebrated Vouk Stephanovich Karajich for the languages of the Servian principality and of south Hungary.

When Vouk undertook the work he was enabled so successfully to carry out, the Servian tongue could scarcely be said to have yet been settled. Most of the literary class considered as their national speech a somewhat artificial idiom formed of old Church Slavonic elements blended with those of the really living and current tongue. The latter was otherwise treated by them as merely a vulgar *patois*. Vouk, however, proposed to adopt this national speech, such as it was, and to radically reform its orthography. The struggle lasted for half a century, but he succeeded in the end, thanks to his perfect knowledge of the Servo-Croatian tongue, as well as to the accuracy and scientific character of his labours.

The essence of the Servo-Croatian literature is the ballad, or national song, the *Pesma*, *Pisma*, or *Pjesma*. A great number of these pieces have been collected and published. Many are undoubtedly very old, and the very form in which they still exist shows how little the language has been changed during the course of centuries. But whilst its grammar has remained intact, the vocabulary, especially of the eastern variety, has admitted far too large a number of Turkish words, to which must be added the inroad of German and French terms into the current scientific and literary speech.

Servia and the Slavonic countries belonging to the eastern rite have had a special literary development, which, if little known, is not unimportant in itself. It dates at least from the beginning of the thirteenth century, although the documents belonging to this early period are of but little intrinsic worth. Before this time, and at most before the twelfth century, there are no records of the Servian tongue beyond a series of words, and of proper names occurring mainly in the Greek and Latin writers.

The written monuments of the western Servo-Croatian territory date from the twelfth century, but the choice literature of Ragusi was not developed till the sixteenth. Nor was it till the end of the same century that the local Croatian literature begins, a literature that at present occupies such an important position in the domain of historical criticism and the science of language.

The special study of the Servo-Croatian tongue is of the greatest importance in the general study of the Slavonic group, ranking perhaps in this respect next to the Church Slavonic itself. In fact, of all the members of this family, the Servo-Croatian and the Slovenian are those that have least suffered in their phonology, and as we have already seen, it is precisely phonology that forms the groundwork of all philological studies. The Slavonic comparative grammar of Miklosich,* a fundamental work for the study of the idioms of this group, at every step supplies the most striking proofs of the vast importance of Servo-Croatian, and the perusal of the excellent works of Danichich, Jagich, and Novakovich must remove the last doubts that could be possibly entertained on the subject.

Servian phonology, which is by no means complex, comprises six vowels, *a, e, i, o, u,* and *r*; and its consonantal system is no less simple, nearly all the sounds possessing English equivalents, with the notable exception of the two liquid palatals *ć* and *gj*. The *ć* has the force of *t* followed by the Scotch *ch*, and *gj* that of an analogous *d*. The Servian accent is very difficult for a foreigner. There are usually reckoned four kinds of accent, which, however, ought to be reduced to two, a strong and weak, each both long and short. Servo-Croatian also has a great advantage over most of its

* "Vergleichende Gram. der Slavischen Sprache." Vienna, 1852.

congeners, in the retention of the organic aorist and imperfect, *bih* = *jui*, *bijah* = *eram*; besides possessing a perfect, formed by means of a participle: *sam bio*, *smo bili* = I have been, we have been.

Slovenian, spoken by upwards of 1,200,000 persons in south Carinthia and south Styria, Carniola, and a part of north Istria, is near akin to the Servo-Croatian, and partakes of its important philological position. Its written literature dates from the middle of the sixteenth century, and though not lacking in merit, was doubtless prevented from acquiring a brilliant future by the preponderance of Servo-Croatian letters. The Protestant works printed at Tubingen are the most important monument of Slovenian literature in the sixteenth century. During the two following centuries it was ably represented by some eminent writers. Murko and Kopitar shed a lustre on their epoch, though the latter wrote in German, an example followed by his fellow-countryman and pupil Miklosich, whose works place him in the foremost rank of scientific writers of Slavonic race.

Bulgarian occupies the greater part of European Turkey, northwards following the course of the Danube from Widdin to Silistria, and even beyond that point westwards, confining with Albania, southwards being separated from the Ægean and Sea of Marmora only by some narrow strips along the coast, where Greek and Turkish are spoken, and eastwards at several points reaching the Black Sea, and sharing with Turkish the extreme north-east corner of the empire. The number of those speaking Bulgarian will easily amount to 6,000,000, if we include those settled in south-western Russia and in Bessarabia, ceded to Rumania by the Treaty of Paris.

Of all the Slavonic tongues, modern Bulgarian is the most corrupt. In common with Rumanian and Albanian, it has the peculiarity of suffixing the article to the end of the word. Its vocabulary also has been greatly affected by the influence of the neighbouring tongues—Turkish, Greek, Albanian, and Rumanian. However, notwithstanding the alteration of its forms, Bulgarian retains some traces of the old Slavonic nasals that have entirely disappeared from its other southern congeners.

Bulgarian literature is quite recent; the few original Bulgarian writers until the middle of this century employing either Russian or the old liturgical language, largely mixed with Russian. Latterly education has spread among the rising generation, which possesses periodicals and a literature daily on the increase. The obstacles thrown by the Turks in the way of the development of the European nationalities in Turkey, unfortunately compel the Bulgarians to study abroad, and there publish their works. A literary society, already occupying a position of some influence, has lately been founded at Braïla, in Rumania.

We may conclude this notice by mentioning the old dialects of the Elbe Slavonians, known by the name of *Polabish*, idioms now extinct, and whose scanty records, greatly affected by German influence, date from the seventeenth and beginning of the eighteenth century.

Reference has already been made to the great importance of the Church Slavonic for the study of the other members of this family. Still it would be in vain to expect to find in the grammar of this tongue a very faithful reflex of the primitive Aryan speech. Its phonology is subject to far more serious modifications than is that either of Lithuanian or Greek. Its vocalismus is not certainly very complex, although the frequent nasalisation of certain sounds is an infallible proof of decay, while the final vowels are greatly affected by certain very uniform laws. On the other hand, its consonants are subjected to laws of attraction and assimilation both very numerous and very delicate; nor, indeed, is this one of the least difficulties presented by the study of the Slavonic tongues. To a series of rather complex phonetic laws must also be added the multiplicity of the consonants. The Slavonic tongues, above all others, may be said to require a careful study of the phonetic elements of speech and of the rules regulating their recurrence. Doubtless the conjugation is relatively simple, but the declension has only too frequently departed from the formula of the common Aryan tongue, while the intricacy of the phonetic laws often presented by the clash of the theme with the endings enhances the difficulty not a little.

THIRD FORM OF SPEECH—INFLECTION.

A rapid glance at the grammar of this old language will at the same time give us an insight into the general structure of all the Slavonic tongues.

Church Slavonic has the vowels *a, e, i, o, u, y* (probably French *u*), a shut *é*, sometimes pronounced as *ya*; further, an *i* and a *u* semi-mute; and, lastly, two nasals, answering in sound to the French *in, on*.

The organic Aryan diphthongs have disappeared, or rather have been contracted to single vowels, and the hiatus is usually avoided either by an intercalated *j* (the English semi-vowel *y*) or by a *v*, both purely euphonic, and both occurring also at the beginning of words formerly commencing with a vowel. Thus the common Aryan *astasi*, the Sanskrit *sthu*, the Greek εστε, the Latin *estis*, the Lithuanian *este*, becomes *jeste* in Church Slavonic; and this "preiotation," as it is technically called, is a leading feature of all the Slavonic tongues, as in the Tscch and Serbian *jeste*, whence *ste*.

Coming to the consonants, Church Slavonic, together with all its congeners, has changed to the simple explosives *g, d, b*, the Aryan aspirates *gh, dh, bh*. On the other hand there have been developed a number of fricatives, such as *sh, z*, and the French *j*, all unknown to the common Aryan, while the influence of strict phonetic laws has often changed the organic *k* to *ch*, transcribed by the sign *č*. The various forms of assimilation have also acquired a great development, so much so that the study of the Slavonic tongues must necessarily be preceded by at least a rapid inquiry into their various laws of assimilation—assimilation, complete or partial, of consonants with the preceding or the following letter, and so on. For want of at least some general notion of these laws the most mistaken ideas are apt to be formed on word-formation.

The principle regulating the suppression of final consonants is also of great importance. In Church Slavonic all final consonants must be suppressed.

Besides the ordinary nominal declension, including adjectives, participles, numerals, and some pronouns, and the pronominal declension proper, Church Slavonic possesses a so-called *compound* declension, peculiar to the Lithuanian also, and (with a fresh element) to the Teutonic tongues. It is composed of the ordinary adjectival forms, to which is added the pronoun *i*, also declined. Adjectives, as a rule, admit of both declensions, the normal and the compound, their employment being a question of syntax; when inflected by the compound declension, the adjective is said to be *definite*, and has the meaning of the Greek or German adjective preceded by the article. All the Slavonic tongues possess this compound declension; thus the Servian says *rast visok* = a lofty oak; *visoki rast* = the lofty oak.

Church Slavonic has retained in its conjugation the three common Aryan numbers, singular, dual, and plural, but the dual has disappeared from the Servo-Croatian, Bulgarian, Ruthenian, and Russian. Of the four simple organic tenses, Church Slavonic has lost the reduplicate perfect (the Greek λέλοιπα) and the imperfect, but has retained nearly all the various forms of the present and aorist. It has also, at least in part, preserved the two primitive compound tenses, future and aorist, whilst further developing a compound imperfect.

Of all Slavonic tongues still spoken the Servo-Croatian and the Slovenian, closely akin to it, possess the clearest and simplest phonology. Not that we do not here also meet with the numerous euphonic laws affecting consonants in juxtaposition, and above mentioned in connection with Church Slavonic. On the contrary, they exist here also, and are quite as exacting as in any other member of the family; but the phonetic element itself is much less complex in Servian than elsewhere, besides which its pronunciation offers no difficulty, while in this respect Polish and Tsech present formidable obstacles. As for Bulgarian, the changes it has undergone in the lapse of centuries have rendered it the most corrupt of all Slavonic tongues.

The classification of these idioms has given rise to serious controversies, which can scarcely be said to have yet been settled. Church Slavonic was at first looked on as the common source of all the others, whence the name of *Palaio-Slave* or *Old Slavonic*, even still occasionally applied to it. No one, however, at present engaged in the study of the Slavonic group dreams of upholding this theory. But after setting aside the pretended paternity of Church Slavonic, the question arose whether it should be placed on the same level as its congeners, and assume that all had alike sprung from a more primitive but now lost common type? Without stopping at this hypothesis, Dobrovsky and Schafarik divided the Slavonic idioms into two principal branches: the western, comprising Polish, Tsech, Lusatian, old Polabish; and the eastern, including all the rest. At first Schleicher proposed some objections against this distribution, but ended by adopting it, and his view of the matter may be conveniently summed up in the subjoined scheme:

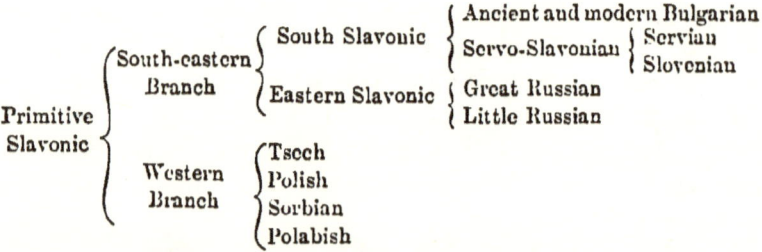

Schleicher may be said to base this division on one solitary fact. In the first group *d* and *t* before *n* or *l* are suppressed, while they are retained in the second. Thus, for instance, the Tsech *oradlo* = a tool or instrument, is more correct than the Church Slavonic *oralo*, and than the Servo-Croatian *ralo*. Danitchitch does not accept the force of this argument, and shows that this *d* and *t* at times disappear in old and modern Tsech also, as well as in Polish and Sorbian, at the same time proving that they were not always suppressed in Church Slavonic and Servo-Croatian. While Schleicher looks on Church Slavonic as the old form of the modern Bulgarian, giving it the name of *ancient Bulgarian*, Miklosich thinks that the old language is now represented by Slovenian, as well as by Bulgarian, and calls it *ancient Slovenian*. This theory was warmly assailed by Schleicher, who, in our opinion, triumphantly proved on phonetic grounds that the present Slovenian could not derive from Church Slavonic, and that, on the other hand, the Servo-Croatian and Slovenian ought to be grouped together, an opinion also shared in by Schafarik.* Danitchitch also has recently, on purely phonetic grounds, broached a very ingenious classification of the Slavonic tongues. His essay being written in Servian is unfortunately accessible to but few readers; but his conclusions may be resumed as under:

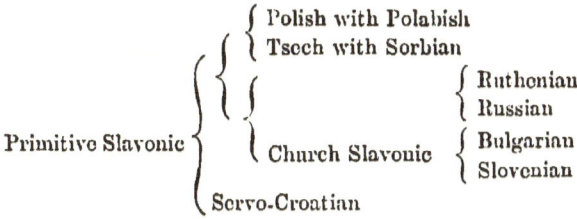

Several other classifications have been proposed, and we have doubtless not yet seen the last of them. Meanwhile, to the two preceding schemes, we may add the following, which a number of authorities seem disposed to accept as final:

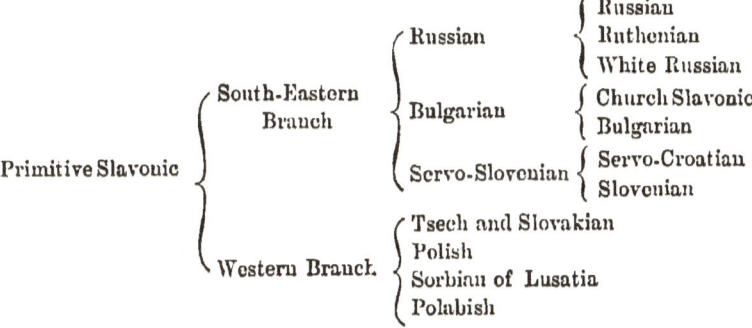

The question, if the truth must be spoken, still seems obscure, and the only points definitely settled appear to be the purity of the Servo-Croatian forms, and the great corruption of Bulgarian. But as to the more or less intimate degrees of kinship existing between the various groups, as to the more or less intermediate common forms that may have at some time existed, as, for instance,

---

* Schleicher, "Ist das Altkirchenslawische Altslowenich?" "Beiträge zur Vergl. Sprachforschung," i. p. 319.

a common Tsecho-Polono-Sorbian, we can say nothing, or at least nothing positive. The future may possibly confirm in part, if not wholly, conclusions already arrived at. Possibly also the day may come when all these Slavonic tongues will come to be looked on as merely a series of so many collateral varieties springing directly from some common source, always, most probably, excepting modern Bulgarian, as deriving from Church Slavonic. Doubtless this would not prevent Ruthenian from resembling Russian more than it does Slovenian or Sorbian, or Polish from being more akin to Tsech than it is either to Bulgarian or Ruthenian. But in the absence of historic records all classifications of this sort should be received with great reserve. And this is no less applicable to the great linguistic classifications, than to more special distributions, such, amongst others, as those of the Slavonic tongues.

§ 9.—*The Lettic Group.*

On the south-east coast of the Baltic, in the Russian provinces of Courland and Covno, and in the extreme north-east of the German province of eastern Prussia, there still survives a little group of Aryan tongues, hemmed in on the west by German, on the south by Polish and Russian, on the east also by Russian, on the north by the Uralo-Altaïc idiom, Esthonian. This group, which must eventually disappear before the Russian and German, is called the *Lettic*, and was formerly represented by three branches: *Old Prussian*, *Lithuanian*, and *Lettish*; but at present by the last two only, Prussian having died out two hundred years ago.

Of all the Aryan tongues, the members of this group are those which in Europe adhere most faithfully to the primitive Aryan type. Our attention must be devoted more particularly to the Lithuanian, which is in truth the most important member of the group.

(1) *Lithuanian,*

Spoken in Germany by from 150,000 to 200,000 persons, in a tract from thirty to thirty-five leagues in length, and occupying the extreme north-eastern frontier of Prussia, but even here in the rural districts only, having disappeared from all the important localities, such as Memel and Tilsit.

The Lithuanian territory in Russia is much more compact, and those occupying it are estimated at 1,300,000, approximately. Without quite reaching Grodno southwards, and Wilna eastwards, it is limited on the north by the Lettish, of which we shall have presently to speak. This northern Lithuanian frontier stretches in nearly a straight line for a distance of upwards of ninety leagues, the most important place within the Lithuanian-speaking district being the little town of Covno.

Schleicher had divided Lithuanian into two dialects, Low Lithuanian, or Jemaïtic, and High Lithuanian, which, however, did not correspond with the political distribution of the Lithuanians into Russians and Germans; the Low Lithuanian being spoken in the north, both in Prussia and in Russia, while High Lithuanian occupies both countries southwards. According to Schleicher, the difference between the two varieties consisted mainly in the fact that the combinations *ti, di*, retained before vowels in Jemaïtic, were changed in High Lithuanian to *ch* and *j*; the transition, however, being very gradual from one to the other.* This twofold division has been warmly assailed; amongst others by Kurschat, who, while admitting that in Prussia, in the neighbourhood of Memel, the sounds *ch* and *j* do not occur, believes that the division cannot be supported by a sufficient number of undisputed facts. The language of the vicinity of Memel may doubtless present some peculiarities, but not enough to constitute it a true dialect.†

The Lithuanian vowel system is very simple, and, next to Sanskrit and the old Iranian tongues, may be said to approach nearest to the common Aryan primitive type. Instead of an organic *á*, it sometimes has a long *o*, as in *moters* = Sanskrit *mátaras* = Greek μητερες = mothers. But a more serious change is that of long to short vowels at the end of words. As regards the consonants we may note, amongst other deviations, the substitution

---

* "Handbuch der Litauischen Sprache," i. p. 4. Prague, 1856.
† "Worterbuch der Litauischen Sprache," first part, p. viii. Halle, 1870.

of the simple unaspirated for the primitive aspirated explosives, the Sanskrit *gh*, *dh*, *bh*, becoming *g*, *d*, *b*. Lithuanian, like the Slavonic group and Zend, possesses the French *j*, which it often substitutes for *g*, or for the organic *gh*. It is transcribed by a *z*, with a dot over it. Lastly, by its retention of the sibilant *s*, Lithuanian shows itself superior to Sanskrit, and to nearly all the other Aryan tongues, which generally replace it by a series of new fricatives.

The Lithuanian declension has been perfectly preserved; it retains the dual forms, and its case-endings are nearly always a faithful reflex of the organic terminations. Lastly, in the conjugation it retains the present and future forms, but having lost the four other organic tenses denoting past time, it has developed a new perfect and an imperfect. The first, as a rule, is distinguished from the present by separate endings, while the second is a compound tense, formed by the root and the past tense of the verb *to do*.

Lithuanian accent is extremely difficult, nor is it much better understood than is that of certain Slavonic tongues. Its orthography is not yet reduced to conformity, several systems prevailing, some of which are more phonetic, and others rather etymological. Each has doubtless its special advantages, rendering a reconciliation all the more difficult.

Lithuanian possesses an important literary monument in the poem of "The Seasons," by Donalitius, in three thousand lines, published by Rhesa, with a German translation, in 1818; by Schleicher, at St. Petersburg, in 1865, and by Nesselmann, in 1869. Donalitius (1714–80) besides "The Seasons," composed some other poetic pieces, some of which are extant, the whole constituting nearly all the Lithuanian literature we possess. A number of national songs, known as "dainas," besides some proverbs and tales in prose, have also been collected, supplying altogether sufficient materials for the study of this valuable language, which, though its days be numbered, must ever be remembered as one of the most remarkable instances of the vitality of human speech.

(2) *Lettish.*

The number of those speaking Lettish is estimated at about 1,000,000, more or less. The northern Lithuanian frontier forms its southern limits; eastwards it confines on the Russian, and on the north with the Uralo-Altaïc Esthonian. It occupies the north of Courland, the south of Livonia, and the west of the province of Vitebsk, and its chief centres are Riga and Mitau.

The Lettish grammar is essentially the same as the Lithuanian, and need not therefore further occupy us. It may, however, be remarked that its grammatical forms are, as a rule, not so well preserved as those of its congener, from which Lettish is certainly not derived, though its main features are less correct and more modern. Like many other languages that possess no other literature, Lettish boasts of a certain number of national songs.

(3) *Old Prussian,*

Which disappeared about two hundred years ago, occupied the shores of the Baltic from the mouth of the Vistula to that of the Niemen. After the conquest of all the old Prussian territory by the Germans, the natives were compelled gradually to give way before feudalism and Christianity, which overspread the country in the thirteenth century, having had recourse to the most violent and unscrupulous means to effect their purpose.

In 1561 the German catechism was translated into Prussian, and this work now forms one of the most important monuments for the study of the language, of which, however, it is not the oldest record. Nesselmann published some few years since a German-Prussian lexicon, containing rather more than eight hundred words, dating from the beginning of the fifteenth century.

Less incorrect than modern Lettish often is, old Prussian inclines more to the Lithuanian. Its forms are perhaps less antique, though at times by far surpassing its congener in this respect. Thus the old Prussian *nevints* = ninth, becomes in Lithuanian *devinats*, the organic nasal being here changed to *d*.

The Lettic group is doubtless nearly connected with the Slavonic, and it is generally supposed that at some remote period both groups were united in one common type, whence they subsequently diverged. Our view of this theory will be given a little farther on; meantime the fact of their great resemblance cannot be gainsaid. It is so striking that many have been deceived by it to the extent of classifying the Lettic tongues with the Slavonic. This, however, involves a fundamental error, for however akin they may be to each other, the two groups are no less essentially distinct than are, for instance, the Sanskrit and the Iranic.

§ 10.—*Unclassified Aryan Tongues.*

The greater part of the Aryan tongues, both living and dead, have been by one writer or another compared, grouped, and classified with one or another language of the same family. In fact, the tendency has always been towards premature classifications, though too great haste in this respect is generally more injurious than profitable, it being in our opinion better not to class at all than to do so on too slight or insufficient grounds. Bopp himself was not proof against the temptation, having at one time essayed to include the Caucasian and the Malayo-Polynesian groups with the Aryan family. The attempt of course proved a failure, but it helped to show how hard it is even for the soundest and most critical minds to avoid at times yielding to the love of such generalisations.

When treating in our fourth chapter of the agglutinating tongues, we may possibly have separated certain groups which may yet be shown to be related. Still we did not hesitate meantime to keep them apart, in the belief that a certain reserve is frequently proof of a sound judgment, while rashness but too often merely betrays a lack of scientific method.

At the same time it is quite possible for a given language to be shown to belong in a general way to such and such a family, though we may be unable perhaps to determine its particular place in that family; that is, to point out the special group with which it ought to be included, or yet to assert confidently that it forms a special division of its own within the family.

U

Such is the case with several Aryan tongues, living and dead, as, for instance, Etruscan and Albanian, and we shall here devote a few words to some of these unclassified tongues.

(1) *Etruscan*.

Few languages have tested the sagacity of linguists to the same extent that Etruscan has, and few have at the same time more readily lent themselves to the most contradictory and unscientific theories. So early as the fifteenth century it was already derived from Hebrew or Chaldee, while some writers even now assign a Semitic origin to it in a general way, if they do not connect it directly with Hebrew. But with Lanzi originated the now generally received opinion that Etruscan is an Italic language in the same sense that Latin, Oscan, and Umbrian are. His famous work appeared in 1789, but it unfortunately necessarily lacked the scientific process, at the time of its composition Aryan comparative grammar not having been yet established. Nor had Lanzi the opportunity of consulting the numerous inscriptions since discovered, and which now supply abundant materials for the study of Etruscan.

Corssen has essayed to resume, in a very important work, the results so far arrived at by those writers that have treated this subject on sound principles, and amongst them he has himself secured a distinguished position.* Etruscan would seem to be decidedly an Italic language, akin to Latin, Oscan, and Umbrian. The forms of all the cases, besides a certain number of verbal and pronominal formations, seem to have been already recognised. Nearly all the Etruscan inscriptions are sepulchral, some being bilingual (Latin and Etruscan), found mostly in the north of Etruria, and these, as may well be supposed, have been of the greatest service in deciphering the language.

The Etruscan alphabet forms, with the Umbrian and Oscan, a branch of the Italic alphabet already spoken of. However, it is divided into several distinct classes, which are successively examined

* "Ueber die Sprache der Etrusker," i. Leipzig, 1874.

by Corssen in the work above referred to. The reader may also consult the writings of Conestabile, which have proved a valuable contribution to the progress of Etruscan epigraphy.*

As regards the language itself, if it is eventually to be classed with the Italic idioms, side by side with Latin, Oscan, and Umbrian, we for our part do not, at all events, believe that the time has yet come for doing so, though it may possibly not be far distant. Doubtless it would be hard to say what Etruscan is, if its right to membership with the Italic group be denied. But that is not the question, for it might still be looked on as simply an Aryan tongue, without forthwith identifying it with the Italic idioms. But in truth, whether it be altogether independent, or belong to some other connection, or is after all akin to the Latin, are points that still remain to be settled. Meantime there is nothing to prevent us from holding this last hypothesis as at least probable enough, though not yet absolutely proven.

(2) *Dacian.*

The old Dacian, limited southwards by the Danube, on the north-east by the Dniester, and on the north-west by the Theiss, comprised the regions now forming the Hungarian circle beyond the Theiss, Transylvania, Bucovina, the Banat of Temes, Wallachia, Moldavia, and Bessarabia.

Of the Dacian language there have survived but scanty fragments—a few names of plants quoted by the physician Dioscorides, and a number of geographical terms, all of which have undoubtedly an Aryan aspect. Thus *propedula* recalls the Gaulish form *pempedula* = cinquefoil. But whether Dacian was Keltic, Teutonic, or Slavonic, or belonged to some other Aryan group, or constitutes of itself a distinct and independent branch of the Aryan family, are questions which in the present state of our knowledge it is impossible to answer.

The Rumanian writer Hájden, who is at present engaged in a great national historical work, fearlessly interprets all the Dacian geographical names occurring in Ptolemy, Strabo, and the table of

* "Iscrizioni Etrusche e Etrusco-Latine," &c. Florence, 1858.

Peutinger. Nay more, he fancies he has lighted upon the old Dacian alphabet, in an alphabet surviving till the last century amongst the Szeklers of Transylvania. But he has altogether overlooked the preliminary question, to what group of languages Dacian may belong.

(3) *The Aryan Languages of Asia Minor.*

That a large number of these idioms were Aryan seems now placed beyond doubt,* and this is unquestionably the case with Phrygian and Lycian. We possess a tolerably large number of Lycian inscriptions, some of which *bilingual,* in Greek and Lycian, a circumstance which will doubtless greatly facilitate the attempts made at deciphering this language. Its alphabet also may be said to be already all but definitely settled. Of Phrygian also we have some inscriptions found in Phrygia itself, besides a series of words occurring in the classic writers. The number of these words is considerable, and as their meaning is clearly determined in the passages where they occur, they may serve as a groundwork for the study of Phrygian. Nor need their transcription be assumed to be radically faulty, though doubtless more or less inexact. In comparing the other Aryan tongues with Greek, or with Iranic, or especially with Armenian, the transcription of their different words in Greek must be relatively correct enough. The old Iranian idioms were in fact not greatly removed from the Greek dialects, and the Aryan tongues of Asia Minor may fairly be supposed to bring these two groups still closer together.

They would thus seem to belong neither to the Iranian group, as many have thought, nor yet to the Hellenic branch, but would rather seem to form a special division of their own, equally allied to Greek, Armenian, and old Persian.

This, however, is a mere hypothesis, which time may or may not confirm. And it may also be discovered that, if certain idioms of Asia Minor are closely related, as for instance the Carian and the Lycian, there are others again but very remotely connected together.

* Renan, " Histoire des Langues Sémitiques," i. ch. 2, § 2.

It may even be necessary to group them in two classes, one leaning towards the Iranic, the other towards the Hellenic family. But the question has not yet advanced beyond the first stage of inquiry, and these various idioms must meantime be included amongst the number of those that still await definite classification.

(4) *The so-called "Scythic" Aryan Tongues.*

In the nineteenth paragraph of our fourth chapter we said that the expressions "Scythian," "Scythic," were merely geographical terms, being applicable to a large number of tribes, differing in race and language. We further stated that certain peoples spoken of by the ancients as "Scythic," spoke an Aryan language.* The reader is referred to this passage, as the matter cannot detain us further here.

(5) *Albanian.*

The questions of the origin of Albanian and of its position in the Aryan family have sorely tried many philologists, nor is the problem yet solved.

Albanian occupies the portion of the Turkish Empire watered by the Adriatic, the Strait of Otranto, and the Ionian Sea. It confines northwards with the Slaves of Montenegro and of the Servian principality, eastwards with the Bulgarians to the north, and with the Greeks of the Ottoman Empire to the south, southwards also with the Greeks. The greatest length of this territory is about ninety-five by an average width of thirty leagues. To the north-east of Scutari it includes some rather important Servian communities, and in the centre, especially southwards, and to the east of Janina, some no less considerable Armenian communities. The Albanians are estimated at about 1,500,000, so that, while much less numerous than the Slaves of Turkey, they on the other hand outnumber the Turks themselves, as well as the Greek subjects of the empire. Their real name is *Skipetar*, or *Highlander*.

* Girard de Rialle, "Bulletins de la Soc. d'Anthropologie de Paris," 1869, p. 46.

Some writers have endeavoured to connect Albanian with the Slavonic idioms, but all such attempts have proved abortive, as they are always likely to do. A more generally received opinion considers it as rather closely allied to Greek, but this view cannot be said to have been scientifically confirmed. Others again have sought to establish a more or less intimate relationship between Albanian and the Italic group, nor would we venture to say that they are nearer the truth than the champions of the Hellenic theory. The matter remains in fact still a moot question. The Albanian adjective we know possesses a sort of ending of pronominal origin, like that of the Slavonic tongues, also that the article is suffixed to the noun, as in Rumanian and Bulgarian; but all else, and especially the conjugation, is very obscure. We therefore hold that, till further proof, Albanian must simply be looked on as an Aryan tongue; so much is certain, but we are scarcely entitled to go further, and connect it forthwith with any particular Aryan group.

§ 11.—*On the Ramification of the Common Aryan Speech, and on its Primitive Home.*

(a)

Scarcely had the affinities of the various Aryan tongues been ascertained, scarcely had their descent been acknowledged from some primitive idiom, of which history has lost all record, when the work of their classification was undertaken. The question was how to group them according to their respective degrees of kindred, to reduce them to families, and thus connect in their turn these families with each other, according to their various mutual relations. In a word, the question was how to divide the common Aryan stock into branches, the branches into offshoots, and so on.

The first connection thus established was between Greek and Latin, an inevitable consequence of the traditions of classical linguistics. It was accordingly assumed that one and the same idiom, breaking away from the main Aryan stem, had given birth to two sister tongues—Greek and Latin. This Græco-Latin ramification seeming to need a name of some sort, was called *Pelasgic*, than which no title was ever less justified. Far from knowing who these Pelasgians were, the very existence of any such people at any time could scarcely be verified, the few passages in Herodotus referring to them, being of a nature calculated to prevent any serious writer from attributing to them any definite meaning.

The labours of Burnouf and of Lassen in the Zend and old Persian domain, enabled the Iranic idioms to be brought into the closest relationship with Sanskrit. A common Indo-Iranian speech was therefore assumed as the source of the Sanskrit on the one hand, and of the Iranian tongues on the other. In the same way the striking resemblance of Lithuanian to the Slavonic group suggested a common Letto-Slavonic speech, which in its turn had a common origin with the prehistoric Teutonic tongue, and so on. Several systems, all defined with equal distinctness, thus came to challenge acceptance. Some writers, for instance, have adopted the subjoined scheme:

$$
\text{Aryan} \begin{cases} \text{Indo-Iranic} \begin{cases} \text{Sanskrit} \\ \text{Iranian} \end{cases} \\ \text{European} \begin{cases} \text{Græco-Italic} \begin{cases} \text{Greek} \\ \text{Italic} \end{cases} \\ \text{Keltic} \\ \text{Slavo-Letto-Teutonic} \begin{cases} \text{Teutonic} \\ \text{Slavo-Lettic} \begin{cases} \text{Lettic} \\ \text{Slavonic} \end{cases} \end{cases} \end{cases} \end{cases}
$$

Schleicher, taking a different view of the Aryan dispersion, tabulated his conclusions as under:

$$
\text{Aryan Mother-Tongue} \begin{cases} \text{Letto-Slavo-Teutonic} \begin{cases} \text{Teutonic} \\ \text{Letto-Slavo} \begin{cases} \text{Lettic} \\ \text{Slavonic} \end{cases} \end{cases} \\ \text{Aryo-Græco-Italo-Keltic} \begin{cases} \text{Græco-Italo-Keltic} \begin{cases} \text{Italo-Keltic} \begin{cases} \text{Keltic} \\ \text{Italic} \end{cases} \\ \text{Greek} \end{cases} \\ \text{Aryan} \begin{cases} \text{Iranian} \\ \text{Hindu} \end{cases} \end{cases} \end{cases}
$$

In this table, therefore, we have no longer any special European speech, some European idioms being more akin to Sanskrit and Iranic than to the other European groups. This theory, in spite of the great weight of its author's name, does not seem to have found much favour, the broad division into Indo-Iranic and European being more generally preferred.* Certain writers, however, while admitting this twofold partition, took different views of the subdivisions, some for instance connecting the Keltic more with the Teutonic group, and others more with the Italic.

Nor is the theory itself of the migrations of the common Aryan stock universally accepted. It has been simultaneously assailed in France and in Germany, in two entirely independent essays, published separately, but at the same date. One of these is by the present writer,† the other by J. Schmidt.‡ Schmidt still admits a linguistic Indo-Iranian unity, and a Letto-Slave unity, but he declines to go farther. He endeavours to show that while on the west the Slavonic and Lettic tongues are indissolubly related to the Teutonic, they are no less intimately related to the Iranian and Indic languages in the east. Hence, he argues, not only was there never a common prehistoric Letto-Slavo-Teutonic speech, but neither was there a special European tongue, clearly distinct from Sanskrit and Iranic. Greek, on the other hand, would be quite as inseparable from the two Asiatic groups as from the Italic, while the Keltic branch could be grouped on no more just grounds with the Italic than with the Teutonic. But this is one of those intricate questions which are not to be settled with a few moments, study.

As regards ourselves, we hold that no intermediate groups have existed between the Aryan mother-tongue, and the Iranian, Hellenic, Teutonic, and other great arteries. Doubtless some Aryan idioms are more allied, all things considered, to some than to others of their congeners; Latin, for instance, more to the Keltic than to the Iranic. But from this we cannot deduce the existence of

---

* Havet, " L'Unité Linguistique Européenne," "Mémoires de la Soc. de Linguistique," ii. p. 261.

† " Notice sur les Subdivisions de la Langue Commune Indo-Européenne," "Comptes-rendus de la Première Session de l'Association Française pour l'Avancement des Sciences," p. 736. Bordeaux, 1872.

‡ " Die Verwandtschaftsverhältnisse der Indo-Germanischen Sprachen." Weimar, 1872.

a common Italo-Keltic speech. We shall probably never know the motives that determined the migrations of the Aryan-speaking races; but it may safely be assumed that before splitting asunder, they occupied a somewhat wide domain, within the limits of which their common speech must necessarily have undergone diverse changes and corruptions amongst the diverse tribes dwelling in this territory. Such modifications could not possibly have been the same everywhere; in one place, for instance, they would affect the fricatives, in another the explosives, elsewhere the forms of the words themselves, and so on. It may be further presumed that in all probability the changes current in one tribe would, on the whole, resemble those taking place in the neighbouring districts, while the more remote the groups, the more such tendencies to corruption would be differentiated. In other words, there must have been a wider severance between the extreme eastern and western groups, than between the latter and any given central group. This kind of gradation and continuity is quite natural in itself, and is no more than what is still met with in modern *patois*.

This is not the place to investigate the causes that determine the general tendencies peculiar to the various tribes; they will probably never be discovered, but we may still confidently believe that the intermediate branches just spoken of, the pretended Italo-Keltic, or Græco-Italic languages never did exist, and never would have been invented but for an excessive love of classification. Still such assumed prehistoric forms of speech have gone on multiplying, nor would it be difficult in the same way to "restore" a common Helleno-Slave, Irano-Kelt, or Italo-Teuton mother-tongue. Once launched on the wide waters of imagination, there can be no reason for stopping short at any particular point.

(β)

Before leaving the Aryan family, we may be allowed a few remarks on the much-debated question of the primitive home of the Aryan speech. And let us in the first place distinguish at once between the question of race and of speech. In dealing with the very formation of articulate speech itself, the element of race is not only all important, but absolutely paramount. The acquisition of the faculty of speech, the formation of the first linguistic systems, and of the first races of mankind are all coincident and simultaneous, as explained in our second chapter, to which no further allusion need here be made. We will merely insist upon the obvious fact that, if the European races come from Europe, or have been developed in Europe, such at least as they now exist, it does not at all follow that the Aryan languages of these regions have also taken their rise here. This distinction, though often overlooked, is essential. We may even say more, and assert that if it is reasonable to speak of Aryan tongues, it is absolutely illogical to speak of an Aryan "race." Such a race has no existence, and those alone may describe and trace its frontiers, and grow eloquent on the theme, who have never entered an anthropological museum. Let us go a step farther. If it is certain that a common Aryan mother-tongue was ever at any time spoken in any region whatsoever, it is not at all certain that those who spoke it belonged to one and the same race. The common Aryan speech was doubtless formed in a single centre by individuals perfectly resembling each other. But its formative period once passed, there was nothing to prevent it from spreading over other tribes very different from each other, as we have seen the "Romana Rustica" spread over the neighbouring tribes of the Guadalaviar, the Somme, and the Lower Danube. Many theories have been advanced on this subject, but after all there is but one well-attested fact that can be relied upon—that is, the existence of this common Aryan tongue, apart altogether from the question of race.

So much established, we may approach the question at issue without fear of further misunderstandings.

Some twenty years ago the home of the common Aryan tongue was generally supposed to be "the vast plateau of Iran," as Pictet writes, "that immense quadrilateral stretching from the Indus to the Tigris and Euphrates, from the Oxus and Jaxartes to the Persian Gulf."* This region answers to the present Persia and to

* "Les Origines Indo-Européennes, ou les Aryas Primitifs." "Essai de Paléontologie Linguistique," i. p. 35. Paris, 1859.

the countries bordering on it east and west [Afghanistan and *Beluchistan* on the east, portions of Mesopotamia, Kurdistan, and Armenia on the west]. But such an extensive area was felt to be much too vague, and attempts were made to restrict it. Relying on the traditions of the "Avesta," it was suggested that Bactriana ought to be looked on as the home of the pretended Aryas, that is of the people speaking the common Aryan tongue. But this was in fact giving to the Iranian tradition a much wider meaning than it really had. The "Avesta" may, strictly speaking, have still had reminiscences of an older Iranian land; but to assume that such a home was at the same time the cradle of the whole Aryan family was a conclusion not at all warranted by the premises. This was readily seen, and it became also evident that philology must be the safest guide in our attempts to solve the difficulty.

Extremely vague, however, is the information to be gleaned from the comparative vocabulary of the Aryan tongues concerning geographical and topographical terms, the names of rivers, mountain-ranges, metals, plants, and animals. They are all equally applicable to a multitude of localities—to Bactriana, for instance, as well as to Assyria, to Assyria no less than to Bactriana.

The most weighty and seemingly the only convincing argument is drawn from the general aspect of the various Aryan tongues. It may be readily admitted that those on the whole most faithfully answering to the common Aryan type are also those that have least wandered from the regions where this common type was spoken. We have already seen that not any one of the Aryan tongues is superior on all points to its congeners, there being none of them but presents some weak side or other. Thus Sanskrit, changing certain organic *k*'s to *ch* is herein surpassed by Latin, which retains them all. But this does not prevent certain idioms from being, all things considered, much more primitive than others. In the very first rank we must unhesitatingly place Sanskrit and the old Iranic tongues, Zend and ancient Persian. Nor is it less certain that the Keltic idioms must occupy the lowest position in the scale. Hence our first conclusion: Of all the Aryan tongues, Sanskrit and Iranic have migrated least from the common Aryan centre, while the Keltic group has wandered farther from it than have any of the cognate idioms.

In the next best state of preservation may be included the Hellenic dialects in the south-east and the Lettic and Slavonic in the north-east of Europe. A third stage would comprise the Teutonic group in the north and the Italic in the south, each of these branches confining on the Keltic, which, as stated, stands in the fourth or lowest rank.

Pictet, whom this unquestioned fact did not escape, drew a conclusion from it. Describing a somewhat oblong ellipse, he makes the focus to the right represent the point where the common Aryan tongue was spoken. A little to the right of this focus he places Sanskrit below and Iranic above [that is, at the extremities of two lines radiating from the focus either way to the right]. Then diverging somewhat to the left, he places the Slavo-Lettic and the Hellenic in central positions, above and below respectively, these two branches thus still remaining near the right focus, though less so than Sanskrit and Iranic. Coming still farther to the left, he places the Teutonic and the Italic in the same way above and below respectively, in the same relative position to the left focus that Sanskrit and Iranic occupy towards the right focus. Continuing still to the left, he places the Keltic branch at the extremity of the horizontal transverse line of the ellipse, between the Teutonic and the Italic groups, Keltic thus occupying the farthest point from the right focus—that is to say, from the assumed centre of departure.

This diagram may easily be constructed [as thus :

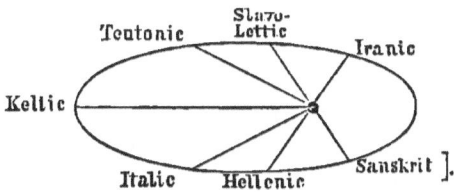

].

The scheme is doubtless very ingenious, and at first sight one feels strongly tempted to adopt it, agreeing, as it also does, with the supposition of Bactriana being the region where the common

Aryan tongue was spoken. But it is in reality liable to two different interpretations, and to two distinct applications, the first being that of Pictet himself. Here is the second : The common centre may possibly not have been in the right focus of the ellipse, but more to the right, and even outside the ellipse itself, that is towards the Chinese frontier. In this case Sanskrit and Iranic would still occupy the first position, Greek and Slavo-Lettic the second, Teutonic and Italic the third, and Keltic the fourth and last.

For our own part, we do not pretend to pronounce on the merits of either of these hypotheses; we merely set them forth without judging, while still expressing our decided opinion as to the Asiatic origin of the Aryan linguistic family.

Latham seems to have been the first to suggest a European origin, which has been adopted by a few writers, some of whom have endeavoured to give a scientific aspect to their view, while others have simply settled the matter offhand with as much boldness as incompetence. Thus certain writers, observing that the Keltic words were shorter than the Sanskrit, have argued that they were also simpler, more primitive, and less removed from the common type, thereby applying the rule of " long measure " to the science of language. By this process Anglo-Saxon would derive from English, Latin from French, Zend from Persian.

Others again, arguing from the fact that the fair blue-eyed type is found more especially in German-speaking countries, conclude, one scarcely sees why, that the common Aryan mother-tongue was spoken in Germany, herein confounding race and language, or rather language and races. It matters little whether the Aryan-speaking tribes were fair or dark, or whether both types were represented amongst them. The question we are concerned with is one not of race but of language. Nor shall we even appeal to the aid of archæology, which yet clearly teaches that at an epoch when the east had reached a certain degree of civilisation, the west was still in a savage state or not far removed from it. The proofs furnished by philology must suffice, and the fact of this series of languages departing more and more from the common type, according as they are situated more to the west, speaks convincingly enough of itself alone. Nor can it matter much whether the home of the common Aryan speech be placed in Armenia, or in Bactriana, or in any other still more eastern region. This is now a question of but secondary interest.

CHAPTER VI.

ORIGINAL PLURALITY OF SPEECH, AND TRANSMUTATION OF LINGUISTIC SYSTEMS.

Having thus come to the end of this long survey, though still necessarily curtailed at almost every page, it remains for us to cast a comprehensive glance at the field travelled over, and in a final chapter sum up its more prominent landmarks. And we must, at the very outset, touch once more on the question of the scientific process, which was the first to challenge inquiry, and must be the last to engage our attention. By it is swayed all present science, or rather they blend together as but one body, the inalienable union of science and method, which cannot be too strongly insisted upon, forming, as it does, the essential characteristic of this new phase of human thought.

§ 1.—*How to Recognise Linguistic Affinities.*

Many writers but indifferently acquainted with the science of language, will often unhesitatingly group together linguistic families, that really competent authorities do not venture to bring into the same category, or will at times even declare to be radically distinct. It is here above all that we see the danger of etymology, which in truth rides recklessly over all obstacles. Its baneful tendencies have been especially fostered by biblical prejudices, it being a foregone conclusion for theological writers, that all the languages of the universe are connected, either directly or collaterally, with the Semitic family. The hope of making Hebrew the origin of all speech they were fain at last to give up, but they still felt the necessity of identifying all languages, Hebrew itself included, with some one common source or mother-tongue.

This theory has now been placed beyond the pale of discussion, and still to speak, even with bated breath, of a so-called common primeval speech, is simply to betray utter ignorance of the science of language.

In comparing idioms, we must, above all, take no heed of the mere likeness of words to each other. Two words of nearly or even absolutely similar meaning in two different languages, may possibly have nothing in common, so that lexical apart from grammatical agreement is nothing to the purpose. The etymologist pounces upon such resemblances, rests satisfied with them, and refuses to look farther afield, while the philologist passes them unheeded. In his eyes the analysis alone of two more or less similar terms can prove their affinity, but he never ventures to compare together two words ready made. Should their formative elements and their roots themselves be the same, they may rightly be looked upon as answering to each other, and as derived from a common source. But should these conditions not be verified, the two terms in question cannot be identified, however homophonous they may happen to be.

The comparison of hundreds of ready-made words in two languages whatsoever, would never advance by a single step the question of their mutual relationship. What requires to be proved, is not the existence of these casual resemblances, but the identity of the roots when reduced to their simplest form, the identity of the formative elements, the identity of the grammatical functions of these elements; in a word, the grammatic identity of the languages compared.

The so-called comparative studies not based on these inexorable principles, can be no longer taken into account; all such trifling belongs to a bygone day.

§ 2.—*Original Plurality of Linguistic Groups and Consequences thereof.*

Not only is there no common grammatical point of identity between the Semitic and Aryan linguistic groups, but, as already explained, inflection itself is differently treated in each of these systems. Their roots are totally distinct, their formative elements essentially different;˙ nor have the.functions of these elements anything in common. The abyss separating the two systems is not merely deep, it is impassable.

"When," asks Chavée, "can two languages be scientifically held as two radically distinct creations? In the first place, when their roots, reduced to their simplest forms, have absolutely nothing in common, either in their phonetic elements or in their syllabic constituents. Secondly, when the laws regulating the first combinations of these simple roots differ essentially in the two systems."*

This is the case with the Semitic and Aryan tongues no less than with a large number of other linguistic systems; and the consequences of this fact are all important. If the faculty of articulate speech constitutes the sole fundamental characteristic of man, as explained in our second chapter, and if the different linguistic groups known to us are irreducible, they must have taken birth independently and in quite distinct regions. It follows that the precursors of man must have acquired the faculty of speech in different localities independently, and have thus given birth to several races of mankind originally distinct.†

* "Les Langues et les Races," p. 13. Paris, 1862.

† This seems to be a very sweeping conclusion to come to on very slight and not yet fully-established premises. In fact, the learned author would appear to be here trespassing beyond the legitimate field of the strict science of language in its present state, and verging on the domain of pure metaphysics, which he himself elsewhere so eloquently denounces. Nor is the statement at all so generally established as he would have us suppose, that families now distinct—such, for instance, as the Aryan and the Semitic—are utterly incapable of being identified. The question cannot here be enlarged upon, and it may be perhaps enough to refer to Andreas Raabe's "Gemeinschaftliche Grammatik der Arischen und der Semitischen Sprachen," Leipzig, 1874, which work may possibly have escaped the

"The French anthropologists," says General Faidherbe, "were usually of accord that articulate speech alone distinguishing man fundamentally from the brute creation, the precursors of man were not entitled to this name before they had acquired the faculty in question. But we readily see that this is merely a question of the conventional use of words. The only important point is to know whether he, this being, called man or not, acquired the gift of speech in one place only and at one particular time, or in more ways than one, both as regards time and place. Now the impossibility of reducing human speech to one source proves the truth of the second hypothesis. Had man acquired this faculty, the consequence of the progressive development of his organisms, in one way only, language would have remained substantially the same to the present time, or at least we should detect in all languages some traces of their common descent. The extreme diversity of idioms and of their formative processes, proves that they were created independently of each other, and probably at

author's notice. It is certainly based on the strict scientific method, and would seem to point at totally different conclusions from those here so confidently proclaimed. Thus, he points out that the perfect is the oldest organic tense both in Aryan and Semitic, and that the *unreduplicate* Aryan perfect, often occurring in the "Vedas," shows a strong likeness to the Semitic perfect, as thus:

Aryan (unreduplicate perfect).	Hebrew.	Ethiopic.
Sing. 1. apátha	אָבַדְתִּי	abadĕku
2. apathitha	תְּ —— fem. תְּ ——	abadĕka, fem. abadĕkī
3. apatha	אָבַד fem. אָבְדָה	abeda, fem. abĕdat
Plural 1. apathimá	אָבַדְנִי	abadena
2. apathá	אֲבַדְתֶּם fem. אֲבַדְתֶּן	abadĕkĕmmu, fem. [abadĕkĕnn
3. apathúh	אָבְדוּ	abĕdū, fem. abĕdā

As Raabe remarks: "The great resemblance of the Aryan and Semitic paradigm is here easily recognised" (p. 23). In any case the author's dogmatism on this subject would seem to be at least somewhat premature.—*Note by Translator.*

x

very different epochs. As, moreover, the principal irreducible linguistic systems correspond in a general way to the leading races of mankind, we argue that speech has sprung up independently amongst sundry distinct varieties of what Fr. Müller calls the *homo primigenius*, and French anthropologists *the precursors of man*."

Thus philology furnishes a new and formidable argument to the polygenists, who were already supplied with so many before. [But it is an argument that the polygenists, who are all necessarily evolutionists in the Darwinian sense, cannot consistently make use of. For surely no form of speech that ever has existed is more. or so much, removed from any other form of speech than is man himself from the lower orders of the animal kingdom, from which on their showing he must yet be descended. Hence, if the impossibility of reducing man now to, say a mollusc, is no argument against the original identity of man with a mollusc, why should the impossibility of now reducing any two or more linguistic systems to a common source be any argument against the original identity of those systems? Speech changes much more rapidly than do the higher orders of the animal kingdom; hence, if there has been time for an oyster to become an elephant or a man, according to the different lines of development it may have taken, why should there not have been time for Chinese, or any other isolating tongue, to become Hebrew or Sanskrit, according to the different lines of development it may have taken through the several isolating, agglutinating, and inflectional phases of its prehistoric and historic life? Thus no argument based on the *present* disparity of human speech ought to have any force for a consistent evolutionist as against the possible primordial unity of all human speech.]

Language being a product of nature herself, being the function of a new organ, it is evident that two irreducible linguistic systems point at two different productive organs. We will not follow Hæckel in reducing to a single race the so-called Indo-Europeans, Semites, Basques, and Caucasians; philology teaches, and would of itself suffice to show, that we have here four distinct races. Their differences may be very slight in all other respects besides that of language, but in this last respect it is decided; and, as philologists, we must conclude for the impossibility of a common origin.

History tells us that a large number of linguistic families have perished without issue, and this is but the result of the struggle for existence pervading all nature in all time and space. The farther back we go, the more numerous do we find the independent linguistic families, and the same is the case with the races of man. It may be asserted without rashness that the precursor of man must have in many places at the same time or successively acquired the faculty of speech that was destined to raise him to the dignity of man. And this is the result that the science of language leads to, in revealing to us a multiplicity of irreducible linguistic systems.

§ 3.—*In their Historic Life Language and Race may cease to be Convertible Terms.*

Thus we see, as already stated, that in the historic period of man no new linguistic systems can arise. The origin of language, the acquisition of the faculty of articulate speech, being coincident with the formation of the first races, it follows that the precursor of man once extinct, the development of new linguistic systems is absolutely impossible. Every effect needs a cause, and the cause disappearing the effect ceases.

But after entering on the historic stage, languages, like races, may die out. Thus it is that modern German has extinguished Polabish, a Slavonic idiom, and old Prussian, a Lettic dialect. Thus also Latin has absorbed her own sisters, Oscan and Umbrian; Spanish is eradicating Basque; and English is sweeping away the North American idioms. In France the Normans lost their Norse tongue, and the Burgundians their Teutonic dialect, as did the Lombards in Italy.

Other languages, again, have attempted violently but unsuccessfully to usurp foreign domain, as is the case with two Uralo-Altaïc tongues in Europe. One of these is the Turkish, which has in vain penetrated to the heart of Europe, but no longer occupies more than a very small portion of European Turkey itself, while in

Candia nearly all the Turks have taken to Greek. The other is the Magyar, which is now rapidly decaying in Hungary, notwithstanding the great privileges it enjoys, and the official countenance given to it at the expense of the surrounding tongues.* But its disappearance may confidently be predicted sooner or later.

Different races often speak one and the same language, just as one and the same race may speak several different languages, facts which are well known, and of which a multiplicity of examples might be adduced. Some of the Basques—the Spanish or genuine Basques—still speak Escaldunac in the neighbourhood of Durango, Tolosa, and Saint Sebastian, while others speak Spanish in the neighbourhood of Vitoria and Pampluna. Some of the Bretons, again, speak French, while others still retain their Keltic tongue. Many Finns speak Suomi, but many also speak Russian exclusively; and in Central Asia other Uralo-Altäic tribes have in the same way adopted Persian. But it would be tedious to prolong the list.

§ 4.—*The Permutation of Species in Philology.*

Once launched on their historic life, the phonetic system and forms of languages soon begin to change, and become gradually modified. Consonants and vowels often change to stronger or weaker consonants, to sharper or more open vowels. Both also frequently influence each other mutually, and such influence becoming more and more pronounced the various branches of a given family, each with their peculiar modifying tendencies, depart daily farther and farther from each other. Persian and French are much more different from one another than were old Persian and Latin; English and German than Anglo-Saxon and old High German. And not only do the forms become modified, but they at times perish altogether. The common Aryan mother-tongue possessed eight cases, of which Latin retained scarcely more than two-thirds, reduced in the Langue d'oïl to two, while in modern French they have quite disappeared. So also the three primitive Semitic cases have been preserved in literary Arabic alone.

* "Les Serbes de Hongrie," p. 310. (Anonyme.) Prague, 1873.

But this is so far a degradation rather than a transformation. True transformation, with which we are now concerned, is a variation of species, a phenomenon in philology which has long been scientifically demonstrated, and which those alone will venture still to doubt who confound etymology with the science of language.

It has been shown in the course of this work that all languages were divided according to their structure into three distinct classes, the isolating, the agglutinating, and the inflectional. In the first class we have neither prefixes nor suffixes, the root itself in its crude state forming the word, so that here the sentence consists of nothing but a series of independent, free, and isolated roots. In the second class the word is formed of two, three, four or more elements, one of these roots alone preserving its full primitive force, while the others, losing a part of their original meaning, are attached to the principal root as relational, that is, secondary elements. In the third class not only are diverse elements agglutinated, as in the preceding, but the root itself may become modified, changing its vowel with its change of meaning. These three stages have been described in their place, with examples calculated to clearly illustrate their peculiar features.

It is now well ascertained that the languages of the second class have passed through the first stage before arriving at their present state, while those of the third have successively passed through the two previous stages. Before being agglutinating, the Uralo-Altaïc idioms were isolating or monosyllabic, and before becoming inflectional, the Semitic had been first monosyllabic and then agglutinating.

The proof of this permutation of linguistic species is self-evident. Thus all the monosyllabic tongues betray clear proofs of a more or less realised tendency towards the agglutinating process, while several agglutinating idioms in the same way manifest tendencies towards inflection. Lastly, in the inflecting tongues themselves there occur numerous traces of the agglutinating and even of the isolating phase.

Thus we have seen that Chinese grammar already distinguishes the roots into *full* and *empty* (p. 37), a distinction which is the first step towards agglutination. Nothing was in fact further needed than to solder the empty on to the full roots, in order to pass completely from the first to the second phase. Of all the isolating tongues, Tibetan seems to show the most marked tendency towards agglutination, so much so that it has at times been wrongly taken for an agglutinating language.

The transition from agglutination to inflection is quite as easy to understand, and all who have studied the Uralo-Altaïc group are aware that the first traces of inflection are much more marked in the Finnic than in the other groups, especially the Tungus.

But the most curious point to observe is the passage from the agglutinating to the inflectional state. Thus a number of Aryan forms are still in the agglutinating period, as, for instance, the vocative, which is nothing but the theme itself: $akra$ = Sanskrit $açva$ = Latin $eque$ = (O horse! where the radical and derivative elements are intimately connected, neither presenting any trace of phonetic modification or of inflection. Nay more, unmistakable traces of the monosyllabic period still linger in the Aryan tongues, as in Sanskrit, which has a somewhat numerous class of nouns, whose theme is nothing but the monosyllabic root itself. It little matters that it modify the vowel, or suffix the case-endings, the fact remains, that we are here evidently dealing with a primitive monosyllabic element. In conjugation also, the augment a, prefixed to the imperfects and aorists (old Persian $abara$ = Greek ἔφερε), is nothing but an old monosyllabic form of the first period.

However, if it is easy to detect in the more recent stages vestiges of the older periods, it is no less easy unhesitatingly to group the various families of languages in their respective periods or classes. Here the broad features are an unerring guide.

The absence of intermediate stages between the existing and the older forms has often been urged as an objection to the theory of transmutation. We have not here to pronounce on a question of zoology or botany, but we would remark that where language is concerned the objection has no force whatsoever, for the process of evolution is here easily followed, and in fact detected in active operation. The transmutation of species is here a patent fact, and one of the fundamental principles of the science of language.* And is not this in itself a fresh and brilliant proof of the truth discussed at the opening of this work, that philology is above all a natural science?

One word in conclusion. We have spoken successively of plurality of origin and of transmutation, terms which to some may seem contradictory, but which are easily reconciled. The doctrine of the original plurality of languages and races in no way pretends to clash with the more general doctrine of cosmic unity. After all, we must still acknowledge that all existing forms, without exception, are but varied aspects of matter, which is *one* as it is *infinite*. But this unity does not at all prevent such and such identical, or even analogous forms from being developed simultaneously in different centres, nor from being reduced directly and without intermediate links to one common form. But whether such analogous but distinct forms have sprung from one original source or not, it is now impossible to determine.

However, this matters little, and the ascertained impossibility of reducing a multiplicity of linguistic families to a common centre is for us sufficient proof of the original plurality of the races that have been developed with them, the acquisition of the faculty of articulate speech being coincident with the appearance of man himself on the earth. [But see Translator's remarks at p. 306.]

* Whitney, "Language and the Study of Language," 3rd ed., p. 175. London, 1870.

APPENDIX.

SYNOPTICAL TABLE OF ALL THE LANGUAGES TREATED OF IN THIS WORK.

NOTE.—Where two names are given in the "Family and Group" column, the first refers to the genus or stock, the second to some particular species, branch, or subdivision of that stock. When one name only occurs, without further explanation, we are to infer that the position of the language in question is not yet thoroughly established. Thus at "Lithuanian" the words "Aryan—Lettic," imply that Lithuanian is a member of the Lettic group or branch of the Aryan family or stock, while at "Albanian," the single word "Aryan" tells us that Albanian is an Aryan tongue, about the further classification of which philologists are still undecided. The terms "Independent" and "Unclassified" imply either that such idioms are not known to be connected with any other, or that their proper classification has not yet been made clear. For instance see "Basque," which is strictly "independent" of all known tongues, and "Munda," whose claim to be included in the Dravidian or any other system has not, so far, been universally recognised, and it is accordingly described as "Unclassified."

In the "Form of Speech" column, the Basque and the American tongues are described as "Polysynthetic," because the Translator does not consider the Author justified in refusing to see any essential difference between polysynthesis and agglutination. At all events, he thinks the term "Polysynthetic" should be retained until the question has been definitely settled. See Translator's remarks at p. 129.

In this same "Form of Speech" column the abbreviations *Is.*, *Ag.*, *Pol.*, *In.*, stand for *Isolating*, *Agglutinative*, *Polysynthetic*, and *Inflectional* respectively.

The numbers to the left refer to the corresponding figures on the philological map, prepared specially for the English edition; those to the right refer to the pages in the work devoted to the languages in question.

Ref. No.	Name.	Family and Group.	Where spoken.	Form of Speech.	Page.
1	Abenaki	Algonquin	State of Maine, New England	Pol.	131
2	Abipon	Independent	Valley of the Salado, Argentine States	Pol.	125
3	Accadian	Unclassified	Mesopotamia	Ag.?	141
4	Æolic	Aryan—Hellenic	Asia Minor	In.	211
5	Afghan	Aryan—Iranic	Afghanistan	In.	207
6	Agaü	Hamitic—Ethiopian	West of Alyssinia	In.	180
7	Aino	Sub-Arctic	Yesso, Japan	Ag.	135

APPENDIX.

Ref. No.	Name	Family and Group	Where spoken	Form of Speech	Page.
8	Akra	Negro—Ewe	Gold Coast	Ag.	58
9	Akusha	Caucasian—Lesghian	Caucasus	Ag.	136
10	Albanian	Aryan	Albania, European Turkey	In.	293
11	Aleutian	Sub-Arctic	Aleutian Archipelago	Ag.	135
12	Alforow	Malayo-Javanese	Dutch East Indies, Moluccas	Ag.	68
13	Algonquin	Independent group	Canada and New England	Pol.	131
14	Amharic	Semitic—Arabic	Abyssinia (south-west)	In.	170
	Andhra	See Telugu			
15	Anglo-Saxon	Aryan—Teutonic	England and Lowlands (extinct)	In.	259
16	Angola	Bantu (Western branch)	Angola	Ag.	61
17	Annamese	Unclassified	Annam	Is.	41
18	Annatom	Malayo-Polynesian — Melanesian	South Sea Islands, New Hebrides	Ag.	68
19	Apache	Athapasque	Nevada and Upper California	Pol.	124
20	Appalache	Independent group	Lower Mississippi	Pol.	121
21	Arabic	Semitic—Arabic	Arabia, Syria, Egypt, Barbary States	Pol.	167
22	Aramaic	Semitic Aramæo-Assyrian	Syria, Chaldæa	In.	155
23	Ararat	Aryan—Iranic	Armenia	In.	202
24	Araucanian	Unclassified	South America, Chili	Pol.	125
25	Arevak	Carib	British and Dutch Guiana	Pol.	121
26	Armenian	Aryan—Iranic	Armenia, Turkey passim	In.	202
	Armorican	See Breton			
27	Assami	Aryan—Indic	Assam	In.	191
28	Assyrian	Semitic—Aramæo-Assyrian	Mesopotamia	In.	157
29	Athapasque	Independent group	Between the Mackenzio and Hudson's Bay	Pol.	121
30	Attic	Aryan—Hellenic	Attica, Eubœa, &c.	In.	212
31	Australian	Independent group	Australia, Tasmania	Ag.	67
32	Auvergne	Aryan—Neo-Latin	Auvergne	In.	236
33	Aware	Caucasian—Lesgian	Lesghistan, between Daghestan and Circassia	Ag.	136

APPENDIX.

Ref. No.	Name.	Family and Group.	Where spoken.	Form of Speech.	Page.
34	Aymara	Kechua group	Peru and Bolivia	Pol.	125
35	Aztek	Independent...	Mexico	Pol.	124
36	Bactrian	See Zend.			
37	Badaga	Dravidian	Neilgherries, between Mysore and Travancore	Ag.	79
38	Baghirmi	Negro—Unclassified	Between Lake Chad and Darfur	Ag.	58
	Baladen	Malayo-Polynesian — Melanesian			
39	Bali	Malayo-Polynesian—Malay	Island of Bali (Dutch East Indies)	Ag.	68
40	Bambarra	African Negro—Mando	Senegambia (south)	Ag.	68
41	Bantu	Independent family	South-east and West Coast of Africa	Ag.	56
42	Barabras	Nubian group	Upper Egypt and Nubia, between 21° & 21° lat.	Ag.	59
43	Bari	African Negro—Upper Nile	White Nile, south of Gondokoro	Ag.	66
44	Basa	African Negro (Kruh branch)	Liberia, Grain Coast	Ag.	58
45	Basque	Independent...	Spanish and French Pyrenees...	Pol.	58
46	Batta	Unclassified—Akin to Mosgu	Central Africa, south of Lake Chad	Ag.	109
47	Battak	Malayo-Polynesian—Malay	Interior of Sumatra	Ag.	58
48	Banro	Malayo-Polynesian — Melanesian		Ag.	68
49	Bayciye	Bantu (Central branch)	South Sea Islands	Ag.	68
50	Beja...	Hamitic (Ethiopian branch)	Interior of South Africa	Ag.	61
51	Beluchi	Aryan—Iranic	N. of Abyssinia, between the Nile and Red Sea	In.	180
52	Benga	Bantu (Western branch)	Beluchistan	In.	207
53	Bengali	Aryan—Indic	Corisco Bay, West Africa	Ag.	61
54	Benguela	Bantu (Western branch)	Bengal, Lower Ganges	In.	194
55	Berber	Hamitic—Libyan	Benguela, West Africa	Ag.	61
56	Bicol	Malayo-Polynesian—Tagala	South of the Barbary States	In.	179
57	Bisaya	Malayo-Polynesian—Tagala	Bicol Island, Philippines	Ag.	68
58	Biscayan	Basque	Bisaya Island, Philippines	Ag.	68
			Spanish Pyrenees	Pol.	115

APPENDIX. 315

Ref. No.	Name.	Family and Group.	Where spoken.	Form of Speech.	Page.
	Bishara	See Beja.			
59	Bohemian	Aryan—Slavonic	Bohemia	In.	274
60	Bola	African Negro—Fedupbranch	Senegal	Ag.	56
61	Bornu	African Negro—Unclassified	About Lake Chad east of Hawsa	Ag.	58
62	Botocudo	Guarani group?	Brazil, east of the San Francisco	Pol.	125
63	Brahui	Dravidian?	Beluchistan, near Kelat	Ag.	138
64	Breton	Aryan—Keltic	Brittany	In.	246
65	Bulgarian	Aryan—Slavonic	Bulgaria	In.	279
66	Bunda	Bantu (Western branch)	Angola	Ag.	61
67	Burgundian	Aryan—Neo-Latin	Burgundy	In.	235
68	Burman	Independent	Burmah	Is.	42
69	Buryetic	Ural-Altaic—Turkic	Chinese Turkestan	Ag.	99
70	Buryetic	Ural-Altaic—Mongol	Shores of Lake Baikal	Ag.	105
71	Bushman	Unclassified	South Africa, Orange River, and Kalahari Desert	Ag.	51
72	Byzantine	Aryan—Hellenic	Eastern Empire	In.	212
73	Calabrian	Aryan—Neo-Latin	Calabria	In.	238
74	Californian	Independent group	California	Pol.	124
75	Cambodian	Unclassified	Cambodia	Ag.?	42
76	Canaanitic	Semitic (Central branch)	Palestine, Phœnicia, Carthage	In.	160
77	Canton	Chinese	China (south-east)	Is.	31
78	Carian	Aryan?—Unclassified	Asia Minor (extinct)	In.?	292
79	Carib	Unclassified	Venezuela and French Guiana	Pol.	124
80	Carora.				
81	Catalonian	Aryan—Neo-Latin	Catalonia	In.	239
82	Cayuga	Iroquois	State of New York	Pol.	131
83	Chactah	Appalache group	Lower Mississippi	Pol.	124
84	Chaldee	Semitic (Aramaic branch)	Mesopotamia	In.	155

316   APPENDIX.

Ref. No.	Name	Family and Group	Where spoken	Form of Speech	Page
85	Cheremissian	Uralo-Altaïc—Volga Finnic	Left bank of Volga, between Nijni Novgorod and Kazan	Ag.	90
86	Cherkessian	Caucasian (Northern division)	Circassia	Ag.	136
87	Cherokee	Appalache group	Lower Mississippi	Pol.	121
88	Chibcha	Independent group	New Granada	Pol.	125
89	Chinese	Independent	China	Is.	34
90	Chippeway	Algonquin	Canada	Pol.	131
91	Chochoni	Unclassified	Sonora	Pol.	124
92	Chudic	Uralo-Altaïc—Finnic	South of Lake Onega	Ag.	91
93	Chukchik (American)	Eskimo group	North-west coast of America	Ag.	135
94	Chukchik (Asiatic)	Sub-Arctic	Extreme north-east of Siberia	Ag.	135
95	Church Slavonic	Aryan—Slavonic	Eastern Europe, limits undefined (extinct)	In.	270
96	Chuvak	Uralo-Altaïc—Turkic	Simbirsk, south-west of Kazan	Ag.	100
97	Ciboney	Unclassified	West Indies (extinct)	Pol.	124
	Circassian	See Cherkessian.			
	Cochimi	See Kochimi.			
98	Continental Saxon	Aryan—Teutonic	Between the Rhine and the Elbe, Westphalia (extinct)	In.	258
99	Coptic	Hamitic (Egyptian branch)	Egypt	In.	177
100	Corean	Unclassified	Corea	Ag.	76
101	Cornish	Aryan—Keltic	Cornwall (extinct)	In.	246
102	Corsican	Aryan—Neo-Latin	Corsica	In.	238
103	Croatian	Aryan—Slavonic	Croatia, Bosnia, Dalmatia	In.	276
104	Dacian	Unclassified	Dacia (extinct)	?	291
105	Danish	Aryan—Norse	Denmark	In.	256
106	Dankali	Hamitic (Ethiopian branch)	Upper Nile, north-west of Abyssinia	In.	180
107	Dayak	Malayo-Polynesian — Malay	Borneo	Ag.	68

APPENDIX. 317

Ref. No.	Name	Family and Group	Where spoken	Form of Speech	Page
108	Dakotah	Independent group	Central and Western States (Sioux and other tribes)	Pol.	124
109	Dauphiny	Aryan—Neo-Latin	South-east of France	In.	236
—	Delaware	See Lenapé			
110	Di-Kele	Bantu (Western branch)	Bight of Biafra	Ag.	61
111	Dinka	African Negro—Upper Nile branch	Right bank of White Nile	Ag.	58
112	Dongola	Nubian group	Nile Valley, about the Third Cataract, north of Khartum	Ag.	66
113	Doric	Aryan—Hellenic	Doria, Peloponnesus, Magna Græcia, &c. (extinct)	In.	211
114	Duallo	Bantu (Western branch)	West Coast of Africa, Bight of Biafra	Ag.	61
115	Echemian	Algonquin group	State of Maine, New England	Pol.	131
116	Egyptian	Hamitic (Egyptian branch)	Egypt	In.	175
117	Ehkili	Semitic (Himyaritic branch)	Southern Arabia, Mahrah	In.	171
—	Elbe Slavo	See Polabish			
—	Elu	See Sinhalese			
118	Emilian	Aryan—Neo-Latin	Emilia, Bologna, Ferrara, &c.	In.	238
119	English	Aryan—Teutonic (Low)	Br. Isles, N. America, Australia, N. Zealand, S. Africa, &c.	In.	259
120	Erromango	Malayo-Polynesian — Melanesian	Erromango, about 21° S. lat., between Loyalty and Fiji	Ag.	68
121	Erse	Aryan—Keltic	Highlands of Scotland	In.	245
122	Erze	Uralo-Altaïc—Finnic (Mordvinian)	Banks of the Volga (Simbirsk)	Ag.	93
—	Escuara	See Basque			
123	Eskimo	Sub-Arctic—Unclassified	Greenland, shores of the Arctic	Ag.	135
124	Esthonian	Uralo-Altaïc—Finnic	Esthonia, Livonia (Dorpat)	Ag.	91

318   APPENDIX.

Ref. No.	Name.	Family and Group.	Where spoken.	Form of Speech.	Page.
125	Etruscan	Aryan? Uralo-Altaïc?	Etruria (extinct)	?	290
126	Ewe or Egbo	African Negro—Unclassified	Slave Coast, 70° N. lat.	Ag.	58
127	Felup	African Negro—Unclassified	The Gambia	Ag.	56
128	Fiji	Malayo-Polynesian — Melanesian	Fiji or Viti Islands, between 10° and 20° S. lat.	Ag.	68
129	Filham	African Negro (Felup branch)	On the Casamanzo	Ag.	56
130	Fingu	Bantu (Eastern branch)	Kafirland	Ag.	60
131	Finnish	Uralo-Altaïc—Finnic (Suomi)	Finland	Ag.	90
132	Fernandian	Bantu (Western branch)	Fernando Po	Ag.	61
133	Flemish	Aryan—Teutonic	Flanders	In.	261
134	Fo-Kien	Chinese	East coast of China, between 21° and 30° N. lat.	Is.	31
135	Formosan	Malayo-Polynesian—Malay	Island of Formosa	Ag.	68
136	French	Aryan—Neo-Latin	France, Belgium, Geneva, Vaud, Canada, &c.	In.	233
137	Frisian	Aryan—Teutonic	North coast of Holland	In.	261
138	Friuli	Aryan—Neo-Latin (Ladin)	Banks of the Tagliamento, below Gorlitz	In.	238
139	Fula	Independent group	Between Senegal and Lake Chad		64
140	Gä	See Akra.			
141	Gaedhelic	Aryan—Keltic	Ireland, Highlands of Scotland, Isle of Man	In.	244
	Galacian	Aryan—Keltic	Asia Minor (extinct)	In.	247
—	Galibi	See Carib.			
142	Galician	Aryan—Neo-Latin	North-west of Spain	In.	239
143	Galla	Hamitic (Ethiopian branch)	South of Abyssinia	In.	180
144	Gascon	Aryan—Neo-Latin	South-west of France	In.	236
145	Gaulish	Aryan—Keltic (Kymric)	Gaul (extinct)	In.	247
146	Gbandi	African Negro (Mande group)	Soudan (west)	Ag.	56
147	Gbese	African Negro (Mande branch)	Soudan (west)	Ag.	56

APPENDIX. 319

Ref. No.	Name.	Family and Group.	Where spoken.	Form of Speech.	Page.
148	Genoese	Aryan—Neo-Latin	Genoa, north-west of Italy	In.	238
149	Georgian	Caucasian (Southern branch)	Georgia, Trans-Caucasia	Ag.	136
150	German	Aryan Teutonic (High)	South Germany	In.	264
151	Gheez	Semitic (Arabic group)	Abyssinia (extinct)	In.	171
152	Ghiliak	Sub-Arctic	South-east coast of Siberia	Ag.	135
153	Gipsy	Aryan—Indic	Europe passim, Western Asia	In.	195
154	Gond	Dravidian	Central India, Nagpore, &c.	Ag.	78
155	Gothic	Aryan Teutonic (Low)	Mœsia (extinct)	In.	254
156	Great Russian	Aryan—Slavonic	Russia	In.	271
157	Grebo	Kruh group	River St. Paul, Liberia	Ag.	58
158	Greek	Aryan Hellenic	Greece, Ionia, Magna Graecia, Sicily, &c. (extinct)		
159	Grison	Aryan—Neo-Latin (Ladin)	Grisons, east of Switzerland	In.	208
160	Gaadalkauar	Malayo-Polynesian — Melanesian		In.	238
161	Guarani	Independent group	South Sea Islands	Ag.	68
162	Guaykuru	Independent group	Paraguay	Pol.	125
			Between the Paraguay and the Pilcomayo rivers		
163	Guipuzcoan	Basque	Spanish Pyrenees	Pol.	125
164	Gujarati	Aryan—Indic	Gujarat	Pol.	115
				In.	194
165	Harrari	Semitic (Arabic division)	Abyssinia (south-east)	In.	172
166	Hawaii	Malayo-Polynesian — Polynesian			
167	Hawsa	Independent Negro	Sandwich Islands	Ag.	68
168	Hebrew	Semitic (Canaanitic)	Between the Niger and Lake Chad	Ag.	56
169	Herero	Bantu (Western branch)	Palestine (extinct)	In.	160
170	High Lithuanian	Aryan—Lettic	East of Benguela, about 19° S. lat.	Ag.	60
			Extreme north-east of Prussia, Baltic Provinces	In.	285

APPENDIX.

Ref. No.	Name.	Family and Group.	Where spoken.	Form of Speech.	Page.
—	High Lusatian	See Sorbian.			
171	Himyaritic	Semitic (Arabic group)	Southern Arabia (extinct)	In.	170
172	Hindi	Aryan—Indic	North-west Provinces	In.	194
—	Hindu	See Sanskrit.			
173	Hindui	Aryan—Indic	North-west Provinces (extinct)	In.	194
174	Hindustani	Aryan—Indic	India (west and north) *passim*	In.	194
175	Hottentot	Independent group	Cape Colony, Orange River, &c.	Ag.	47
176	Huastek	Maya group	Mexico (north-east)	Pol.	124
177	Huzváresh	Aryan—Iranic	Persia (extinct)	In.	203
178	Ibo	Unclassified	Niger Delta	Ag.	58
179	Icelandic	Aryan—Norse	Iceland	In.	256
—	Ife	See Ewe.			
180	Ingush	Caucasian (Northern)—Kistian	West of Daghestan	Ag.	136
—	Innuit	See Eskimo.			
181	Ionic	Aryan—Hellenic	Ionia, Asia Minor (extinct)	In.	212
182	Irish	Aryan—Keltic	Ireland (west and south-west)	In.	241
183	Iroquois	Independent group	New York, southern shores of the great lakes	Pol.	131
184	Isubu	Bantu (Western branch)	Bight of Biafra	Ag.	61
185	Italian	Aryan—Neo-Latin	Italy	In.	237
186	Jagataic	Uralo-Altaic—Turkic	Turkestan	Ag.	100
187	Japanese	Independent	Japan	Ag.	72
188	Javanese	Malayo-Polynesian—Malay	Java, Sunda Islands	Ag.	68
—	Jemaitic	See Lithuanian.			
189	Kabyle	Hamitic (Libyan branch)	South of Algeria	In.	179
190	Kafir	Bantu (Eastern branch)	South-east of Africa	Ag.	61

APPENDIX.

Ref. No.	Name.	Family and Group.	Where spoken.	Form of Speech.	Page.
191	Kahita	Unclassified	Sonora	Pol.	124
192	Kaluillo	Unclassified	Sonora	Pol.	124
193	Kalmuk	Uralo-Altaic—Mongolian	Western Mongolia, Caspian (west)	Ag.	105
194	Kamassic	Uralo-Altaic—Samoyede	South Siberia	Ag.	89
195	Kamchatdale	Sub-Arctic	Kamchatka	Ag.	135
196	Kamiloroi	Australian (Eastern group)	New South Wales, River Barwan	Ag.	67
197	Kanarese	Dravidian	Southern India	Ag.	78
—	Kanem	Akin to Bornu, which see.			
—	Kannada	See Kanarese.			
198	Kanuri	Bornu group.	Central Africa, about Lake Chad	Ag.	58
199	Karabulak	Caucasian (north)—Kistian	between Daghestan and Circassia	Ag.	136
200	Karelian	Uralo-Altaic—Finnic	Finland, between Lake Ladoga and Lapland	Ag.	90
—	Kasdo-Scythic	See Accadian.			
201	Kashmiri	Aryan—Indic	Kashmir	In.	194
202	Kasi-Kumuk	Caucasian (north)—Lesgian	Daghestan	Ag.	136
203	Kassia	Independent	Assam, left bank of Brahmaputra	Is.	34
204	Kataba	See Appalache.			
205	Kazak	Uralo-Altaic—Turkic, Kirghiz	Aral Sea, Caspian (north)	Ag.	99
206	Kechua	Independent group	Peru, Chili (north)	Pol.	125
207	Kenai	Independent group	North-west of north America	Pol.	124
208	Khora, or Khorana	Hottentot group	Cape Colony, Orange River Free State	Ag.	48
209	Kiabi	Australian (Eastern group)	Queensland, north of Moreton Bay	Ag.	67
210	Kirghiz	Uralo-Altaic—Turkic	Turkestan	Ag.	99
211	Kistian	Caucasian (north)	Between Daghestan and Circassia	Ag.	136
212	Kizh	Unclassified	Sonora	Pol.	124
213	Ki-hiau	Bantu (Eastern branch)	Mozambique, 13° S. lat.	Ag.	60
214	Ki-Kamba	Bantu (Eastern branch)	Zanzibar district	Ag.	60
215	Ki-Nika	Bantu (Eastern branch)	Coast of Zanzibar	Ag.	60
216	Ki-Pokono	Bantu (Eastern branch)	Zanzibar, a little south of the Equator	Ag.	60

Y

Ref. No.	Name.	Family and Group.	Where spoken.	Form of Speech.	Page.
217	Ki-Sambala	Bantu (Eastern branch)	East Coast of Africa	Ag.	60
218	Ki-Suaheli	Bantu (Eastern branch)	Zanzibar, about 5° S. lat.	Ag.	60
219	Kochimi	Californian group	California	Pol.	121
220	Koiuberri	Australian (Eastern group)	New South Wales	Ag.	67
221	Kokai	Australian (Eastern group)	Maranoa and Kogun rivers	Ag.	67
222	Koldaji	Nubian group	West of Kordofan	Ag.	66
223	Kolocho	Independent	Extreme west of Canadian Dominion	Pol.	124
224	Komancho	Unclassified	Sonora	Pol.	124
225	Kond, or Ku	Dravidian	Orissa	Ag.	78
226	Kongo	Bantu (Western branch)	Kongo	Ag.	60
227	Konjari	Nubian group	Darfur and Kordofan	Ag.	66
228	Kora	Unclassified	Sonora	Pol.	121
229	Koryak	Sub-Arctic	Extreme north-east of Siberia	Ag.	135
230	Kota	Dravidian	Neilgherries	Ag.	78
231	Kotte	Sub-Arctic	Heart of Siberia	Ag.	135
232	Kree	Algonquin family	Canada	Pol.	121
233	Krewinian	Uralo-Altaic—Finnic	Courland	Ag.	90
234	Krik	Appalache	Lower Mississippi	Pol.	124
235	Kru	Independent Negro	Windward and Grain Coast	Ag.	58
236	Kudagu	Dravidian	Southern India, west of Mysore	Ag.	78
237	Kueva	Independent	North of Panama	Pol.	124
238	Kumanji	Aryan—Iranic	Kurdistan	In.	207
239	Kumuk	Uralo-Altaic—Turkic	Caucasus (north-east)	Ag.	100
240	Kurdish	Aryan—Iranic	Kurdistan	In.	207
241	Kurilian	Sub-Arctic	Kurile Archipelago	Ag.	135
242	Kurine	Caucasian (north)—Lesgian	Daghestau	Ag.	136
243	Labourdin	Basque	Pyrenees	Pol.	115
244	Ladin	Aryan—Neo-Latin	Grisons, Tagliamento	In.	238

APPENDIX. 323

Ref. No.	Name.	Family and Group.	Where spoken.	Form of Speech.	Page
245	Ladrone	Malayo-Polynesian—Malay	The Ladrones	Ag.	68
—	Lanur	See Ingush.			
246	Lamutic	Uralo-Altaic—Tungus	North-east of Siberia	Ag.	103
247	Landoro	African Negro (Mande group)	Senegambia	Ag.	56
248	Langue d'oc	Aryan—Neo-Latin	South of France	In.	236
—	Langue d'oïl	See French.			
249	Lapponic	Uralo-Altaic—Finnic	Lapland	Ag.	90
250	Latin	Aryan—Italic	Latium and Western Empire (extinct)	In.	218
251	Lazian	Caucasian (southern)	Lazistan, Turkey in Asia	Ag.	136
252	Lenapé	Algonquin family	New Jersey, Delaware, Pennsylvania	Pol.	131
253	Lesbian	Aryan—Hellenic, Æolic	Lesbos (extinct)	In.	211
254	Lesgian	Caucasian (north)	Daghestan	Ag.	136
255	Lettish	Aryan—Lettic	North Courland, South Livonia, Riga, Mitan	In.	288
256	Libyan	Hamitic (Western division)	Barbary States	In.	179
257	Liège	Aryan—Neo-Latin, Wallon	Belgium (east)	In.	235
258	Lifu	Malayo-Polynesian — Melanesian	Loyalty Islands	Ag.	68
259	Limousin	Aryan—Neo-Latin	Limousin, south of France	In.	236
—	Little Russian	See Ruthenian.			
260	Lithuanian	Aryan—Lettic	North-east Prussia, Baltic Provinces	In.	285
261	Livonian	Uralo-Altaic—Finnic	North-east corner of Courland	Ag.	90
262	Logone	Akin to Mosgu, which see.			
263	Lombard	Aryan—Neo-Latin	Lombardy	In.	238
264	Londa	Bantu (Western branch)	West Africa, about 22° S. lat.	Ag.	60
265	Low Lithuanian	Aryan—Lettic	North-east Prussia, Baltic Provinces	In.	285
—	Lusatian	See Sorbian.			
266	Lycian	Aryan—Hellenic?	Lycia, Asia Minor (extinct)	In.	292
267	Maba	Negro—Unclassified	South-east of Lake Chad	Ag.	58

Y 2

324 APPENDIX.

Ref. No.	Name	Family and Group	Where spoken	Form of Speech	Page
268	Macedo-Rumanian	Aryan—Neo-Latin	Rumelia, Thessaly, Albania	In.	242
269	Madura	Malayo-Polynesian—Malay	Dutch East Indies	Ag.	68
—	Magadha	See Pāli.			
270	Magyaric	Uralo-Altaïc—Finnic	Hungary	Ag.	94
271	Makua	Bantu (Eastern branch)	Mozambique, north-east of the Shiré	Ag.	60
—	Malabar	See Tamil.			
272	Malagasse	Malayo-Polynesian—Malay	Madagascar	Ag.	68
273	Malay	Malayo-Polynesian—Malay	Malacca, Singapore, coast of Sumatra	Ag.	68
274	Malayālam	Dravidian	Malabar Coast	Ag.	78
275	Mallikolo	Malayo-Polynesian — Melanesian	South Sea Islands	Ag.	68
276	Maltese	Semitic (Arabic group)	Malta	In.	170
277	Mame	Unclassified	Mexico	Pol.	121
278	Mandarine	Chinese	China	Is.	34
279	Mandehn	Uralo-Altaïc—Tungus	Manchuria	Ag.	103
280	Mande	African Negro (Mande group)	Senegambia, Upper Guinea	Ag.	56
281	Mandingau	African Negro (Mande group)	Southern Senegambia, Upper Guinea	Ag.	56
282	Mankasar	Malayo-Polynesian—Malay	Dutch East Indies	Ag.	68
283	Mano	African Negro (Mande group)	Senegambia	Ag.	56
284	Manx	Aryan—Keltic	Isle of Man	In.	244
285	Maori	Malayo-Polynesian — Polynesian	New Zealand	Ag.	68
286	Marāthi	Aryan—Indic	Western India	In.	68
287	Marianne	Malayo-Polynesian—Malay	The Mariannes	Ag.	194
288	Marquesas	Malayo-Polynesian — Polynesian	The Marquesas	Ag.	68
289	Massachusetts	Algonquin family	Massachusetts	Pol.	131
290	Maya	Independent group	Yucatan	Pol.	124
291	Mazahua	Unclassified	Mexico	Pol.	124

APPENDIX.

Ref. No.	Name	Family and Group	Where spoken	Form of Speech	Page
	Median	See Arcadian.			
292	Memphitic	Hamitic (Egyptian group)	Lower Nile (extinct)	In.	178
293	Mendean	Semitic—Aramean	Irak Arabi	In.	156
294	Menomeni	Algonquin family	Canada	Pol.	131
295	Mexican	Independent group	Mexico	Pol.	124
296	Miami	Algonquin family	Ohio	Pol.	131
297	Michi	Negro—Unclassified	East of Lower Niger, about 7° N. lat.	Ag.	58
298	Mikmak	Algonquin family	Nova Scotia	Pol.	131
299	Mingrelian	Caucassian (Southern branch)	Mingrelia, Imeritia	Ag.	136
300	Mixtek	Unclassified	Mexico	Pol.	124
301	Modern Greek	Aryan—Hellenic	Greece, Archipelago, Candia, &c.	In.	212
302	Mohawk	Iroquois family	Upper Canada, New York (extinct)	Pol.	131
303	Mohican	Algonquin family	Connecticut (extinct)	Pol.	131
304	Moki	Unclassified	Sonora	Pol.	124
305	Moksha	Uralo-Altaic—Finnic	Banks of the Volga, Stavropol, &c.	Ag.	93
306	Mongolian	Uralo-Altaic—Mongolian	Mongolia, Lake Baikal	Ag.	105
307	Monki	Californian group	California	Pol.	124
308	Mordvinian	Uralo-Altaic—Finnic	Banks of the Volga, below Kazan	Ag.	90
309	Mosarabic	Semitic (Arabic group)	South of Spain (extinct)	In.	170
310	Mosgu	Negro—Unclassified	Central Africa, south of Lake Chad	Ag.	58
	Moska	See Chibcha.			
311	Mpongwe	Bantu (Western branch)	Kongo	Ag.	60
312	Multani	Aryan—Indic	Lower Indus	In.	194
313	Munda	Unclassified	South-west of Calcutta	Ag.	138
314	Murio	Bornu group	Central Africa, about Lake Chad	Ag.	58
315	Muscogi	Appalache group?	Lower Mississippi	Pol.	124
316	Nabatean	Semitic—Aramean	Chaldea (extinct)	In.	156
—	Nahuatl	See Aztek.			

Ref. No.	Name.	Family and Group.	Where spoken.	Form of Speech.	Page.
317	Namaqua	Hottentot group	Namaqualand	Ag.	48
318	Namur	Aryan—Neo-Latin	Belgium (south, south-east)	In.	235
319	Nano	Bantu (Western branch)	Benguela	Ag.	60
320	Narragansets	Algonquin family	Rhode Island (extinct)	Pol.	131
321	Natchez	Appalache group	State of Mississippi	Pol.	121
322	Navarrese	Basque	Navarre	Pol.	115
323	Neapolitan	Aryan—Neo-Latin	Naples	In.	138
324	Nepáli	Aryan—Indic	Nepál	In.	191
325	Netela	Unclassified	Sonora	Pol.	124
326	Netherlandish	Aryan—Teutonic (Low)	Holland, Belgium	In.	261
327	Ngurn	Bornu group	Central Africa, near Lake Chad	Ag.	58
328	Nogairic	Uralo-Altaic—Turkic	Astrakhan, Crimea, Lower Don	Ag.	99
329	Norman	Aryan—Neo-Latin	Normandy	In.	235
330	Norse	Aryan (Norse branch)	Scandinavia (extinct)	In.	255
331	Norwegian	Aryan (Norse branch)	Norway	In.	256
332	Nubian	Independent group	Upper Egypt, Nubia	Ag.	66
333	Nuer	African Negro (Upper Nile group)	White Nile, north of Gondokoro	Ag.	58
334	Nupo	Unclassified	Niger Delta	Ag.	58
335	Oji	Ewe group	Gold Coast	Ag.	58
336	Ojibway	See Chippeway.			
—	Old Prussian	Aryan—Lettic	North-east Prussia, Courland (extinct)	In.	288
—	Old Saxon	See Continental Saxon.			
—	Old Slavonic	See Church Slavonic.			
337	Omagua	Guarani group	Paraguay and Parana	Pol.	124
338	Ompqua	Athapasque group	South of the Columbia River	Pol.	124
339	Oneida	Iroquois group	State of New York (extinct)	Pol.	131
340	Onondago	Iroquois group	State of New York (extinct)	Pol.	131

APPENDIX.

Ref. No.	Name.	Family and Group.	Where spoken.	Form of Speech.	Page.
311	Opata	Unclassified	Sonora	Pol.	124
312	Oregon	Independent group	Oregon	Pol.	124
—	Orna	See Galla.			
343	Oscan	Aryan—Italic	Campania, Samnium (extinct)	In.	218
—	Osmanli	See Turkish.			
344	Ossetian	Aryan—Iranic	Caucasus	In.	207
345	Ostyak	Uralo-Altaic—Finnic	Banks of the Obi	Ag.	90
346	Ostyak	Uralo-Altaic—Samoyede	Western Siberia	Ag.	89
347	Ostyak-Yeniseï	Sub-Arctic	Shores of the Arctic, Siberia	Ag.	135
348	Othomi	Unclassified	Mexico	Pol.	124
349	Ottawa	Algonquin family	Canada	Pol.	131
—	Otyi	See Oji.			
—	Pahlavi	See Huzvâresh.			
350	Pah-Utah	Unclassified	Sonora	Pol.	124
351	Paiamba	Australian (Eastern group)	Queensland	Ag.	67
—	Pakkhto	See Afghan.			
352	Pali	Aryan—Indic	Magadha (extinct)	In.	192
353	Pampanga	Malayo-Polynesian—Malay	Pampanga, Philippines	Ag.	68
354	Papago	Unclassified	Sonora	Pol.	121
355	Papuan	Independent group	New Guinea, Solomon Isles, &c.	Ag.	66
356	Parsi	Aryan—Iranic	Persia (extinct)	In.	205
357	Pawnee	Unclassified	Western States	Pol.	124
—	Pazend	See Parsi.			
355	Pegu	Burman	British Burmah	Is.	34
—	Pehlvi, or Pehlevi	See Huzvâresh.			
359	Pepel	African Negro (Felup group)	Bisagos Islands, coast of Senegambia	Ag.	56
360	Pericu	Californian group	California	Pol.	124
361	Permian	Uralo-Altaic—Finnic	Peru, west of the Upper Kama	Ag.	93

APPENDIX.

Ref. No.	Name.	Family and Group.	Where spoken.	Form of Speech.	Page.
362	Persian (old)	Aryan—Iranic	Persia (west) (extinct)	In.	200
363	Persian (new)	Aryan—Iranic	Persia, Afghanistan, India	In.	206
364	Phœnician	Semitic (Canaanitic group)	Phœnicia	In.	161
365	Phrygian	Aryan—Hellenic (?)	Asia Minor (extinct)	In.	292
366	Picardy	Aryan—Neo-Latin	Picardy	In.	235
367	Piedmontese	Aryan—Neo-Latin	Piedmont	In.	238
368	Pikunbul	Australian (Eastern group)	Queensland	Ag.	67
369	Pima	Unclassified	Sonora	Pol.	124
370	Platt-Deutsch	Aryan—Teutonic (Low)	North Germany	In.	261
371	Polabish	Aryan—Slavonic	Banks of the Upper Elbe (extinct)	In.	280
372	Polish	Aryan—Slavonic	Poland	In.	272
373	Portuguese	Aryan—Neo-Latin	Portugal, Brazil, Goa, east and west coasts of Africa	In.	240
374	Prâkrits	Aryan—Indic	India, north of the Nerbuddah (extinct)	In.	192
375	Provençal	Aryan—Neo-Latin	South of France	In.	236
—	Prussian	See old Prussian.			
376	Puelche	Independent	West of Buenos Ayres	Pol.	125
—	Pul	See Fula.			
377	Punic	Semitic (Canaanitic branch)	North Africa, Carthage, &c. (extinct)	In.	166
—	Pushtu	See Afghan.			
378	Qualihoqua	Athapascque	North of the Columbia River	Pol.	124
379	Quiché	Maya group	Yucatan	Pol.	124
—	Quichua	See Kechua.			
380	Rajmahal	Dravidian	Central India	Ag.	78
381	Rarotonga	Malayo-Polynesian — Polynesian	Cook's Archipelago	Ag.	68
382	Rheto-Romance	Aryan—Neo-Latin	Grisons	In.	238

APPENDIX. 329

Ref. No.	Name.	Family and Group.	Where spoken.	Form of Speech.	Page.
383	Romaic	See Modern Greek.			
384	Roman	Aryan—Neo-Latin	Rome	In.	238
385	Rumanian	Aryan—Neo-Latin	Moldavia and Wallachia	In.	240
385	Rumansh	Aryan—Neo-Latin	Grisons	In.	238
—	Rusniak	See Ruthenian.			
386	Russian	Aryan—Slavonic	Russia	In.	270
387	Ruthenian	Aryan—Slavonic	South Russia, Galicia, north-east of Hungary	In.	272
—	Salcan	See Mexican.			
—	Sabellian	See Oscan.			
388	Sahapti	Unclassified	Oregon	Pol.	121
389	Saho	Hamitic (Ethiopian group)	West of Abyssinia	In.	180
390	Saki	Algonquin family	Ohio	Pol.	131
—	Samnite	See Oscan.			
391	Samoa	Malayo-Polynesian—Polynesian	Samoa Isles, east of Figi, and north of Navigator group	Ag.	68
392	Samoyede	Uralo-Altaic	Extreme north of European and Asiatic Russia	Ag.	89
—	Sandwich	See Hawaii.			
393	Sanskrit	Aryan—Indic	India, north of the Nerbuddah (extinct)	In.	190
394	Sardinian	Aryan—Neo-Latin	Sardinia	In.	238
—	Saxon	See Anglo-Saxon and old Saxon.			
—	Scandinavian	See Norse.			
395	Scythic	A geographical term		...	138
396	Sechuana	Bantu (Central branch)	South Africa, between 20° and 25° S. lat.	Ag.	60
397	Schlapi	Bantu (Central branch)	South Africa, west of the Bechuanas	Ag.	60
398	Sena	Bantu—Eastern branch	Lower Zambesi	Ag.	60
399	Seneca	Iroquois group	State of New York (extinct)	Pol.	131
400	Serere	African Negro (Felup group)	Senegambia	Ag.	56

APPENDIX.

Ref. No.	Name.	Family and Group.	Where spoken.	Form of Speech.	Pago.
401	Serolong	Bantu (Central branch)	South Africa, west of the Bechuanas	Ag.	60
402	Servian	Aryan—Slavonic	Servia, Montenegro, Herzegovina	In.	276
	Servo-Croatian	See Servian and Croatian.			
403	Sesuto	Bantu (Central branch)	South Africa, Basutoland	Ag.	60
404	Sharra-Mongol	Uralo-Altaic—Mongolian	East Mongolia, west of Manchuria	Ag.	105
405	Shiluk	African Negro—Upper Nile group	West bank of White Nile	Ag.	58
406	Siamese	Independent	Siam, Laos	Is.	42
407	Sicilian	Aryan—Neo-Latin	Sicily	In.	238
408	Sindhi	Aryan—Indic	Lower Indus	In.	194
409	Sindonga	Bantu (Western branch)	Ovambo, south-east of Benguela	Ag.	60
410	Sinhalese	Unclassified	Ceylon	Ag.	137
411	Siryenian	Uralo-Altaic—Finnic	North-east of European Russia	Ag.	90
	Skipetar	See Albanian.			
	Slavonic	See Church Slavonic.			
412	Slovakian	Aryan—Slavonic, Tsech	Moravia	In.	274
413	Slovenian	Aryan—Slavonic	Carinthia, Styria, Carniola, Istria	In.	279
414	Somali	Hamitic (Ethiopian group)	South-east of Abyssinia	In.	180
415	Sonora	Unclassified groups	Sonora	Pol.	121
416	Sonrai	Unclassified	Niger, south-east of Timbuktu, about 15° N. lat.	Ag.	56
417	Souletin	Basque	Pyrenees	Pol.	115
418	Sorabian	Aryan—Slavonic	Upper Spree, Lusatia	In.	275
419	Sorbian				
420	Spanish	Aryan—Neo-Latin	Spain, Mexico, Central and South America	In.	239
421	Suanian	Caucasian (Southern branch)	Imeritia, north-west of Georgia	Ag.	136
	Sumerian	See Accadian.			
	Sunda	See Javanese.			
422	Suomi	Uralo-Altaic—Finnic	Finland	Ag.	90

APPENDIX. 331

Ref. No.	Name.	Family and Group.	Where spoken.	Form of Speech.	Page.
123	Suriquois	Algonquin family	State of Maine ...	Pol.	131
	Susiana	See Arcadian.			
124	Susu	African Negro (Mande group)	Senegambia (south-east)	Ag.	56
125	Swedish	Aryan—Norse	Sweden, coast of Finland	In.	256
126	Syriac	Semitic—Aramean ...	Syria ...	In.	155
127	Tagala	Malayo-Polynesian—Malay	Philippines ...	Ag.	68
128	Tagwi	Uralo-Altaic—Samoyede	Siberia (north) ...	Ag.	89
129	Tahiti	Malayo-Polynesian—Polynesian	Society Islands ...	Ag.	68
130	Ta-masheq	Hamitic (Libyan branch)	South of Algeria	In.	173
131	Tamil	Dravidian	Southern India, Madras, Pondicherry, &c.	In.	77
132	Tana	Malayo-Polynesian—Melanesian	New Hebrides	Ag.	68
133	Tarahumara	Unclassified ...	Sonora ...	Pol.	124
134	Tarasca	Unclassified ...	Mexico ...	Pol.	124
135	Tebu, or Tedâ	Bornu group ...	North and north-east of Lake Chad	Ag.	58
136	Tegeza	Bantu (Central branch)	Central Africa, west of Zanzibar	Ag.	60
137	Tegua	Unclassified ...	Texas	Pol.	124
138	Tehuelcho	Unclassified ...	Patagonia	Pol.	125
139	Tekele	Nubian family	Nubia ...	Ag.	66
140	Telugu	Dravidian	Southern India ...	Ag.	78
141	Teno	African Negro (Mande branch)	North-west of Liberia ...	Ag.	56
142	Tepeguana	Unclassified ...	Sonora ...	Pol.	124
143	Tette	Bantu (Eastern branch)	Lower Zambesi ...	Ag.	60
	Thai ...	See Siamese.			
144	Thelan	Hamitic (Egyptian branch)	Upper Egypt (extinct) ...	In.	178
145	Thessalian	Aryan—Hellenic, Æolic	Thessaly (extinct)	In.	211

APPENDIX.

Ref. No.	Name	Family and Group	Where spoken	Form of Speech	Page
446	Tibetan	Independent	Tibet	Is.	43
447	Tigré	Semitic (Arabic group)	Abyssinia (north)	In.	172
448	Tlaskanni	Athapasque	Mexico	Pol.	124
449	Toda	Dravidian	Neilgherries	Ag.	78
450	Toma	African Negro (Mande group)	North of Kong Mountains	Ag.	56
451	Tonga	Malayo-Polynesian — Polynesian	Navigator Archipelago	Ag.	68
452	Totonak	Unclassified	Mexico	Pol.	124
453	Tsech	Aryan—Slavonic	Bohemia	In.	274
454	Tubar	Unclassified	Sonora	Pol.	124
455	Tulu	Dravidian	Mangalore, south-west coast of India	Ag.	78
456	Tumal	Nubian group	South of Kordofan	Ag.	66
457	Tungus	Uralo-Altaic	Upper Yenisei	Ag.	103
458	Tupi	Guarani group	Parana and Paraguay	Pol.	125
459	Turkish	Uralo-Altaic—Turkic	Ottoman Empire *passim*	Ag.	99
460	Turkoman	Uralo-Altaic—Turkic	Turkestan	Ag.	100
461	Turrubul	Australian (Eastern group)	Queensland, near the River Brisbane	Ag.	67
462	Tuscan	Aryan—Neo-Latin	Tuscany	In.	238
463	Tuscarora.				
464	Tush	Caucasian (northern)—Kistian	South of Caucasus—Upper Alasan	Ag.	136
465	Ude	Caucasian (Northern branch) —Lesgian	Daghestan	Ag.	136
466	Ugric	Uralo-Altaic—Finnic	Russia (north-east)	Ag.	90
467	Uiguric	Uralo-Altaic—Turkic	Turkestan (east)	Ag.	99
468	Umbrian	Aryan—Italic	Italy (north-east) (extinct)	In.	218
—	Umpqua	See Ompqua.			
469	Uraon	Dravidian	Central India	Ag.	78

Ref. No.	Name	Family and Group	Where spoken	Form of Speech	Page
470	Urdu	Aryan—Indic	India (north and west)	In.	191
471	Uriya	Aryan—Indic	India, (east)	In.	191
472	Uscara	See Escuara			
472	Utah	Unclassified	Sonora	Pol.	124
473	Vei	African Negro (Mande branch)	North of Kong Mountains	Ag.	56
474	Venetian	Aryan—Neo-Latin	Venetia	In.	238
475	Volscian	Aryan—Italic	Umbria, &c. (extinct)	In.	224
476	Wailwun	Australian (Eastern branch)	Between the River Barwan and Fort Bourke	Ag.	67
477	Wallon	Aryan—Neo-Latin	Belgium (east and south-east)	In.	235
478	Welsh	Aryan—Keltic (Kymric)	Wales	In.	245
—	Wendic	See Sorbian			
479	Wepsic	Uralo-Altaic—Finnic	Lake Onega	Ag.	90
480	Wiraurei	Australian (Eastern group)	New South Wales	Ag.	67
481	Wogulic	Uralo-Altaic—Finnic	North-east Russia, east of Siryenian	Ag.	90
482	Wolaroi	Australian (Eastern group)	Queensland	Ag.	67
483	Wolof	African Negro—Wolof	Senegambia	Ag.	52
484	Wotic	Uralo-Altaic—Finnic	Lake Onega	Ag.	90
485	Wotyak	Uralo-Altaic—Finnic	Peru (Viatka)	Ag.	90
486	Yakutic	Uralo-Altaic—Turkic	Siberia (south)	Ag.	99
487	Yenisei	Uralo-Altaic—Samoyede	Siberia (north)	Ag.	89
488	Yenisei	Sub-Arctic	Siberia (north)	Ag.	135
489	Yoruba	Ewe group	Lower Niger, east of Dahomey	Ag.	58
490	Yukagiric	Sub-Arctic	Siberia (north)	Ag.	135
491	Yuma	Independent group	Lower Colorado	Pol.	124
492	Yurak	Uralo-Altaic—Samoyede	Siberia (north-east)	Ag.	89

APPENDIX.

Ref. No.	Name.	Family and Group.	Where spoken.	Form of Speech.	Page
493	Zaconic	Aryan—Hellenic (Doric?)	Morea	In.	213
494	Zambesi	Bantu (Central branch)	South Africa, Zambesi	Ag.	60
495	Zaza	Aryan—Iranic (Kurd)	Kurdistan	In.	207
496	Zend	Aryan—Iranic	Persia, Bactria (extinct)	In.	197
497	Zopotek	Unclassified	Mexico	Pol.	121
498	Zulu	Bantu (Eastern branch)	South Africa, Kafirland	Ag.	60
499	Zuni	Unclassified	Sonora	Pol.	124

INDEX.

	PAGE
Abyssinia, Semitic languages of	170
Accadian, Double meaning of	140
Accent, Latin	222
„ Its influence on the Neo-Latin tongues	229
Afghan, Eastern Iranian dialect	207
Agglutination, Second linguistic form	44
„ Its various kinds	45
Albanian, An unclassified Aryan tongue	293
Algonquin, Grammar of	131
American languages, Their great number	123
„ Their common features	125
„ Not distinct from other agglutinating tongues	127
„ Vocabulary of	134
Amharic, Akin to the *Gheez*	172
Anglo-Saxon	258
„ The term vindicated	259
Annamese, An independent language	41
„ An isolating idiom	41
Anthropoids, Arrested in their development	30
Arabic, Group of the Semitic family	166
„ Proper, Its alphabet	168
„ Its position	168
„ Dialects of	170
Aramean group	155
Armorican, or *Breton*	246
Aryas, Meaning of the term	188
Aryan Family of languages	181
Asia Minor, Aryan idioms of	292

	PAGE
Asia Minor, Greek spoken in	214
„ Turkish spoken in	103
Assyrian, A Semitic tongue	157
Australia, Languages of	67
"*Avesta*," Sacred book of the Zoroastrians	198
„ The Huzvâresh translation	203
Bactrian, *Zend*, So-called	198
Bantu group (*African*)	59
Basque, Limits of	109
„ Yielding to Spanish	111
„ Isolated position	113
„ Oldest traces of	114
„ Numerous varieties of	115
„ Phonology of	116
„ Word formation of	116
„ Incorporates the direct object	117
„ Not allied to the American tongues	119
„ Its vocabulary	120
„ Origin of	121
Beja (*Bishara*), An Ethiopian dialect	180
Beluch, An Iranian tongue	207
Berber, General name of modern Libyan	179
Bohemian, See *Tsech*.	
Burman, An isolating tongue	42
Buryetic, Its importance in the Mongol group	106
Bushman language	51
Breton, A Keltic idiom	246
Bulgarian, Limits of	279
„ Its forms badly preserved	279
Byzantine, Medieval Greek	212

INDEX.

	PAGE
Cases, The three common Semitic	153
„ The eight common Aryan	186
„ Two in the old French	232
Catalonian, Grouped with the Langue d'oc	236
Caucasus, Languages of	136
Chaldee, Its place in the Aramean group	155
Canaanitic, Group of the Semitic family	160
Chinese, Dialects of	34
„ Its grammar purely syntactic	35
„ Its graphic system	38
Coptic, Represents old Egyptian	177
Corean, Agglutinating, but little known	76
Cornish, A Kymric dialect	246
Croatian, See *Servo-Croatian*.	
Dacian, Not yet finally classified	291
Danish, Its place in the Norse group	257
Dankali, An Ethiopian dialect	180
Devanāgari alphabet	191
Dravidian, Extent of its domain	77
„ Languages	77
„ Former limits of	79
„ Simple grammatical system	81
„ Poverty of its vocabulary	85
Dutch, A Netherlandish dialect	261
Egyptian, A Hamitic tongue	175
„ Its grammar	176
Ehkili, Akin to the *Himyaritic*	171
Elbe, Slavonic of the	280
Elu, or *Sinhalese*	137
English, Different periods of	259
Erse, Scotch Gaelic	245
Escuara, Original name of the Basque	112
Ethiopian group of the Hamitic tongues	180
Etruscan, Different opinions on its origin	290
, Belongs to the Aryan family	291

	PAGE
Etymology, Dangers of	13
„ Its true nature and province	14
Finnic group of the Uralo-Altaïc tongues	90
Flemish, A Netherlandish dialect	261
Forms, Threefold, monosyllabic	31
„ Agglutinating	44
„ Inflecting	146
French, Formation of	230
„ Two classes of words in	230
„ Two cases in its old declension	232
„ Dialects of old	235
Friuli, Eastern *Ladin*	238
Frisic, A Low German branch	261
Fulu, or *Pul*, An African language	64
Gaedhelic, or Gaelic branch of the Keltic	244
Galatian, Old	247
Galician, Akin to Portuguese	240
Galla, An Ethiopian dialect	180
Gáthás, Zend dialect of the	199
Gaulish, Ancient	247
German, Characteristics of modern	266
„ Its orthography	267
Gheez, South Arabic group	171
Gipsy dialects	195
Glagolitic alphabet	269
Gothic, Its proper spelling	254
„ Position of in the Teutonic family	254
Greek branch of the Aryan family	208
„ Not to be grouped with the Latin	209
„ Grammar	210
„ Dialects	211
„ Common dialect of	212
„ Byzantine	212
„ Modern	212
„ Extent of modern	213
„ Pronunciation of ancient	214
Hamitic family	174
„ Inadequate title	174
„ Hypothesis on former limits of	174

INDEX.

Hamitic Akin to the Semitic family ... 174
,, General Grammar of ... 175
,, Divided into three branches ... 175
Harari, Akin to *Ghees* ... 172
Hebrew, Various periods of ... 160
,, Its grammar ... 162
,, Its alphabet ... 163
High German, Three periods of 264
,, Two kinds of ... 267
Himyaritic, Member of the south Arabic group ... 170
Hindi, Its limits in medieval times ... 194
Hindu group of the Aryan tongues ... 190
,, Neo-Hindu languages 193
,, Phonology of ... 190
Hottentot language ... 47
Huzváresh version of the "Avesta" ... 203
,, Aramean influence on 204
,, Its grammar ... 204
,, Its alphabet ... 205
Iberian theory... ... 121
Icelandic, Its place in the Norse group ... 256
Incorporation differs from polysynthesis ... 128
,, In *Basque* ... 119
,, In the American tongues 128
,, In the Uralo-Altaic tongues ... 97
Indo-European, See *Aryan*.
Indo-Germanic, Inadequate title ... 188
Inscriptions, Cuneiform, Language of the Second Column of ... 139
,, Assyrian ... 157
,, Persian ... 200
Intonation, Importance of in the isolating tongues ... 34
Iranian group of the Aryan family ... 195
Irish, Importance of in the Keltic group... ... 244
,, Grammar ... 249
Iroquois ... 131
Italian, Its place in the Neo-Latin group... ... 237

Italian, Its dialects ... 238
Japanese, wrongly grouped with other agglutinating idioms ... 72
,, Grammar ... 75
Kabyle, A Libyan dialect ... 179
Kafir languages ... 59
Kasdo-Scythic, or *Sumerian*... 141
Keltic group ... 242
,, Two branches of ... 244
Keltomania ... 250
Kurdish, An Iranian tongue... 207
Kymric, Branch of the Keltic family ... 245
Ladin, The three groups of 237
Languages, The life of ... 8
,, Mixed do not exist ... 8
,, Isolating and monosyllabic ... 31
,, Original plurality of ... 304
,, Affinities of, how detected... ... 302
,, Not always identical with race ... 307
Latin, Its degree of affinity with *Greek* ... 217
,, Old and classic ... 218
,, Phonology of ... 219
,, Pronunciation of classic 220
,, Accent... ... 222
,, Vulgar, the source of the Romance tongues 227
Lettic group ... 285
,, Its dialects ... 285
,, Distinct from *Slavonic* 289
Lettish, Limits of ... 288
,, More corrupt than *Lithuanian* ... 288
Libyan group of the Hamitic family ... 179
Linguistics distinguished from philology ... 1-7
,, Its real domain ... 3
,, Its use in philology ... 10
Lithuanian, Highly preserved 286
,, Limits of ... 286
,, Grammar ... 287
Little Russian, or *Ruthenian*... 272
Low German group ... 257
,, Proper, or *Platt-Deutsch* 261
Lusatian ... 275

z

INDEX.

	PAGE
Lycian, An Aryan idiom (Asia Minor)	292
Magyar, Its importance in the Finnic group	94
" Its limits and grammar	95
Malay group of the Malayo-Polynesian family	68
Malayo-Polynesian family classified	68
" Their common origin	68
" Form an independent system	69
" Grammar of	70
Maltese, Its Arabic origin	170
Man distinguished by the faculty of speech	18
" The precursor of, and Philology	30
Mandchu, A member of the Tungus group	103
Manx, A Gaedhelic idiom	244
Metamorphosis, Period of	9
Mongolian group of the Finno-Altaïc tongues	105
Monosyllabic languages	31
" Their grammar	32
Morphology, Its meaning	9
" Cannot alone determine affinity	14
Mosarabic, Of Arabic origin	170
Neo-Latin languages	227
" Formation of	227
" Foreign elements in	229
" Their seven groups	229
" Play of accent in their formation	230
Negrite languages of Africa	51
Netherlandish	261
Norse, Ancient	255
Norwegian, Its place in the Norse group	256
Nubian languages	66
Oc, Langue d', Dialects of	236
" Present limits of	236
Oïl, Langue d', in the Middle Ages	234
" Dialects of	235
" Present limits of	235
Oscan, An Italic tongue	224
Ossetian, An Iranian dialect	207
Pâli, Place of in the Prâkrit tongues	192

	PAGE
Papuas, Their dialects	66
Parsi, A medieval Iranian tongue	205
Pázend, Parsi, Incorrectly so-called	205
Pehlvi, or Pahlavi, See Huzváresh	203
Persian, The widest spread of modern Iranian tongues	206
" Ancient discovery of	200
" Cuneiform inscriptions	201
Phœnician, A member of the Canaanitic group	164
" Nearly related to Hebrew	165
" Of Africa, or Punic	166
Philology, Distinct from linguistics	1-3
" Its true province	4
Phrygian, An Aryan idiom	292
" Akin to the Iranian tongues	292
Physiology and philology	19
Plurals, Broken or fractæ	168
Polabish, or Slavonic of the Elbe	280
Polish, Limits of	272
" Its grammar	273
Polyglot, Not to be confounded with philologist	11
Polysynthesis, How differing from incorporation	129
Portuguese	240
Prâkrit, Its relation to Sanskrit	192
Provençal, Langue d'Oc	236
" Its semi-analytic period	236
Prussian, Old, an extinct Lettic idiom	288
Pul, See Fula.	
Punic, Phœnician of Africa	166
Race, Not always convertible with language	307
Romaic, or modern Greek	212
Romance, or Neo-Latin idioms	227
" Language, Theory of	227
Root, Definition of	32
" In the isolating idioms it constitutes the word	32
" How modified in the inflecting tongues	147

INDEX. 339

Root, Semitic, how far reducible ... 149
Rumanian, Its place in the Neo-Latin group ... 240
„ Its article, phonology, &c. 241
Rumansch, or *Western Ladin*... 238
Rusniak, or *Ruthenian* ... 272
Russian, Limits of 270
„ Its grammar 271
„ White, dialect... ... 271
Ruthenian, Limits of 272
„ How differing from Russian 272
Saho, Ethiopian dialect ... 180
Samoyede group of the Uralo-Altaïc tongues 89
Sanskrit, First essays on ... 189
„ Place in the Aryan system 189
„ Grammar 191
„ Alphabet 191
„ Literature 193
Sa con, Old 258
Scandinavian, See *Norse*.
Scythic language, mythical ... 138
„ A geographical expression 138
Semitic inflection 152
„ Radically distinct from Aryan... 148
„ The term defective ... 151
„ Roots, how far reducible 152
„ Noun 152
„ Verb 153
„ Alphabet 154
„ Languages classified ... 155
„ Primitive, where spoken 174
„ How related to Hamitic 175
Servian, or *Serro-Croatian* ... 276
„ Limits of 276
„ Dialects of 277
„ Literature of 278
„ Importance of... ... 278
„ Grammar of 278
Siamese, An isolating idiom... 42
Sinhalese, Difficult to classify 137
Skipetar, See *Albanian*.
Slavonic group 268
„ Limits of, in medieval times 268
„ Alphabet 269

Slavonic Tongues, now spoken 270
„ Classification of ... 283
„ Church, its limits and grammar 280
Slovakian, Akin to *Tsech* ... 274
Slovenian, A south Slave tongue 279
Somáli, An Ethiopian dialect 180
Sorabian, or *Lusatian* ... 275
Spanish, Its place in the neo-Latin group 239
„ Absorbing the Basque 111
Species, Permutation of, in philology 308
Sub-Arctic idioms 135
Sumerian, Meaning of ... 141
Suomi, Its importance in the Finnic group 90
Swedish, Its place in the Norse group 256
Syntax, Precedes accidence ... 33
Syriac, Its place in the Aramean group... 155
Syro-Arabic, Synonymous with Semitic 151
Ta-Masheq, A Libyan dialect 179
Tamil, Importance of in the Dravidian family ... 77
„ Its alphabet, &c. ... 86
Tatar, or Turkish group ... 99
„ Crimean 100
Telugu, A Dravidian idiom ... 78
Tenses, The two of the common Semitic tongue ... 153
„ The eight of the common Aryan 187
Teutonic group 252
„ Meaning of the term ... 252
„ Characteristics of ... 253
„ Position of Gothic in... 254
Tibetan, An isolating tongue 43
Tigré, Akin to *Gheez* ... 172
Tone, Importance of in the isolating idioms ... 34
„ In Chinese 38
„ In Annamese 42
„ In Siamese 42
„ In Burman 43
Tsech, or *Bohemian*, Limits of 274
„ Its orthography ... 274
„ Its grammar 275
Tulu, A Dravidian idiom ... 77

	PAGE
Tungus group of the Uralo-Altaïc family	103
Turanian, A meaningless term	144
" Languages, false theory of	145
Turkish group of the Uralo-Altaïc tongues	99
" Its grammar	101
Umbrian, An Italic language	224
Uralo-Altaïc family, its five groups	88
" Their differences	88
" Their common features	89
" Their incorporating system	89
" Their vowel harmony	106
Verb, Semitic	153
" Aryan	186
Wallon, A dialect of the Langue d'oïl	235
Welsh, A Kymric tongue	245
Wendic, See *Sorbian*.	
Writing, Chinese system	38
" Annamitic system	42
" Siamese "	42

	PAGE
Writing, Tibetan "	43
" Japanese "	73
" Malayo-Polynesian	72
" Corean "	76
" Tamil "	86
" Semitic "	154
" Assyrian "	158
" Arabic "	167
" Himyaritic "	171
" Egyptian "	176
" Devanâgari "	191
" Zend "	198
" Persian "	201
" Armenian "	203
" Huzvâresh "	205
" Italic "	226
" Slavonic "	269
Zaconic, a modern Greek dialect	213
Zend, Discovery of "	197
" An Eastern Iranian tongue	198
" Its grammar	199
" Its epoch, &c.	199

CHARLES DICKENS AND EVANS, CRYSTAL PALACE PRESS.

www.ingramcontent.com/pod-product-compliance
Lightning Source LLC
Chambersburg PA
CBHW030310240426
43673CB00040B/1116